With Trumpet and Bible
The Illustrated Life of James Hembray Wilson

Frontispiece. A photographic portrait of James Hembray Wilson (1880-1961), circa 1908.

With Trumpet and Bible

The Illustrated Life of James Hembray Wilson

by

Frank Tirro

AMERICAN MUSIC AND MUSICIANS SERIES No. 2

Pendragon Press
Hillsdale, NY

American Music and Musicians Series

No. 1 *George Whitefield Chadwick: An American Composer Revealed and Reflected* by Marianne Betz

Cover design by Stuart Ross

Library of Congress Cataloging-in-Publication Data

Tirro, Frank, author.
  With trumpet and Bible : the illustrated life of James Hembray Wilson / by Frank Tirro.
    pages cm. -- (American music and musicians series ; No. 2.)
  Includes bibliographical references and index.
  ISBN 978-1-57647-222-4 (alk. paper)
  1. Wilson, James Hembray, 1880-1961. 2. African American musicians--Alabama--Biography. 3. African American college teachers--Alabama--Biography. 4. Southern States--Social conditions--20th century. I. Title.
ML423.W75T57 2015
780.92--dc23
[B]
                              2015003810

Copyright 2012 Frank Tirro

Table of Contents

Prologue		vi
Chapter 1.	Nicholasville, Kentucky:1850—1893	1
Chapter 2.	Cincinnati, Ohio, and Nicholasville: 1893—1902	21
Chapter 3.	A Period of Indecision:1902-1904	47
Chapter 4.	On the Road Again:1904-1908	63
Chapter 5.	A Pivotal Year:1908	77
Chapter 6.	The Return to A.&M.	101
Chapter 7.	The Big Change:1908—1910	123
Chapter 8.	The Buchanan Years:1910-1920	143
Chapter 9.	New Presidents and a Reshaped Identity: the1920s	167
Chapter 10.	The Omnipresent Professor: 1930—1941	195
Chapter 11.	The War and Post-WarYears: 1941—1951	221
Chapter 12.	Coming Full Circle	257
Appendix 1. James H. Wilson Journal: January 1— June 30,1908		284
Appendix 2. James H. Wilson Band and Tour Booklet		320
Appendix 3. Known Compositions and Arrangements by James H. Wilson		331
List of Illustrations		333
Acknowledgements		340
A Brief Recommended Reading List		344
Locations and Acknowledgments for Illustratiions		347
Index		351

Prologue

In 2009 the enthusiastic television commentator for Huntsville's station WHNT laid on the hyperbole as uniformed college students marched past the cameras on a cloudy autumn Saturday:

> Mother Nature did not stop Alabama A. & M. fans from celebrating this weekend. Thousands turned out to watch the Alabama A. & M. homecoming parade. The parade [is] a longstanding tradition here in the "Rocket City." Also today the loudest, best, and classiest band in the South walked the walk and played through the talk . . . .[1]

Although the more than 200 student musicians of the modern "Marching Maroon & White" band who strutted and played through the streets of Huntsville on that chilly and damp fall day may indeed have earned a place of regional if not national distinction, the band's history traces back to a time of truly modest beginnings.[2] Ten years after the end of the American Civil War, the Huntsville State Normal School, an "Institution for the Education of Colored teachers,"[3] opened its doors and admitted its first class of students. Five years later, this school boasted a band in addition to a thriving

---

[1] The parade was held on 26 September 2009 and a brief video was published on the web (accessed 8 May 2011): http://www.whnt.com/whnt-alabama-am-band-performances,0,135854.htmlstory.

[2] In 1875, the present day university opened its doors as the Huntsville Normal School with 61 students enrolled for credit. Under the leadership of William Hooper Councill, a former slave and the school's founder and first president, the institution underwent several name changes due to its growth and expanding mission: first Alabama State Normal and Industrial School, then State Normal and Industrial School of Huntsville, and next the State Industrial and Mechanical College for Negroes. In 1919 it received a new title again, the Alabama State Mechanical and Industrial Institute for Negroes. In 1939 the two-year school became a four-year college, and its name was appropriately changed in 1949 to reflect its senior college status, the Alabama Agricultural and Mechanical College. With the addition of graduate programs, the college became a university in 1969. [Summarized from Richard David Morrison, *History of Alabama Agricultural and Mechanical University: 1875-1992* (Huntsville, Alabama: Liberal Arts Press, 1994).]

[3] *Huntsville Gazette*, "Huntsville State Normal School," (Huntsville, AL: September 16, 1882), v. 3, no. 44, p. 3.

vocal music program.[4] At the head of the infant music curriculum stood a talented music teacher, William Grant Still, Sr., father of the now famous 20th-century composer and conductor, William Grant Still, Jr.[5] The senior Still was in charge of both the choir and the band, and in 1891 the school newspaper reported that:

> We are now having some excellent music at Sunday morning services. Mr. Still has a first class choir. . . . Mr. Still is well pleased with the progress made by his band boys.[6]

The founder of the institution, Principal William Hooper Councill, had both a personal love of music and a humanistic regard for the importance of music in general education. Aware of the artistic and financial successes of the Fisk Jubilee Singers as they toured through several northern states in the 1870s, this hard-working and practical man, a former slave, was also mindful that music might offer him an opportunity to carry the message of his school and of African-American culture and excellence to the general population of the southern states. In 1894 he undertook an "Educational Campaign" to raise funds for and an awareness of African-American higher education. With a male quartet and two young lady musicians from the school in tow, he personally oversaw a successful concert and lecture tour throughout northern Alabama and southern Tennessee.[7]

The following year his head music instructor, W. G. Still, Sr., died, and Councill, now President Councill, had to make do for the next few years. In 1900 he recognized an opportunity when he heard cornetist William Christopher Handy play in Sheffield, Alabama, and he immediately recruited Handy as musical director of A. & M. to lead the band, orchestra, and vocal instruction programs. At that time W. C. Handy had not yet earned his title "Father

---

[4]Lynn Abbott and Doug Seroff, *Out of Sight: The Rise of African American Popular Music, 1889-1895* (Jackson, MS: University Press of Mississippi, 2002), p. 355.
[5]William Grant Still, Jr. is best known for his *Symphony No. 1 "Afro-American"* (1930) and his opera, *Troubled Island* (1937-39) [produced by New York City Opera in 1949], with libretto by Langston Hughes and Verna Arvey.
[6]*Normal Index* (January 1891).
[7]Lynn Abbott and Doug Seroff, *Out of Sight,* pp. 352-355.

Figure P1. W. C. Handy and the Alabama A. & M. Band, ca. 1900. In the photo one might notice that some of the young musicians are probably only grade-school and high-school age.

of the Blues," a nickname derived from his 1941 autobiography,[8] but he had already achieved considerable recognition on a national level as cornetist and bandmaster of Mahara's Colored Minstrels. Blackface minstrelsy, begun in America before the Civil War by white actors in "blackface" makeup, thrived during the late 19th century, and both white and black companies of actors and musicians toured and performed in the theaters and opera houses of the United States. These touring companies performed for white, black, and mixed audiences, and although the importance of the genre began to wane by the end of the first decade of the 20th century, this form of entertainment continued as a popular genre in America even as late as the Second World War.

Although male white Americans had the full gamut of employment and educational opportunities available to them from the earliest days of this nation to the present day, post-Civil-War

---

[8]William Christopher Handy, *Father of the Blues: An Autobiography by W. C. Handy* (New York: Macmillan, 1941).

Figure P2. James Hembray Wilson with the Alabama A. & M. College R.O.T.C. band in 1919. Wilson, hatless, stands with his trumpet at the center of the back row.

African Americans were not so fortunate. For the most part, menial jobs, both domestic and hard labor, were their lot, but just as sports during the second half of the 20th century became another gateway for African Americans to achieve equality, and sometimes even wealth and fame, black men of talent found similar opportunities in late 19th-century minstrelsy. As the *Iowa State Bystander* announced in 1897, "W. C. Handy, of Mahara's Minstrels, is making quite a reputation as a cornet sol[o]ist."[9] In fact, the young Handy served as bandmaster for Mahara's traveling entourage when, there in his minstrel show band, he met and traveled with an even younger James Hembray Wilson, a fellow cornetist who played under his direction. When Handy resigned his position at A. & M. after only serving two years,[10] this same James H. Wilson stepped into his shoes and became Handy's successor on the faculty.

---

[9] "Race Echoes," *Iowa State Bystander* (Des Moines, Iowa: March 26, 1897), p. 4.
[10] Handy's reasons for leaving after only two years are not clear, but popular web sites tend to emphasize his love of African-American music and the school's preference for "inferior foreign music considered to be 'classical'." [http://www.una.edu/library/about/collections/handy/biography.html] Most likely it was a combination of reasons involving personal ambitions and more rewarding opportunities elsewhere.

This book relates the story of James Hembray Wilson who, for over forty years directed instrumentalists and singers at A. & M.; participated in the founding of the school's first social sorority; taught the Sunday School as well as A. & M.'s future Sunday School teachers; served as postmaster of the community at Normal; and eventually became the first African-American treasurer of the college. A man of talent, conviction, and industry, he generously divided his productive life among music, church, college, and family.

Wilson began his professional career playing cornet in a minstrel show when he was but fifteen years of age. He had a lot of growing up to do before he reached manhood, and for several years he led a happy-go-lucky life as a rising young star on the road. Let us move backward in time and imagine for a moment that we are present among the theatergoers on a Saturday evening in 1899. We have purchased tickets to see the famous Mahara's Colored Minstrels at the local opera house. That afternoon we stood on the Front Street sidewalk and watched the black minstrel troupe parade down the main street of our own home town. There we saw the twenty-five-year-old W. C. Handy leading the band but hardly noticed the slender, even younger, eighteen-year-old Jimmie Wilson blowing and marching alongside two other fellow cornet players. This evening we have taken our seats in the opera house—whites on the first floor, blacks in the balcony—and the show is about to begin. When all is ready the band opens the entertainment with a snappy ragtime number, and as the music moves into its second chorus the costumed members of the troupe of minstrel actors and comedians enter from the rear and sing and dance their way down the aisles, through the audience and past the band onto the stage. Their improvised banjo, fiddle, and rhythm-bones playing contrasts with the orchestrated sound of the brass band in the pit, and all this joyous music accompanies singing voices and prancing feet. As the entertainers of the opening act gather on the stage, each before his chair, the master of ceremonies in high hat and tuxedo struts to center stage and inspects the audience and his company. This tall and dignified interlocutor moves to stand before his chair in the center of the stage, while to his right and left bounce the boisterous banjo-strumming and fiddle-playing singers and dancers. These stage performers are flanked by Tambo and Bones, the tambourine tapping and bones snapping percussionist-jokesters. When the accompanying music comes to the final cadence, we know that both the performers and the audience are ready to proceed. Responding to this cue the stately interlocutor removes his top hat, taps his cane once, spreads wide his arms, and addresses his cohorts in stentorian tones, "Gentlemen, be seated!"[11] And so our story begins.

---

[11] An introductory summary history of American minstrelsy is available on the web: John Kenrick, "A History of the Musical Minstrel Shows" (http://www.musicals101.com/minstrel.htm, accessed February 3, 2012).

CHAPTER ONE

Nicholasville, Kentucky: 1850—1893

Were you to drive to Nicholasville, Kentucky, today, you would discover a small but growing city of 20,000 residents situated just beyond the reach of Lexington, a prosperous and spreading metropolis. Urban sprawl connects one city with the other, but the two remain distinct entities, the county seats of two different areas—Jessamine and Fayette counties. Lexington harbors the state's land-grant research university and a huge medical center, boasts a bustling modern airport with direct flights to Chicago, Atlanta, Dallas and elsewhere, and thrives on the wealth of corporate centers and racing horses. Nicholasville is too small to claim any of these metropolitan features, but it is blessed with charm and a bustling local economy, and it blends into the surrounding natural beauty of the Kentucky bluegrass country. The rolling plains and modest hills of the central piedmont where it is situated inevitably lead downhill toward the Kentucky River. The undulating land serves as a massive watershed reaching south toward the impressive cliffs of the Kentucky River Palisades near historic Camp Nelson, one of the largest recruiting and training centers for African-American troops entering the Union Army during the American Civil War. Lexington sits only thirteen miles from Nicholasville, almost due north on US-27, and where the large city displays its gleaming high-rise buildings, Nicholasville, in contrast, boasts its Jessamine County Court House that was completed in 1878 and its Old Jail, that was built in 1870 when General Ulysses S. Grant was well into his first term as President of the United States. Throughout Nicholasville, low-rise modern structures serve the needs of civic and private offices, but the atmosphere of this city derives from its 19th-century past.

Figure 1-1. Jessamine County Court House, Nicholasville, Kentucky.

At the same time, today's Nicholasville is also cursed by the inconvenience of urban renewal, something one might expect only in larger municipalities. However, even in a village of 20,000 residents, the all-too-familiar problems of adequate parking and utilities never dreamed of by the builders of the antique buildings that still stand proudly on or near Main Street is causing a fair amount of inconvenience and upheaval. As the downtown revitalization project proceeds apace in 2011, cars and trucks steer around traffic cones and torn up streets, and proprietors of small shops on Main Street wait anxiously for the recession to end and the work to be completed.

Even though much remains from its 19th-century past, we should note that today's Nicholasville is much changed from the old Nicholasville and the even older and more rural Jessamine County where Jacob Wilson, the father of our protagonist James Hembray Wilson, was born in 1853 during the pre-Civil-War years, and this is where and when our tale begins. Although the few old buildings that stand and function today remind us of that earlier time, the reality of Jacob Wilson's town[1] of Nicholasville was immensely different from today's small southern city. As an African American, there were many places he was forbidden to go, items he could not purchase, and people to whom he must not speak. The various equal opportunity laws, provisions, and the civil rights movements of the 20th and 21st centuries that so altered our nation are only some of the significant transformations that have taken place since 1850, the year that Millard Fillmore became the 13th President of the United States upon the death of President Zachary Taylor. At that time, forty percent of the population of Jessamine County was African American, and virtually all of these men, women, and children were slaves. In 1850, this spacious county contained but 10,249 residents—6,256 whites, 168 free colored, and 3,825 black slaves.[2] Most of the male population of Kentucky, white and black,

Figure 1-2. South Main Street, Nicholasville, Kentucky. The cupola of the Court House towers above the shops.

---

[1]Designated a "Town" in the 1860 United States Federal Census.

worked with their hands and muscles. To travel from place to place, everyone walked, sat astride a horse or mule, or rode in an animal-drawn cart or carriage. There was one major, revolutionary exception to this rule—travel by railroad. By that time railroad lines connected the urban centers of the eastern half of the United States with fast, efficient transport, and The Cincinnati Southern Railroad linked both Lexington and Nicholasville to Ohio and the eastern half of the United States.

A large percentage of Kentucky males were employed in, or forced into, agricultural work in the fields tending crops or livestock. Most of the remainder were busy in coal mines, cotton and woolen factories, bagging factories, iron foundries, furnaces, and rolling mills, flour and grist mills, saw mills, distilling plants, and tanning and currying businesses.[3] Although most white citizens could read and write, only 38 percent of the free colored were able to do so in 1850 [that would mean only about 68 free African Americans in the entire state could read and write]. No statistics of literacy among slaves were collected at that time.[4] It is highly unlikely that more than a handful of black slaves could read, although household and office servants were taught those skills that would profit their masters. We might note that:

> In 1794 the governing body of the Presbyterian Church of Kentucky resolved that slaves belonging to members of the Presbyterian Church should be taught to read the Scriptures and prepare for freedom. . . . [and the Church even] urged immediate emancipation of all slaves who had been thusly prepared. . . .[5]

These good intentions had little effect in the real world. The major churches of Kentucky during this period, as enumerated by

---

[2]United States. Census Office, *The Seventh Census of the United States: 1850* (Washington, D. C.: Robert Armstrong, Public Printer, [G. P. O.] 1853), p. 611.
[3]U. S. Census Office, *Seventh Census . . . 1850,* p. 623.
[4]U. S. Census Office, *Seventh Census . . . 1850,* p. 622.
[5]Frank Robert Cannon, Jr., *Bethel Methodist Church, Jessamine County, Kentucky* (Nicholasville, KY: n. p., 1996), p. 5.

the 1850 census, were the Baptist and Methodist Churches, and they had no desire to press for these reforms. The Presbyterian Church was third in size, and it was followed by various congregations with a smaller representation throughout the state including Roman Catholic, Lutheran, and Episcopal Churches.[6] Although it is possible that Jacob Wilson might have been born a free man, this is statistically unlikely, and no evidence to support this possibility has yet been uncovered. Documentary evidence for African Americans during the pre-Civil War 19th century is spotty at best, but one should at least note that some free Black settlers moved to Kentucky from northern states and were able to maintain their status as "free people" and even own property. Their children, of course, would have been born free in this border state. However, it still remains most likely that Jacob Wilson, James H. Wilson's father, entered this world in bondage. Public records do not always provide definitive information, and we have a case in point with the Kentucky 1860 Slave Schedule, essentially a property inventory with no individual slave names listed. The 1860 Schedule informs us that Sophia Wilson, a white woman of Jessamine County, owned sixteen slaves and housed them all in a single building. Slaves were allowed no family names, but on achieving their freedom after the war they commonly took the family name of their master for their own. One of Sophia Wilson's slaves, number 10, was a black male child eight years of age, and this data closely approximates the facts known about the birth and place of birth of Jacob Wilson. Number 10 could have been someone else, but this boy may well have been James H. Wilson's father.[7]

James H. Wilson's mother, Hester Monroe Wilson, was born in June of 1862, one year after the beginning of the Civil War and six months before President Abraham Lincoln issued his Emancipation Proclamation. Hester Monroe, like Jacob Wilson, was also born in bondage, and at the earliest she could have gained her freedom

---

[6] U. S. Census Office, *Seventh Census . . . 1850,* pp. 633-641.
[7] 1860 Slave Schedule Kentucky, Jessamine County, Town of Nicholasville, p.39, col 1, lines 37- 40, col.2 lines 1-12 [printed number "310" in upper right hand corner].

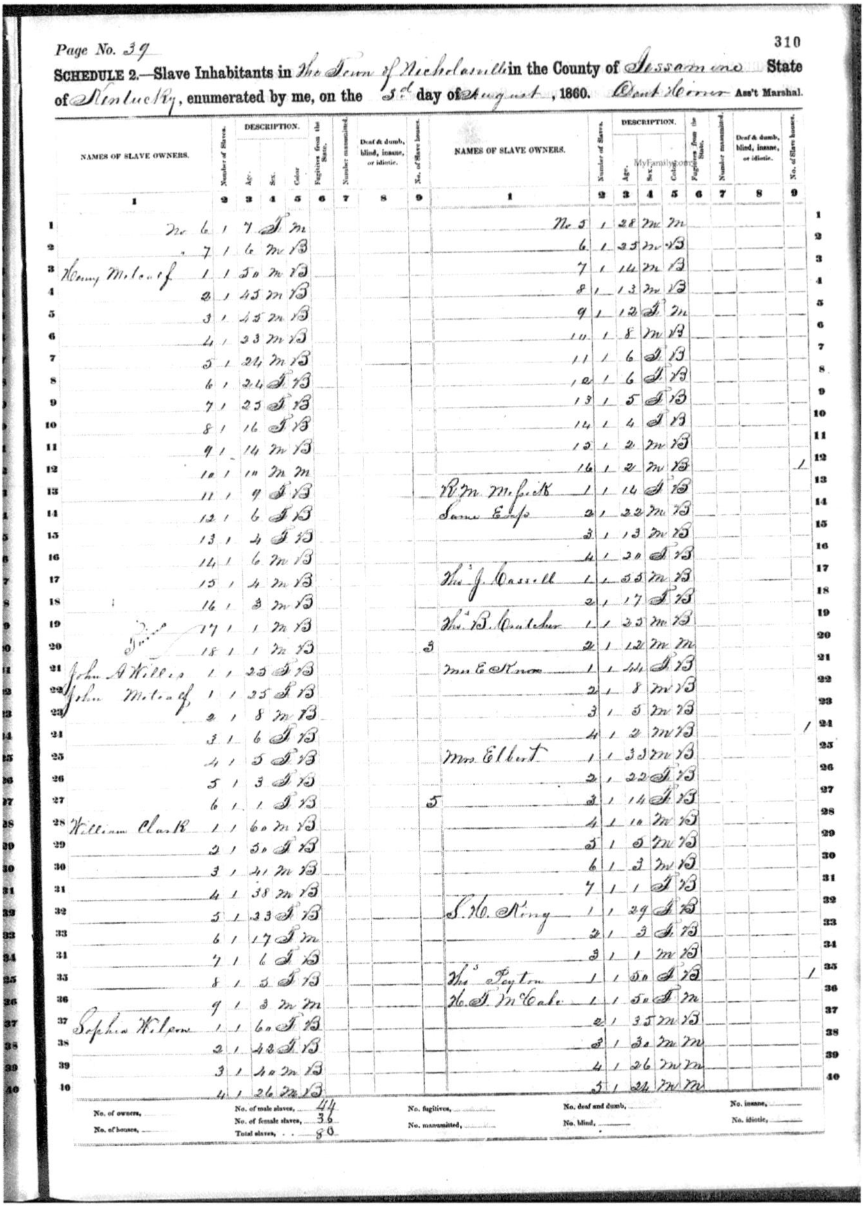

Page No. 39 310

SCHEDULE 2.—Slave Inhabitants in the Town of Nicholasville in the County of Jessamine State of Kentucky, enumerated by me, on the 3rd day of August, 1860. Dent Horner Ass't Marshal.

	NAMES OF SLAVE OWNERS. (1)		Number of Slaves. (2)	Age. (3)	Sex. (4)	Color. (5)	Fugitives from the State. (6)	Number manumitted. (7)	Deaf & dumb, blind, insane, or idiotic. (8)	No. of Slave houses. (9)
1		No 6	1	7	F	M				
2		7	1	6	M	B				
3	Henry Metcalf	1	1	50	M	B				
4		2	1	45	M	B				
5		3	1	45	M	B				
6		4	1	33	M	B				
7		5	1	24	M	B				
8		6	1	24	F	B				
9		7	1	25	F	B				
10		8	1	16	F	B				
11		9	1	14	M	B				
12		10	1	10	M	M				
13		11	1	9	F	B				
14		12	1	6	F	B				
15		13	1	4	F	B				
16		14	1	6	M	B				
17		15	1	4	M	B				
18		16	1	3	M	B				
19		17	1	1	M	B				
20		18	1	1	M	B				3
21	John A Willis	1	1	23	F	B				
22	John Metcalf	1	1	25	F	B				
23		2	1	8	M	B				
24		3	1	6	F	B				
25		4	1	5	F	B				
26		5	1	3	F	B				
27		6	1	1	F	B				5
28	William Clark	1	1	60	M	B				
29		2	1	50	F	B				
30		3	1	41	M	B				
31		4	1	38	M	B				
32		5	1	23	F	B				
33		6	1	17	F	M				
34		7	1	6	F	B				
35		8	1	5	F	B				
36		9	1	3	M	M				
37	Sophia Wilson	1	1	60	F	B				
38		2	1	42	F	B				
39		3	1	40	M	B				
40		4	1	26	M	B				

	NAMES OF SLAVE OWNERS. (1)		Number of Slaves. (2)	Age. (3)	Sex. (4)	Color. (5)	Fugitives from the State. (6)	Number manumitted. (7)	Deaf & dumb, blind, insane, or idiotic. (8)	No. of Slave houses. (9)
1		No 5	1	28	M	M				
2		6	1	25	M	B				
3		7	1	14	M	B				
4		8	1	13	M	B				
5		9	1	12	F	M				
6		10	1	8	M	B				
7		11	1	6	F	B				
8		12	1	6	F	B				
9		13	1	5	F	B				
10		14	1	4	F	B				
11		15	1	2	M	B				
12		16	1	2	M	B				1
13	R M McFick	1	1	14	F	B				
14	Sam Epps	2	1	22	M	B				
15		3	1	13	M	B				
16		4	1	20	F	B				
17	Thos J. Cassell	1	1	55	M	B				
18		2	1	17	F	B				
19	Thos B. Crutcher	1	1	25	M	B				
20		2	1	12	M	M				
21	Mrs E Knox	1	1	44	F	B				
22		2	1	8	M	B				
23		3	1	5	M	B				
24		4	1	2	M	B				1
25	Mrs. Elbert	1	1	33	M	B				
26		2	1	22	F	B				
27		3	1	14	F	B				
28		4	1	10	M	B				
29		5	1	5	M	B				
30		6	1	3	M	B				
31		7	1	1	F	B				
32	S. H. Roney	1	1	29	F	B				
33		2	1	3	F	B				
34		3	1	1	M	B				
35	Thos Peyton	1	1	50	F	B				1
36	H. S. McCabe	1	1	50	F	M				
37		2	1	35	M	B				
38		3	1	30	M	M				
39		4	1	26	M	M				
40		5	1	22	M	M				

No. of owners, — No. of houses, — No. of male slaves, 44 No. of female slaves, 36 Total slaves, 80 No. fugitives, — No. manumitted, — No. deaf and dumb, — No. blind, — No. insane, — No. idiotic, —

Figure 1-3. 1850 Slave Schedule, Jessamine County, Kentucky.

when she was three years old. Kentucky, a border state that joined the Confederacy late and did not officially declare secession from the United States, never officially released its slaves until forced to through defeat. African Americans had to wait out the war or hazard an escape to the north. Even then, as is well known, segregation remained dominant in both the North and the South for many decades.

Hester Monroe probably met the older Jacob Wilson some years later when she was in her teens and he in his twenties. When she was eighteen years old she gave birth to James Hembray Wilson in or near Nicholasville on December 19, 1880. At first theirs would have been a common-law marriage, not uncommon in America at that time, but Jacob and Hester soon obtained the blessings of church and state and were married at a friend's home the year following James' birth.

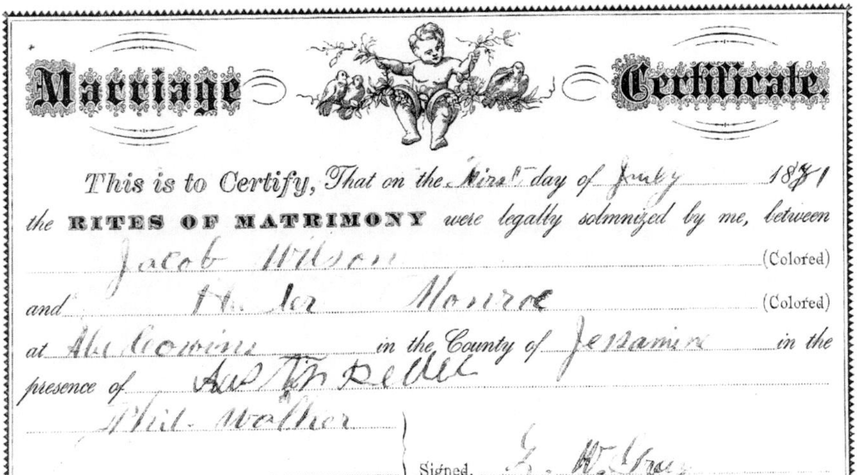

Figure 1-4. Marriage Certificate, Jacob Wilson and Hester Monroe [ceremony at Abe Cowins' home].

From the Marriage Certificate we learn that the couple were married at Abe Cowins',[8] a black man who worked as a mason and owned his own home on Hervey Street in the African-American district called Hervey Town in Nicholasville, the same area where Jacob rented a house.[9] The black section of town received its informal name from a local nurseryman who died in 1888, James O. Hervey.[10] He owned this land and built inexpensive homes on it that he then sold or rented to accommodate the black population of the town. Since Hervey, a Caucasian, owned

Figure 1-5. One of the older period homes in Hervey Town still in use in 2011 in Nicholasville, Kentucky. In the 1880s the house would have lacked the additions in back, electricity, and indoor plumbing.

---

[8]From the marriage document the last name might be "Cowin" or "Cowins," for there is no possessive apostrophe. The last name was spelled "Cowan" with an "a" in the 1920 US Census, Kentucky, Jessamine County, Nicholasville. To confuse matters further we find it spelled "Cowans" on the man's 1923 death certificate. Since he could neither read nor write I am sure that correct spelling was not a matter of prime importance to him.

[9]1910 US Census. Kentucky, Jessamine County, South Nicholasville.

[10]1860 US Census. Kentucky, Jessamine County, Town of Nicholasville.

Figure 1-6. Map 1. Nicholasville in 1877 with Court House, Jail, Hervey Town, Phillip Walker's house, and three "colored" churches located.[11]

[11]In 1877 a few plots and buildings in Hervey Town were still owned by James O. Hervey. To use space more efficiently the mapmaker indicates these with the initials "JOH" and "JH." His last name is spelled out fully on one of his buildings, "J. Hurvey." The modern annotations on the lower left portion of the map plus the oval, the connecting lines, and the shading of the annotated buildings are mine. The identification of the three churches as "colored" was made in 1877 by the mapmaker. [Beers (D. G.) and Company, *Atlas of Bourbon, Clark, Fayette, Jessamine, and Woodford Counties, Ky.* (Philadelphia, D. G. Beers & Co., 1877), image 22.]

seventeen black slaves of his own before the war,[12] it is likely that Hervey Town was a business venture for profit and not a humanitarian gesture. These real estate transactions also served unofficially but effectively to restrict the Blacks of Nicholasville to one area of town.

Jacob Wilson was a house plasterer,[13] and Abe Cowins was a mason, and these neighbors likely met while working together in the building trade for some local contractor. They surely became friends through this relationship. One of the witnesses on the certificate is Phillip Walker, and he, too, was a house plasterer like Jacob. Unlike Jacob, who rented his house, Walker owned his own home, and his house is plotted on an 1877 map of Nicholasville. Walker lived there with his wife, Belle, on Lincoln Street in Hervey Town[14], and on the 1877 map we can see his house drawn next to the "L" of Lincoln Street. Hervey Town had no legal borders; it was and is just an area in Nicholasville where most of the African Americans of the town lived then and live now. The general area is indicated by an oval drawn onto the map, and note that two "colored" churches fit into this area and that the third is close by.

James' father, Jacob, could read and write, but it is not known whether he had any formal schooling, since slaves were not normally afforded that luxury unless there was the possibility of potential profit from it for the master. One might expect the same would be true with respect to formal music lessons as well. Paul Alan Cimbala informs us that:

> Few of these slave musicians had "scientific training" but some owners who were aware of the possibility of personal gain from such an investment encouraged and facilitated formal lessons. . . . This was probably one slaveholder's reasoning when he at least permitted if not openly encouraged "a white man named Sneed" to teach one of his slaves the fiddle and another the banjo.[15]

---

[12]1860 Slave Schedule   Kentucky, Jessamine County, Town of Nicholasville, p. 37, col 1, lines 17- 32 [printed number "310" in upper right hand corner].

[13]1910 US Census. Kentucky, Jessamine County, South Nicholasville.

[14]1900 US Census. Kentucky, Jessamine County, Nicholasville.

[15]Paul Alan Cimbala, "Fortunate Bondsmen: Black 'Musicianers' in the Antebellum Southern United States" (unpublished master's thesis, Emory University, 1977), pp. 10-11. Cimbala points out (p.40): (cont.)

NICHOLASVILLE, KENTUCKY: 1850—1893

W. C. Handy, in a letter to his friend, William Grant Still, Jr., tells a slightly different tale about music instruction for African Americans in the South before and after the Civil War:

> I read an article in the *Daily News* about Negro music. . . . It glorified our music, but said we know how to make good music, but did not know how to read it. So, I wrote a letter about music in the south before and after the Civil War; and the theatres had Negro musicians that played all travelling shows, like Reuben Brooks at Vicksburg . . . . I told him of the Germans and Italians who came to the South and were ostracized and had to come to the colored homes; and [there they] taught some very fine musicians that were as good as any musicians at that time, but were held back.[16]

We know that Jacob Wilson had musical talent and that he learned to play horn well enough before the turn of the century to perform in a brass band. We find his name listed on the 1900-1901 roster of Elmore's Cyclone band, a small, 12-member community ensemble of Nicholasville, Kentucky, and on that same roster we find his son, James, listed too. By 1900 the son was already an experienced professional musician. The roster shows that James had become the director of the Cyclone band and that his father played horn in the ensemble.[17] Jacob's instrument was the alto or baritone horn, not likely the French horn, and it is he who first gave music lessons to "Professor Wilson," the honorary title commonly bestowed upon band directors. James' youngest daughter, Marian, said with certainty that her grandfather was a musician and that her father had first learned to play

---

The slave musician was a noticeable fixture of the antebellum South and the owners of these talented bondsmen clearly valued them. As members of the occupational hierarchy musicians were an important element in Southern life. Slaveholders used them to entertain at all types of social functions including military drills and parades. Masters attempted to capitalize further on their talents and used musicians to facilitate social control in the quarters and to earn extra cash. Since many owners believed it to be to their advantage, they encouraged their musicians whenever possible.

[16] W. C. Handy and Eileen Southern, "Letters from W. C. Handy to William Grant Still," in *The Black Perspective in Music*, v. 7, n. 2 (Autumn, 1979), p. 222.

[17] James H. Wilson Band and Tour Booklet, p.7.

from his father,[18] which is confirmed by Browne, a man who wrote using his last name only, saying, "While still a young lad he [James H. Wilson] was taught to play the horn by his father who was manager of a band."[19] Instrumental ensemble musicians must read music, especially those playing a concert band repertoire, and even though Jacob worked with his hands for a living, he must have received some music instruction somewhere along the way.

From about 1880 to approximately 1893, Jacob and his family lived somewhere in Hervey Town. Unfortunately the 1890 census was mostly destroyed by fire and so leaves an unfortunate gap in the historical record during the time of James' grade school years. We know there was a public school set aside for the African-American children of Nicholasville, and if it was Dunbar School, as some current residents of Hervey Town have suggested, it would have been located on present-day Walnut Street. Sadly, this school is not shown on the 1877 map. In later life James H. Wilson composed a brief autobiography and referred to his Kentucky educational experience in this manner:

> Mr. Wilson was born in Nicholasville, Ky., December 19, 1880, and after "going through" the public schools at that place he finished his education in the public schools of Cincinnati, O.[20]

We know that young James' early years in Nicholasville were the source of many pleasant memories, for he returned there many times over the years and even made "My Old Kentucky Home," a minstrel song by Stephen Foster, one of his signature solo pieces for cornet. James family surely were members of a "colored" Protestant church in his hometown, but which one is still a puzzle. In later life James maintained membership in a Baptist Church in Huntsville, Alabama, but

---

[18]Interview with Marian Floredia Wilson Turner, September 16, 2010.

[19]Browne [no first name], "The Man Himself: Prof. James H. Wilson, Sr." *The State A. & M. Campus Journal* (Normal: The State A. & M. Institute, [1943]), p. 3.

[20]"Woodbine" [pen name], "The Stage," *The Freeman* (Indianapolis, IN: January 2, 1904), v. xvi, n. 2, p. 5.

his father, Jacob, was a member of the "Colored Christian Church" on East Street in Nicholasville.[21] It is possible the family worshiped together in this attractive brick building with gothic windows, Figure 1-7. Notice the horse carriage parked to the left of the entrance and the African-American man leaning on the fence. The bell tower is attractive. The gothic windows appear to contain clear glass and would provide good illumination. The round window, high above the front of the church, seems to be decorated with stained glass. The white house to the right was probably the parsonage.

There were three "colored" churches indicated on the 1877 map of Nicholasville, all on East Street, and James later attended and served in a leadership role with all three.[22] In Hervey Town, the congregation of Bethel African Methodist Episcopal Church completed their new church building in 1868 one block south of the courthouse and one block east of Main Street. This sanctuary eventually served as the worship space for most of the African-American community of Nicholasville for many years.[23] When James returned to Nicholasville some years later he "presided" at the organ for the Bethel A. M. E. Sunday evening service. It is also possible that Jacob, Hester, James, and his sister, Maggie, worshipped here in the A. M. E. church during James' early years.

---

[21]James H. Wilson, *Journal*, February 22, 1908.
[22]James H. Wilson, *Journal*, February 23, 1908.
[23]See Cannon, *Bethel Methodist Church, op. cit.* Also note James' Journal entries, Appendix 1, February 22-24.

WITH TRUMPET AND BIBLE

Figure 1-7. Colored Christian Church, Nicholasville, Kentucky.[24]
[Photo ca. 1890].

[24]Bennett Henderson Young, *A history of Jessamine County, Kentucky, from its earliest settlement to 1898*. S. M. Duncan, associate author. (Louisville, Ky.: Courier-journal job printing co., 1898), p. 192

Figure 1-8. Bethel Methodist Church [formerly Bethel African Methodist Episcopal Church] in 2011.

In later life James and his family maintained membership in the First Baptist Church of Huntsville, Alabama, and there he served as a deacon and worked diligently in the Sunday school programs. The early "Colored Baptist Church," of Nicholasville, pictured below, Figure 1-9, is also located on East Street and is the third possibility for a house of worship for Jacob and his family. This simple frame and clapboard structure with its attractive Roman-arch windows over the entryway could have been young James' boyhood church. We simply do not know, but what is certain is that when he later returned to visit his home town in 1908, he addressed the morning Sunday school of the Nicholasville Colored Baptist Church and then remained there for the Service as well.[25]

---

[25]James H. Wilson, *Journal*, February 23, 1908.

Figure 1-9. The early "Colored Baptist Church" in Hervey Town, Nicholasville.[26]

---

[26]Young, *History of Jessamine County, op. cit.*, p. 186.

The religious beliefs and church involvement of James Hembray Wilson were central to some of his most meaningful activities and accomplishments in the years to come. Although his early years on the road as a minstrel musician seem to contradict some of his religious and moral views in later life, James' home religious training and church experiences in Nicholasville seem to have played a decisive role in shaping his spiritual, ethical, and moral development of later years. These principles clearly affected the professional decisions he made during his adult years. In his church he found meaning and purpose, as well as security and comfort from all the tribulations inflicted upon him and his loved ones. Years later, on his final minstrel venture he rode the train from Nashville, Tennessee, to Princeton, Kentucky. On that leg of his trip he wrote in his Journal to remind himself of his daily activities. There we see that he read his beloved and well-worn Bible and noted the chapters he studied that day.[27] Near the beginning we find words that seem to encapsulate feelings he carried deep in his heart for his church and his brothers and sisters in Christ:

> We are bound to thank God always for you, brethren, as it is meet, because that your faith groweth exceedingly, and the charity of every one of you all toward each other aboundeth; So that we ourselves glory in you in the churches of God for your patience and faith in all your persecutions and tribulations that ye endure:
>
> 2 Thessalonians 1: 3-4.

Wilson came back often to Nicholasville—to get married, to live with his first wife, Georgia, to visit his father, to direct a band, to sell copies of a national African-American newspaper (the Indianapolis *Freeman*), and to sue for and obtain a divorce. In the years after his first marriage he likely set up a household with Georgia somewhere in town, but its location is not known. The couple may have shared space in his father's house. Truly, "My Old Kentucky Home" meant a great deal more to James H. Wilson than just the title of a popular song he frequently played in public recitals.

---

[27]James Wilson's Journal, p. 30. [Appendix 1]

Life took a quick turn and circumstances changed dramatically and unexpectedly for young James sometime around the beginning of his high school years. His mother, Hester, packed her bags, boarded the Cincinnati Southern Railroad, and left her husband to move north to Cincinnati, Ohio. We do not know why or precisely when she left, but she took her two children, James and his younger sister, Maggie, with her and moved into an apartment far away from Jacob. Perhaps she sought a better life and greater educational opportunities for her children; could be she dreamed of greater opportunities for herself; obviously her marriage had deteriorated; or conceivably some other reason intervened to force the move. But when she got to her chosen destination, the best she could manage for herself as an illiterate woman of color in the 1890s, was employment as a washerwoman in the court house district of a large northern city. Maggie did little better, but huge new vistas were about to open up for James Hembray Wilson.

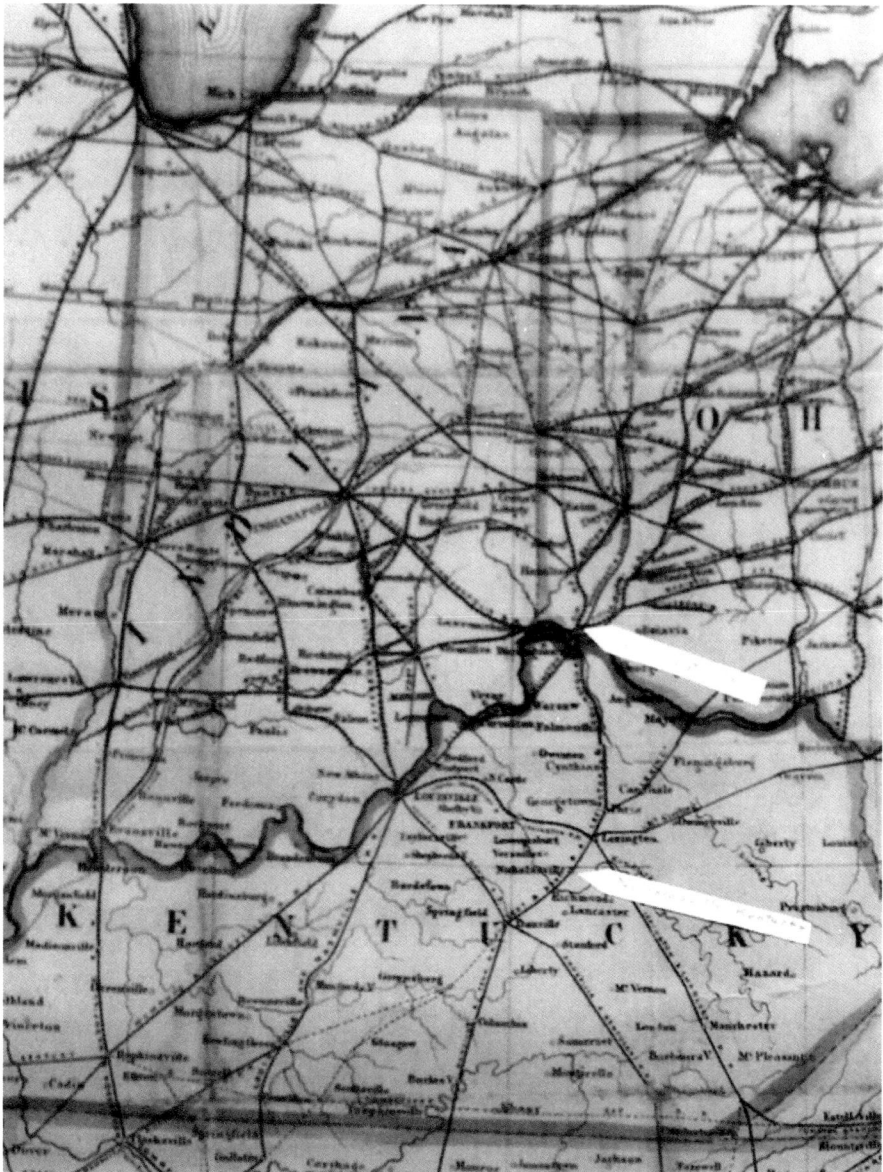

Figure 1-10. Map 2. Nicholasville, Kentucky to Cincinnati, Ohio. [100 miles]. From *Map of all the Railroads in the United States in Operation* ... (New York:, H.V. Poor ... [1855]).

Figure 2-1. A vintage building on the opposite side of East Court Street [photo taken 2011].

CHAPTER TWO

Cincinnati, Ohio: 1893—1902

Young James H. Wilson was clearly precocious, musically talented, and filled with boundless energy. Once he left Nicholasville he was able to enjoy an enriched lifestyle as he ventured from his new home in downtown Cincinnati on East Court Street near Main. Living in Cincinnati was totally unlike life in small-town Kentucky, and to this smart teenager the opportunities must have seemed boundless. The theme song of the popular television sitcom series of the 1970s and '80s, *The Jeffersons*, would have been appropriate for James Wilson and his generation of African Americans as it was for Mr. and Mrs. James Jefferson when they moved from Archie and Edith Bunker's working-class neighborhood to the upper-middle-class lifestyle of Manhattan. Though there are many differences between the historical Wilsons and the fictional Jeffersons, both families were on the move and striving to advance—socially, culturally, and economically:

> Well we're movin' on up,
> To the east side,
> To a deluxe apartment in the sky.
> Movin' on up,
> To the east side.
> We finally got a piece of the pie.
>
> Fish don't fry in the kitchen,
> Beans don't burn on the grill . . . .
>   Lyrics by Jeff Barry and Ja'net Dubois

The Wilsons had not yet become members of the middle-class, but James H. Wilson was about to take his first step up the ladder. It was much more difficult for his mother, who could neither read nor write, and for his sister, who could, but who, as a young black woman, had to contend with both the sexism and racism of late-Victorian America.

By 1900 James had already climbed onto the first step up the socio-economic ladder toward middle-class stature. In that year, this nineteen-year-old African American had his occupation recorded on the U. S. Census as a "musician."[1] As we shall soon see, it is quite likely that by this time he was earning good money and making a substantial contribution to the family income. In fact, the various types of music he performed also elevated his respect in the public eye—both the minstrel music and the concert band repertoire. The snappy ragtime pieces were in vogue as *the* popular music of the day; sentimental songs were still drawing tears from late-Victorian audiences who attended these shows, often performed in local opera houses; classical favorites, such as Rossini's "William Tell Overture" were incorporated into the minstrel show productions to add an element of class; and the concert bands were special in their own way as America's favorite outdoor musical entertainment. The leading performers were popular heroes, in some ways comparable to today's pop stars and rock musicians, and we shall see that James H. Wilson received his fair share of attention in the public press.

James' mother rented an apartment on the "East Side" of Cincinnati near the Court House, and she made her living laundering clothes and renting a room to a boarder, Nicholas Worthy, an African-American day laborer. James' younger sister, Maggie, worked as a "servant," which in 1900 Cincinnati meant a domestic servant—a maid, housekeeper, or kitchen help. We know Hester Wilson moved to Cincinnati a few years before 1900. By this date she had become head of the household at 106 East Court Street. We can only speculate why Jacob remained in Nicholasville. As for the apartment that was now Hester's home, one can travel to Cincinnati today to view some of the turn-of-the-century buildings on Court Street that have been preserved and still function well. Some, of course, have been leveled and

---

[1] 1900 U. S. Census, Cincinnati, Hamilton County, Ohio.

Figure 2-2. A vintage five-story building directly across the street from where 106 East Court Street would have stood ca. 1900 [photo 2011].

replaced, and unfortunately the Wilsons' residence at number 106 was demolished and the location turned into a parking lot. However, period buildings just across the street still preserve the four- and five-story brick walk-up structures characteristic of the era with businesses on the first floor and apartments above.

As one studies census documents of the period it becomes apparent that the census takers walked from residence to residence and collected information in an order based on location. In the case of an apartment building, especially in the days before elevators were common, common sense tells us that the "enumerator" began his task by interviewing residents on the ground floor first and then slowly worked his way up to the top floor. Judging from the number of families interviewed at this location before reaching the apartment of Hester Wilson, her name appears at the end of the list, and considering that a washerwoman is likely to seek out one of the least expensive rentals, the Wilsons and Mr. Worthy, their boarder, probably lived on the fourth or fifth floor of their building. They probably had no more than two bedrooms, a kitchen, a living room, and a bath, if that, but running water and steam heat were luxuries they probably had not enjoyed in Kentucky. It is not difficult to imagine the struggle this family underwent, as did many other American apartment dwellers in the late 19th century, as they hauled food, supplies, and other shopping, and perhaps even Hester's laundry, up all those stairs. Hester, born in 1862, died in 1912 at the age of fifty. James' sister Maggie, who was seventeen in 1900, seems to have disappeared from the records. Perhaps she married and changed her name, or perhaps she died young. We do not know.

When James first moved to Cincinnati, probably around 1893 to 1895, he attended Games High School.[2] As a youngster he learned to play the cornet, and it is possible that he was first coached in Nicholasville by his father, who played horn in Elmore's Cyclone Band.[3] However, James probably received his first professional instruction on the instrument while attending a public high school in the big city. The cornet, a brass instrument similar to the trumpet but producing a mellower tone, was a very popular musical instrument in America during these turn-of-the-century years. Cornet soloists were regularly featured on concerts of many of the famous bands of the day, such as those of Patrick Gilmore and John Philip Sousa. Concert-hall and outdoor band concerts were extremely popular as forms of public entertainment in the days before radio, sound recordings, and movies, and virtually every band—local, national, and military—had its cornet soloist.

Wilson not only earned his high school diploma from a large, metropolitan high school, an accomplishment about which he boasted more than a few times in the years to come, but he also learned to play cornet well enough to make his entrance into the world of professional music at the age of fifteen. Before his 20th

---

[2]Fleming, G. James and Christian E. Burckel, eds. *Who's Who in Colored America*, 7th ed. (New York: Who's Who in Colored America Corp, 1950), p.565. In 1950 the school had been renamed Western District High School.
[3]Journal No. 2, p. 7.

birthday he would earn his reputation as a solo cornet virtuoso and become the director of more than one professional band. By age thirty he had composed music for minstrel bands that would gain attention in the public press. James was a young man of great musical talent and developing intellectual gifts, and he began his professional life when he seized an opportunity for paid employment in the "Pickaninny Band" of a successful musical/theatrical production. Although "Pickaninny" was a derogatory slang expression for an African-American child, similar to "Wop" or "Dago" for an Italian-American, "Kike" for a Jewish-American, or "Chink" for a Chinese-American, Wilson, like all Black members of minstrel companies, accepted these degradations as the unavoidable dues to be paid for entrance into the world of professional entertainment at a time when there were virtually no other similar options for African-Americans.

In 1895 Jacob Litt's minstrel theater piece, "In Old Kentucky," earned these words in the *Parsons* [Kansas] *Weekly Blade*:

> "In Old Kentucky" drew a crowded house last Friday night. The streets in the afternoon were crowded with spectators to see the Picniny [Pickaninny] band.[4]

It was during the following year, the 1896-1897 season that our young cornetist, Jimmy Wilson, was playing and strutting in that same band.[5]

When the show opened two years earlier in 1894 it enjoyed a seven-month run at the New York Academy of Music. Writer/promoter Jacob Litt wanted to capitalize on his New York success, so he booked the show for an extensive U. S. tour. The entertainment editor for the St. Paul, Minnesota, *Broad Axe* wrote this glowing announcement:

---

[4]*Parsons Weekly Blade* (Parsons, KS: January 12, 1895), p.3.
[5]Fleming and Burckel, eds. *Who's Who in Colored America*, 7th ed., pp.565-6. [Biographees, all living when the book was compiled, supplied their own biographical information. Although Wilson's name does not appear in any of the historical newspaper accounts of Litt's production, for our purposes this listing is considered a primary source verifying Wilson's engagement with the *In Old Kentucky* Company.]

Figure 2-3. Lithograph poster advertising Jacob Litt's production, *In Old Kentucky*.

The second annual tour of Jacob Litt's very successful drama of Blue Grass Life, "In Old Kentucky," has been auspiciously inaugurated and another season of prosperity is undoubtedly in store for this capital play.... [The New York success] prevented the production from visiting many cities and therefore it will be entirely new to a great majority of theatre-goers, especially in the west. Its prime features, however, have been made more or less familiar through the general attention given them by the dramatic writers of the country. The striking novelty of a brass band composed entirely of diminutive darkies and the genuine racing scene will particularly arouse interest among theatre-goers, and the general excellence of the play itself will doubtless combine to attract large audiences everywhere. This immense attraction will appear at the Grand, Thanksgiving week, commencing Sunday, Nov. 25th.[6]

---

[6] *The Broad Axe* (St. Paul, MN: November 15, 1894), v. 4, n. 10, p.1.

Today we recognize that these romanticized tales of "darkies" happily living in bondage are entirely figments of the imagination of white writers[7] of the antebellum, wartime, reconstruction and post-reconstruction eras, but the fact remains that black actors and musicians were also able to capitalize on these notions and join the theater world through minstrel genres previously reserved for costumed white entertainers in blackface makeup. Many black musicians earned fame and fortune in a manner not possible before for African Americans, especially in the South. Today, as repulsive as we find both this simple-minded portrayal of slavery and the derisive portrayal of African Americans in general, blackface minstrelsy remains a historical fact that continued well into the 20th century. James H. Wilson, like W. C. Handy, not only profited from it, but he, like Handy, was proud to be a part of this form of theatrical entertainment.

Having tasted the excitement and challenges of living and working on the road, sixteen-year-old Jimmy Wilson found himself a new job for the next two years touring with Al Martin's production of Harriet Beecher Stowe's *Uncle Tom's Cabin*.[8] Wilson must have been gaining musical skills at a prodigious rate, for he started this tour as a cornetist in the production's band and became one of their bandmasters by age eighteen, probably of the company's second band, before the company completed its second-year's tour.[9] The show was elaborate and expensive, and when it toured Michigan in 1896, the *Jackson Citizen Patriot* printed:

ANNOUNCEMENTS.
"UNCLE TOM'S CABIN"

The Salter & Martin mammoth original, three-car Uncle Tom's Cabin company at the opera house, Saturday afternoon and evening, is actually a $20,000 production of this grand, old historical play—a magnificent scenic production. It requires a

---

[7]The playwright Charles Turner Dazey was born in Illinois in 1855 and graduated from Harvard in 1881. His play, written for Jacob Litt, *In Old Kentucky*, ran without interruption for 26 years.

[8]*Who's Who in Colored America*, ibid.

[9]*Philadelphia Inquirer* (Philadelphia, PA: April 3, 1898), v. 138, no. 86, p. 14.

whole train of three 60-foot palace cars to transport this mammoth spectacle: 40 people, 20 ponies, donkeys and burros, mules, oxen, horses, eight original jubilee singers, a pack of seven man-eating Siberian and Cuban bloodhounds; Eva's golden chariot, "a thing of beauty," costing over $3,000; two big bands of music; Uncle Tom and his typical southern ox-cart. The grand free street parade is the finest ever witnessed. The sight of a life-time![10]

It would appear that young Wilson had arrived when he joined Al Martin's company, and both his playing and his conducting for this show would serve to establish his musical credentials and his uniquely personal musical identity. But the road furthered his education in other ways as well. Not only did he now have the opportunity to travel—he later claimed to have visited forty-four of the then forty-seven states and Canada—but he also began to encounter some of the more unpleasant aspects of life. While on tour in New Jersey in 1897, two of the expensive show dogs, a Great Dane and a Siberian bloodhound, were poisoned. The performers' reaction to the incident was reported in the newspaper:

"Bounce" was a Great Dane 27 months old and was considered the feature of the street parade. It was also a very affectionate animal and a great favorite with every member of the company. His death so affected them that many of the performers wept when they heard the sad news.[11]

During these same two years, 1897 to 1899, Wilson also served as cornetist in the band of Mahara's Minstrels. How he divided his time between two different shows is uncertain, and it would have been tricky at best, even for a young man full of energy and ready to take on the world. Perhaps he played part of the touring season with one company and part with the other, or perhaps the two companies had different touring schedules that allowed the young musician to shuttle back and forth between the two. Either way, W. C. Handy, the bandmaster of Mahara's Minstrels, confirms that James played cornet in his band. In his 1941 autobiography, when Handy wrote about his decision to leave his teaching post at Alabama A. & M., he said:

---

[10]*Jackson Citizen Patriot* (Jackson, MI: October 23, 1896), v. xxxii, no. 184, p.7.
[11]*Trenton Evening Times* (Trenton, NJ: November 28, 1897), p. 1.

Figure 2-4. Lithograph poster copyrighted by Al. W. Martin ca. 1899.

At any rate, the next season saw me back with Mahara again, and James Wilson, cornetist in our minstrel band, became musical director at A. & M., a position he has held almost forty years.[12]

Handy and Wilson remained friends for the rest of Handy's life, and whenever the older man returned to A. & M. as a visiting dignitary he made a point of going over to James' home and spending time with his former band member and successor at the college.

These minstrel band experiences led to professional opportunities with concert bands as well. James Hembray Wilson never enlisted in nor was drafted into the army,[13] but he was not ashamed to say that:

> Mr. Wilson has the distinction of being one of the leading trumpeters in America regardless of race . . . . [One] of the coveted positions held by Mr. Wilson . . . . [was] Soloist [with the] 9th Cavalry Band, Douglas, Arizona, [for] two weeks.[14]

and he added elsewhere that:

> Mr. Wilson has the distinction of being the first civilian ever to be appointed to a position of rank in the U. S. Army. He was appointed chief trumpeter in the 9th Cavalry Band.[15]

The African-American 9th Cavalry, dubbed the "The Buffalo Soldiers" by Native Americans, was raised shortly after the Civil War by General Philip Sheridan as a regiment of "colored" cavalry. The 9th Cavalry, distinguished itself and earned great fame while serving in the American West.

---

[12]W. C. Handy, *Father of the Blues: An Autobiography*, ed. by Arna Bontemps, Foreword by Abbe Niles (reprint, Da Capo, NY: 1985 [originally published Macmillan, NY: 1941]), p.63.

[13]Wilson did register for the draft on September 12, 1918 (Local Board, County of Madison, City of Huntsville, State of Alabama, Registration Card, Serial Number 810).

[14]Recital program (June 24, 1940), "The Alabama A. & M. College Presents Mr. James H. Wilson in Trumpet Recital."

[15]Recital program (June 9, 1948), "The Alabama A. & M. College Presents Mr. James H. Wilson in Trumpet Recital."

There it [the 9th Cavalry] was charged with protecting stage and mail routes, building and maintaining forts, and establishing law and order in a vast area full of outlaws, Mexican revolutionaries, and raiding Comanches, Cheyennes, Kiowas, and Apaches. To compound their problems, many Texans felt that they were being subjected to a particularly harsh form of post-war reconstruction by Washington, and saw the assignment of the Black troopers as a deliberate attempt by the Union to further humiliate them. As such, the relationship between the troopers and locals was often at or near the boiling point. Despite prejudice and the almost impossible task of maintaining some semblance of order from the Staked Plains to El Paso to Brownsville, the 9th established themselves as one of the most effective fighting forces in the Army.[16]

U. S. Army regulations authorized regiments to enlist musicians, and these musical units were used to attract recruits, comfort tired soldiers, inspire troops into battle, lead the soldiers on the parade grounds, and entertain the officers and men with concerts and dances. The 9th Cavalry Regimental Band of African-American musicians was no exception, and apparently James H. Wilson was invited to perform as a uniformed member with rank because of his virtuosic solo abilities, even though he was a civilian.

In the following photograph, Figure 2-6, probably taken at the Army Post in Douglas, Arizona, we see a handsome young James H. Wilson seated in the front row, on the left next to the bass drum, smiling and relaxed, holding his trumpet on his knee. He seems pleased with himself, as well he might be, a man recognized for his achievement at a very early age.

In the detail of this photo, Figure 2-7, we can just discern two stripes on the sleeve of Wilson's jacket near the cuffs, the chevron insignia of rank of Corporal in the army. Perhaps that is what Wilson was referring to when he said he was "the first civilian to be appointed to a position of rank. . . ." Notably, this "chief trumpeter" smiles slightly as he looks to his right, in contrast to the more military directness of most others' gazes.

---

[16]Ninth Cavalry Timeline, http://www.9thcavalry.com/history/timeline.htm, accessed January 18, 2012.

Figure 2-5. Buffalo Soldiers band on parade.

Figure 2-6. 9th Cavalry Trumpet Corps with soloist James H. Wilson (seated front row on left, next to bass drum).

Figure 2-7. 9th Cavalry Trumpet Corps, detail, James H. Wilson.

In the fall of 1899 two separate minstrel companies, The Original Nashville Students and Gideon's Minstrel Carnival, joined forces and toured as a combined unit. Together they numbered fifty entertainers, employed two bands, and traveled in two railroad cars. The Chicago agency of Rusco & Holland billed them, together with the Georgia Minstrels, and advertised an attraction they called "The Largest Minstrel Show in the World." The Richards and Pringles Famous Georgia Minstrels numbered another forty-five people, two bands and a special train for its own touring. This large production must have drawn resources from all three companies to offer a combined show, a Big Minstrel Festival, with 55 people and three bands, all of which were transported in special trains. These musicians and stage entertainers were ready to impress Chicago and then America with minstrel magnificence. This was big-time entertainment at its extravagant best, and James Hembray Wilson was dead center in the middle of it.

During the fall season of that year James began work with The Nashville Students, a professional entertainment company whose band had earlier earned a reputation for its excellent performance of "classical" music under the direction of Harry Prampin.

> Harry Prampin's peerless concert band will soon be heard in concert, rendering the following overtures: "Faust," "Wm. Tell," "Wang," "Bridal Rose" and many other classical selections.[17]

---

[17] *The Freeman* (Sept. 9, 1899), v. xii, n. 34, p. 5.

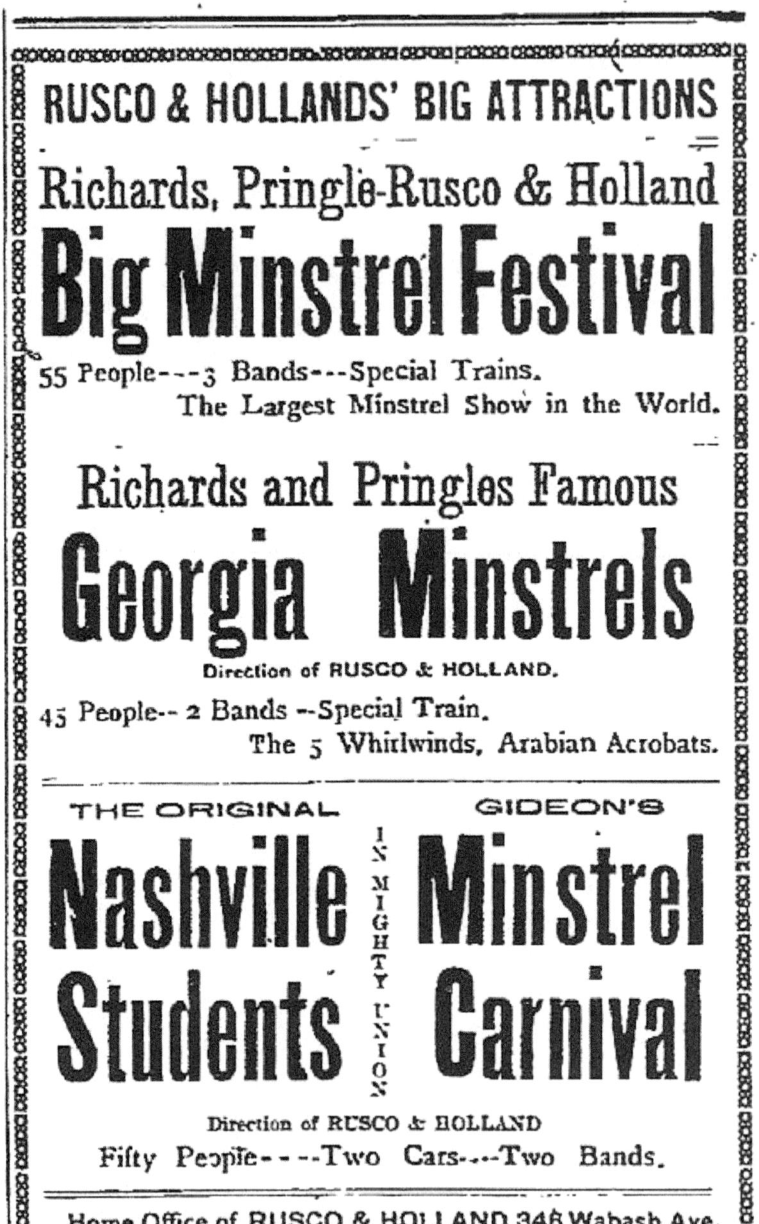

RUSCO & HOLLANDS' BIG ATTRACTIONS

Richards, Pringle-Rusco & Holland

Big Minstrel Festival

55 People---3 Bands---Special Trains.
The Largest Minstrel Show in the World.

Richards and Pringles Famous

Georgia Minstrels

Direction of RUSCO & HOLLAND.

45 People-- 2 Bands --Special Train.
The 5 Whirlwinds, Arabian Acrobats.

THE ORIGINAL Nashville Students

IN MIGHTY UNION

GIDEON'S Minstrel Carnival

Direction of RUSCO & HOLLAND

Fifty People----Two Cars----Two Bands.

Home Office of RUSCO & HOLLAND 346 Wabash Ave. Chicago, Ill., care National Printing Co.

Figure 2-8. Minstrel Festival Announcement in the Indianapolis *Freeman,* September 23, 1899.

When the Nashville Students teamed up with Gideon's Big Minstrel Carnival for a combined tour, the troupe advertised two military bands under the direction of Prampin, ten soloists, and a "symphony orchestra" conducted by Dan Desdunes.[18] These musicians went into rehearsal during August of that year at Mt. Carroll, Illinois, and their season opened on September 4th. Shortly thereafter while on tour the company reported to *The Freeman*:

> The Nashville Students and Gideon's Big Minstrel Carnival are now in their third week packing them nightly. E. J. Carpenter our business manager is determined that our company shall lead minstrelsy so you can imagine the rest. Our street parade is superb. Sam Robinson our drum major stands pre-eminent as a baton manipulator. Our walking gents, ten in number, are most gorgeously attired, presenting within itself a true picture of minstrelsy.... Harry Prampin spent the week rehearsing his famous band.... Jas. H. Wilson is with the Students playing trombone in orchestra and cornet in band.[19]

At this time the eighteen-year-old musician had not yet earned his title of "cornet virtuoso," but he was gaining experience and making important professional contacts posthaste.

Not every minstrel company was as lucky in its travels as was theirs. For example, we see in a neighboring article from the same journal that Melroy, Chandler & Co.'s Real Negro Minstrels had a difficult time in Texas. It is interesting to note the change in writing style and choice of words used by the reporter for the Real Negro Minstrels as he writes of their trying experiences in the Southwest. There is little of the enthusiasm found in the Nashville Students' account.

> Notes from Melroy, Chandler & Co's. Real Negro Ministrels [sic].—Owing to the Yellow fever scare in Louisiana we have changed our route and [are] now heading northward through the [Cherokee] "Nation" [Oklahoma] over into Missouri, Wisconsin, Iowa and Minnesota. While our business far exceeded expectations in the Lone Star State, everybody was glad enough to say good-by to Texas at Whitesboro last Wednesday night, and

---

[18] *The Freeman* (Aug. 26, 1899), v. xii, n. 22, p. 5.
[19] *The Freeman* (Sept. 30, 1899), v. xii, n. 36, p. 5.

the majority of the members of the company declare it their last visit to Texas—"You aint nothing but a nigger no how in Texas," so they say.[20]

James' advancement in the profession was rapid, for after only a few months on tour with the company we read:

> Ray Trusty of the Nashville Students and Gideon's Minstrel Co., writes: — "We are in our 14th week. Every member of the above company is well. Mr. Gideon has added to his company Simon Bonimor's No. 2 Troupe of Arabs, late of the Buffalo Bill's Wild West Show, known as the Six Whirlwinds. . . . Our roster is as follows. . . . Harry Prampin, leader of No. 1 band; Mr. James H. Wilson, leader of No. 2 band; . . .[21]

And just one week after this announcement we see another advancement posted in the *Freeman*, "J. Wilson, solo cornet." And then, further down in the same article we also read, "Jas. H. Wilson has proven himself quite a trombonist with Prof. Desdune's superb orchestra."[22] The other band members are rarely mentioned, so this is high praise indeed. So much attention devoted to this youngster by a major touring group is a clear indication of his great talent and skill as well as his intelligence, willingness to work, and amiable personality.

During the summer of 1899 Wilson found himself another job. Not long before, R. H. Barnett of the Leland Melroy Minstrels wrote *The Freeman* to explain that their manager, Melroy, had skipped out on them and that their show under his banner was closing but was opening again with new management as the New Orleans Minstrels.[23] When Wilson finished touring the regular season with Mahara's Minstrels and Martin's Uncle Tom's Cabin Company, he accepted a summer job as bandmaster of the New Orleans Minstrels.[24] Word was getting around that this 18-year-

---

[20]*Ibid.*
[21]*The Freeman* (Nov. 11, 1899), v. xii, n. 42, p. 5.
[22]*The Freeman* (Nov. 18, 1899), v. xii, n. 44, p. 5.
[23]*The Freeman* (Oct. 29, 1898), v. xi, n. 44, p. 5.
[24]Fleming, G. James and Christian E. Burckel, eds. *Who's Who in Colored America*, 7th ed.(New York: Who's Who in Colored America Corp, 1950), pp.565-6.

old was good. He was certainly not lacking for employment opportunities, and he parted company with the New Orleans Minstrels in the fall to follow other pursuits.

While he was touring with the Nashville Students, a friend inserted a personal notice in *The Freeman*, "Nathan Wilkins sends regards to Prof. Jas. Wilson, Oliver Perry, C. J. Scotte and all members of the Cyclone Band."[25] "Professor" was a title of respect generally used by musicians for the leader of the band, certainly not an academic rank in this case. Wilson now had a fair amount of conducting experience under his belt—Al Martin's *Uncle Tom's Cabin* company, the New Orleans Minstrels, the Nashville Students, and his own hometown musical organization, Elmore's Cyclone Band. In this case, he was its musical director and conductor.

Wilson's tour with the Nashville Students came to an end in 1900, and about this same time he became infatuated with a young woman who would soon become his first wife, Georgia Miller from Lexington, Kentucky. During the last month of 1900 a newspaper article happily proclaimed that James married this girl. The announcement appeared as front page news in the Indianapolis *Freeman*, and it was probably sent to the paper by young Wilson, himself:

> Lexington, Ky., Special.—James H. Wilson, the cornetist, has retired from the road and is band instructor of Elmore's Cyclone Band, Nicholasville, Ky. He has taken unto himself a rib by the name of Georgia Miller, now Georgia Wilson. Regards to friends.[26]

Little is known about James' first wife, Georgia Miller. She apparently was almost two years older than James, born in January of 1879, rented a room at 22 Hawkins Avenue in Lexington, about ten miles north of Nicholasville, and worked as a cook. She and her parents were all born in Kentucky, and although she could read English she could not write it. Also, at the time of the 1900 census, she had been unemployed for about eight months.[27]

---

[25] *The Freeman* (Oct. 14, 1899), v. xii, n. 39, p. 5.
[26] *The Freeman* (Dec. 22, 1900), v. xiii, n. 51, p. 1.

Their marriage was not to last long, although James would not obtain a legal divorce for another ten years. With James constantly on the road, this marriage was arguably doomed from the start, and we know almost nothing about this woman or their relationship. She surfaces once again in the 1920 U. S. Census, still living in Lexington but at an address not too far from the one listed in the 1900 census, 538 Toner Street. At this time the 41-year-old woman is cooking for a hotel and lists herself as a widow. [28]

During the year 1900 James apparently took leave of the road as he announced he would and directed rehearsals and concerts with Elmore's Cyclone Band. It may have been Georgia's insistence that he do so, but James would have seen a drastic cut in his income as well as a dramatic change from the excitement of travel and the company of bright, glamorous professional musicians. In January of 1901 a brief notice of a band concert appears in *The Freeman*:

> Lexington News Items.
>
> Lexington, Ky. Special: .... Elmore['s] Cyclone Band of eighteen, conducted by James H. Wilson, the cornet soloist, will give an open air concert in front of the Ph[o]enix Hotel some time in the near future. Watch for the date.[29]

No management, no commitment, no money. James had taken a step back in his profession and it must have caused some

---

[27] 1900 U. S. Census, Lexington, Fayette County, Kentucky, 20th Precinct. Another Georgia Miller, four years younger, lived in Lexington and appears in the 1900 census as well. However she is white and not likely James' fiancée. Georgia Miller turns out to be a very common name in this area of Kentucky during these years. Another good possibility for Wilson's first wife is the younger sister of Earl Miller, the trombonist (photo, Figure 2-10, below). She would have been two years younger than James, could read and write, and was also a cook. She appears in the 1900 U.S. Census living with her mother, Cora, and her younger brother "Earlie," who was still in school. For no better reason than James' announcement appeared as "Lexington, Ky. Special," I selected the Fayette County girl as the more probable candidate. Also, "Earlie" Miller is Earl Miller, the trombonist and friend of James Wilson. When Wilson became infatuated with a Louisiana belle, Toula Morrison (see Chapter 5), the newspaper report said Earl Miller attended the party and looked on approvingly. That seems incongruous to me, since his sister, Georgia, would still have been married to Wilson at that time.

[28] 1920 U. S. Census, Lexington, Fayette County, Kentucky, ,

considerable stress at home. Two months later Wilson was on the road again with the Richards & Pringle's Minstrels as they began their outstandingly successful tour of Canada.

Before his marriage in 1900 it is likely that James had earned sufficient money playing and conducting with the *In Old Kentucky*, *Uncle Tom's Cabin*, Mahara's Minstrels, Nashville Students, and New Orleans Minstrels organizations to make him think he could afford marriage and retire from the life of the traveling minstrel shows. He had garnered self-esteem as well as confidence in his own abilities to compete successfully with the best African-American musicians of the day. His rapid advancement from cornet and trombone player to cornet soloist and director of Elmore's Cyclone Band and two touring bands would have told him much about his talent and potential. All along he would have been measuring the musical prowess of his musician friends and rivals on a daily basis while working alongside and in front of them. He knew just where he stood amongst his peers and where he might be able to go in the future. All looked bright until the Nicholasville Cyclone Band started to push him into obscurity. Their concerts were few, the pay was substandard, and the responsibilities were substantial. After a European solo engagement never materialized, he, with or without Georgia's blessings, began a tour with the Famous Georgia Minstrels, and life turned into a roller coaster ride.

In 1901 Richards & Pringle's Famous Georgia Minstrels toured the northwest United States and southern Canada. These entertainers appeared in Olympia, Washington, on January 30th, worked engagements throughout the local area, and then moved on to a four-night run at the Grand Opera House in Butte, Montana, beginning Sunday, March 10th. The amusement column of the regional Montana newspaper, the *Anaconda Standard*, spread word of their upcoming appearance, first the half week in Butte and later the single performance in Anaconda at the Margaret Theater:

> Richards & Pringle's Famous Georgia Minstrels, which will be seen at the Margaret on Thursday, March 14, number 50 prime

[29]*The Freeman* (Indianapolis, IN: January 19, 1901), v. xiv, n. 3, p. 2.

performers, including such well-known names as Harry Fidler, the Alabama quartette, Arnie Stevenson, Kid Langford, Dick Thomas, James Moore, the Houseleys brothers, the only Sheids, Christian, "the Black Watch Drill," a host of the funniest end men and an elaborate first part introducing the entire company. The attractive street parade takes place at 11:30 a. m. This will include two brass bands, stylish English dogcarts drawn by Kentucky thoroughbreds and other good features.[30]

Blackface Minstrelsy was quite an elaborate and sophisticated entertainment form by the turn of the century, and the better known companies traveled with their own "Pullman Palace" railroad cars that not only transported their entertainers but provided housing for their black employees in all-while cities and towns. This minstrel show had a multitude of song, dance, and comedy stars and acts. They brought horses and other animals with them as well as performers, managers, technicians, and laborers, and the company always had one or more bands not only to accompany but to entertain on their own. When the troupe advertised an orchestra, this title usually indicated a small band plus three to five string players, often musicians from the band who "doubled" on violin, cello, or string bass. Obviously minstrelsy was an expensive entertainment form, and in its heyday the name entertainers were well paid. Usually the white troupes commanded higher fees than the black companies, but African-American artists, donning burnt cork and white greasepaint to perform in blackface, earned substantial salaries at a time when black men had few opportunities for well-paying employment other than hard labor or as porters on the railroads. Sadly, black women had even fewer work choices than men. African-American women were lucky to get steady employment as laundresses, housekeepers, or cooks.

In 1901, a 20-year-old James Hembray Wilson joined Richards and Pringle's Famous Georgia Minstrels while their tour was in progress. He already had five years of professional band and minstrel show experience to his credit when he began work with this company, and now he was added as one of this renowned

---

[30]*The Anaconda Standard* (Anaconda, MT: March 10, 1901), v. xii, n. 181, p. 5.

```
         AMUSEMENTS.

Grand Opera House    DICK P. SUTTON
       Butte, Montana        Manager.

Four Nights Commencing with Matinee
         Sunday, March 10,
      RICHARDS & PRINGLE'S
    Famous Georgia Minstrels
  50—People—50   2—Bands—2   A Carload
 of Special Scenery   4—Big Comedians—4
 (Thomas, Fidler, Stevenson, Langford),
 4—Swell English Boulevard  Traps—4,
 drawn by Kentucky thoroughbred horses.
 Special Train of Pullman Palace Cars.
 14 Comedians, 21 Solo Singers 16 Dancers,
 10 Big Olio Acts  Famous Alabama Quar-
 tette  Strongest Singing Turn Ever In-
 troduced by a Minstrel Company  A Mag-
 nificent Free Street Parade takes place
 daily at 11 30 a. m.
```

Figure 2-9. Announcement in the *Anaconda Standard,* March 10, 1901[31]

company's featured attractions. Even though the Famous Georgia Minstrels achieved considerable success during their northwest United States tour, their reception in Washington State was almost paltry in comparison to their jubilant welcome in Canada. In August of 1901, *The Freeman* reported news of the company's progress over the border:

> We have now been in Canada just two weeks, and doing, so far, the banner biz of the season. This show without exaggeration is certainly setting the Canadians wild; on an average the houses being sold out before we get into the different cities [in which] we show . . . . Our reception in Winnepeg [sic] and press notice on Dominion Day and our opening day in Canada were simply superb. The traveling men and business men from that city have spread the news of the famous Georgias all up and down the Canadian Pacific R. R. to such an extent we hardly need billing

[31] *The Anaconda Standard* (Anaconda, MT: March 10, 1901), v. xii, n. 181, p. 9.

Figure 2-10. James H. Wilson, cornet, on stage with a minstrel show colleague, trombonist Earl Miller.

matter at all. . . . Another big feature and factor in way of making friends, and also advertising us so grandly, is our base ball team, which has played 7 games over here and lost one, that being with the champion team of this country . . . . In one or two places over here the citizens made an appeal to the Crown Justice to appoint a half holiday so the clerks could attend the ball game. You can imagine what large crowds we have at the grounds . . . . Our team is a good one and very prominent in Canada now. James H. Wilson, cornet virtuoso, joined the company in Marshfield, Wis., and has proved a valuable addition to this aggregation in his work and is a perfect gentleman.[32]

Obviously the Canadians loved the Georgia Minstrels. It would seem that to some extent these entertainers must have been able to mix socially with the locals as well as engage them in sport, and the Canadians clearly were ready to spend their hard-earned money on tickets for black American minstrel entertainment. The company's reception north of the border was nothing short of triumphant. And in the United States, African-American minstrelsy flourished and drew large crowds and appreciative audiences everywhere at the turn of the century. Still, the reality of life on the road did not always play out as smoothly as that just described, especially in the South. Only six months after this Canadian tour the same but now twenty-one-year-old James Hembray Wilson was still performing with Richards and Pringle's Georgia Minstrels, but this time he was playing south of the Mason-Dixon line when racial hatred turned to violence. One of the troupe was lynched, and Wilson was shot and jailed.

> Information comes that at [New] Madrid, Mo, last Sunday night, masked men overpowered the jailer and took a Negro, Louis Wright, a short distance from town and hanged him. Richards & Pringle's Negro Minstrels gave an entertainment there Saturday night, when an altercation arose between one of the musicians and some of the white town boys. Several of the boys undertook to take the musicians out, when the Negroes on the stage began to shoot. Several whites in the audience were hit, but no one was seriously hurt. . . . All the Negroes were put in jail, and as the result of an examination the name of the one who did the shooting was discovered. He was lynched and the others were released. Several of the prisoners were badly beaten Saturday night.[33]

Newspaper reports varied when telling the details of the incident, but young Wilson was now coming face-to-face with

---

[32]*The Freeman* (Indianapolis, IN: August 3, 1901), v. xiv, n. 31, p. 5.
[33]*The Freeman* (Indianapolis, IN: Febr. 22, 1902), v. xv, n. 8, p. 4.

circumstances that could not help but affect his personality as well as his mission in life.

> It will be recalled that in the latter part of February, 1902, that Louis F. Wright, who resided at 20 Bishop Court, this city [Chicago], was murdered by a white mob at New Madrid, Mo. At that time Louis Wright was traveling with the Richards & Pringle's minstrels, and because he resented an insult heaped upon him by some of the Christian gentlemen of that city, he was arrested by the sheriff, who deliberately turned him over to the mob, which promptly hung him up to a tree and riddled his body with bullets.[34]

Another paper modifies the details somewhat:

> A special dispatch from Ottawa [Kansas] says: Louis Wright, who was lynched in New Madrid, Mo., for shooting into a crowd at a theater, was an Ottawa Negro. He had been out with a minstrel company for several seasons. He was a singer of considerable local note . . . . The minstrels were attacked while making their parade in the streets, and a fight averted by the interference of the city marshall. At night a large audience gathered with evident determination of making trouble. When the entertainment closed members of the audience went upon the stage to clean out the minstrels. In the shooting that ensued some slight wounds were inflicted, but no one was badly hurt. Four of the minstrels were arrested. During the night Wright was taken from the cell and hanged.[35]

One of those black men arrested and released was Wilson. He had been shot and possibly badly beaten. An eye witness and participant in the event, a member of his own minstrel company, sent this report to *The Freeman*:

> James H. Wilson, cornetist with the Famous Georgia Minstrels, who was shot while in the orchestra pit during our recent trouble at New Madrid, Mo has displayed wonderful nerve. He laid all night in jail without the aid of a doctor until the next day and not then until they saw fit to send one, with not one of us out to assist in any way, yet Mr. Wilson for the love and respect of his fellow

---

[34]*Broad Axe* (Chicago, IL: April 4, 1908), p. 1.
[35]*Plaindealer* (Topeka, KS: Febr. 21, 1902), v. iv, n. 8, p. 2.

members and manager, G. A. Tryser, has played every show that we have been able to make. We were disabled for two nights to show at all. We take the very best care of Mr. Wilson as we have among us a man quite handy in that line of work, George A. Swan recently from the Ninth Cavalry. Mr. Wilson is hauled to and from the Opera house nightly and is improving rapidly.[36]

Perceptive road musicians know that touring with a band provides an education in life and human nature unlike that of almost any other experience. In a way the sidemen and the bandleader are separated from the "real world" about them by a stage or an orchestra pit, and from that vantage point the musicians will begin to play or conduct the music by memory of often repeated performances. They thus, like flies on the wall, have the unusual opportunity to unobtrusively observe the rest of the world about them. Sometimes the best, occasionally the worst, of human nature erupts and comes to the surface as men and women out for a good time relax, drink, and open up to their emotional natures. Usually the musician gazes from a safe and protected vantage point among like-minded companions and protected from this other, outside world by his stage or pit. That February night in 1902 the castle wall was breeched. New Madrid, Missouri, became the low point in minstrelsy for James H. Wilson, and later that same year he sought employment elsewhere.

---

[36]*The Freeman* (Indianapolis, IN: March 8, 1902), v. xv, n. 10, p. 5.

Figure 3-1. Cuban Military Band, Spanish-American War, 1898.[1]

---

[1] My sincere thanks to the West Haven Veterans Museum and Learning Center in West Haven, Connecticut, for access to their library materials and help in identifying the band by their uniforms, environment, and equipment

CHAPTER THREE

A Period of Indecision: 1902-1904

James H. Wilson had had enough. He decided to walk away from the minstrel business for good in the spring of 1902 shortly after having been shot and jailed in Missouri on the terrible, frightening night that his friend, Louis Wright, had been dragged from the jail and lynched. He had a wife and a father in Kentucky and he returned home to sort out his life. The Indianapolis *Freeman* had published information about the shooting and lynching on March 8th, and just one month later the same newspaper posted a notice from his colleagues in the Richards & Pringle's Famous Georgia Minstrels that not only indicated they missed him but unashamedly pled with him to come back and rejoin the troupe:

> Notes from the Famous Georgia Minstrels:—We closed our season and have reorganized for the coming season, opening at Rochelle, Ill., March 31, to the capacity of the house as usual .... The entire company sends regards to James H. Wilson, our soloist in the role of Nick Carter and want him to come home and get into the office again. Lots of work here for the office. Beverly cannot keep up. Wake up Jim, cherries are ripe. Our base-ball teams are coming together again.[2]

Wilson paid them no heed, but once home in Kentucky, he discovered he had new problems to contend with. To keep busy in

---

[2]*The Freeman* (Indianapolis, IN: April 19, 1902), v. xv, n. 16, p. 5. Nick Carter was the master detective of popular dime novels and pulp magazines of the time published by Street & Smith. The first Nick Carter dime novel, written by John R. Coryell, appeared in 1886 under the title *The Old Detective's Pupil; or, The Mysterious Crime of Madison Square*. Beverly almost certainly refers to Beverly Housley, a trap drummer with the Minstrels' band who, like Wilson, worked in the business office of the troupe on the road. Three years earlier four Housleys all played in the band at the same time: Goldie on cornet, Matt on alto horn, Angelo on euphonium, and Beverly on drums. (*The Freeman* (Indianapolis, IN: September 2, 1899), v. xii, n. 33, p. 5.).

Nicholasville and to make a living, the best he managed to come up with was to take charge of music at his Baptist Church, sell newspaper subscriptions for the Indianapolis *Freeman*, become involved in the community's affairs, and try to keep his life as a concert band director and cornet soloist going as best he could from a distance.

> News Items from Old Kentuck.
>
> Nicholasville, Ky., Special.—Subscribe for *The Freeman*. The December rally at the First Baptist church was a grand success, ... Our people, the Baptists, are fast learning to patronize home industries, much to the credit of C. C. Goines, our pastor. . . . James H. Wilson, our musical director, is soon to make a trip to Europe with the famous Armant 8th Battalion Band of Chicago as cornet soloist. . . . Every one that has read *The Freeman* pronounces it the greatest Negro journal published. James H. Wilson, agent, says read *The Freeman* and see how fast the Negro problem is being solved.[3]

One wonders whether that last remark is edged in sarcasm or just a reflection of his natural optimism and industrious nature. However, the European tour apparently fell through, for had James actually soloed overseas with the 8th Battalion Band from Chicago he would have lost no opportunity to inform the world of his international successes. Not a mention can be found in any of the black or white newspapers of the day. The newspaper notice is inaccurate in one detail, for the Chicago military unit is the 8th Regiment, not 8th Battalion, a volunteer regiment commanded entirely by African Americans that was organized in 1898. That Wilson soloed with this regimental band is confirmed by the heading of a concert tour program from later years preserved among Wilson's personal belongings.

This military unit, later nicknamed "The Fighting Eighth," first served in the Spanish-American War when the United States intervened against Spain in the Cuban War of Independence. It was probably during Wilson's collaboration with this unit that he collected a fascinating photo of a Cuban Military Band. See Figure

---

[3]*The Freeman* (Indianapolis, IN: January 3, 1903), v. xvi, n. 1, p. 8.

Figure 3-2. Header of Wilson Concert Tour Program.

3-1, above. Even though Wilson neither enlisted in nor was drafted into the army, and he certainly never traveled to Cuba, he did have many professional associations with American military units as a featured soloist. On these occasions he would have developed friendships with other military musicians, and that probably explains how this interesting photo came into his possession.

Once settled in Nicholasville, James found a second local band to conduct, and he traveled ten or twelve miles north to direct the musical activities of the Cooke Peerless Band of Lexington, Kentucky.[4] On the handwritten roster of his Band and Tour Booklet he listed another man, Thadius [no last name], as the solo cornet player of the ensemble,[5] but that would not have precluded him from programming solos for himself or duets with his associate. Still, it was a noticeable step down from the fame and attention he had been receiving during the recent years touring with the Famous Georgia Minstrels. James, of course, continued to direct the hometown band in Nicholasville, Elmore's Cyclone Band,[6] but the limited musical activities of that small town brass ensemble would have earned him little income. He tried to make ends meet as best he could, but earning sufficient money to support a woman who had married him at the height of his public success, when he was not only a well-known popular entertainer but a highly paid soloist, became increasingly difficult. Sometime during this period of his life he and Georgia grew apart and permanently separated.

[4]*The Freeman* (Indianapolis, IN: February 7, 1903), v. xvi, n. 6, p. 6.
[5]James H. Wilson, Band and Tour Booklet, p. 2.
[6]James H. Wilson, Band and Tour Booklet, p. 7.

And that was not the end of his troubles. Another clipping from the Indianapolis *Freeman* seems to indicate that he had been receiving petty criticism from some of the "holier than thou" Nicholasville locals about his minstrel past. This comes as no real surprise for two reasons—some fellow African-Americans, of course, would have been jealous of his celebrity, and then some conservative churchgoers would have labeled his former activities as sinful. The music of ragtime, the blues, and jazz were not welcomed into the early-20th-century African-American churches. These new American musical forms were commonly labeled "the Devil's music."[7] Though the following newspaper article is not signed, and although James claims no authorship for any of the newsy bits published in the *Freeman*, which was one of the best read, nationally distributed black newspapers of the day, it should be remembered that Wilson was the local agent for the paper and was most likely the local reporter as well. The writing of this March, 1903, article is especially revealing, for the line of reasoning and the method of argument used to defend minstrelsy in the following snippet of the article are very similar to those used in articles he published elsewhere in later years that he signed with his by-line. Finally, at the end of this newsy excerpt we can read a notice confirming that some of his activities, although useful for his church and probably fun for him, were offered *gratis*. Who knows how wife Georgia might have reacted to such generosity while money increasingly became a serious issue?

Special News.

Nicholasville, Ky., Special.—Protracted meeting going on at the Christian Church. . . . B.Y.P.U. [Baptist Young People's Union] meets every Sunday at 6 o'clock not 7. . . . Some people want to go and find the meaning of the word "minstrel." They have the wrong conception of the word. After you find the word then tell me the difference between an old folks concert

---

[7]Several authors have touched on this subject. An interesting book and a Ph. D. dissertation are two of the better studies: Giles Oakley, *The Devil's Music: A History of the Blues* (London: British Broadcasting Corporation, 1976) and Tammy Lynn Kernodle, "Anything you are shows up in your music': Mary Lou Williams and the Sanctification of Jazz" (Ph.D. dissertation, Ohio State University, 1997).

A PERIOD OF INDECISION: 1902-1904

and a minstrel. Then tell me the difference between a musical concert and a minstrel. Which is worse, a preacher's wife acting a minstrel in church or a preacher's wife playing for a musical entertainment in a hall? The Clayborn aggregation will go to Keene Camp Nelson and Lexington under the direction of Jas. H. Wilson. The Baptists will organize a convert [sic] choir of twenty five-voices in the near future. Read The Freeman, 5 cents per copy. J. H. WILSON, Agent.[8]

We know for certain that Wilson loved his old home town, but it is also clear that he had been going through a very difficult period at this time. His relationship with Georgia was deteriorating. He was not earning enough money, he was discovering how fleeting fame can be, and he was unable to grasp a satisfactory work option that would prove fulfilling and materially rewarding for his future years. Then Dr. William Hooper Councill entered into his life.

1902 and the first half of 1903 was a troubling period as well for Prof. William Hooper Councill, the founder and president of Alabama A. & M. College. For two years Councill had enjoyed the excellent work of bandmaster William Christopher Handy. Councill's band director had left Frank Mahara's Minstrels in 1900 to join the faculty at A. & M. and had successfully reorganized, taught, and conducted a brass band for the college that was reportedly quite good. Handy's importance to the college went beyond directing the band, however, for music teacher training was an important element in the Normal School curriculum of the day and, therefore, a crucial component in Councill's vision of the future of African-American higher education. His future teachers needed solid preparation in music. He was not working alone in this task of preparing African-American teachers, for many of America's Historically Black Colleges and Universities that developed rapidly after the Civil War did so as well. Fisk University in Nashville,

---

[8]*The Freeman* (Indianapolis, IN: March 14, 1903), v. xvi, n. 11, p. 5. This article has numerous spelling and grammatical errors, and I have tried to correct them as best I could without destroying the flavor of the writing. To have shown all the changes in square brackets [ ] would have made the quotation nearly illegible.

Tennessee, famous for its Fisk Jubilee Singers, opened its doors as a Normal School in 1867. In Councill's own state of Alabama, his distinguished contemporary, Booker T. Washington, was leading the Tuskegee Institute. It, too, had been founded as the Tuskegee Normal School for Colored Teachers and later gained its splendid reputation for academic and scientific excellence.

By 1895 Councill's State Normal and Industrial School for Negroes was growing and thriving on its new campus. The school had opened its doors as a land grant institution five years earlier and proudly announced its accomplishments and purpose:

> ... it stands among the best schools in the land as a powerful lever in elevating the great masses of the Negro race to intelligent, industrious, Christian citizenship. . . . The school has grown rapidly in its "new home," and finds it impossible to accommodate hundreds who yearly apply for admission. . . . Normal has the confidence and support of the entire white population of this section and throughout Alabama.[9]

At that time the school owned 182 acres of land on which stood six main buildings, eleven small buildings, and seven cabins. Much of the construction had been accomplished by the students themselves, and though the main buildings had been outfitted with bathrooms and sewer connections, much of the faculty housing had not. Fortunately, the campus was well supplied with excellent drinking water, for there were three wells and two springs on campus, and their own water works connected them with the "Huntsville Big Spring."

The college had graduated 293 young men and women during its first five years on the Normal campus, and 197 of those degree recipients had earned their degrees in the Normal Course, that is, teacher education.[10] For this reason three departments of the school taught most of the students: English Language, Mathematics, and Vocal Music. By 1902 Councill's college had developing programs in agriculture, practical trades,

---

[9] William Hooper Councill, *Normal, Alabama, or Information about the State Normal and Industrial School for Negroes* (Montgomery, AL: Roemer Printing Co., [1896]), p. 3.
[10] *Ibid.*, pp. 4-5.

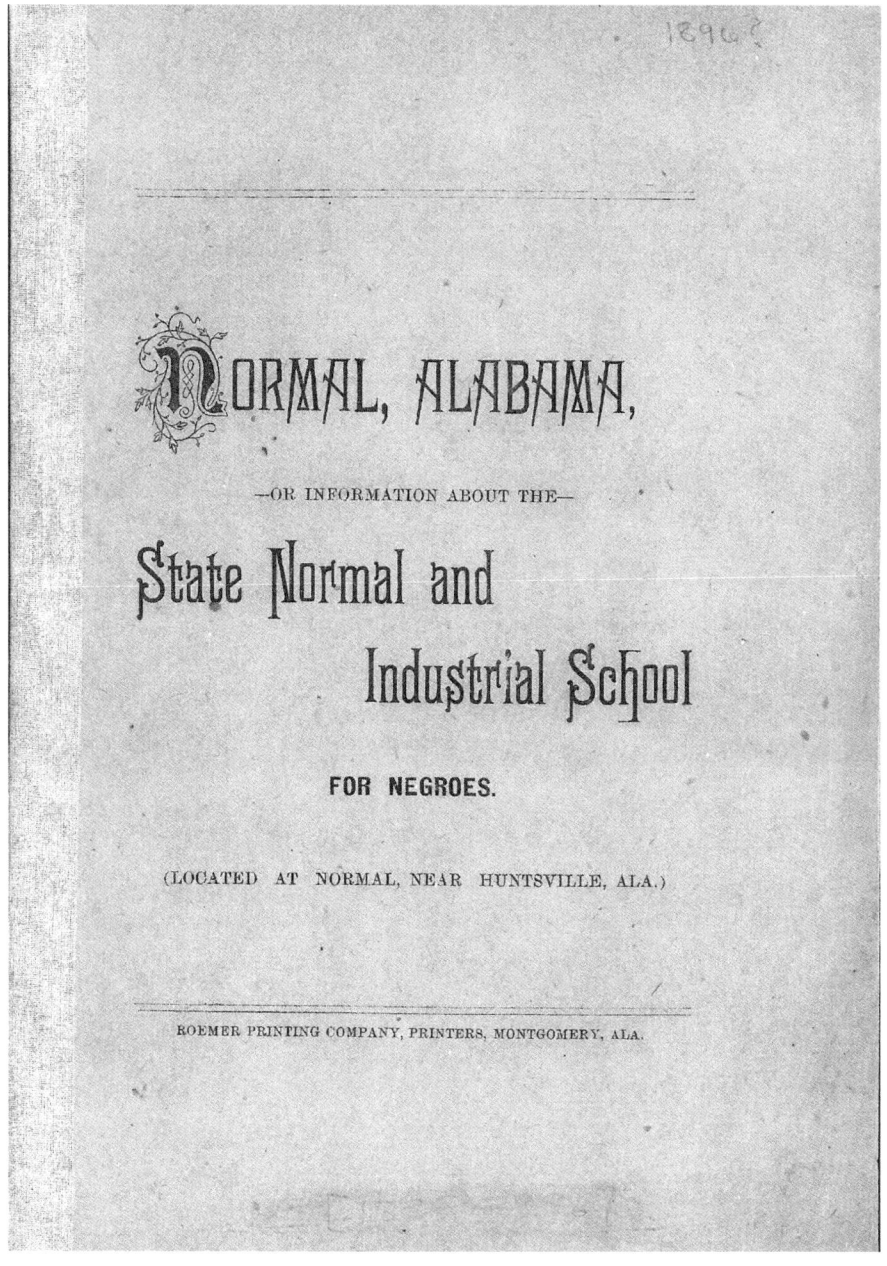

Figure 3-3. Bulletin, Alabama State Normal and Industrial School for Negroes [1896].

Figure 3-4. The "Old Mountain Spring," Normal, Alabama.

home economics, and the liberal arts, but teacher education was the central and largest course of study in the college and it was still centered in the Normal School. That area of instruction included a laboratory school for the faculty children, a place where young future teachers could practice their craft as well as help educate the campus youngsters. It was from the Lab School that Handy had recruited additional talent for his college band, and Wilson would do the same after he arrived on the campus.

During the 1902-1903 academic year, without a musical leader for the education program of the college, the Normal School suffered a severe deficiency. Music education as a core program of the curriculum had been introduced into the public schools of America in the earlier 19th century largely through the influence and efforts of Lowell Mason in Boston. The teaching of music methodology at the Normal School level had followed suit. The National Education Association had even added a music component to their organization in the 1890s, the same decade in which Councill was building a college four miles northeast of Huntsville. Even though Councill wanted a band director to replace W. C. Handy, he absolutely needed a competent professional musician to guide the program in vocal music. Additionally, educating competent music directors for the African-American churches was even more than a cultural or recreational necessity. African-American churches were, and still are, a powerful focal point of leadership in the black communities of America. The music directors of those churches ranked just below the minister in order of importance. Councill had recognized the qualities he was seeking in William Christopher Handy, but apparently there had gradually developed some difference of opinion between the two men. Some emotional words had been exchanged about the superiority and propriety of one type of music versus another. Councill later had second thoughts about the matter and regretted the split once Handy was committed to leaving, but the deed was done. Handy had firmly decided to pursue more fruitful ventures elsewhere, first in minstrelsy and later in composition and publishing in New York City.

Concerning his departure from the college, Handy described the events in this way:

> Among the letters [I received] were two envelopes with pictures of sliced watermelons on the outside. The melons had big black seeds which, examined closely, proved to be the pictures of various Negro minstrel stars. These letters were from the Maharas. Each contained an offer: fifty a week—come at once. So I accepted F. L. Mahara's offer.
>
> My increased mail attracted attention, and Councill began to suspect something. Apropos, he delivered a chapel lecture on Negro minstrels. The tone of his remarks was sarcastic and

derisive in the extreme. . . . Before it was over I found myself making an impassioned defense of my former associates. The minstrel show at that time was one of the greatest outlets for talented musicians and artists. . . . I concluded, "who shall say that minstrel men may not lead parades through pearly gates and up streets of gold?" . . . . Councill stood apart, silent and grim. . . . He looked disappointed and sad. Suddenly I lost my bitterness. . . . I found no pleasure in adding to the burdens of the lonely man who was trying so hard to keep his school going against great odds.[11]

Fifty dollars per week in 1902 was a very handsome salary, far more than A. & M.'s president could afford to pay. Knowing that Handy would leave probably precipitated the incident, for Councill had felt betrayed, but it also seems clear that Handy had not discussed the situation with his superior before finalizing his decision. Handy must already have felt some restriction from trying to work within the bounds of Councill's concept of music, music fit and proper for the education of the next generation of African-American leaders, for the "sarcastic and derisive" comments made in chapel would not have been cooked up overnight by this kind and thoughtful leader. On the positive side, the parting seems to have served to open Councill's eyes about music beyond his own sphere of experience and personal taste, for he quickly came to realize that the pool of highly qualified professional black musicians in minstrelsy was a rich source of talent not to be ignored. This realization paved the road for James H. Wilson, a man of modest schooling but of great talent, intelligence, and Christian purpose, and this situation allowed him to enter the world of higher education without any college degree.

For an entire academic year, 1902-1903, the music post at A. & M. remained unfilled.[12] Councill experienced some real difficulty finding a satisfactory replacement for Handy. Then this grand old man of the college learned about Wilson and sometime

---

[11]William Christopher Handy, *Father of the Blues: An Autobiography*, ed. Arna Bontemps, Foreword by Abbe Niles (New York: Macmillan, 1941), pp. 62f.

[12]My sincere thanks to the Rev. Dr. Henry Bradford, Jr. for sharing a typescript that clarifies the succession of music faculty at Alabama A. & M. by listing all the bandmasters by name with the years in which they served. The portion of interest to us with respect to James H. Wilson reads as follows:

before the fall of 1903, he approached and recruited him, offering him the opportunity to start down a new path. In many ways Councill and Wilson, despite their age difference and educational backgrounds, were men of like mind and purpose. Councill, like the Benedictine Monks of ages past, believed in the intrinsic value of work and the necessity and power of prayer. So did Wilson. Just as the motto of the Benedictines, *Ora et Labora*, Pray and Work, ordered the lives of its initiates, the same motto could have been justifiably appropriated for the State A. & M. College at Normal, Alabama. The A. & M. students were required to work hard physically and intellectually, and all were also required to attend chapel every day. Both of these two men believed that work and prayer would pave the road toward their goal of raising their race from its then low status to one of social equality, and when Councill offered Wilson a teaching position, James could hardly say "no." It was not an easy decision for him, for he had just spent a year among friends at home building professional connections to the best of his abilities, but Councill was not to be denied. Although James was off to a bumpy and hesitant start, this moment marked the turning point in his life.

William Still	1898-1899	[vacant 1899-1900]
William C. Handy	1900-1902	[vacant 1902-1903]
James H. Wilson	1903-1904	[vacant 1904-1905]
Wade Hammonds*	1905-1906	
E. Hill	1906-1907	[vacant 1907-1908]
James H. Wilson	1908-1947	(Consultant 1947-1951) [retired in 1951]
Wilton Robinson**	June 1947-June 1948	
James H. Wilson	1948-1949	
Jonathan Ford	1949-1951	
Phillip Cooper	1951-1952	
James H. Wilson	1952-1953	[after retirement]

* [Wade H. Hammond]
** [Wilton Robertson]

Figure 3-5. Alabama A. & M.'s founder and first president, William Hooper Councill.

A PERIOD OF INDECISION: 1902-1904

Wilson joined the faculty of Alabama A. & M. College three months before his twenty-third birthday. He was then the youngest member of the faculty, and at that time he had been married to Georgia for but a year and a half. He left his home in Kentucky and relocated to Alabama for this first academic appointment, and we do not know whether or not Georgia accompanied him on his move from Kentucky to the college. His first academic responsibilities were twofold: bandmaster and teacher of vocal music. When he stepped off the train at the Normal Station, this, in Councill's words, is what he would have discovered when he made his first appearance on campus:

> A Good School.
> ———
>
> Are you looking for a good school
> to attend, or to send your children?
> If so, the state Normal and Indus-
> trial School at Normal Alabama,
> near Huntsville, is the place. Its
> various departments of Mathematics,
> Latin, Music, English, Scientific,
> Blacksmithing, Carpentry, Printing,
> Wheelwright, Painting, Farming,
> Sewing, Housekeeping, Cooking,
> Nursing, Laundrying, etc. offer su-
> perior advantages to young people
> seeking both literary and Industrial
> education. Board only $7 per month.
> Tuition free. Limited amount of
> work furnished each student to aid in
> paying expenses. For catalogue
> and further information, address
>   Prof. W. H. Councill
>   Normal, Ala.[13]

---

[13]*Huntsville Gazette*, vol. xiii, iss. 38 (Huntsville, AL: August 20, 1892), p. 3.

The carpentry classes actually erected buildings to house students and faculty, the agriculture classes provided food to eat, and the cooking and laundry students lent both their talent and sweat to provide a sizable share of the necessities for a financially struggling institution. The college was small, very small by today's standards. Although we do not have a faculty and student roster for 1903, the 1905 faculty and staff roll totaled twenty-eight people: four administrators, two ministers, and twenty-two others including a secretary and a laundress.[14] In addition to the traditional subjects one might expect to find in a college—English, Latin, History, Chemistry, Mathematics, and the like—the school also offered cooking, typing, stenography, agriculture, carpentry, stone and brick-masonry, shoe repairing, printing, sewing, millinery, and nursing. In music, instruction was offered in band, vocal music, and piano, and another person, not Wilson, taught piano. Of the approximately 200 students enrolled at the time, and this included high-school age students in the Normal Preparatory Category, a majority were female. Home Economics was then called "Female Industries," and the young women of A. & M. studied to become teachers, nurses, secretaries, cooks, and housewives as the men, in small numbers, studied the various trades available at the college. Achievable ambitions were important to Councill. In his own words:

> The races of the south, side by side, moving in parallel lines, must work out all the problems naturally growing out of our new relations, as well as get rid of the ill feelings, like tares sown among the good wheat by 'an enemy.' External forces can avail nothing. We alone must correct our errors and set right our wrongs. . . . I want my race to learn the hardest lessons of labor, for thereby may it have that continued resistance which labor brings regardless of denominational creeds or the defects and triumphs of political parties. . . . [T]he negro will blot out his illiteracy, lessen the number of criminals, normalize his morality, build up his fortunes and again take his stand among men of integrity and industry.[15]

It was into this charged environment that James H. Wilson stepped when he began his first semester of teaching at Alabama A. & M.

---

[14]Rev. Dr. Henry Bradford, Jr., "Faculty 1905-1906," [typescript].
[15]*Age-Herald*, vol. 26, iss. 120 (Birmingham, AL: October 13, 1899), p. 3.

College in 1903. In the Christmas issue of the *Freeman* his change of occupation was announced to the world:

> The subject of this sketch, Mr. James H. Wilson, is one of the best known colored musicians in the country. He has composed and arranged several beautiful pieces of music for the cornet, and as a cornet soloist he stands second to none. Mr. Wilson has traveled extensively throughout this country and Canada with different well known musical organizations. He is now professor of music at the A. & M., College, of Normal, Ala. Mr. Wilson was born in Nicholasville, Ky., December 19, 1880, and after "going through" the public schools at that place he finished his education in the public schools of Cincinnati, O. Mr. Wilson is a constant reader of The Freeman and wishes us with all professional friends a merry Christmas and a Happy New Year.[16]

James was a happy young man and proud to display his accomplishments. In fact, the *Freeman* ran an identical article one week later and included his photograph.

Nattily dressed, bright-eyed and confident, a cross prominently displayed on a gold chain extending from his vest pocket, James was the picture of self-assurance and composure. But for some unknown reason he resigned at the end of the academic year, Spring, 1904.

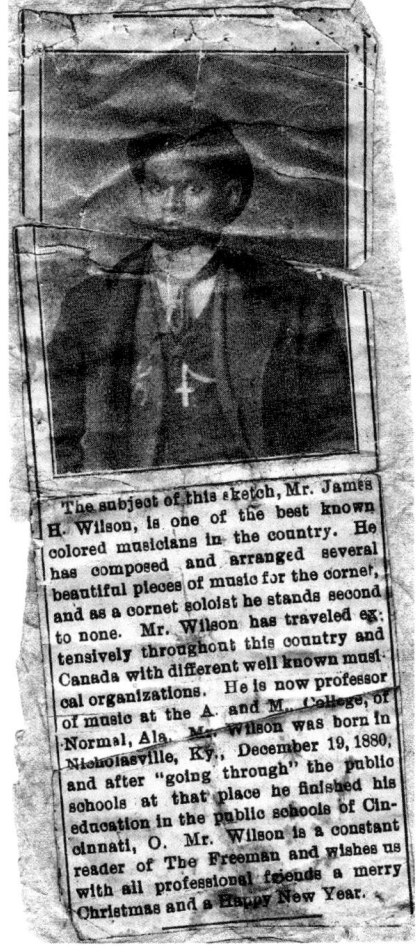

Figure 3-6. *The Indianapolis Freeman*, January 2, 1904.

---

[16]*The Freeman* (Indianapolis, IN: December 26, 1903), v. xvi, n. 51, p. 5.

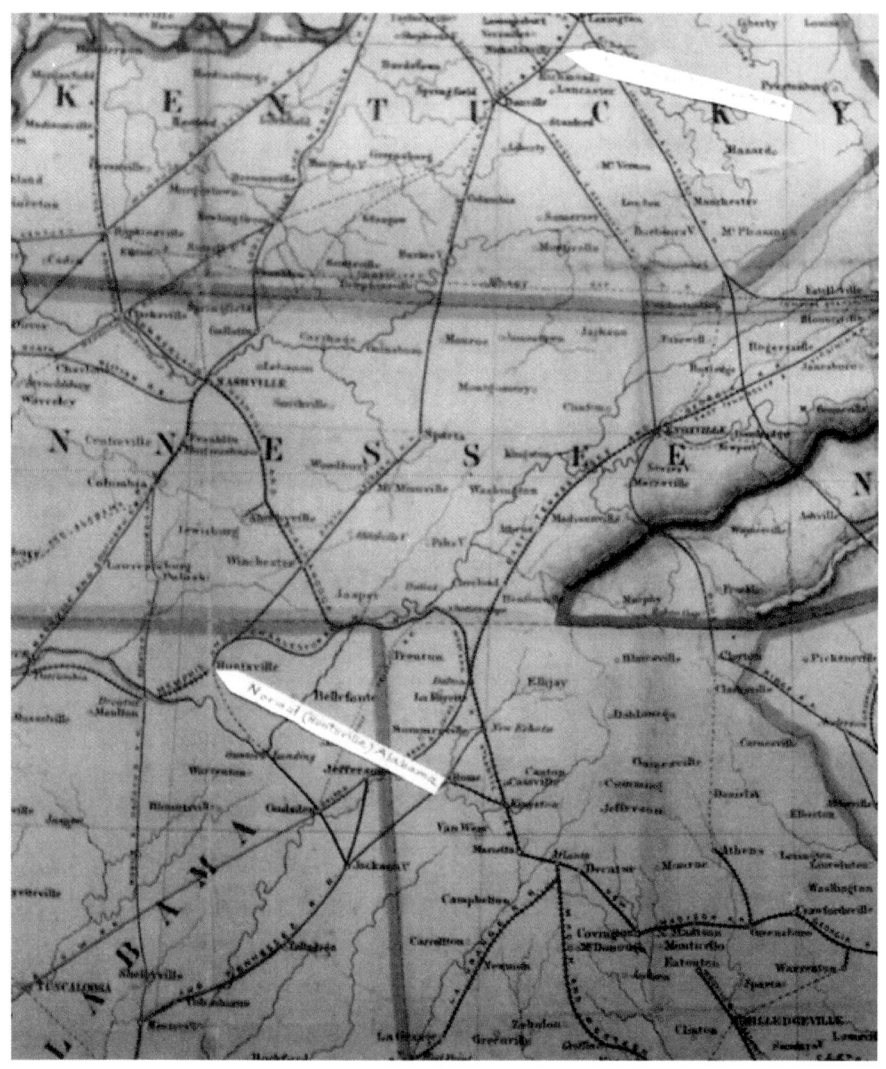

Figure 3-7. Map 3. Nicholasville, Kentucky, to Normal [Huntsville], Alabama. [325 miles]

From *Map of all the Railroads in the United States in Operation* . . . H. V. Poor . . . [1855]

CHAPTER FOUR

On the Road Again: 1904-1908

For some reason, the first year of teaching at Alabama A. & M. College did not work out for Wilson. We can be certain that he left in the school's good graces, for had there been a problem with his teaching or deportment he would never have been rehired a few years later by the same president who hired him the first time. A. & M. in those days was too small for secrets, and the community of teachers and college families was too tight for problems not to have been known by everyone on campus. Most likely his wife felt out of place, for she could not write, and this was an academic community. Also, she may not have taken well to the religious expectations of this very Christian college. There are many reasons to speculate that Georgia led James to leave the campus, but there is no surviving evidence to draw upon to ferret out the truth in this matter. If she did not accompany him to Alabama and remained in Kentucky, that, too, could have been reason enough for him to return home and try to salvage his marriage. It is truly unfortunate that Georgia Miller Wilson and her personality have faded so completely into the cobwebs of history. What little we have been able to glimpse of her has been gleaned from a newspaper report of their wedding and a pair of census documents that tells us almost nothing about this woman. And, of course, money would certainly have been an issue. James was not getting rich and famous as a beginning teacher in the high school and college. Why James left Normal after his first year will most likely always remain a mystery, but we do know for certain that once he boarded the outbound train from Normal and headed home, he did not sit around feeling sorry for himself. Upon his return he quickly found work, first as a cornet soloist and a band conductor, and then, when the opportunity presented itself, as a star musician with the most famous black minstrel show of the day, the Billy Kersands Minstrels.

When he first returned to Nicholasville after leaving Normal, he apportioned some of his time to work in Lexington, Kentucky, as musical director and soloist for Hamilton's Military Band. He had worked for Hamilton before and they welcomed him back as their musical leader. Then he began to commute by train to Columbus, Ohio, as the cornet soloist for the People's Band, a professional ensemble based in that city under the management of Thomas Howard. This big-city band regularly played concerts 150 miles southwest of Columbus at Gray's Armory in Cincinnati. They also were the featured band for the Ohio State Fair at the fairgrounds just outside of Columbus. Then, because band concerts were arguably the most popular public entertainment of the day, they played a regular series of summer concerts in the public parks throughout the city of Columbus. Additionally, this musical organization booked single engagements at other venues as well, for their fame was more than local. The People's Band even played for five years running at a festival close to James' home in Nicholasville, at the Afro-American Fair in Lexington, Kentucky.[1] Thomas Howard most likely heard James when the People's Band was in Lexington at a time when the young artist performed cornet solos with Hamilton's Military Band. It was probably after one of these concerts that Howard made James' acquaintance and invited him to join his Ohio band as a featured cornet soloist.

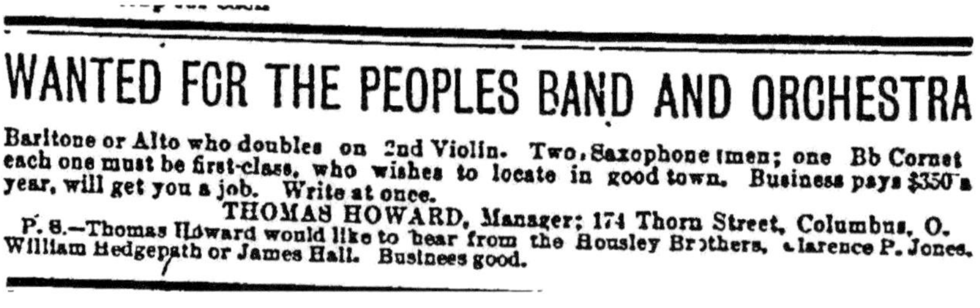

WANTED FOR THE PEOPLES BAND AND ORCHESTRA

Baritone or Alto who doubles on 2nd Violin. Two, Saxophone tmen; one Bb Cornet each one must be first-class, who wishes to locate in good town. Business pays $350 a year, will get you a job. Write at once.
THOMAS HOWARD, Manager; 174 Thorn Street, Columbus, O.
P. S.—Thomas Howard would like to hear from the Housley Brothers, Clarence P. Jones, William Hedgepath or James Hall. Business good.

Figure 4-1. Advertisement for musicians, People's Band of Columbus, Ohio.[2]

---

[1]Fleming and Burckel, eds., *Who's Who in Colored America*, 7th ed., p.565, and *Cleveland Gazette* (April 15, 1905), p. 3.
[2]*The Freeman* (May 17, 1902), v. xv, n. 20, p. 5.

ON THE ROAD AGAIN: 1904-1908

From this advertisement that was posted in the *Freeman* shortly before the time when Wilson first started to work for Howard we learn that the going rate for a musician performing in the band and orchestra was $350.00 per year. Assuming the band season to cover no more than seven or eight months, the average professional musician employed as a section player would have earned $40 to $50 per month, a decent wage for an African-American working during the first decade of the 20th century. The featured soloist would earn more, of course, but his pay most likely would have been irregular, for he would have been paid by the concert rather than with a yearly stipend or monthly salary.

The People's Band was excellent, and when it was scheduled to play a concert and dance in Cleveland, the *Cleveland Gazette* ran this announcement:

> The People's band and orchestra of Columbus, which will give a concert and ball at the Grays' armory on Easter Monday, is one of our best organizations and comes to us with such recommendations. You will certainly enjoy a rare treat in hearing this wonderful band and in dancing "after" [to the music of] their fine orchestra. This is the band that has played for the past five years at the great Afro-American state fair held annually at Lexington, Ky., and was the official band at the Ohio state fair, Columbus. It has played in public park concerts for the last three years, and when we say they are first-class, we mean it. The Peoples band claims to be the best band of the race and stands ready to defend the claim at all times against any similar race organization in America. Their concert and ball will prove a grand treat for all who love good music and wish to enjoy an evening in dancing.[3]

Both the concert and dance at Gray's Armory were a grand success, and a post-concert review informs us that over 700 people were in attendance. Also, when the Columbus band arrived at the train station in Cincinnati that Easter Monday, another band, the Buckeye Band,[4] was there to greet them and escort them to the armory. This was elegant treatment indeed!

---

[3]*Cleveland Gazette* (April 15, 1905), p. 3.
[4]*Cleveland Gazette* (April 29, 1905), p. 3. This "Buckeye Band" is not likely to have been the college band of the Ohio State University of Columbus.

Not long after this concert the People's Band switched from private to public ownership when it was mustered into the Ohio National Guard.[5] Beginning March, 1906, it changed names and was to be known thenceforth as the Ninth Infantry Band, Ohio National Guard. James continued to be invited as a guest soloist with the National Guard band as well, and he performed with them when it fit into his now busy schedule.

Upon his return to Nicholasville in 1904 and continuing through the summer of 1907, Wilson resumed his position as soloist and director for Henry Hamilton's Military Band of Lexington, Kentucky. James had worked with Hamilton a few years earlier when he first moved back to Kentucky, and as this unit's musical director he would have been kept busy with both the rehearsals as well as the concerts of the organization. In the following photograph of the band, Hamilton is seated with his horn immediately behind the bass drum, and Wilson, with baton in one hand and trumpet, not a cornet, in the other, is standing next to Hamilton on his left.

Then, in 1906, a new and exciting opportunity was offered Wilson, and he quickly accepted. He left these other posts during the minstrel touring season to become the cornet soloist and assistant bandmaster for the Billy Kersands Minstrels. Kersands, the star, had an unusually large mouth, and he was noted for using it to good advantage on the stage for his comic routines. During his younger years he was an excellent acrobatic dancer, and he was also skillful as a singer and banjo player—a very talented man. He scripted his own routines and created a stage persona that unfortunately reinforced a bigoted stereotype of the dim-witted black man that was so much a part of the minstrel show expectations of the day.

By 1906, Billy Kersands had become the grand old man of the business, the most famous minstrel star still living. He was the featured attraction, and he brought audiences that packed the opera houses and civic auditoriums from coast to coast. He was still the most popular African-American comedian of his day and a household name among whites as well as blacks. For most of the

---

[5]*The Freeman* (March 10, 1906), v. xix, n. 10, p. 3.

ON THE ROAD AGAIN: 1904-1908

Figure 4-2. Hamilton's Military Band, ca. 1905.

Figure 4-3. Poster for Callender's Georgia Minstrels. Billy Kersands in his 30s [1870s].

year Wilson's new job would again require a life of constant travel, but apparently James was looking to regain some of the excitement, fame, and money to which he had become accustomed just a few years earlier. Now he would be the featured instrumental soloist of this leading company's band.

By this time James may have given up on Georgia, but he would have had another reason to want to move away from Nicholasville—smallpox.

Nicholasville, Ky., News.

Local Odd Fellows held appropriate services at the cemetery Sunday afternoon and decorated the graves of their dead and friends. Rev. A. L. Guthrie delivered the address and the choirs of the Methodist, Baptist and Christian churches furnished music. . . . Two cases of smallpox and a family were taken to the pest house.[6]

Everyone feared smallpox, and this event must have frightened all the inhabitants of Nicholasville, black and white. Although no full-blown epidemic developed in the United States in 1905, there had been one in Montreal, Canada, just twenty years earlier in which over three-thousand citizens died and many more were ravaged by the long-term effects of the disease. Nicholasville was but a somewhat isolated small town, and its gossip network would have quickly spread the news and fear of pestilence to all its citizens. The one certain option to safety for those who had the means to get away would be to seek refuge elsewhere.

During the Kersands Minstrels' spring tour the year before James joined the company, Kersands was scheduled to appear in Hopkinsville, Kentucky, 200 miles southwest of Nicholasville. The local newspaper decided to quote a review the company had recently received when they had performed in Montgomery, Alabama.

---

[6]*Cleveland Gazette* (June 24, 1905), p. 1.

On the Road Again: 1904-1908

OLD TIME

Southern Negro Minstrelsy to
Be Seen Wednesday Night.

Concerning Billy Kersands' Minstrels, which will appear at Holland's Opera House next Wednesday night, April 12, the Daily Advertiser, of Montgomery, Ala., says:

"Fine performance by Billy Kersands and Minstrels. Large audiences at both matinée and night witnessed the performance of Billy Kersands' Georgia Minstrels at McDonald's Theatre yesterday. It was easily and above question the best minstrel show ever given in this theatre, and it is doubtful if a brighter or better performance of minstrelsy was ever put on the stage anywhere by negroes. Oftentimes in a minstrel performance the soloists are good and the jokes bad, or vice versa. A minstrel show has always from the beginning, it seems, had either one defect or the other. A most equally balanced and excellent combination of genuine old time Southern negro minstrelsy has been put together this season by Billy Kersands. There was nothing coarse or vulgar about the entertainment which was exceptionally good and deserving of patronage."[7]

While the racial terminology may grate on contemporary ears, one can also hear the high praise in "it is doubtful if a brighter or better performance of minstrelsy was ever put on the stage anywhere by negroes," particularly from a reviewer who appears to have had years of experience attending minstrel shows. It was with this company that James H. Wilson began his final stint of touring, and for the next two years James could honestly say that he was working at the pinnacle of the minstrelsy profession.

In the fall of 1906 the company opened its new tour in Illinois, and both Billy Kersands and his wife, Louisa, were featured on the program. The company also included Juggling Johnson and Hoop Controller Billy Earthquake. Dancing comedian Slim Henderson performed in a sketch entitled "The Phillipina Dance," and the

[7]*Hopkinsville Kentuckian* (April 8, 1905), p. 5.

Alabama Quartet sang ragtime specialties and popular music of the day. There was a trick bicycle act, band numbers, and lots of scenery and animals, all in all a full evening's worth of entertainment for a ticket-paying audience. The band, counting its director, contained fifteen musicians, and the orchestra, a smaller ensemble of nine members, drew their musicians from the band roster. The leader, James Lacy, played 1st violin in the orchestra; Calvin Miller, a trombonist in the band played 2nd violin; Charles Watts, the first horn in the brass band was the orchestra violist; and Lloyd Cooper, the band tubist, played string bass. This quartet of strings plus a small ensemble of brass and winds with one trap drummer constituted an orchestra in the world of minstrelsy. It was certainly not a symphonic orchestra, and it just as certainly was not able to do justice to the symphonic repertoire. But the Kersands' musicians knew that and did not attempt to do so.

> Our concerts are of a pleasing nature. Our leader, Mr. Lacy, has common sense enough to know that a small band can not render successfully such selections as Wm. Tell, Morning, Noon and Night, Zampa and a few others, so we are satisfied with a few popular selections and a little ragtime.[8]

However, an orchestra added a touch of class, and it was able, with four string players, to offer romantic accompaniment for the sentimental ballads of the day. The band provided excitement; the orchestra set the stage for love and melodrama.

Wilson was a careful man, a methodical bookkeeper, and he carefully listed his instrumental compatriots alongside their musical responsibilities in his handwritten Band and Tour Booklet:[9]

---

[8]*The Freeman* (November 30, 1907), v. xx, n. 46, p. 5.
[9]James H. Wilson Band and Tour Booklet, p.7.

Billy Kersands' Minstrel
Season 1906-1907

Lacy's Challenge Band

Jas. S. Lacy	Director
Jas. H. Wilson	Solo Cornet
P. M. Logan	Solo Cornet
C. Johnson	First " [Cornet]
B. S. Gaten	Clarinet
Chas. T. Watts	First Horn
Benj. W. Lee	Second
W. A. Law	Trombone
Chas. S. Crossen	Trombone
W. Cal Miller	Trombone
Walter Watkins	Baritone
Lloyd Cooper	Tuba
Skip Farrel	S. Drum
J. A. Watts	Cymbals
Jakie Smith	B. Drum

Lacy's Orchester [sic]

Jas. S. Lacy	Leader
W. Cal. Miller	2^d Violin
Chas. T. Watts	viola
B. S. Gaten	Clarinet
Walter Watkins	Sax
Jas. H. Wilson	Cornet
Chas. S. Crossen	Trombone
Lloyd Cooper	Bass
Skip Farrel	Traps

James spent two years on the road with these musicians, and these men became his close friends as well as colleagues. They affectionately called their young cornetist "Jimmie."[10]

It was during this period of his life that we see James first taking a serious interest in composition and arranging. We know he was a virtuoso soloist on the cornet, but the style of solo he performed in the past was the decorative and embellished light-

---

[10] *The Freeman* (September 1, 1906), v. xix, n. 35, p. 5.

classical repertoire that dominated the concert band repertoire of the period. These solos, often based on familiar operatic arias such as "Caro nome" from Verdi's *Rigoletto*[11] or popular songs like "Silver Threads Among the Gold"[12] by Rexford and Danks, were very popular among late 19th-century American concert audiences. The familiar melody would serve as the basis for a standard "theme and variations" format upon which the soloist could demonstrate his prowess—ensemble introduction, an ornamental opening cadenza, a lightly-decorated melodic first chorus, successive choruses of increasing difficulty where the soloist could add double and triple tonguing or fast arpeggiated passages, perhaps a slow chorus in the relative minor for contrast, and a flashy final chorus with another virtuosic cadenza ending in a long, high note just before the final cadence. Instrumental soloists had been using this formula for many years, and it was familiar territory for James. Now, we learn that he added a masterful ragtime style to his previous accomplishments and that he had composed some ragtime numbers that had become "hits" in the city.

Billy Kersands Minstrels.

> . . . Our band is still knocking rag time cold with the rag time king and cornetist, Jimmie Wilson, the real author of the recent Pittsburg hits, "Drag Lotz" and "Shame Lotz." We handle quite a number of Mr. Wilson's rags and some of his marches which are very fine compositions, especially the one entitled "United."[13]

Two weeks later, while the company was working in Louisiana, the troupe reporter sent another message to the *Freeman* in which he commented that "Lacy's band is playing compositions especially written for it by the enterprising young cornetist, Jimmie Wilson."[14] And one month later as the company was making their exit from the state of Texas the minstrel company heaped even more praise

---

[11] Giuseppe Verdi, *Rigoletto* (1851), "Caro nome che il mio cor" [Sweet name that first made my heart flutter].

[14] Eben E. Rexford and Hart Pease Danks, "Silver Threads Among the Gold" (1873).

[13] *The Freeman* (September 15, 1906), v. xix, n. 37, p. 5.

[14] *The Freeman* (September 29, 1906), v. xix, n. 39, p. 6

upon their cornet soloist, "Jas. H. Wilson, the Bronze Kryl[15], is without a peer . . . the tones alone . . . [that issue] from the golden bell of his instrument, easily place him as one of the greatest and noblest cornet soloists before the public to-day."[16] Of course much of what was written in these articles was typical overstatement meant to sell their product to the general public, but not every member of the company was so honored. Clearly this company thought very highly of their young virtuoso, Jimmie Wilson.

As the tour was about to enter the eastern phase of their circuit in January, 1907, another of James' band compositions, "The Bugle Call," won public praise in the Kersands report to the *Freeman*.[17] What these compositions and performances sounded like is left for the educated guess, because none of the scores or parts from Wilson's minstrel days have survived and none of those minstrel performances could have been recorded live in 1906. Still, his compositions must have achieved a high level of professional competence, equal at least to contemporary minstrel music of the day, for the leader of the band, James Lacy, was a well-known and respected musician in the trade. He would never have used anything for the Kersands' public repertoire that might harm the show, and it is unthinkable that he would have allowed such repeated praise for Wilson's compositions to have gone into print had the music not been deserving.

The show continued its tour through the spring of '07, and in April James' playing was then compared to that of British cornetist Jules Levy, arguably the most famous cornet soloist of the era. Levy immigrated to the United States, played and soloed in Patrick Gilmore's famous band, and was billed as "The World's Greatest Cornetist." The *Freeman* had this to say about Wilson:

---

[15]The comparison is surely to the noted Czech-American cornetist and bandmaster, Bohumir Kryl (1875-1961). Kryl was a pioneer recording artist, and his work may be sampled on youtube: http://www.youtube.com/watch?v=8BMMGqJYONY (accessed 9/26/2014).
[16]*The Freeman* (October 27, 1906), v. xix, n. 43, p. 5.
[17]*The Freeman* (January 26, 1907), v. xx, n. 4, p. 6.

THE BILLY KERSANDS FAMOUS MINSTRELS.

.... Prof. Lacy has been away a few days on business. He has returned smiling and happy to his post again.... Jas. H. Wilson has just finished arranging one of his selections for the orchestra, "Gloomorian." Mr. Wilson has quite a selection of very beautiful solos and wins for himself "multi laudis." To hear him one would not wonder why he is so styled as the black Jules Levy.[18]

The record of James H. Wilson's minstrel days is copiously documented, but the evidence of his concert band work during this period is nowhere near as complete. Had he himself not listed bands, years, and colleagues in one place or another, most of these activities would have evaporated into the ether. One of the reasons for this lack of evidence is that every American city and town had its band, and commonplace does not equal newsworthy. Band music was a very popular entertainment form in the days before motion pictures, radios, and sound recording, and it has been estimated that in 1890 as many as 10,000 bands were active in the United States.[19] Hamilton's Military Band concerts were considerably less remarkable than Patrick Gilmore's or John Philip Sousa's, and reports of Hamilton's performances or actual concert programs have not yet been discovered. Still, when James finished his 1906-1907 tour with the Kersands we know he returned to Nicholasville and continued his directorial and solo activities with Hamilton's Band in addition to his local Elmore's Cyclone Band concerts. When his summer concert band activities came to a close, he returned to Illinois to start another tour with the Billy Kersands Minstrels. This musical circuit through Illinois, Kansas, Missouri, Oklahoma, the Indian Territory, Texas, Louisiana, Mississippi, Tennessee, Alabama, Georgia, and Kentucky would be his last.

---

[18] *The Freeman* (March 9, 1907), v. xx, n. 10, p. 6.
[19] Stephen L. Rhodes, *A History of the Wind Band*, http://www.lipscomb.edu/windbandhistory/index.htm (accessed April 23, 2012). This exemplary book, complete, appears on the above website. This information referenced here can be found in Chapter 9, "The American School Band Movement," in the third subsection, "Decline in Professional Bands," which can be accessed from Table of Contents at the above web location.

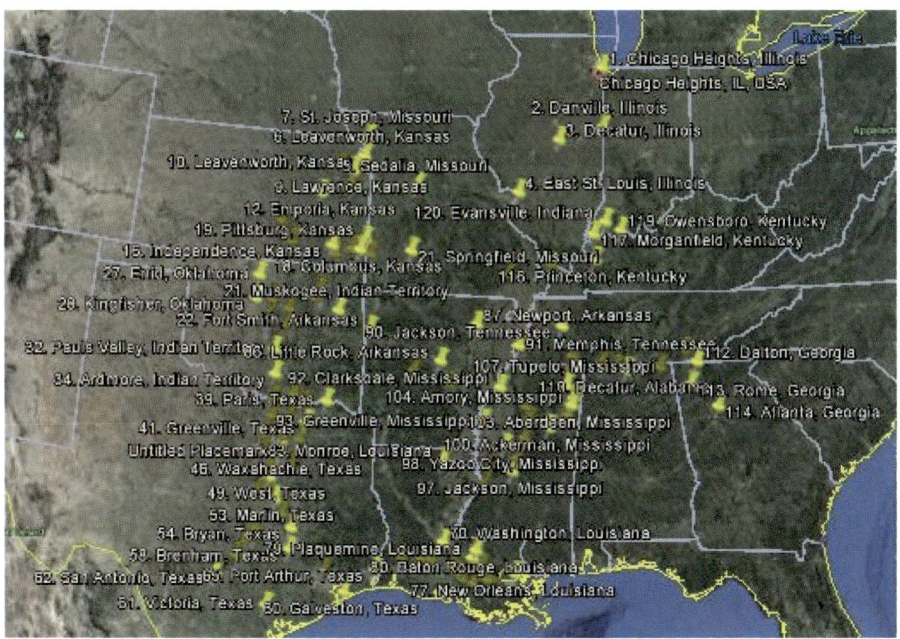

Figure 4-4. Map 4. Wilson's railroad tour with Kersands Minstrels, Sept. 2, 1907 to Febr. 21, 1908. [120 locations in 173 days!]

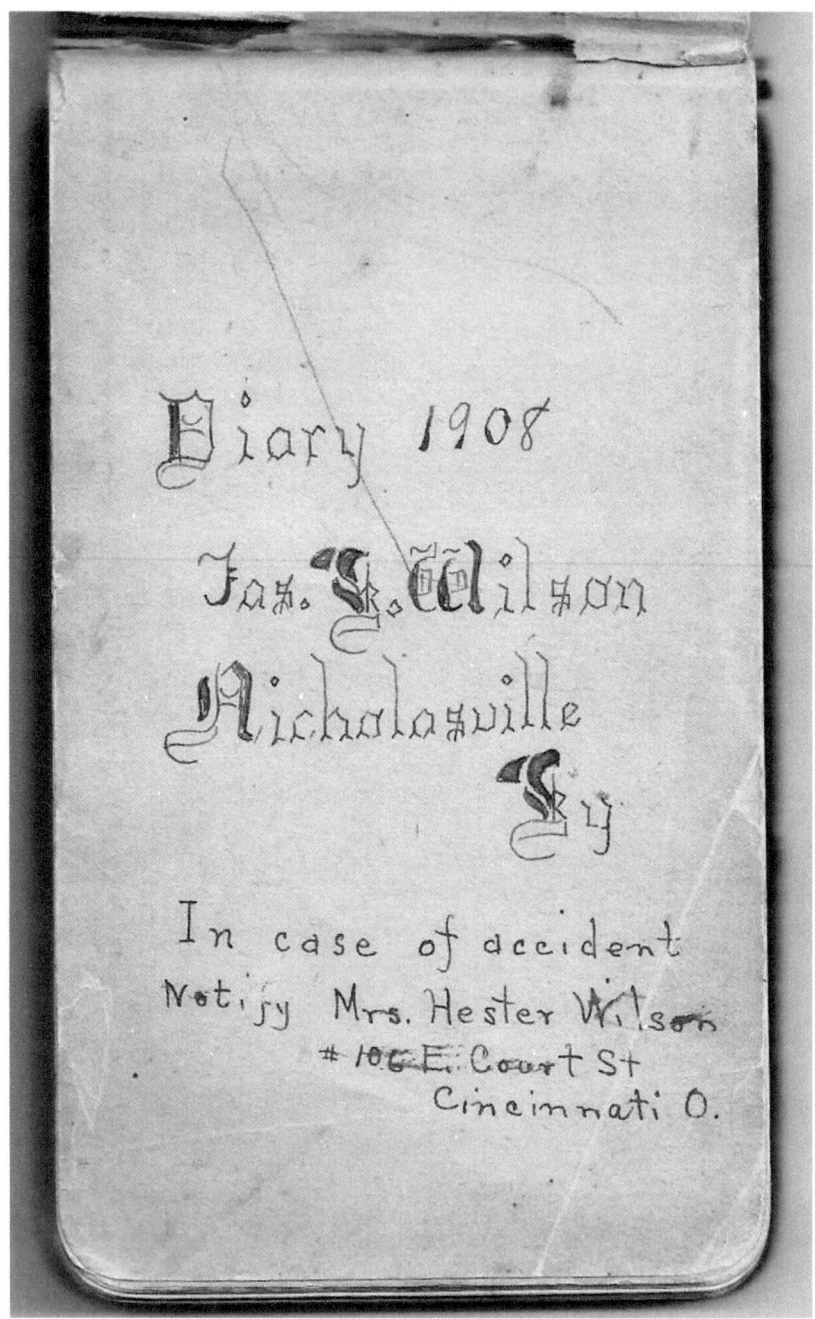

Figure 5-1. James H. Wilson Journal. Flyleaf.

CHAPTER FIVE

A Pivotal Year: 1908

Throughout his adult life James Hembray Wilson kept a journal of his daily activities,[1] and in these tiny booklets, small enough to fit comfortably into a shirt pocket whether traveling about the country or working behind a desk, Wilson preserved in abbreviated form many intimate details of his life. Sadly only one journal remains today, and it records his activities for but one-half of one year, from January 1st to June 30th of 1908, six months of names, places, and events during a busy time in his life when he traveled with the Billy Kersands Minstrels troupe for the last time before returning to Alabama Agricultural and Mechanical College permanently. What better way might there be to get to know a man long gone than to read his own account of his life as it was happening? These daily jottings are not the romanticized and edited remembrances of distant and blurry memories, as one usually finds in most autobiographies, often inaccurate and sometimes intentionally changed; here we find a series of brief personal notations recording events of the day shortly after they occurred. Many connections are trivial but others are significant and hold some real fascination for us today.

---

[1] James H. Wilson's youngest daughter, Marian Wilson Turner, first related information about the journals' existence to the author in the 1970s, saying that they were then in the possession of her older sister, Hester Orr. They were not available for study at that time. Two other booklets of the same age, paper, and dimensions (3⅜ X 5¾ inches, leatherbound) have also been preserved, but they are not journals. One records the personnel of several of the bands Wilson played with or directed during this period (it is a collection of loose leaves, the cover having disappeared), and the other is a bound series of notes for homilies he planned to deliver as well as notes he made after reading passages of the Bible. The three booklets will be referred to in my notes as Journal, Band and Tour Booklet, and Homilies Booklet. Wilson did not number his pages. I have numbered the Journal pages lightly in pencil in the lower right hand corner, and the Journal page references in these footnotes are mine, not Wilson's.

In the fall of 1907 Wilson rejoined the Billy Kersands Minstrels in Chicago and began his final tour with this famous old company. Kersands was about sixty-five-years old when this tour started, a senior citizen of the minstrel business, and he had received some unexpected criticism just a few years earlier. In 1903 a negative and highly critical article portrayed this former superstar as a has-been and a wastrel:

> Rialto Notes.
>
> Kersands' Humiliation.—The published reports of the waning ability of Billy Kersands is a direct object lesson to coming minstrel stars to husband their talent—and finances, too—for the period when Dame Nature demands that the vital forces shall be given a rest from its strenuousness. That Kersands should struggle on despite the fact that his powers of attractiveness are each day becoming diminished . . . . Had Kersands retired five years ago, it would in no way have affected his reputation, but now—Ah![2]

Not all theater critics agreed, and, in fact, most disagreed. In the very next issue just one week later Sylvester Russell rushed to Kersands' defense:

> During the early traditions of minstrelsy there was one phase of individuality that advanced many of the comedians of those days, no matter how illiterate they were, to the rank of a notable.
>
> This phase was a common form of easy grace called naturalness.
>
> Billy Kersands was one of the lucky number whose old time naturalness gained for him the undisputed reputation which he now enjoys, and which will live in the brightest pages of history long after his voice will cease to echo with other voices as it once did in days of yore. . . . Billy Kersands has not lost his popularity to any great extent. He has not wilted with age. I can name comedians whom he can triply discount in voice, age, and beauty. . . . All he needs is a modern monologue written to order by some proficient man of his race who understands his business. . . . [Billy Kersands] is the only colored minstrel man who has a household

---

[2]*The Freeman* (Indianapolis, IN: July 11, 1903), v. xvi, n. 27, p. 5.

reputation the world over.... His name is unblighted. He is still Billy Kersands—the grand old minstrel man.[3]

If there was a problem that needed attention, Kersands and his company pulled it all together quickly, as no other critical articles appeared. Still, these two reviews, opposed as they are, reflect the fame and importance of the star of the show. In the year before Wilson's final tour with Kersands, someone from his minstrel show reported on the company's current success to *The Freeman*:

THE KERSANDS MINSTREL.

The old ship is still sailing smoothly along, playing to excellent business at Corinth, Miss. Business was above the average. At Memphis we played to capacity for three performances. We were also tendered two very grand receptions. We never had more hospitality shown us by citizens . . . than by those in Memphis. . . . The New Orleans press is still commenting on Prof. Lacy's Band and Orchestra in the most glowing terms. Mr. James H. Wilson has composed a new EX "THRE" ACT,[4] entitled "Reveille," [Wake Up!] a very beautiful march of a brilliant nature, the same was quite a musical treat to our great band and company.[5]

For the 1907-1908 Kersands Minstrel season Wilson had been rehired as the company's cornet soloist and second bandmaster, and the touring company boarded their Pullman cars in Chicago to play their first engagement at Chicago Heights, Illinois, on September 2nd. Thus began their extensive tour of the United States.[6] A steam locomotive of the Illinois Central Railroad pulled them to most of the cities they would visit.[7] Wilson and the

---

[3]*The Freeman* (Indianapolis, IN: July 18, 1903), v. xvi, n. 28, p. 5.
[4]I have been unable to find a definition of "ex 'thre' act." I suspect it is meant to contrast with "entre act," a piece or number meant to be performed between the acts, an *intermedio*. If so, my best guess is a reference to a free-standing concert piece meant to stand alone. More likely it is a misspelling [*Reveille* was also misspelled] for "*ex* théâtre' act," a lively march to be performed outside the theater to induce listeners to buy a ticket and enter the theater.
[5]*The Freeman* (Indianapolis, IN: December 29, 1906), v. xix, n. 50, p. 5
[6]James H. Wilson, Band and Tour Booklet, p. 17.
[7]My thanks to Jerry Pitts, railroad historian, who traced the entire route of the tour and determined that the Illinois Central Railroad tracks accounted for the majority of the stops on the company's itinerary.

Kersands began in Illinois—September 3rd and 4th, then one night stands in Danville and Decatur; and then three consecutive nights, the 5th through the 7th in East Saint Louis. They passed through Sedalia, Missouri, on the 8th of September to play that evening in Leavenworth, Kansas. The next day the troupe backtracked (and here the word has literal meaning) to St. Joseph, Missouri, for two nights, before they returned to Kansas for almost three weeks in this Midwest agricultural state—two nights in Topeka, one each in Lawrence, Leavenworth, Ottawa, Emporia, Wichita, and Winfield, before two in Coffeyville, and on and on.

From Kansas they worked their way through Missouri, the Indian Territory, and Oklahoma, and their coal-fired locomotive puffed and pulled them into Texas on the 12th of October. That giant state gobbled up all of the remainder of October and almost three weeks of November, and finally the company said goodbye to the Lone Star State in Port Arthur on the 19th. As they moved into Louisiana for the continuation of their touring schedule, someone from the company once again sent a report to the Indianapolis *Freeman*:

Billy Kersand's Minstrels

We have just emerged from "The Lone Star State," where we did a phenomenal business. In Dallas and Ft. Worth we played to capacity. We played two days in San Antonio and the white patrons turned out in a large body each night. The show pleases easily. We are not so egotistic as to think that we have the greatest minstrel show traveling, but it is the consensus of opinion of the public that the Kersands Minstrels are the greatest that have visited the South so far. The band and orchestra are composed of real musicians and are receiving daily from both press and public much praise . . . . Mr. J. H. Wilson is arranging a solo to be played by himself, which when finished will add much to our daily concerts. Prof. J. J. Smith is proving himself a man on both cornet and cello. The Toney Trio may be termed the invincibles. Mr. Wilson, our cornet virtuoso, has received a very encouraging letter from a young lady of New Orleans stating that the girls of the Crescent City were prepared to make his second visit there a memorable one. The main factors in the event will be Misses

Toula J. Morrison and Pearl Hobson, two very dear friends of his, and whom he esteems very highly. Earle Miller, alias "Old Kentucky,"[8] is still happy and getting fatter every day.

The Kersandites send regards to all friends.[9]

We will soon see evidence that James did esteem Miss Toula, the New Orleans Belle, very highly indeed.

The day after the show closed in Port Arthur, the Kersands Minstrels performed their first Louisiana engagement at Lake Charles. The Louisiana opener was followed by ten more one-night stands, eleven consecutive days of travel and performances in the Bayou State. On December 1st the Billy Kersands Minstrels opened in New Orleans for a full week's engagement at the Elysium Theater, December 1st through the 7th. Shortly after the company left New Orleans to continue their tour in Louisiana someone from the company sent another report to *The Freeman*, and this article, in conjunction with the journal of Wilson's that we are about to study, will tell us much about James' relationship to Miss Toula, without question a New Orleans "belle of the ball."

THE FAMOUS BILLY KERSANDS MINSTRELS

We have just emerged from the Crescent City, leaving quite a respectable reputation. We are more than proud to grat[u]itously acknowledge the same from all the leading papers of the city. All readers of The Freeman will be able to agree about the comments of the citizens of New Orleans this season as well as [the] previous season.

The Tramps Social Club, Dec. 6th represented by Paul Steele, stage manager of the Elysium Theatre, presented Mr. L. D. Henderson (alias "Slim" Henderson) with a gold headed cane as a symbol of their appreciation of Mr. Henderson and his masterly work as a comedian.

---

[8] See photo, Figure 2-10, Chapter 2.
[9] *The Freeman* (Indianapolis, IN: November 30, 1907), v. xx, n. 46, p. 5. This article contains an unusually high number of misspellings and typos and I have chosen to correct most so as not to impede the reader's enjoyment of this quotation with a constant series of "sic" roadblocks.

Mr. Kid Langford and the Tony Trio, and our great minstrel king, Billy Kersands, are the prime factors with producers. The Tonys are considered as having no peers in their line for the American stage.

On Wednesday, Dec. 4, Miss Toula J. Morrison, a friend of Mr. Jas. H. Wilson, our cornet virtuoso, gave a reception in his honor. The affair was quite an elaborate one, and was attended by some of the elite of New Orleans. The majority of the guests invited was a select crowd of Creole belles. After dinner had been served Mr. Wilson was called on to render a cornet solo, which he did in a pleasing manner. Long live Miss Morrison and her friends, and may she always think of Mr. Wilson as one of her dearest friends. Among those of the company that did him honor by their presence was Mr. E. L. Miller, trombonist.

Regards to all friends. Happy New Year to all.[10]

James must have left New Orleans with a smile on his face. Very few young men are regaled with more royal treatment than a big-city party in his honor, surrounded by Creole belles, and the full and pleasant attention of one Miss Toula J. Morrison. Perhaps this is she:

Figure 5-2. An unidentified photograph from James H. Wilson's personal collection. [Toula? or Georgia?]

[10]*The Freeman* (Indianapolis, IN: December 28, 1907), v. xx, n 50, p. 5.

A Pivotal Year: 1908

After New Orleans the company played only four more engagements in Louisiana and then moved on to Mississippi. They had exited the Bayou State with a show at Baton Rouge before entering the Magnolia State for another one-night stand at Port Gibson. After that they slowly worked their way north via Vicksburg, another one-nighter back across the border to Monroe, Louisiana, then re-crossed back once again to continue through Mississippi by way of Pine Bluff, Hot Springs, Little Rock, and Newport. A dizzying, exhausting life for some, it was an exciting, exhilarating life for the true road warrior. It is difficult to determine, at this point in his career, whether James was tiring of the road and looking forward to returning to academic life, a home, a wife or possibly a new wife and family, or whether he was watching with regret as his shadow began to lengthen while the limelight of the theater moved farther and farther into the distance.

The remainder of that year, 1907, saw him travel more in Mississippi and then through Missouri, Illinois, and Tennessee. He spent Christmas and the New Year in Memphis, where he began his new diary for 1908. This little booklet is the single journal of his life that is still preserved for us today. The leather covers have dried and frayed, and the paper of the pages has darkened with age. The black ink has turned a shade of dark reddish-brown as the mild acid of its formula continues to transform the original carbon color with age. On the flyleaf inside this small leatherbound booklet, less than four by six inches in size and thin enough to slip comfortably into a pocket, he writes:

Diary 1908

Jas. H. Wilson
Nicholasville
Ky

In case of accident
Notify Mrs. Hester Wilson
#106 E. Court St.
Cincinnati O.

Figure 5-3. James H. Wilson Journal. Cover.

We might note that James claimed Nicholasville as his home in 1908 even though the 1900 census, collected midyear and just before his marriage to Georgia, placed him in his mother's Ohio apartment at that time. This helps confirm that after the marriage he must have moved out of his mother's home to set up a household of his own somewhere in his old home town. However, by 1908 he already must have been estranged from Georgia, for in this little booklet he does not request the finder to notify his wife in case of accident, nor his father in Nicholasville, but rather his mother in Cincinnati. If indeed he and Georgia were then separated, we do not know for certain where he and she were living at that time nor where she was working. He might have been staying with his father in Herveytown or with a friend when he returned to work or visit in Kentucky, or he may have had a place of his own. If he did its location has not yet come to light.

On the 1st of January, 1908, Wilson was still in Memphis and he wrote:

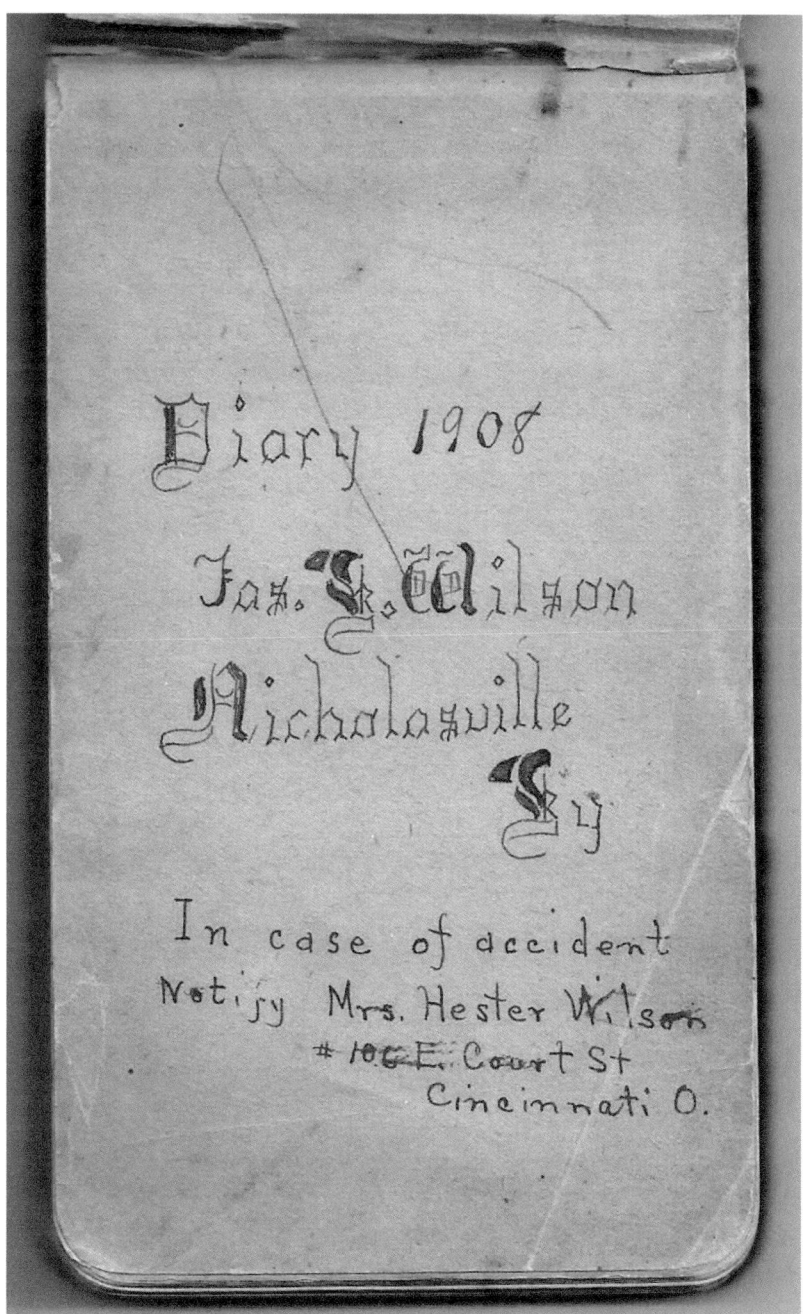

Figure 5-4. James H. Wilson Journal. Flyleaf.

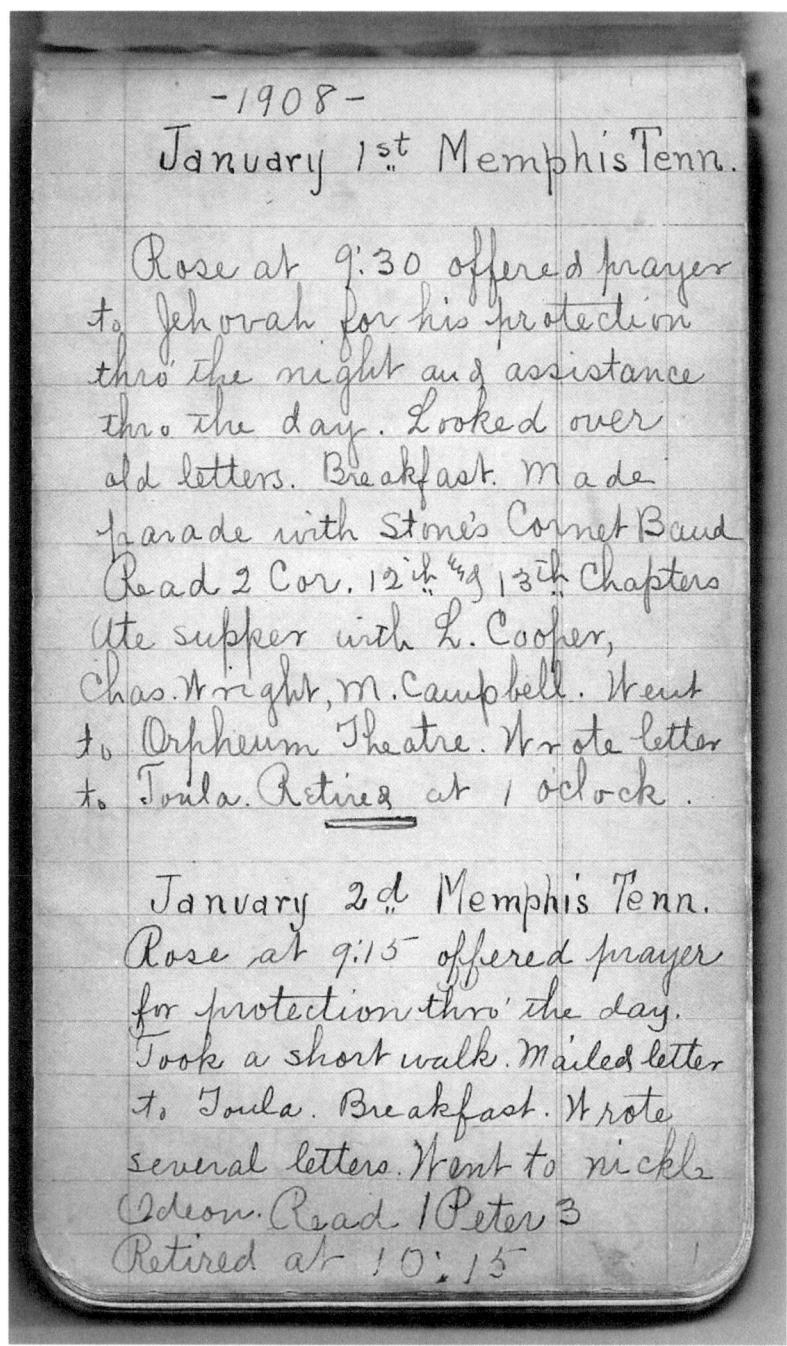

Figure 5-5. James H. Wilson Journal. Entries for January 1st and 2nd, 1908.

A Pivotal Year: 1908

> January 1st Memphis Tenn.
>
> Rose at 9:30 offered prayer
> to Jehovah for his protection
> thro' the night and assistance
> thro the day. Looked over
> old letters. Breakfast. Made
> parade with Stone's Cornet Band
> Read 2 Cor. 12th and 13th Chapters
> Ate supper with L[loyd]. Cooper,
> Chas. Wright, M[anzy]. Campbell. Went
> to Orpheum Theatre. Wrote letter
> to Toula. Retired at 1 o'clock.

This entry is typical of those to come—religious observances; two meals [almost never three]; rehearsals and performances; other business of the day; personal correspondence; and the times of his arising and retiring.

Sometimes he attended church services and Sunday schools, and when he did he usually critiqued both the sermons and the music. From time to time he rated them as fair or poor, but just as often he praised the thoughtful homilies and excellent performances. Wilson displays a serious religiosity in these notes, written not for posterity but for himself, and all these jottings also help to keep order in his life, to remind him of all the people he must remember for professional reasons, and to jog his memory for pleasant reflections of people and events gone by. These diary entries were never written for the public, but we now intrude on his privacy to learn those things about the man that only his own daily record might reveal to us.

On New Year's Day in Memphis, 1908, he arose late. Because of evening performances, (and here we should note that entertainers work late and therefore rotate their work and body clocks by three or four hours to accommodate their work schedules) he got up late and went to bed late. On this day our twenty-seven-year-old musician offered prayers of thanks and for deliverance and then began the activities of his new day and year. He read letters, had breakfast, participated in the street parade that advertised their show to the town's folk and attracted customers to the evening performance. In the afternoon he read his Bible, not just a verse or two, but a chapter or two almost every day. For supper he was accompanied by three members of the troupe—Lloyd Cooper, a bass player and possibly a road manager as well; Manzy Campbell, later known as an outstanding drummer but now one of "The Six Campbell Brothers," siblings celebrated for their eccentric singing and dancing; and Charles Wright, another member of the company. He went to perform at the Orpheum Theater where the Kersands' Minstrels had been playing for a week, and on his return to the railroad car, just before he went to bed, he wrote a letter to Toula. He clearly had become smitten by this vivacious woman of New Orleans, and this letter is but the first of many sent to Toula and recorded in the journal.

No performance is indicated in the entry for the next day, January 2nd, but it may be that the same routine in the same place for over a week obviated the need. On this day it would seem that Wilson also decided to enjoy a little inexpensive entertainment, the Nickelodeon, an early silent-film motion-picture theater where a movie, actually about an hour's worth of entertainment including a few short movies accompanied by organ plus a little audience sing-along and maybe even a comedian, could be had for a nickel, or more usually a dime.[11] The pattern of this entry is generally the same as the first—get up, say a prayer, do something and eat breakfast, do some more, read the Bible, and go to bed. With this day's notes to prod our imaginations we can picture him walking to the mailbox or post office to send yesterday's letter to his new girlfriend, and we can just as easily imagine him singing a popular song of the day to the accompaniment of the movie house reed organ

---

[11]Russell Merritt, "Nickelodeon Theaters, 1905-1914: Building an audience for the movies," *The American Film Industry*, ed. Tino Balio (Madison, WI: University of Wisconsin Press, 1976), pp. 83ff.

A Pivotal Year: 1908

or watching with amazement the flickering wonder of pictures that move. That January 2nd was a Thursday.

> January 2d Memphis Tenn.
>
> Rose at 9:15 offered prayer
> for protection thro' the day.
> Took a short walk. Mailed letter
> to Toula. Breakfast. Wrote
> several letters. Went to nickle
> Odeon. Read 1 Peter 3
> Retired at 10:15

Friday's activities included some creative work:

> Memphis Tenn. Jan 3d
> Rose at 8:50 Offered prayer.
> Read 2 Peter 2d & 3d Chapters
> Wrote to sister Goines. Breakfast.
> Sent off telegrams for Mme
> Kersands. Bathed. Wrote Toula
> Began an arrangement on
> Melody in F. Walked out in
> town. Retired at 11:18

Prayers, Bible reading, and Toula, again. The times of rising and retiring are unusually precise—8:50 a.m. and 11:18 p.m., but the events of his waking day are in essence the same: prayers, Bible reading, correspondence, breakfast, and business—this time for Madame Kersands. On that day he took a walk in town, and he wrote another letter to Toula Morrison.

The Friday bath is interesting, for bathing in the 1900s was not as easily accomplished as it is today, especially if your home was but a small compartment in a railroad car. Hot water was scarce, and there would have been no shower or full-size tub. Even in their own private homes, middle-class Americans in 1908, both white and black, usually bathed but once a week, because most homes had no water heaters. So, a bath meant heating water on the kitchen stove, repeatedly carrying pots of boiling water to a tub half filled with cold, and perhaps even reusing the warm water for more than one bather.

The musical arrangement Wilson was completing that Friday is particularly fascinating. The "Melody in F" is probably Anton Rubinstein's Opus 3, No. 1, for piano, a composition that was first published in 1852. This work quickly earned great popularity in both Europe and America, and this type of arranged "classical" melody that Wilson was working on is but one of a large genre of accessible classical compositions that helped serve to bridge the cultural gap between "upper-class" concert hall compositions and "lower and middle-class" public entertainment music. Though Wilson's arrangement is now lost, the reference still tells us something about his musical taste as well as the kind of music that had popular appeal to an early-20th-century minstrel audience. His arrangement surely would have been written for solo cornet and band, and he most likely, in performance, would have embellished the well known melody in a style of decorative ornamentation favored by virtuoso instrumentalists of the day.[12]

On that same day James also wrote a letter to "sister Goines," the wife of the minister of the First Baptist Church in Nicholasville. An editor of the Indianapolis *Freeman* collected a miscellany of disparate tidbits about Nicholasville a few years before:

Kentucky Items Picked Up. Nicholasville, Ky., Special.— . . . .
A man can no more live out of the church than a fish can out of water, so come back, brother. If eating meat hurt my brother I eat no more meat. If dancing hurts the church, and it does,

---

[12] A YouTube performance of Anton Rubinstein's *Melody in* F by Josef Hoffmann followed by a jazz performance by Teddy Wilson is available: http://www.youtube.com/watch?v=rvC5kzUqFzw&feature=related (accessed February 12, 2012). Although James H. Wilson's and Teddy Wilson's styles are very different, the idea of converting a composed work first to a new style or genre and then using the arrangement in an ornamented theme and variations manner is similar

why don't we stop? . . . The Christian Church has organized an aid society. Rev. W. M. Richards is their able pastor. Rev. C. C. Goines, pastor of the First Baptist church, and his wife, Mrs. R. M. Goines, are the greatest church workers that Nicholasville has ever had, both are for the upbuilding of the race and church. Six hundred dollars is their report for nine months. Subscribe for The Freeman; five cents per copy; James H. Wilson, agent.[13]

Although James' name appears at the end of this brief newspaper notice, it is there to announce the name of the local agent from whom a reader might subscribe to *The Freeman*, not because James was claiming authorship for its contents. He may, however, as the Nicholasville representative, have sent some or all of this information to Indianapolis for publication.

Another article, contemporary with the above tells us a little more about Rev. Goines:

Special News. Nicholasville, Ky., Special.—Protracted meeting going on at the Christian church. . . . Rev. C. C. Goines will preach a series of doctrinal sermons when he comes home. He delivered his first sermon Febr. 22nd [1903].[14]

Apparently James' abilities to write clearly and keep private matters to himself came to the attention of Billy and Madame Kersands during the progress of this tour, and though they hired him as an instrumental musician they frequently took advantage of his secretarial talents. During the continuation of the 1907-1908 tour Wilson wrote several "important" letters for Madame Kersands and others. We know James possessed an aptitude for handling business affairs, and it certainly proved useful on this trip. On January 4th he wrote a "letter of importance for Mme. Kersands," and on January 16th he again "Wrote letter of importance for Mme. Kersands." The day before this latter remark was entered into the journal, the company's train had been involved in a railroad accident. Mrs. Kersands was injured, property was destroyed, and she must have had need to inform someone of the problem and their needs.

---

[13]*The Freeman* (Indianapolis, IN: January 10, 1903), v. xvi, n 2, p. 4.
[14]*The Freeman* (Indianapolis, IN: March 14, 1903), v. xvi, n 11, p. 5.

Winona Miss. Jan. 15

Rose at 9 Offered prayer. Read 1 Cor 4 Parade. Wrote letter to T[oula] Dinner first meal of the day. Quite an accident with the car in which Mme [Louisa] Kersands and L. D. Henderson ["Slim" Henderson, an entertainer in the company] were hurt. Dishes broken. Stove broken. Breakfast lost. Card to Ga [Georgia, his wife] Concert. Show. Mrs. McMahon visited us from Chi[cago] Retired at 11:45[15]

Utilizing someone like Wilson was of special importance in this instance since neither Billy Kersands nor Madame Kersands could read and write. James Wilson would not have been the only person in the troupe capable of writing letters for Mme. Kersands, but genuine business correspondence required good English, an ability to state things clearly and fully, and, most importantly, discretion, the personal character trait of keeping confidential matters confidential. That James was called upon to act in this capacity for the Kersands indicates that Wilson had become known to the owners of the show as a capable and trustworthy associate. This talent for handling business would soon become apparent to President William Solomon Buchanan, Councill's successor in 1909, after Wilson returned to the college.[16] President Buchanan and his two successors at the institution quickly took advantage of these formerly unsuspected talents of Wilson and made them major factors in Wilson's career development at Alabama A. & M. College.

Reading between the lines one might discern that James H. Wilson was not easily ruffled. He always took issues seriously, but tended to keep matters to himself, internalizing difficulties when they arose until his solutions to the various problems were worked out to his satisfaction. Consequently, he appeared to others as having an unflappable personality. Much evidence for this conclusion will appear as we progress through his later life, but

---

[15]James H. Wilson Journal, pp. 7f.

[16]In 1910 Wilson indicated his trade or profession as "teacher." (1910 U. S. Census, [Normal], Alabama, Madison County, Meridianville, Precinct 11, Eastern Part, Alabama Agricultural and Mechanical College.)

here in 1908 we have a clear example. The journal entry one day after the railroad accident is particularly informative for both the events recorded and a view of Wilson's reaction to them. We might note that Wilson seems to have taken everything in stride that day, items large and small—routine morning, railroad accident, no first meal, injured people and broken property, a card written to his wife after having written a letter to his girlfriend, a concert and a show, a visitor to entertain, and then bed. Not many people would have been able to handle so many disparate elements of life in so short a span of time with such equanimity and aplomb, but Wilson seemed able to do so with ease.

The journal also reveals that James was an active participant in the work of his church, and not just his home church. In his journal he recorded visits to several houses of worship during his travels. When he visited a new church he sometimes spoke to the Sunday school participants, and when he attended the morning or evening worship service he always took special note of both the sermons and the music. On more than one occasion he "presided" at the organ. There were no electronic organs in those days, so the various houses of worship where organs are referenced in the journal would have had either pipe or reed organs. The smaller and poorer churches would most likely have had the latter, a treadle organ that required the organist to pump the bellows with the feet while playing the music of the service on the keyboards with the hands.

Although we do not know the content of nearly all the letters James sent while he traveled with the Kersands, as early as January 3rd he sent some message related to church matters to the wife of the minister, Rev. C. C. Goines, of his hometown Baptist Church. Wilson and sister Goines, "brother and sister in Christ," were probably making arrangements for his participation in services at his home church upon his return to Nicholasville in February.

> Louisville Ky. Feb. 22 [Saturday] . . . . Left Lexington en route for Nicholasville at 6:50 arr. 7:30 Had lunch. Attended supper given by the B.Y.P.W. [Baptist Young People's W?] and candy pulling given by members of my father[']s club of Christian Church. Retired at 12.

> Nicholasville Ky. Feb 23 [Sunday] Rose at 8:30 Arranged toilet. Breakfast. Attended Sunday School at Baptist Church. Very nice school. Addressed the same. Remained to morning service. Text John [?] Sermon by John Fisher D.D. good Congregation small. Choir poor. Accompanied Mrs. M. E. Smalley home for dinner. Attended evening services at the Christian Church. Text 1 Cor 16: 2 Sermon by Eld Morrison of A. M. E. Church good. Congregation large. Choir fair. Rally in which my father was a contestant. Had lunch at home. Attended B. Y. P. U. [Baptist Young People's Union] services very good. Addressed the same. Remained to evening services and assisted the choir by presiding at the organ. Text Matt 25: 24 by Jno. Fisher D.D. fair choir good. Congregation small. Went to the Christian Church to hear the result of rally. My father was the winner. Stopped by a restaurant and had a piece of pie. Wrote T[oula] retired at 11:50

While James' business acumen seems certain and trustworthy, his relationships with members of the opposite sex, at least during this young hormonal stage of his life, might be considered a little surprising for a man so intent on studying the Bible and actively participating in the work of his church. On Saturday, January 18th, after the minstrel train pulled into Yazoo City, Mississippi, James went to the post office and collected six letters and two packages from General Delivery. One of the packages, and the only one about which he comments, contained "a handsome present from Toula." While it is possible that their relationship was purely platonic, this handsome gift would seem to indicate a growing affection between the two. He, of course, immediately wrote another letter to Toula. In the first eighteen journal entries, James referenced his New Orleans girlfriend on nine of those days. His Kentucky wife, Georgia, appears but once. Toula was sent letter after letter; but Georgia would have received but a single penny post card during that time. Their marriage would end officially in less than two years, and by then another woman, not Toula, would steal the show and his heart to become his wife.

As we read these journal entries we begin to learn that James Hembray Wilson was indeed very human, a man of remarkable abilities and lofty ideals but also of certain normal weaknesses as well. He was no mythological icon of Christian perfection; he was a real human being, a young man of emotion and passion, a successful artist away from home and traveling alone, and a handsome figure surrounded by admiring young women. He loved music, worked hard, enjoyed life, helped others, had concern for his race, and did many things well. He was not, however, a recluse. He enjoyed the company of his friends from the troupe, the men and women of his church, and many of the various people he encountered on his travels. Undeniably he welcomed the attention of members of the opposite sex. Part of his own personal struggle in life was not just to succeed, not just to help others to do so as well, but to come to grips with balancing a full, robust, and pleasure-filled life with the dramatic admonitions delivered from the Baptist pulpit he had experienced throughout his life. Somehow he had to find a way to reconcile his church upbringing and the teachings of his beloved Bible with the realities of human nature and life on earth.

During the month remaining on tour with the Kersands and before his return to Nicholasville, there are a few additional items in Wilson's journal of particular interest. From photographs preserved from this period we see that Wilson was a careful dresser. In the following photograph, Figure 5-6, both of the handsome young men's suits are flawlessly pressed, perfectly fitted, and modern in taste. Their white shirts are spotless, starched, and pressed, and Wilson's shirt sports a stylish collar that exposes the necktie carefully wound around his neck. Wilson's white tie has a faint pattern woven into the fabric, tasteful not gaudy, and it is held in place with a pearl stickpin. Manzy Campbell's diagonally patterned tie also boasts an ornamental stick pen. In Wilson's jacket pocket we can see his ink pen neatly clipped in place, and from Campbell's jacket-collar buttonhole, the ornamental end of a gold chain dangles while presumably its other end reaches into the nearby pocket to secure a watch or wallet resting out of sight. Careful dressers indeed!

Figure 5-6. Wilson, left, and his minstrel show colleague, Manzy Campbell.[17]

[17]Manzy Campbell is one of the slipperiest people I have encountered in my researches of James H. Wilson. Other than newspaper references to Manzy, the Campbell Brothers, and his brother Bunk, little else has surfaced. However, since he was a friend and colleague of Wilson's, and since one of the most respected drummers in jazz referred to him positively, I suspect he is another African American worthy of serious study. Papa Jo Jones, perhaps the best known and most respected drummer of the Count Basie Orchestra, who was also a student of Wilson's at Alabama A. & M. College, is reported to have said on the recording that accompanied his 1973 book, The Drums, "... that Manzie played with The Silas Green Show and was without a doubt THE world's greatest drummer." http://www.dannybritt.com/JoJones.htm (accessed February 17, 2012)

Wilson's diary entries show an attention to sartorial details. Earlier, in Memphis, Wilson bought a box of shoe polish. Then as the company continued its tour he purchased a vest and shirt in Canton, Mississippi and a pair of shoes in Morganfield, Kentucky. Perhaps he is wearing his Mississippi shirt and vest in this next photo, Figure 5-7. It would appear that the shirt he wears in this portrait has a celluloid collar, for it seems very stiff and has no wings. The jacket is not the same as the one worn for the portrait with Manzy Campbell; the lapel has a different cut. Based on these and other details we can be certain he had a fairly extensive wardrobe. From a buttonhole in his vest a golden chain dangles downward, and it is probably attached to a gold cross that Wilson wore for years. The clothing in both these photographs seems to be of good quality and excellent fit, luxury items that few African Americans in the early 1900s could afford.

That Wilson cared about his looks and could afford dress clothes and professional photographers reflects on his values, aspirations, and earning power at that time. When he arrived in Louisville, Kentucky, on the evening of February 21, he took a taxicab to the studio of Mr. Neighbors, the photographer. It was after hours and the photographer was not in, but Wilson, now the successful, well-paid artist, had returned to Kentucky with new clothes and money in his pocket for the taxi, the photographer, a room for the night, a couple of books, and a meal. Though he might not get his photograph taken that evening, he would soon have a record of this new chapter in his life.

Earlier that day James had said goodbye to his employer and minstrel friends when the tour ended and the train returned to Evansville, Indiana. He had packed up, got a haircut, and took the 2:15 train for Louisville, Kentucky. He stayed in a boarding house that night, woke up early, and caught the 7:35 am train for Lexington. Four and a quarter hours later he arrived at his destination, ate at Campbell's Restaurant,[18] and "Went to Neighbors. Spent the Afternoon with Mrs. Hawthorne."[19] This

---

[18] Possibly the father of Manzy Campbell and the minstrel troupe's Campbell brothers.

[19] James H. Wilson Journal, pp. 34ff.

Figure 5-7. A photographic portrait of James Hembray Wilson, circa 1908.

A PIVOTAL YEAR: 1908

is a perplexing journal entry. Did he have a home with Georgia in Lexington, and was Mrs. Hawthorne the neighbor mentioned or just some other friend? He does not mention Georgia, his wife, so one wonders whether or not he saw her at all on his return. If she lived in Lexington this would partly explain why, a few days later in Nicholasville, he would write a letter to Georgia rather than speak with her in person. If they shared a home in either of these two cities it would appear that he chose not to see her. Yet, for some unknown reason he still maintained an occasional correspondence with his estranged wife.

What is clear is that James had much affection for his father, and that he loved and trusted his mother. In his journal he mentions an Aunt Maggie and a Cousin Rosie, and one might assume his sister was named in honor of his Aunt Maggie.[20] One can see in these few Nicholasville entries the things that are particularly meaningful to this traveling man—friends, family, his public school, church and Sunday school. He is pleased and proud when his father wins a contest at a church gathering, and they celebrate in a quintessentially American fashion: "Stopped by a restaurant and had a piece of pie." These Nicholasville entries also show that Wilson was comfortable and familiar with all three of the African-American churches in town. "Attended . . . candy pulling given by members of my father's club of Christian Church." "Attended Sunday School at Baptist Church." "Attended evening services at the Christian Church. . . . Sermon by Eld[er] Morrison of A. M. E. Church — good." "Attended supper given by the A. M. E. Church." And on this day he wrote letters to both Georgia and Toula.[21] We can only guess the content of those writings. What we do know is that he paused to write these two important women in his life before embarking on his new career at Normal, the career that would define the rest of his life.

---

[20] James H. Wilson Journal, p. 37.
[21] James H. Wilson Journal, pp. 35ff

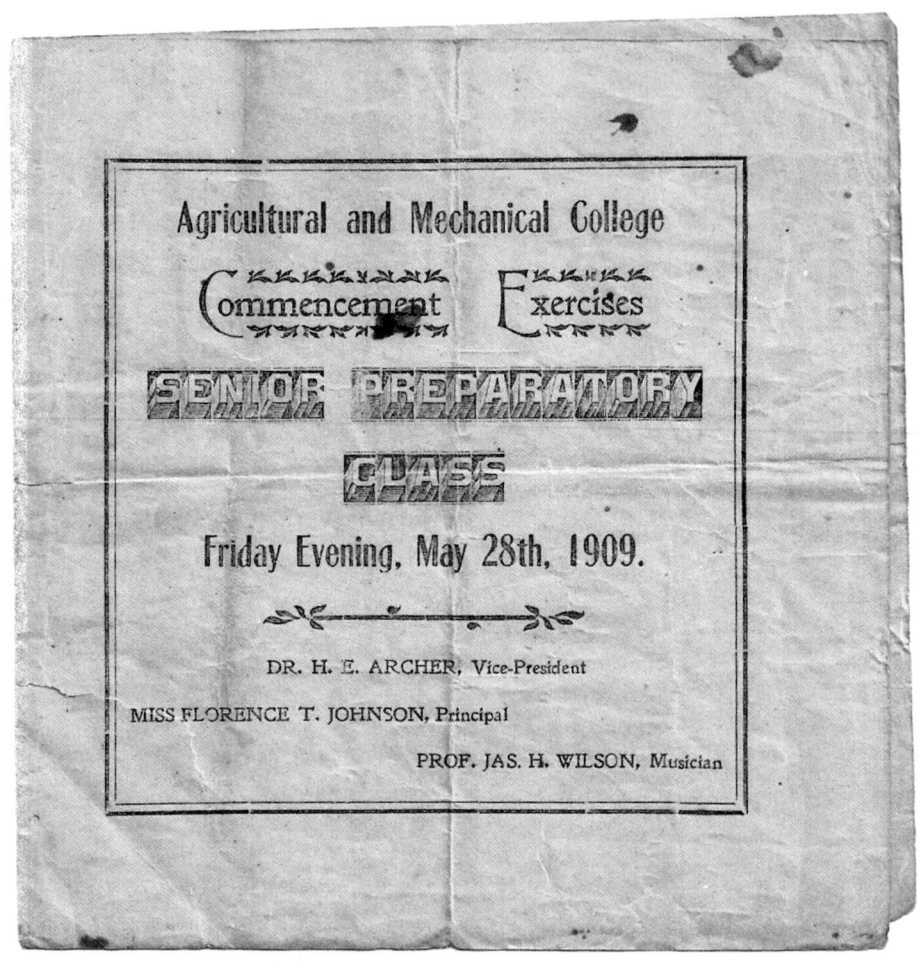

Figure 6-1. Program cover, Commencement Exercises, Senior Preparatory Class, 1909

CHAPTER SIX

The Return to A. & M.

On February 24th, 1908, Wilson left Nicholasville to begin his journey to the college in Normal, Alabama. He had earlier transferred his bags to a locker at the railroad station and he caught the 10:45 pm train after an event-filled day. En route he had breakfast with a friend in Chattanooga, Tennessee, and when he arrived in Normal at 2:10 on the afternoon of the 25th, he immediately reported in to President William Hooper Councill. The President was especially pleased to welcome him back, because following his departure in the spring of 1904 the position had lain vacant for a year. His first replacement, Wade Hammond, lasted only one year, and Hammond's replacement, George F. Hill, remained on campus the same length of time. Consequently, A. & M. had no bandmaster for another academic year, 1907-1908. Despite Councill's best efforts, the music program had fallen into a state of disrepair.[1] James was a welcome addition to the faculty in 1908, and he began work in earnest as bandmaster and instructor of vocal music before the academic year had come to a close. *The Freeman* reported that President Councill had taken ill about this time,[2] but if Wilson no-

---

[1]Rev. Dr. Henry Bradford, Jr., "A. & M. Music Faculty," [typescript with manuscript additions]. In this document Hill is listed as "E. Hill," but the 1905-1906 faculty roster lists his name as George F. Hill. Also, a George F. Hill accepted the position of director of the Odd Fellows band of Edgefield, Tennessee, in the northeast corner of the state in December of 1904 *Freeman*, "Nashville. Nashville, Tenn., Special," (Indianapolis, IN: December 31, 1904), v. xvii, no. 52, p. 2), and the newspaper article would seem to confirm the faculty roster. Also, the roster lists Dement Councill, the president's 18-year-old son, as "Instructor of band and Assistant Commandant." It would seem that Councill asked his son to help out until Wilson's return after finishing his responsibilities with the Kersands Minstrels.

[2](*Freeman* (Indianapolis, IN: April 24, 1909), v. xxii, no. 17, p. 1. Richard Davis Morrison reports that Councill's illness had begun around 1906 and that two Vice Presidents, H. C. Hopkins and Dr. H. E. Archer, had served as Administrative Assistants until Councill's death in 1909. (Morrison, *History of Alabama Agricultural and Mechanical University, 1875-1992* (Huntsville, AL: Liberal Arts Press, 1994), p. 97.)

ticed any signs of his employer's poor health, he makes no mention of it in his journal. After this initial conference with the President, James took the time to meet a few of the teachers and then strolled around the campus to reacquaint himself with the grounds and buildings to observe whether any changes had taken place since his departure in 1904.

That evening after dinner Wilson attended the devotional exercises required of all the students in the college. One might note that it made no difference whether or not A. & M. was a land-grant, state-supported public institution, for at that time in history Alabama A. & M. was clearly a Protestant Christian college. At this first evening religious service Wilson was introduced to the students, and on this occasion he had an opportunity to offer a few remarks. After the meeting he visited "the judge," whoever that might have been. Perhaps he was seeking advice about a divorce. Later he enjoyed some Coca Cola and peanuts "on Mr. Griffin," the commandant of the college.[3] The last thing James did before retiring for the night was write another letter to Toula, the woman who had become his touchstone.

Wednesday, February 26th, was Wilson's first day on the job. He had joined the faculty late in the year, and the second semester was well underway. After attending the morning devotional exercises, he went to the band room, examined the musical instruments, and found them to be in very bad condition. He immediately reported the situation to the president, and to Councill's great credit he straight away instructed the young faculty member to draw up a list and order new instruments. Even though musical instruments were expensive, school-owned instruments would have been essential in black colleges at that time, for African-American students rarely had the resources to own their own band instruments and bring them to school. If

---

[3]James H. Wilson Journal, p. 39. The Morrill Act of 1862 established land grant colleges, and the federal government required these publically supported institutions to include military science in their curriculum. This developed into the modern Reserved Officers Training Corps (ROTC), and the Commandant was the military officer in charge of the program. On March 7th Wilson wrote in his Journal, "Witnessed military drill by students." (p. 48.)

The Return to A. & M.

Councill wanted instrumental music performed at A. & M., and we know that he did, the college would have had to provide most, if not all, of the instruments. Wilson spent part of that day in the office of the bookkeeper, presumably filling out forms to order new cornets, alto and baritone horns, trombones, clarinets, drums, and a tuba, and then he went to meet the band. Since the students had no serviceable instruments on which to learn and perform, Wilson gave a short lecture and dismissed them. His task was not going to be easy, but very little came easy for African Americans in the south in those days.

On the day following his first meeting with the band, Wilson sent Toula some Bible readings for the week beginning March 1st.[4] This is one of the few times when he specifically cited the content of any of his letters, and in this case one might wonder whether Bible readings and religious instruction from a boyfriend would sit well or ill with a high-living New Orleans belle. New Orleans, then as now, was proud of its reputation as a pleasure palace, and Toula gave every evidence of thoroughly enjoying that life style. Their mutual affection would soon wither on the vine, and it is difficult to know whether this journal entry is evidence of what might have contributed to their rift. It does, however, seem unusual and out of keeping with his previous record on the road of many letters and a valentine to this girlfriend.

During his first few days on the campus, Wilson began adjusting to the new environment by participating in a variety of activities—teaching, attending meetings, getting together with teachers, visiting campus facilities, and composing and arranging music. Some of these arrangements were for his old bandmaster, James Lacy, but most were for his fledgling band. If his students were to perform music of quality, he would need simplified arrangements, because he was restarting a program essentially from scratch. In the journal we can see that he began his music teaching duties with lessons for the band and conducting rehearsals of the glee club. And in the same journal entry we might note that he sent a money order to someone and mailed a letter to

---

[4]James H. Wilson Journal, p. 41.

C. F. Geiger & Co., a music instrument dealer.[5] That important transaction of providing satisfactory musical instruments for his students had been quickly effected.

Once he completed the dealings necessary to restart his instrumental music program, he began to involve himself in campus religious affairs. The college had many chapel services and a variety of religious meetings for its students each week, some required and others elective. Councill was not ambiguous about his minimum expectations for all members of the campus community, students and faculty alike, and he had this outline of daily activities printed as part of the "Rules and Regulations" in the 1907-1908 *A. & M. Catalogue*:

Rules and Regulations

Rising Taps	5:00 a.m.
Dressing/Arranging Rooms	5:00 – 5:45 a.m.
Study Hour	5:45 – 6:45 a.m.
Devotions	6:45 – 7:00 a.m.
Breakfast	7:00 – 7:30 a.m.
General Information	7:45 – 8:00 a.m.
School	8:00 – 1:00 p.m.
Dinner	1:00 – 2:00 p.m.
Industrial School	2:00 – 4:00 p.m.
General Work	4:00 – 5:30 p.m.
Supper	5:30 – 6:00 p.m.
Recreation	6:00 – 6:45 p.m.
Devotions	6:45 – 7:00 p.m.
Study	7:00 – 9:15 p.m.
Retiring Taps	9:30 p.m.
Preaching (Sundays)	10:30 – 12:00 p.m.
Sunday school	3:00 – 4:00 p.m.[6]

---

[5]*Ibid.*
[6]Morrison, p. 78.

Wilson regularly attended many of these gatherings, and he began to participate in several early upon his return to Normal. Before each day ended he would usually evaluate both the message and the delivery of the various preachers he heard, and he would do the same for all the musical performances as well, entering a "good," "fair," "poor," or "interesting" into his journal. For example:

> A. and M. College. March 1. . . . Attended Y. M. C. A. meeting and took a part in discussion from Daniel 1:8. Subject: "Stand up for the right." Good meeting. Read Titus. Attended morning services in chapel. Text: Romans 8:13. Sermon good. Eld[er] Ramsey chaplain. Choir very good. . . . Went to Sunday School. Large attendance. Taught Senior Class of Boys. . . . Attended Sunday Evening Meeting in the chapter [chapter house]. Chaplain read Romans 12. Meeting good.[7]

Not every sermon met his criteria:

> A. and M. College. April 16 Rose at 7:00 Breakfast. Chapel . . . Visitors from Oak Wood School. Elder Leak preached. Text Revelation 22:3. Subject the soul. Argument was without substantial foundation.[8]

On Monday, March 2nd, Wilson began a series of classroom activities for which he was not hired but for which he was qualified by experience to teach. He earlier had met two of the classroom teachers, Miss Johnson and Miss Gibson, who worked in the "Normal School," a division of A. & M. that offered a two-year course to high school graduates for the specific purpose of training them to become elementary-school teachers. Florence T. Johnson was an English teacher and Principal of the Preparatory Department, and her colleague, Mary J. Gibson, also taught English. In his role as a guest classroom instructor Wilson taught penmanship to both levels of the Normal School classes, and he coached Miss Johnson's upper level class for "rhetorical," the craft of effective, even eloquent, public speaking. Though he may or may not have had formal training in these skills, he had professional experience

---

[7]James H. Wilson Journal, p. 44.
[8]James H. Wilson Journal, p. 72.

and considerable natural talent in both these areas. His on-the-job training served to qualify him for his new teaching tasks. His business letters for Billy and Madame Kersands and the quality of penmanship demonstrated in his journal both attest to his competence in this subject. His observation of stage elocution during his many years in the minstrel business, a skill vitally important for communicating well to a paying audience in the days before microphones and amplification, also served him well. His ability to speak readily and effectively to both religious groups and to professional musicians in rehearsal as their conductor and musical director provided additional qualification for teaching "rhetorical," perhaps even more than most teachers at A. & M. would have possessed from their traditional training. His bona fides came from life experiences, and they afforded him the privilege of teaching and coaching Normal students in two practical areas not related to music.

Even though today's computers are making good penmanship a dying craft, its importance at the beginning of the 20th century needs no further explanation. But "rhetorical," or rhetoric as a particular subject, has not been common in the American school curriculum for many years. We might ask what the content of the rhetoric class syllabus at Alabama A. & M. in 1908 was, and to what purpose did the students use these skills while still enrolled at the college. Commonly, the classroom teacher would select uplifting passages or brief works of literature, both poetry and prose, appropriate for the students' age group. Students would then be called upon to memorize and recite the selections. While this task was in process, the teacher would drill the students in the classroom with and without their notes, thus aiding the memory process. Also, the teacher would explain meanings and give instruction in both diction and dramatic accent. The class would be asked to stand and recite in unison one of the selected works, and the teacher, like a music conductor, would set tempo, indicate dynamics, point out accent, and both criticize and praise the performance. Of course, some students would show greater talent and ability in this area than others, and these better orators would be rewarded with opportunities to perform solo for other students or for a general public as the various occasions presented themselves on campus.

Normal School Preparatory Division commencement exercises were such occasions, and we can see from a preserved printed program for the very next year the nature and variety of these rhetorical offerings (Figure 6-2, below). On Friday evening, May 28th, 1909, the Senior Preparatory Class presented a program of music, readings, and declamations. The band played, the chorus sang, and two vocal solos were performed. The eleven members of the senior class were required to stand before the audience of teachers, students, and relatives and display their accomplishments in an appropriate manner. One read the class history, another the class prophecy, and yet a third the class poem. Two sang vocal solos and two presented declamations, "Failures" and "Manhood." The remainder delivered a variety of short prose works. To conclude the program, everyone sang James Hembray Wilson's favorite song, Stephen Foster's "My Old Kentucky Home." The variety of this program shows the importance that the Normal School placed on the ability of its graduates, male and female, to speak publicly and to exhibit grace and self-possession.

For Wilson, this would be a special graduation, though he may not have realized it at the time. One of those young women reading a selection to the assembly that evening, the senior class secretary Miss Exeline Polk from Nashville, Tennessee, would become Mrs. James H. Wilson in but little more than a half year after her graduation. Between March of 1908 when Wilson first started teaching penmanship and rhetorical in the Normal School and December of 1910 when he married for a second time, Toula and Georgia would disappear into the tangled cobwebs of yesterday's mistakes, and young Miss Exeline Polk would step in to become Mrs. Wilson for the remainder of James' life. In 1908, however, Wilson seems to have taken no special notice of this seventeen-year-old junior, for her name never appears in his journal.

From the journal entries for the months of March, April, and May we learn that James enjoyed baseball and pitching horse shoes. He must have had at least a modicum of athletic ability. "March 7 . . . . Played a game of ball. First of the season."[9] "March

```
              PROGRAM
Processional  "Paradise"..................................Barnby
              A. and M. College Band
Chorus  "In May Time".....................................Speaks
              Treble Clef Club
Class History.........................................Henrietta James
Reading  "Duty".............................................Vida Lacy
Vocal Solo  "Mighty Lak a Rose"..............................Nevin
              Elizabeth Saffold
Declamation  "Failures"................................William Fennoy
Reading  "Mother, Home and Heaven"..................Lucenda Bose
Reading  "God in Nature"................................Isora Simmons
Vocal Solo  "Nazareth"...................................Emma Jackson
Declamation  "Manhood"...................................Harvey Clark
Reading  "Home".............................................Exeline Polk
Intermezzo  "Iola"...........................................Johnson
              A. and M. College Band
Class Prophecy........................................Benjamin E. Ware
Class Poem  "Farewell"..........................Dwight Lormar Clanton
Song  "My Old Kentucky Home"..............................Foster
```

Figure 6-2. Program, Commencement Exercises, Senior Preparatory Class, 1909.

18 .... Pitched horse shoes."[10] Since notations of these activities are repeated elsewhere we can assume these are normal activities he continued throughout his healthy younger years. We also discover that his school activities soon became routine. Instead of writing a brief description of each he began to regularly enter "Usual work" or "Usual duties."[11] A very important entry teaches us something about his attitude toward himself and his work. From it we learn that he is willing to be self-critical and admit shortcomings. On March 27th he writes, "Industrial parade. Band played. Very shabby indeed."[12] On that day he again wrote Toula, and one wonders whether he might have been seeking a little comfort and understanding about his day's unsatisfactory work.

The next day, James arranged a piece for band, a lullaby

---

[9] James H. Wilson Journal, p. 48.
[10] James H. Wilson Journal, pp. 54ff.
[11] March 9, 10, 11, 12, 13, 17, and following.
[12] James H. Wilson Journal, p. 60.

Figure 6-3. "Arrah Wanna: An Irish Indian Matrimonial Venture" by Jack Drislane and Theodore Morse.[13]

---

[13] And indeed it is used as a camp song today! Camp Arrah Wanna, "nestled in the foothills of majestic Mr. Hood," in Welches, Oregon, keeps the memory alive over a hundred years after the publication of the song. http://www.camparrahwanna.org/, accessed March 19, 2012.)

Figure 6-4. "Arrah Wanna: An Irish Indian Matrimonial Venture" by Jack Drislane and Theodore Morse.

composed by Miss Hopkins, the daughter of a mathematics professor and principal of the Normal Department. The day after that, the 29th, he worked on an arrangement of a popular song published in New York two years earlier, "Arrah Wanna" with words by Jack Drislane and music by Theodore F. Morse. Subtitled "An Irish Indian Matrimonial Venture," we see the creative musician/teacher adapting a current popular song for his young beginning students. Though we may chuckle today at the simplistic *naïveté* of both the lyrics and the music, they demonstrate a common genre of American popular music taste of the early 1900s. This song quickly became well known and successful through both its sheet music sales, live performances, and a 1906 Edison cylinder recording sung by Arthur Collins and Byron Harlan. The music has a simple melody and a repetitive accompaniment, useful material for beginning students. The words revamp the familiar 17th-century John Smith and Pocahontas story into a situation where Barney tricks the Indian maid into accepting his proposal of marriage with a pun on "race." The lyrics also employ a cute rhyme—Barney Carney from Killarney. "Arrah Wanna" is little more than a fireside camp song, but it struck the public's fancy and proved useful in class.[14]

An Irish Indian Matrimonial Venture

Verse:

> 'Mid the wild and wooly prairies lived an Indian maid,
> Arrah Wanna queen of fairies of her tribe afraid
> Each night came an Irish laddie buck, with a wedding ring.
> He would sit outside her tent and with his bagpipes sing.

Chorus:

> "Arrah Wanna, on my honor, I'll take care of you,
> I'll be kind and true, we can love and bill and coo,
> In a wigwam built of shamrocks green, we'll make those red men smile,
> When you're Misses Barney, heap much Carney, from Killarney's Isle."

---

[14]Duke University, David M. Rubenstein Rare Book and Manuscript Library, Item ID: a2203, URL: http://library.duke.edu/digitalcollections/hasm_a2203/, accessed 3/13/12, Used with permission.

Verse 2:
>While the moon shone down upon them Arrah Wanna sighed,
>"Some great race must call you Big Chief, then I'll be your bride,"
>"Sure, that's easy" whispered Barney, with a smiling face,
>All my family were good runners and were first in every race."

Chorus: [repeat above]

Why might Wilson have chosen to arrange this piece for his band? Part of the answer is to be found in the band itself—the members are rank beginners, some probably still of grade school age. He needed elementary band music that would teach fundamentals to young musicians yet still provide a sense of accomplishment and some level of enjoyment. The repetitive left-hand part of the vocal score would serve to teach his tubist and horn players how to play the omnipresent "oom-pah" rhythms of American march music without the introduction of complexity, and the melody, a current popular song, would be a cinch for young cornet players. Wilson probably was introduced to the number while traveling with the Kersands, and even though the melodic line does not exceed the range of an octave, it has just enough of a catchy rhythm and funny words to make playing it enjoyable.

The sounds of the 1906 original recording are available to us on YouTube.[15] We are doubly fortunate, because the Edison cylinder recording of this song also preserves for us a performance by a typical early-20th-century popular-entertainment orchestra, one likely to have been very similar to ensembles in which Wilson played as he toured the country with minstrel troupes and military bands. Of course the instrumental sounds are distorted by the primitive recording techniques available at that time, but if one listens sympathetically to the enthusiastic vocalists and the

---

[15]The YouTube recording is available free at: http://www.youtube.com/watch?v=4gt2O0jlHRM. "Arrah Wanna" was recorded by Collins and Harlan, with orchestra, November 14, 1906 (E-4043). (Accessed March 19, 2012.)

boisterous orchestra, the listener will be rewarded with a telling audio representation of James H. Wilson's minstrel environment.

On March 28th Wilson also attended a banquet given by the Frederick Douglass Debating Society. Douglass was arguably the most famous African American of the pre-and post-Civil-War years, and naming the college debating society in honor of this great orator and outspoken black abolitionist reflects the lofty goals of the college's founder and first president, William Hooper Councill. Wilson's attending and enjoying the debate society's event soon after returning to campus gives us some indication of his wide-ranging interests. Another similar event on April 18th, the annual banquet of the Adelphic Literary Society, may have been a precursor to his active participation as a faculty sponsor of the student social organizations of the campus. On this same April evening he notes that he "Accompanied Miss Marguerite Thompson to table and hall"[16] before returning to his room to start a letter for Toula and to retire for the night.

As the month of April progressed, performance activities at the college intensified. Wilson became much involved rehearsing the band, glee club, other vocal ensembles, and the rhetoricians for their various roles in end-of-the-semester concerts and for the all important commencement exercises. At the beginning of May there was a special ceremony for the celebration of the thirty-third anniversary of the institution. On the morning of May 1st he simply attended a special chapel service, but in the evening he directed both the band and the chorus. He remained busy teaching and conducting for the remainder of the month, but he does find time to umpire a baseball game, pitch horse shoes,[17] and keep up both his correspondence and his Bible reading. One day he had to discipline some of his students, writing, "Penmanship in which the time was taken in talking to Juniors about the conduct of some of the male members of the class."[18] Nowhere in the journal do we find evidence of his hesitating to own up to his responsibilities,

---

[16]James H. Wilson Journal, p. 74.
[17]James H. Wilson Journal, pp. 81-85 [band and chorus, 81; baseball, 83; horse shoes, 85].
[18]James H. Wilson Journal, pp. 87f.

and one might think that disciplining some junior boys was likely one of his more unpleasant tasks. In the middle of the month he received a "basket of fruit from First Normal Class as a token of their appreciation of my services rendered them."[19] He must have been a good teacher; certainly the students thought so. On the 21st, he went to Huntsville to purchase four books as gifts for four members of the senior class. He, too, was willing to reward excellence with gifts purchased with money from his own pocket. Wilson seems to have found contentment in his return to Normal, and one senses him settling in and enjoying his new environment as the pages progress through the months of March, April, and May.

The graduation exercises began on Friday, May 22nd, and eleven seniors received their diplomas that year. At the chapel ceremony Professor Henry Hopkins, principal of the Normal Department addressed the graduating class. The next day the students, teachers, and families again gathered in the chapel, this time for a service of devotions specially prepared for the campus literary societies. Wilson's Minstrelnola Club, a musical organization that sang popular music, jubilee hymns, and the like, performed two numbers at the ceremony. He was pleased, for he graded their performance "Excellent." He also informs us that he "Presided at the organ for devotions."

The highlight of the 1908 commencement weekend, for Wilson, took place on Sunday, May 24th, and he joyously writes, "A. and M. College   May 24   A day long to be remembered."[20] On this day he met and had breakfast with Dr. Charles H. Parrish, the guest speaker for the day's baccalaureate service, and Wilson found him to be an inspiration. Parrish, a former slave, a Baptist, and an 1886 graduate from Simmons College of Kentucky, the only school of African-American higher education in Kentucky until 1930, spent much of the day with Wilson. After breakfast James took Dr. Parrish on a tour of the campus, and then they parted because Wilson had to attend to his final rehearsal of the choir. For the baccalaureate sermon Parish spoke on "Obedience," and

---

[19] James H. Wilson Journal, pp. 90f.
[20] James H. Wilson Journal, p. 96.

James rated the sermon "Excellent." He was also pleased with his own handiwork, rating the music for the service "Superb." There was an afternoon Sunday School at 3:00, and that evening, in the chapel, a special meeting took place for the religious societies at which Parrish delivered a "Fine Lecture [about the Holy Land]. . . . Instructive" to the attendees.[21] This was meat and potatoes for Wilson, and through the abbreviated jottings of his journal we can sense him thriving in this enriched educational and Christian environment.

The final graduation exercises for Alabama A. & M. College took place on Monday, the 25th, and the ceremony for the Industrial School took place first in the morning. Wilson conducted both the Glee Club and the Minstrelnola Club as they performed for the event. Later, a separate ritual took place for twenty-five graduating seniors of the College and the Normal School, and he comments that two received the Bachelor of Science degree.[22] We can only imagine how special and precious those degrees must have been for black men and women in Alabama in 1908. There were so many barriers operating in the early 20th century, some legal and others brutal, that prevented African Americans from participating fully in society and succeeding in life. One can envisage the measure of accomplishment and raw determination a college degree from a state supported institution required of each of these very few black citizens of Alabama who walked away that day with certified college credentials.

During the next few days Wilson saw students off, took inventory, and kept busy around campus and in Huntsville cleaning up loose odds and ends as he prepared to leave for Kentucky. He took his last meal on campus on June 1st, bought a typewriter for himself, said goodbye to his colleagues, and boarded a train for Chattanooga, Tennessee, where he stayed for three days with an actor friend, David Smith. He visited other friends, went sightseeing, made a few purchases, and played and practiced both cornet and piano.[23] On June 4th he continued on his way home,

---

[21] James H. Wilson Journal, p. 97.
[22] James H. Wilson Journal, p. 98.
[23] James H. Wilson Journal, pp. 103ff.

again stopping en route for three days in Somerset, Kentucky, to do a little more of the same.[24] After a few months of long and active days on campus, Wilson seems to have been ready to move into a relaxed and recuperative mode. When he finally arrived in Nicholasville on the evening of the 6th he went to his father's next-door neighbor's home on Lincoln Street to have supper with Mrs. Elmore, and although he had gotten up at five minutes to six that morning, he did not get to bed that day until midnight. His next day was chock-a-block full, too. It was Sunday and he rose at 6:00 am, went to Sunday school and taught some lesson from a chart. Then at the morning service he again "presided" at the organ. He was enough of a professional musician to know that it is not the minister who leads the service but the organist. The pastor may be in charge, he may officiate and preach, but the tempo and the continuity of the service are truly in the hands of the organist. He consistently used the word "preside" for this church responsibility rather than "play" or "perform." It would appear that after this service he then attended another worship service, this time at the Baptist Church. Perhaps the Sunday School and first service took place at his father's Colored Christian Church. At the Baptist service he particularly enjoyed the sermon by E. U. Hantham, Doctor of Divinity, and James wrote, "Sermon excellent."[25] At this service he played a cornet solo, probably right after the sermon during the collection of the offering. Still his Sunday activities were not yet complete. He attended an evening service as well before returning to his bed and retiring for the night. His involvement in the church had become much more than just a once-a-week interest. It was developing into a genuine calling.

    On Monday morning, James visited with Sister Dickerson, the wife of Elder Dickerson from his own Baptist church. He boarded the train in the early afternoon for the short ride north to Lexington, and there he visited more friends and referred to some as "Neighbors." It seems possible that he might once have had a home in Lexington with Georgia, but he never mentions a visit to see her. And, on Tuesday when he is ready to go back to

---

[24]James H. Wilson Journal, pp. 105ff.
[25]James H. Wilson Journal, pp. 107f.

Nicholasville he writes, "Left Lexington at 6:45 for home."[26] This time on his return to Nicholasville he sends his wife no letters. They obviously now have become totally estranged. Even though he wrote to her several times over the course of the six months recorded in the journal, and even though he sent her $17.00 from Normal, Alabama, on April 13th, there is no reason to think he harbored any warm feelings for her at this point in his life.[27] Perhaps in his letters to her he had been trying to negotiate a divorce, perhaps something else. The journal does not reveal all.

One additional item of importance is presented to us at the end of his journal, a little more information about his concert band activity and solo cornet career, especially as it relates to Kentucky. On Saturday, June 13th, he went to the Union Station in Lexington to meet Beulah Price from Fisk University and also Henry Hamilton, the owner of Hamilton's Military Band.[28] He returned home to Nicholasville for Sunday services but came back to Lexington on Monday to begin rehearsals with this impressive musical organization with which he first soloed in 1902.

Hamilton's band had core members, musicians who played every concert and parade, and to this group were added additional changing personnel of professional musicians as might be demanded by different engagements. The numbers varied from fourteen to seventeen to twenty-two and a high of twenty-five, an unusually large ensemble for a military organization or a civilian band that fashioned itself in the military manner. After all, regimental bands of the Civil War were only authorized to enlist up to twenty-four musicians and were in practice often fewer in number.[29] Hamilton's Military Band both marched in parade and performed in concert, and for these two different functions Hamilton engaged two different leaders, both a drum major and a musical conductor.

---

[26]James H. Wilson Journal, p. 109.
[27]James H. Wilson Journal, p. 70.
[28]James H. Wilson Journal, p. 111.
[29]General Order 15 (May 4, 1861) for volunteer units. General order 16 authorized the same for the regular army. Cavalry regiments were limited to sixteen band members. See Raoul F. Camus. "Band." Grove Music Online. Oxford Music Online. [Section 2, Brass Bands]. Oxford University Press. Web. 27 Sep. 2014. <http://www.oxfordmusiconline.com/subscriber/article/grove/music/A2252742>.

Figure 6-5. "Hamilton's Military Band. Lexington Ky. Jas. H. Wilson, Ban[d Director.]"

James Hembray Wilson was the musical director. Hamilton, the owner, was probably but an average musician himself, for on one band roster recorded by Wilson, there were four horn players, and Hamilton was listed as fourth. He must have enjoyed performing, however, for in every photo preserved of the band we see him sitting or standing proudly holding his instrument. Based on his appearance in the photos, he may have been Caucasian or perhaps a very light-skinned mulatto. Either way, he was the boss and had the good sense to hire an outstanding musician for his musical director and cornet soloist, James H. Wilson.

In the first photo (Figure 6-5.) Hamilton stands in the back left with his mellophone while Wilson, front and center, cockily displays his sergeant stripes and conductor's baton. Richard Curd, the drum major, is seated just to Wilson's right. The twenty-three performing musicians of this brass band show off their five Albert system clarinets, one tenor saxophone, four cornets, one mellophone

THE RETURN TO A. & M.

Figure 6-6. "Hamilton's Military Band in Camp with U. R. of K. of P. . . . July 26-7-8-9-30. 1908"[30]

and two alto horns, three baritone horns, three trombones, a tuba, a bass viol, one snare drum, and a bass drum. A drum major and a conductor bring the total to twenty-five.

The second photograph (Figure 6-6.) was taken in July of 1908, only one month after Wilson's journal comes to a close. Wilson stands on the left with baton in hand, the drum major lounges in the center foreground, and Hamilton sits cross-legged on the right. All the musicians are identified below the photo, and they are in uniforms different from those worn in Figure 6-5. In this photo Wilson was twenty-seven years old and we notice that he has begun to wear eyeglasses. If he consistently wore his spectacles and did not let vanity remove them for photographic portraits, we might assume the picture in Figure 6-5 represents an earlier version of Hamilton's Military Band.

---

[30]Uniform Rank of Knights of Pythias. I thank Alfred A. Saltzman, PSC, Supreme Lodge of Pythias. He explained that the Uniform Rank ". . . was a branch of the Pythian Order around the 1900's. The last group ceased to exist around 1950. Several members at that time wanted a more military use of the ceremonies and use of the sword, in which they were very proficient. The group used military designations for their lodges and addressed themselves with military titles. They went to "encampments" instead of lodge meetings and their rules were designed to follow the pattern of the U.S. Army regulations." (Email communication, March 17, 2012.)

After Wilson returned to Lexington on Monday the 15th of June to begin band rehearsals he remained in the city for three days, not returning to Nicholasville until Thursday. The musicians would rehearse in the evening, and on Wednesday he went to the Hamilton home for supper before rehearsal.[31] He does not inform us where he was staying, but it was not at the Hamiltons' house. James returned to his own home in Nicholasville the next day and quickly continued on to Camp Nelson, five miles south of Nicholasville.[32] By this time Camp Nelson had become an African-American community, and Wilson remained there overnight before returning home to Nicholasville on the 20th. He filled the next day with his usual Sunday church-related activities and returned to Lexington on Monday to sightsee and again rehearse the band in the evening. Another three evening rehearsals and the band was ready for their Thursday evening concert in Paris, Kentucky, the county seat of Bourbon County. This concert they performed outdoors on the street, perhaps only for donations. Before the band left town the next morning they played a few numbers at the railroad depot and then boarded for a trip to Frankfort, the state capital, to play for the Independent Order of Odd Fellows' picnic.[33] The occasion was special, for the organization was dedicating their new building, and Hamilton's Military Band was there to contribute some pomp and circumstance to the occasion. That Friday became a very long day, for they caught a 2:20 am. train to return to Paris. Wilson crawled into bed at 3:00 am. and rose again at 6:30 am. to leave Paris at 7:00 am. for Lexington. The band was engaged to play at the Lexington Union Station for the arrival of some delegates to the city, and once again Wilson had another long day before he could return home to Nicholasville. There he spends three days in routine activities, and the journal ends abruptly on June 30th.

---

[31] James H. Wilson Journal, p. 113.
[32] Camp Nelson is still in use today as a Civil War Living History Museum. The camp website offers a historical overview at http://www.campnelson.org/introduction.htm (accessed March 16, 2012).
[33] James H. Wilson Journal, p. 118.

The Return to A. & M.

All in all the first half of 1908 was a telling period in the life of James Hembray Wilson. During those first six months he ended his minstrel life on the road, began his teaching career in earnest, and struggled to maintain his professional standing as a cornet virtuoso soloist and professional concert band conductor. Those same six months tell of his involvement with Toula, his separation from Georgia, and his early contact with Exeline. His church activities also became intense, and last, but not least, we discovered his athletic proclivities—baseball and horse shoes. The people and institutions that would give shape to his adult life were coming into focus.

Figure 7-1. The Alabama A. & M. campus [ca. 1938].

CHAPTER SEVEN

The Big Change: 1908—1910

When Wilson returned to A. & M. in the fall of 1908 he was about to embark on the most meaningful voyage of his life, a whole-hearted, full-time commitment to education, family, music, and Christian service. The 27-year-old Wilson rejoined a faculty and staff of 32, and these officers, teachers, and administrators provided for the intellectual and physical needs of a student body of 120 males and 147 females on a campus of only 182 acres.[1] On "the hill," a plot of land just over a quarter square mile in area, the students not only attended academic classes but raised poultry, cattle, and a variety of row crops, and they were also instructed in the household and mechanical crafts of homemaking, printing, carpentry, blacksmithing, shoemaking, stone and brick masonry, and similar practical skills by which they might earn a respectable living.

Of the total 267 students registered in 1908, 136 were engaged in teacher preparation and certification in the Normal Department, and 80 of this group were those younger students of the preparatory program.[2] In comparison with today's giant state universities, Alabama A. & M. in 1908 was intimate indeed, hardly more than an extended family dedicated to delivering personal attention to the needs of students easily intimidated, for they often traveled to Normal from repressive circumstances and truly humble backgrounds. There were exceptions of course, such as Ida Councill, the daughter of the university president, who graduated from the college in 1901, studied at a German conservatory of music, followed that with additional study at Oberlin College for another two years, and then was appointed a notary public by Governor Jelks of Alabama in 1907, an uncommon and much-

---

[1] Richard David Morrison, *History of Alabama Agricultural and Mechanical University, 1875 – 1992* (Huntsville, AL: Liberal Arts Press, [1994]), p. 98.
[2] Morrison, *History of Alabama Agricultural and Mechanical University*, pp. 59f.

Figure 7-2. Advertisement for the agricultural program, A. & M. Brochure [ca. 1930].

Figure 7-3. The Mechanical Arts Building, A. & M. Brochure [ca. 1930].

prized certification for an African American that enabled her to "discharge the duties of that office before Judge Lawler."[3] During that same school year, 1907-1908, Ida Councill held an academic appointment at the college teaching piano and vocal music to the A. & M. students. Her enriched educational upbringing was exceptional. In contrast, the majority of Normal students came to A. & M. with much hope, promise, and determination, but they also arrived on campus having left impoverished family circumstances, and just as often they came equipped with substandard preparatory educations as well.

In today's academic environment a father and daughter teaching at the same college, especially if the father is the president of the institution, would raise suspicions of nepotism. However, during the early 20th century it was a common practice and, in the case of the fledgling black colleges, a useful and necessary means of acquiring qualified and devoted teachers when salary money was insufficient to attract and keep high quality faculty. In addition to the Councills we find among the names on the faculty roster the Archers providing another campus example of this practice. In 1908 Dr. Hiram E. Archer, Professor of Natural Science, was the Vice-President of the College. His wife, Professor Henrietta M. F. Archer, was on the faculty, too, a teacher of Mathematics, Pedagogics, and Literature. In addition, she was also the Secretary of the Faculty, an important administrative post. In those days very few if any of the full-time faculty were able to enjoy the luxury of specialization expected today, for all were called upon to wear the varied but necessary hats required to keep this struggling institution afloat. Even non-academic family members were frequently called into service and asked to participate in their share of the necessary work. For those appointed to the faculty, not all of their tasks were related to their primary teaching, administrative, or research responsibilities. Like all colleges then and now, faculty may be required to serve on committees, supervise student discipline, take inventory, or evaluate equipment, and to these various charges their administrators would determine which person should be

---

[3]*The Freeman* (January 12, 1907), v. xx, n. 2, p. 2.

W. H. COUNCILL, Ph. D.,
PRESIDENT.
H. E. ARCHER, M. S., M. D.,
VICE-PRESIDENT.

AGRICULTURAL and MECHANICAL COLLEGE,

TRUSTEES:
HON. S. J. MAYHEW,
HUNTSVILLE, ALA.
HON. D. A. GRAYSON,
HUNTSVILLE, ALA.
HON. BEN. P. HUNT,
HUNTSVILLE, ALA.

NORMAL, ALA., Sept. 18, 1908

Prof. H. Hopkins,

    Prin. Normal Department,

Dear Sir:-

    I am requested to notify you that you are chairman of the Committee on Industrial Inspection - the full committee being:-

        H. Hopkins

        O.J. Jordan

        M.J. Gibson.

You are also a member of the following committees:-

        Inspection of Programs - W.J. Ramsey, Chr.

        Text -Books - H. M. Archer, Chr.
        Literary Courses - H. M. Archer, Chr.

You are also appointed chairman of the committee on admission to the Literary School - the full committee being:-

        H. Hopkins.

        H. M. Archer

        O.N. Jordan.

                Very respectfully,

                              H. M. Archer

                              Secretary.

Figure 7-4. Letter, from Henrietta M. Archer to Henry Hopkins, September 18, 1908.

THE BIG CHANGE: 1908—1910.

matched to each of the obligations. Mrs. Archer, performing her duties as Secretary of the Faculty, wrote, at the beginning of the fall semester, a letter to Professor Henry Hopkins, Principal of the Normal Department and Professor of Mathematics. In it we read that she was writing to inform him of his various committee obligations.

Hopkins was to chair the Industrial Inspection committee, serve as a member of three more committees—Text Books, Literary Courses, and Inspection of Progress, and also chair the Committee on Admission to the Literary School. And if these responsibilities were not enough to keep the poor man out of trouble, her husband, Vice President H. E. Archer, wrote to him six days later:

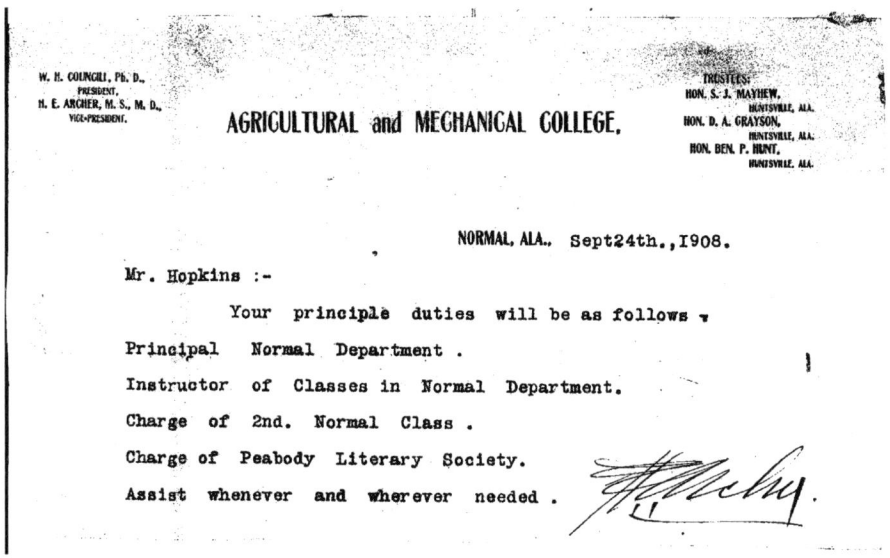

Figure 7-5. Letter, from Henry E. Archer to Henry Hopkins, September 24, 1908.

As was mentioned before, President Councill believed in the uplifting value of work, but who today would not run to his attorney after reporting to work and receiving the ominous notice that he or she was expected to "Assist whenever and wherever needed."? Notably, Archer herself was sharing in the listed committee work while also managing and administering the assignments. This is the environment into which James H. Wilson entered in the fall of

1908. He would have been called upon to do his share, too, and he was ready for the challenge.

Wilson's primary teaching responsibilities were Band Director and Vocal Music. The latter task meant conducting vocal ensembles. His colleague in music was the President's daughter, Ida Councill, and she taught piano and vocal music, but in her case "vocal music" meant classes in music appropriate for elementary school children and private instruction in vocal technique, solo singing and repertoire. Wilson had great respect for Ida Councill, and he never, then or later, indicated any difficulty working with her, nor did he ever show any disrespect for her musical or teaching skills. He would never have considered her appointment the result of favoritism, for indeed she was much better instructed in music, formally and traditionally, than he—she had studied at a German conservatory and had earned a college degree from Oberlin. He could only boast a high-school diploma and years on the road.

During these first few months of the fall semester, Wilson continued those same teaching activities he had pursued when he arrived on campus in February at the end of his Kersands Minstrels tour. This academic year, however, while coaching in the Normal Department he took serious notice of an eighteen-year-old senior, Miss Exeline Polk from Nashville. Little evidence remains of their courtship, but one small but charming document tells much. We know for a fact that by the middle of the second semester of that academic year James was actively courting Exeline. She was fascinating—pretty, intelligent, and educated. And he, too, had his charms—handsome, talented, and, by all standards of the day for African Americans, successful and respected.

After failing in his first marriage, then somehow losing the affection of his New Orleans girlfriend, Toula, James understandably would have been looking for a wife who would willingly share his life and future at Normal. He was lucky and found her in the teacher training program of the college. In March of 1909 he mailed her a penny post card, illustrated with a poem, "The Love Untold," a card she cherished until her death.

THE BIG CHANGE: 1908—1910.

Figure 7-6. An oil portrait of the young Exeline Polk Wilson [artist unknown].

The message James penned on the reverse of the card to his sweetheart illustrates once more his desire to find a woman who could understand his wish to raise a Christian family and share his life, not in the limelight of public acclaim but in the world of service to his race. The next four decades would prove Exeline to be the perfect match for his desires.

Figure 7-7. Postcard from James Wilson to Exeline Polk.[4]

---

[4]A possible source for the poem on this card is: Benjamin Franklin Johnson, compiler, *The Beautiful Tree of Life . . . Helpful Hints . . . Christian Living* (Richmond, VA: B. F. Johnson & Co., 1892), p. 420. It appears elsewhere, e.g. George Albert Lomas and Henry Clay Blinn, eds., *The Shaker Manifesto*, v. 12, n. 40 (Shaker Village, NH: November, 1882), p. 253.

THE BIG CHANGE: 1908—1910.

Figure 7-8. Message side of card from James to Exeline, March 5, 1909.

Precisely when he proposed to Exeline and when she accepted is not known, but this romance was suddenly put on hold, because the month following the mailing of this card, tragedy struck the campus of A. and M. Wilson's attention had to be diverted to exceedingly serious and pressing matters. President William Hooper Councill suddenly passed away in April. The man who had first brought James to campus, who had welcomed him back after his earlier resignation and who had supported him as he tried to untangle the various threads of his life, was dead.

Councill's death became front page news in the Indianapolis *Freeman*, and his lengthy obituary retold the much-loved man's tale of hardship, accomplishment, and service.

DEATH OF W. H. COUNCILL
NOTED EDUCATOR PASSES TO ETERNAL REWARD
SUCCUMBS AFTER YEAR'S ILLNESS
Head of Successful Institution
at Normal—Hard and Constant
Worker—Carved Out His Own
Sphere in Life

The death of William Hooper Councill was the startling intelligence that flashed over the wires April 17. Professor Councill had been ailing for something over a year, but his early demise was not expected. Long ago he was one of the few great Negro educators, especially along educational lines. His work contrasted with that being done by Prof. Booker T. Washington. . . .

Prof. Councill was born in Fayetteville . . . North Carolina, July 12, 1849. It is needless to say that he was born a slave. . . . Councill's father escaped to Canada . . . . his mother and brothers were sold and carried to Alabama. . . . the boys escaped to the Union ranks, the mother escaped, also . . .

[William] worked for board and clothing, that he might have the privilege of school . . . . He was beset with difficulties: the night riders of that day were in evidence—the Ku Klux. . . . He pursued his course persistently . . . . sought opportunities when others were asleep or at play. It is said of him that he procured chemical and philosophical instruments, walked eight miles once a week and paid a dollar to hear a lecture in these branches. He paid six dollars per month for instruction in Latin and higher mathematics, finally developed into a full-fledged professor, and prized his possession, since he knew the fearful cost. . . .[5]

Although we do not have a program of the music Wilson performed at Councill's funeral, we know that "James H. Wilson, trumpeter and bandmaster of the A. and M. College Band and Minstrelnola Club of the A. and M. College at Normal, Ala., conducted the music for the funeral of Prof. W. H. Councill."[6] James would have had much work to accomplish in a brief amount of time in order to do musical justice to this great man. When Councill's wife, Maria, died just one year after her husband, two favorite African American hymns were sung at her services:

WIFE OF NOTED EDUCATOR DIES

Mrs. Maria Howard Councill, wife of the late President William Hooper Councill . . . [died] as the result of a major operation at a Nashville infirmary. . . . The funeral services, which were held in Palmer Hall Chapel, were short and simple, the Rev. Mr. W. M. Jones of the M. E. Church, Huntsville, read the obituary. . . . Resolutions offered by the faculty were read by Professor Henry Hopkins of the faculty. Miss Isora Garrett of the faculty sang "Crossing the Bar." . . . . the funeral procession marched to the grave [of her husband] directly in front of the Carnegie Library. Here the body was lowered into the vault above the remains of the late President Councill. The slab was rolled over the tomb and on this was placed the many floral tributes of the family . . . . Before the completion of these last funeral rites, Miss Isora Garrett and Miss Odell Robinson of Huntsville sang "I Shall See Him Face to Face." The services closed with the audience singing "God Be With You Till We Meet Again," and the benediction. . . .

A few days before grim Death claimed his victim she had remarked, "I am ready to meet God." Whenever I think of it I am reminded thus.

"Lay me down to peaceful slumber,
I am weary and must rest;
Mourn not that I've left your number,

---

[5]*The Freeman* (April 24, 1909), v. xxii, n. 17, p. 1.
[6]*The Freeman* (April 24, 1909), v. xxii, n. 17, p. 5.

> Can you grieve that I am blest?
> Dry your tears; I soon shall greet you,
> When your earthly work is done;
> At the pearly gates I'll meet you
> While the Master says "Well done."
>
> D. E. Dortch[7]

Ida Councill must have been devastated by her father's sudden death, a loss that would be redoubled with the passing of her mother the next year. But, cut from the same quality cloth as her parents and raised with their devotion to education, she faithfully carried out her teaching responsibilities at the college through her mourning. Quickly, the state addressed the death of W. H. Councill and the problem of leadership at A. & M., and the Alabama Board of Commissioners, at their June meeting, selected his replacement from outside the college. For their new president they chose the Principal of the Corona Industrial Institute of Corona, Alabama, Ida's fiancée, Walter Solomon Buchanan.

At the June meeting the state committee first appointed Buchanan to the post for only one year, but shortly thereafter they changed his presidential appointment to that of the continuing head of the institution.[8] Buchanan began his duties in July of 1909, and he and Ida were married before the beginning of the next academic year. Both their marriage and his appointment cemented her commitment to A. & M. In September and October of that year we again find evidence of Ida and James working together as colleagues in music at A. & M., this time she under her married name.

Early in the semester a student, Miss Winona Agatha Mason, offered a vocal recital in the college chapel on the evening of September 17th. Newlywed Ida Buchanan accompanied Miss

---

[7]*The Freeman* (August 20, 1910), v. xxiii, n. 34, p. 3. The two verses of the 8787-meter gospel hymn added at the end of the obituary were composed by David Elijah Dortch, an evangelical singer and music publisher born in Maury County, Tennessee, March 5, 1851 [anon., *Century Review, 1805-1905, Maury County, Tennessee* (Columbia, TN: Board of Mayor and Aldermen, 1905), p. 66].

[8]Morrison, *History of Alabama Agricultural and Mechanical University*, pp. 97f.

THE BIG CHANGE: 1908—1910.

Figure 7-9. A. & M.'s second president, Walter Solomon Buchanan.

Figure 7-10. "If Life Be a Dream" by Harry T. Burleigh, words by Frank L. Stanton [1904].

THE BIG CHANGE: 1908—1910.

Vocal Recital

BY

Miss Winona Agatha Mason

Assisted by

Mrs. Ida C. Buchanan

A. & M. COLLEGE CHAPEL

Friday, Sept. 17, '09, 7:30 P. M.

Progam

Lascia Ch'io Pianga . . . . . *Handel*
Admonition . . . . *Watts*
      Miss Mason

Prelude . . . . *Rachmaninoff*
Ballade . . . . *Rhinberger*
      Mrs. Buchanan

Lungi dal caro bene . . . . *Secchi*
Mon desir . . . . *Nevin*
      Miss Mason

Polonaise op. 27, No. 1 ⎫
                     ⎬ *Chopin*
Etude op. 25, No. 7 ⎭
      Mrs. Buchanan

Im Herbst . . . . *Franz*

A Little While . *Mary Turner Salter*
Acushla Machree . . . . *Old Irish*
If Life be a Dream . *Harry Burleigh*
Were I Sunbeam . . . *Saint Saens*
      Miss Mason

Valse . . . . *Schutt*
      Mrs. Buchanan

Wanderer's Night Song . . . *Liszt*
Where Corals Lie . . . . . *Elgar*
Mother O' Mine . . . . . . *Tours*
      Miss Mason

Figure 7-11. Vocal and Piano Recital, September 17, 1909.

Mason and also performed solo piano numbers. The repertoire of both performers contains standard western European classical numbers, as one might expect, plus a few lighter vocal pieces near the end of the recital. Among this group of songs it is interesting to note that Miss Mason included "If Life be a Dream," composed in 1904 by Harry Burleigh, a contemporary African American. Although spirituals and jubilee hymns had long been used in the repertoire of this and other Black colleges' vocal works, the inclusion of music composed by living African-American artists who were not members of the faculty was extremely rare in the first decade of the 20th century. Wilson might program his own marches on his own band concerts, but the inclusion of Harry Burleigh's work signals a growing awareness of quality music being produced by African-American composers.

Ida and James were now not only colleagues in the music program, they were also taking their places among the new generation of leadership at Alabama A. & M. Two weeks after this performance, James took charge of a campus recital where various students and faculty members volunteered or were asked to perform for a campus audience. On this program he directed both the band and the singers of the Minstrelnola Club, and then he played a selection of trumpet and cornet solos accompanied by a Professor Fentress. The program also offered vocal solos, the reading of an essay, a declamation, an oration, and a recitation. These cultural enrichment programs were standard fare for the students of Alabama A. & M., and James H. Wilson became deeply involved in supervising as well as performing in these elective concerts..

Wilson successfully continued his teaching and performing duties at the college for the remainder of the academic year. At the same time, his life became increasingly intertwined with A. & M.'s Councill-Buchanan dynasty. Just before commencement in May of 1910, the U. S. Census was taken in Alabama during the spring of that year. From it we discover that he, or someone in the household, told the census taker that the "divorced" Mr. James H. Wilson was living in the residence of President Walter Buchanan and his wife, Ida Councill Buchanan. Their home on Meridianville

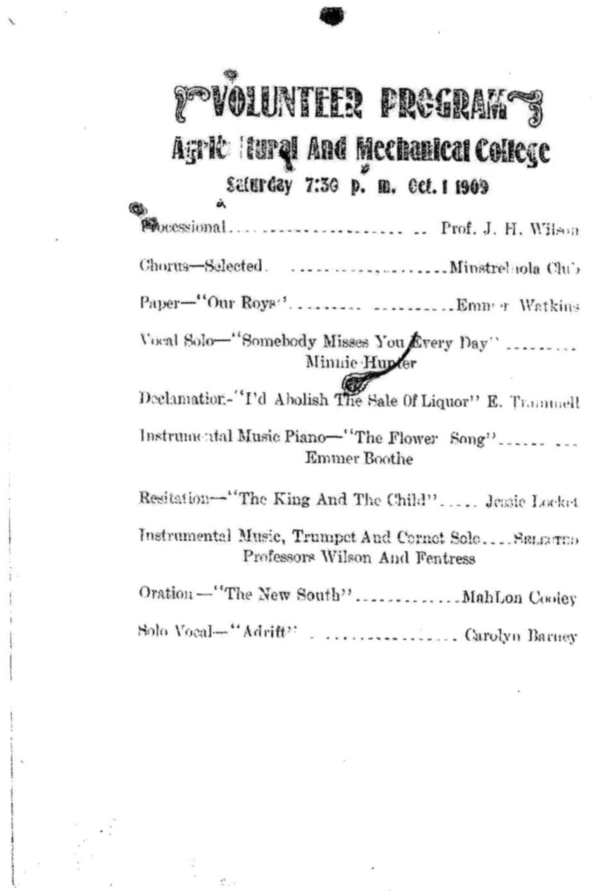

THE BIG CHANGE: 1908—1910.

VOLUNTEER PROGRAM
Agricultural And Mechanical College
Saturday 7:30 p. m. Oct. 1 1909

Processional	Prof. J. H. Wilson
Chorus—Selected	Minstreliola Club
Paper—"Our Boys"	Emmer Watkins
Vocal Solo—"Somebody Misses You Every Day"	Minnie Hunter
Declamation.-"I'd Abolish The Sale Of Liquor"	E. Trammell
Instrumental Music Piano—"The Flower Song"	Emmer Boothe
Recitation—"The King And The Child"	Jessie Locket
Instrumental Music, Trumpet And Cornet Solo	Selected Professors Wilson And Fentress
Oration —"The New South"	MahLon Cooley
Solo Vocal—"Adrift"	Carolyn Barney

Figure 7-12. Vocal and Instrumental Recital Program, October 1, 1909

Pike was certainly an interesting household; in the president's abode there were nineteen adult inhabitants living in the same building. These people, besides Walter and Ida, included his mother and sister, Harriet and Mollie Ardis; his mother-in-law, Maria Howard Councill; his brother-in-law, Dement H. Councill; Miss Gibson, one of the English teachers in the Normal Department for whom James offered help in rhetoric and penmanship; and our protagonist, James Hembray Wilson.

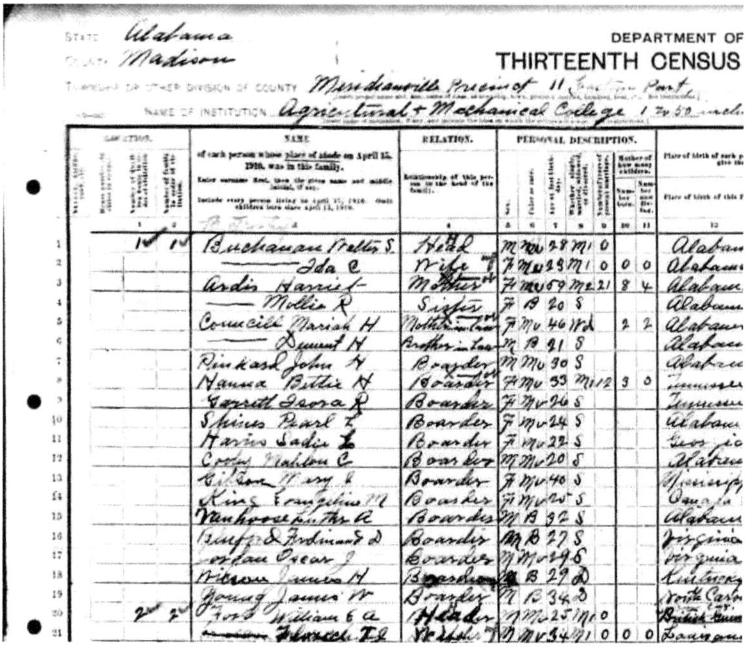
State: Alabama
County: Madison
Township or other division of county: Meridianville Precinct 11
Name of institution: Agricultural + Mechanical College

DEPARTMENT OF
THIRTEENTH CENSUS

Figure 7-13. 1910 U. S. Census, Madison County, Alabama, Meridianville Precinct 11.

This census indicates that James had a serious problem to solve. On April 15th, the day the census enumerator collected this information for the U. S. government's ten-year enumeration and analysis, in spite of what was recorded therein, we know James was not divorced. He was still married to Georgia Miller Wilson. By this time he probably had proposed to Exeline, perhaps he had even met her parents, Austin and Elizabeth Polk of Nashville, Tennessee. He needed to address this issue immediately, and he wasted no time. In June, he caught the train from Normal to his former home in Nicholasville and went before the judge of the June Circuit Court that was meeting there at the county court house.

From the document in Figure 7-14 we can see that James had pled his case before Judge J. M. Benton and won his suit. Then the Clerk of the Jessamine Circuit Court, S. E. Holloway, certified the action on June 14th, 1910, which turned out to be just in time. James and Exeline were married August 15, 1910, just two months

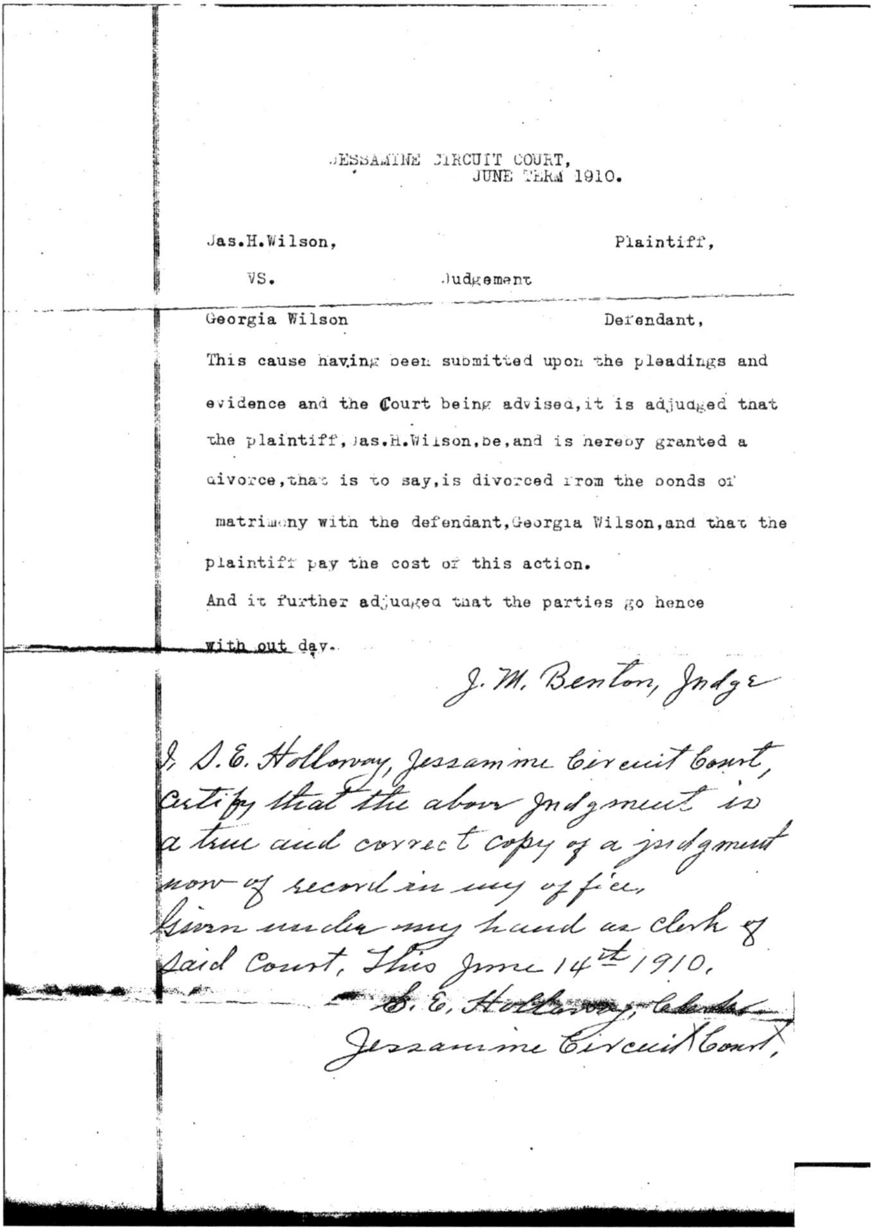

JESSAMINE CIRCUIT COURT,
JUNE TERM 1910.

Jas.H.Wilson,   Plaintiff,

VS.   Judgement

Georgia Wilson   Defendant,

This cause having been submitted upon the pleadings and evidence and the Court being advised, it is adjudged that the plaintiff, Jas.H.Wilson, be, and is hereby granted a divorce, that is to say, is divorced from the bonds of matrimony with the defendant, Georgia Wilson, and that the plaintiff pay the cost of this action.

And it further adjudged that the parties go hence with out day.

J. M. Benton, Judge

I, S. E. Holloway, Jessamine Circuit Court, Certify that the above Judgment is a true and correct copy of a judgment now of record in my office. Given under my hand as clerk of said Court, This June 14th 1910.

S. E. Holloway, Clerk
Jessamine Circuit Court,

Figure 7-14. James H. Wilson's certificate of divorce from Georgia Wilson.

later. One might hope that this misadventure had taught this young man a lesson and that his life would now find a semblance of order and sense of deep purpose that he seems to have been seeking for years. But little besides music came simply and easily for James Hembray Wilson.

CHAPTER EIGHT

The Buchanan Years: 1910—1920

James was a happy man when school opened at Normal in the fall of 1910. He began that academic year with a new wife, a home on campus, and a satisfying and busy job to keep him productively occupied. What he probably did not realize when classes reopened was that a major change was about to take place on campus that could significantly affect his appointment and his future. During President Buchanan's first year in office it seemed that the college would carry on under its new leader in exactly the same manner as it had under its founder and first president, William Hooper Councill, and that is precisely what happened during the 1909-1910 school year. James, like the other members of the faculty and staff, must have felt both contented and secure when the classes commenced again in September of 1910, and we can observe that his responsibilities and related activities were indeed similar if not identical to those he had under Councill and, the previous year, under Buchanan. In December, the eighth grade class of the elementary school performed its public rhetorical exercises in the college auditorium, and Wilson had taken responsibility to prepare all the musical offerings on the evening's agenda—individual numbers by the band and chorus, two vocal solos, and a piece by an *a cappela* quartet of eighth graders to close. The program was just as one might have expected, including the class motto, which could very well have been a quotation of W. H. Councill, "Work is the measure of success."

Eighth Grade Rhetorical
Agricultural and Mechanical College
Saturday Eve. December 8, 1910
College Auditorium, 7:30 P. M.

Processional ------------ A. & M. College Band
Address of Welcome --------------- H. J. York
Chorus—"A Song of Nature" -------------Class
Roll Call ---------------------- Quotations
Indolence ----------------- Nannie B. Whitfield
Keep Pegging Away ---------- Charlie Williams
Solo—"In the City of Sighs and Tears" ---------
   Charles Henderson
Over the hill to the Poor House ------ Allie Turner
Tuberculosis—How to Prevent It - - -Mary Robinson
Solo—"Tender Little Flower" ------ Marion Segura
The Power of a Dollar ----------- Linnie Stratton
Oration—"Leave things better" - - Gertrude Roberts
    ⎡ ------------------ Marion Segura
Quartett ⎢ -------------- .Nannie B. Whitfield
    ⎢ ------------------- Bennie Haynes
    ⎣ ----------------- -Chas. Henderson

  Class Colors, Purple and White
   Class Flower, Carnation
 Motto, "Work is the measure of success"
 Henry York, Pres. Marion Segura, Secty.
  H. Hopkins, teacher in charge.
   J. H. Wilson, musician

From this program we might glimpse some of the surprisingly mature concerns of black eighth graders attending school at Alabama A. & M. in 1910—tuberculosis, earning a living, the moral value of work and the sinful nature of laziness, as well as the obligation to improve society—somewhat cheerless topics for thirteen-year-old children and just as weighty subjects to have been taught and discussed in an eighth-grade classroom. On a happier note we also sense the romantic taste of early 20th-century society in the titles of the choral number and the second vocal solo: "A Song of Nature" and "Tender Little Flower." Still, the first vocal solo seems an unexpected choice by today's standards for the musical interests of an eighth-grade boy—"In the City of Sighs and Tears."

> "Papa, tell me where is Mamma?" cried a little girl one day,
>
> "I'm so lonesome here without her. Tell me why she went away?
>
> You don't know how much I'm longing for a loving goodnight kiss."
>
> Papa placed his arms around her as he softly whispered this:
>
> "Down in the City of Sighs and Tears, under the white light's glare,
>
> Down in the City of Wasted Years, you'll find your Mamma there,
>
> Wand'ring along where each smiling face hides its story of lost careers,
>
> And perhaps she is dreaming of you tonight, In the City of Sighs and Tears."[1]

This program of a routine public exercise reflects well James H. Wilson's participation as a leader in the education of Alabama A. & M.'s students as he begins to engage more fully in the struggle to upgrade the young people of his race. He was vitally concerned with uplifting both the physical and moral wellbeing of his people through his teaching and, from this time forward, through example. It is even possible that by this date he was coming to realize that he just might be underqualified, as measured by traditional credentials, for the job. His high school diploma was sufficient for President Council at the time he was

---

[1] "In the City of Sighs and Tears," by Andrew B. Sterling and Kerry Mills (New York: F. A. Mills, 1902). Words transcribed from the 1903 recording sung by J. W. Myers (YouTube, http://www.youtube.com/watch?v=-uYNESf7ruw [accessed December 4, 2012]).

hired, but the climate on campus was changing. It may have been incidental, but on this program he is not listed as "Professor," as he was before. His title is simply recorded as "musician." Was there a significant change taking place on the A. & M. campus, and if so, how was he to meet the challenge?

President Buchanan took charge during the summer of 1909 with a faculty hired by Councill, students already enrolled for the fall semester, and an established framework of courses inherited from his predecessor. However, the evidence suggests that when the Alabama Board of Commissioners hired Buchanan for the job they made it clear that they were selecting him because they thought he was capable of improving the college, not just maintaining the status quo. It seems he was deliberately selected for this purpose, a choice for change. Although no minutes of the state educational board meetings survive to settle whether or not this was the case, his appointment has been interpreted by a later president of the college, Richard David Morrison, as having come with the mandate to move the college forward from its present state.[2] Both Buchanan's and Councill's emphases were placed on educating for practical skills that would lead to gainful employment, income, and self-respect through productive work, primarily practical crafts, but either the state board or Buchanan seems to have viewed the college as being deficient in the credentials of its academic faculty. It would be easy to say that the Caucasian commissioners of the State Agricultural and Mechanical College at Normal, Alabama, were simply inventing roadblocks for the man and this African-American institution, but granting the institutionalized racism of the 1910s, they seem also to have had the school's welfare in mind and had simply made clear their expectations for change. They visited the campus periodically for various occasions and even participated in some of its public events. For example, at the graduation exercises on May 22, 1912, the Honorable S. J. Mayhew, chairman of the Board of Commissioners, presented certificates to the graduates of the Industrial Department of the college. Two years later, on May 27,

---

[2]Morrison, *History of Alabama Agricultural and Mechanical University: 1875-1992*, pp. 97ff.

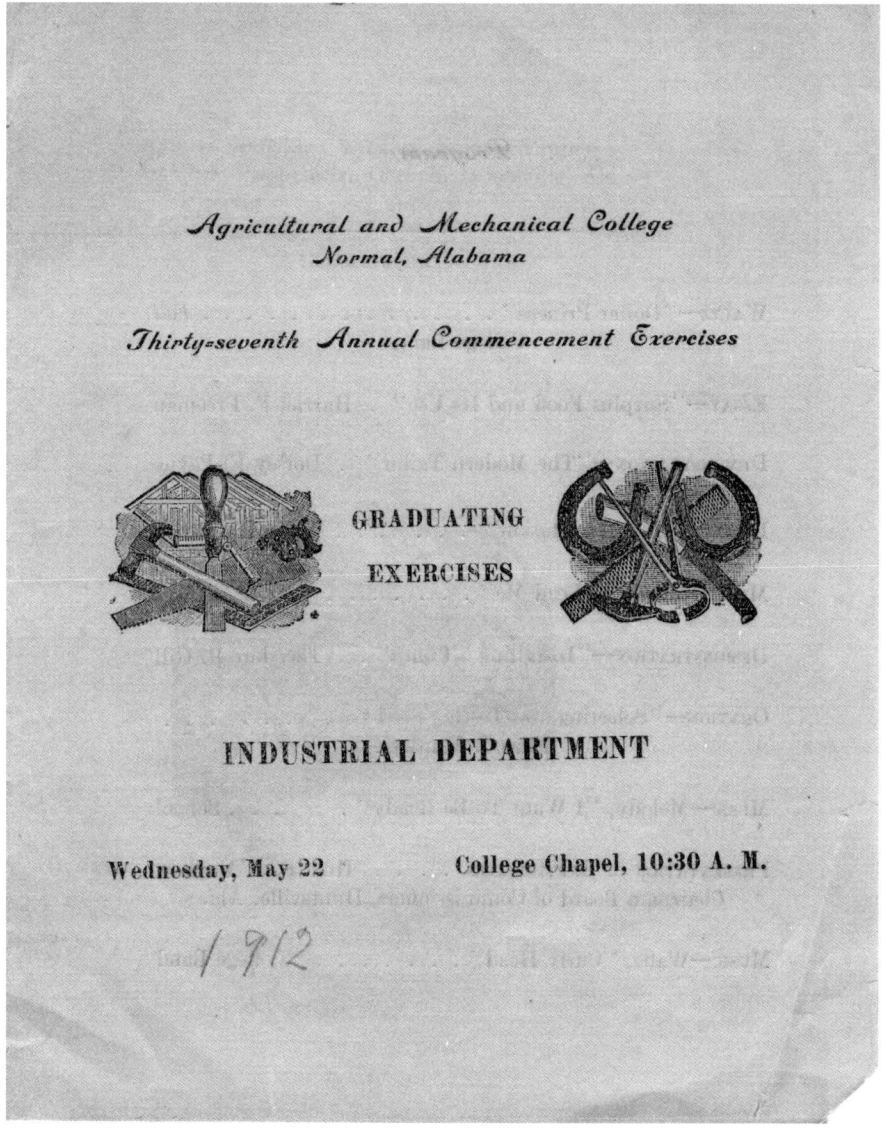

Figure 8-1. Cover, program of A. & M. Industrial Department Graduation, 1912.

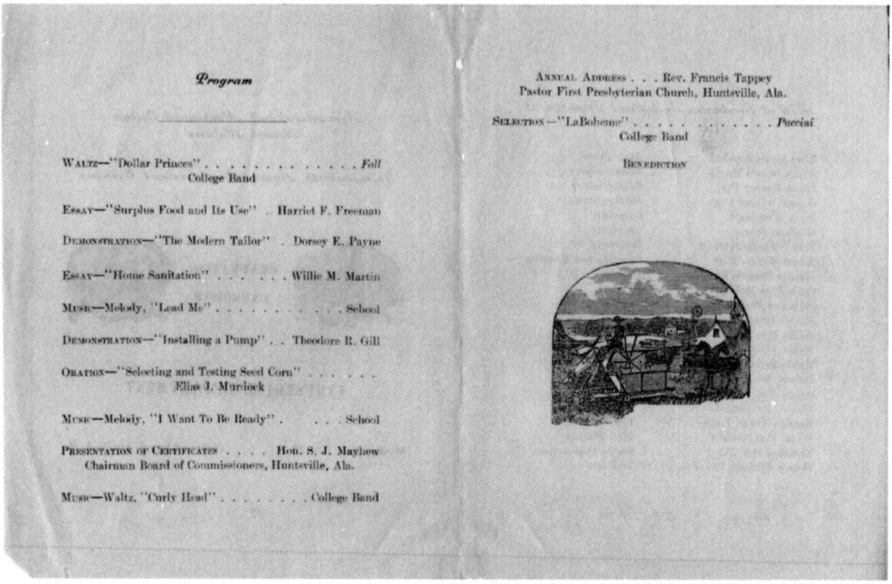

Program

Waltz—"Dollar Princes" . . . . *Fall*
College Band

Essay—"Surplus Food and Its Use" . Harriet F. Freeman

Demonstration—"The Modern Tailor" . Dorsey E. Payne

Essay—"Home Sanitation" . . . . Willie M. Martin

Music—Melody, "Lead Me" . . . . School

Demonstration—"Installing a Pump" . . Theodore R. Gill

Oration—"Selecting and Testing Seed Corn" . . . .
Elias J. Murdock

Music—Melody, "I Want To Be Ready" . . . . School

Presentation of Certificates . . . . Hon. S. J. Mayhew
Chairman Board of Commissioners, Huntsville, Ala.

Music—Waltz, "Curly Head" . . . . College Band

Annual Address . . . Rev. Francis Tappey
Pastor First Presbyterian Church, Huntsville, Ala.

Selection—"LaBoheme" . . . . *Puccini*
College Band

Benediction

Figure 8-2. Program of the Commencement Exercises, Alabama A. & M. College Industrial Department, 1912.

1914, another board member, the Honorable David A. Grayson, performed the same function for graduates of the Teachers' College. Both of these white men were serving on the three-member Board of Trustees in 1909 when Buchanan was offered the presidency of Alabama Agricultural and Mechanical College, and their interest in the college's welfare seems genuine.

Buchanan must have agreed with the trustees who offered him his new office, for he hesitated no longer than was necessary before beginning a dramatic process of hiring and firing.

> Therefore, for the first year, it was business as usual. The following year a noticeable change occurred in the faculty. There were new faces and the absence of many of the previous 24 faculty members. The 1911-1912 faculty roster showed only five members were retained from the previous year. They were Henry C. Hopkins, Ida C. Buchanan, James H. Wilson, Thomas W. Maddux and J. Walter Ramsey. This meant that 19 new faculty members were employed during this period. The following year 1912-13, ten of the 26 faculty members returned to this job. . . . Two causative factors appeared in the faculty

situation with President Buchanan. The first one came into prominence when he demonstrated in his hiring practice that he desired highly qualified persons who had graduated in his discipline from an educational institution of recognized quality; ... Lincoln University ... Berea College ... Chicago University ... Atlanta University ... University of Illinois .... [3]

Five retained and nineteen replaced in 1911-1912; ten retained and fourteen more fired and replaced in 1912-1913. These were extraordinary rates of turnover for any institution, particularly an educational one. That Wilson escaped this faculty purge is either a testament to the exceptional quality of instruction he must have been providing the students of the college or to his resourcefulness and adaptivity, or both. His musical skills as a band teacher were proven and clearly outstanding, and that was his primary appointment, but he continued on the faculty rosters with three listings:

> FACULTY 1912-1913
> James H. Wilson, Bandmaster, Vocal Music, English branches
> FACULTY 1913-1914
> James H. Wilson, Bandmaster, Vocal Music, English branches
> FACULTY 1915-1916
> James H. Wilson, Bandmaster, Vocal Music, English branches[4]

Why might President Buchanan have allowed him to continue teaching "English branches" and even "Vocal Music"? One wonders whether Ida Councill Buchanan might not have been helpful in explaining to her husband just how fine a musician James was and that his abilities in music were not likely to be replaced at the same qualitative level by some young holder of an academic degree. She certainly would have been aware of

---

[3] Morrison, *History*, p. 99.
[4] Rev. Dr. Henry Bradford, Jr., "A. & M. Music Faculty," [typescript with manuscript additions].

the special nature of music as a discipline, for her academic *and* musical credentials were impeccable. When Charles E. Stump, a roving reporter for the Chicago *Broad Axe* visited Normal in 1915, he mentions her in his report:

Charles E. Stump Still Continues His Travels Throughout the South Land; He Lately Visited Normal, Ala., Where He Held a Pleasant Interview with Walter S. Buchanan, President of the A. & M. College

Normal, Ala.—You will see from this letter that I am just a little more in the south. . . . I spent all the time I could in Nashville . . . and Tuesday I got myself together to start for another part of the world. I . . . got on the N. C. & St. L. wagon . . . headed for Chattanooga, but I wanted to come to Normal. Of course I found my way to the place set apart for us to ride, and I did not fail to find my way there. I am not going to get mixed up in the least with this law down here, but intend to be a law-abiding citizen, but I am not going to tell you that I am satisfied. . . .

Perhaps you have not heard of this place. This is the location of the Agriculture and Mechanical college, started by that great educator, Prof. W. H. Councill, who now sleeps in front of the library. Prof. Councill laid a foundation and now comes along his son-in-law, Prof. W. S. Buchanan, a brilliant young man who is just building. He is doing something. Here I find 250 young men and women preparing for life's work. . . .

Right by the side of Prof. Buchanan is his wife, who is the daughter of the late W. H. Councill. She is well educated. Her father had her trained so that she could be of some use. One of the finest musicians of our race in America. . . . I never dreamed of finding such an institution in Alabama, and they tell me there are some others. . . . There have been several changes in the faculty, looking towards the strengthening of the teaching force.

"President Walter S. Buchanan, announces the following faculty:
. . . , A. B., Dartmouth, L. L. B., Harvard, . . . A. B., Howard, A. M., Clark Univ., . . . A. B., Univ. of Ill., . . . A. B., Ohio Wesleyan and Ohio State, . . . A. M., Columbia, . . . A. B., Talladega, B. A. S., Ohio State, . . . Mrs. Ida C. Buchanan, Oberlin Conservatory, Head of the Department of Music, . . . B. S., Cornell, . . . B. A.

S., State Agric. College, Ames, Iowa, . . . Mr. James H. Wilson, Cincinnati High School, Bandmaster, Vocal Music, English Branches . . . .[5]

Still, within the context of this list of colleges and degrees, James' paper certification without doubt would have been considered less than impressive, and he could not help but worry. Though there is no evidence to prove this conjecture regarding Ida Buchanan's support of her colleague, it seems more than logical that she would have had a role in explaining James' unique qualities and qualifications to her husband, Walter. After all, she was Head of the Department of Music and she had earned her degree from the best conservatory in America open to African-American musicians at that time, the Oberlin College Conservatory of music in Ohio. President Buchanan was not about to fire his wife, and he just might prefer some peace at home. But James must have become concerned as he observed the decimation of the old faculty and the transient nature of the new. He might even have considered what could happen to him were Ida to resign her post to raise a family, and it appears that during this period he took steps to open three additional options that might secure his retention at Normal—work related to his interest and expertise in the Bible, a staff position in the business office, and campus employment for his wife, Exeline. After all, she had an earned degree from Normal and, therefore, was qualified to teach in the college. In 1912 the couple were just starting a family of their own, and for James to return to the road amidst a waning public taste for minstrelsy surely would not have seemed a satisfactory option to either of them.

James' and Exeline's first child, a girl, Hester Elizabeth, was born in 1912, and she was named in honor of both James' and Exeline's mothers, Hester Wilson and Elizabeth Polk. A second child, a boy, arrived two years later, and he received his father's name to become James Hembray, Jr.

A second son joined the family in 1917, Karl Talmadge, and the Wilsons' youngest child, a second daughter, was born in 1919,

---

[5]*Broad Axe* (Chicago, IL: November 6, 1915), p. 5.

Figure 8-3. A snapshot of James, Jr. and Hester posed beside their home, circa 1917.

Figure 8-4. A studio portrait of James, Jr., age 2 years and 4 months.

Marian Floredia. James could not have known during the fall of 1910 that he and Exeline would be blessed with four children before the decade ended, but the couple likely had a family in mind after their marriage, and before the faculty purges of 1911-1913, they had every reason to plan for a lifetime at Alabama A. & M. College. Their new home, faculty housing, was a small cottage on campus with clapboard siding. It was modest by most standards of the day. It had no indoor plumbing, so the family used an outhouse in the back yard. At first the house was lighted by kerosene lamps, and only later was their home connected to electricity. There was no basement, and the only heat in the winter was provided by fireplaces in the bedrooms and living room as well as the warmth which radiated from the kitchen wood stove. The floor plan was simple, but there were a sufficient number of rooms: three bedrooms—one for James and Exeline, one for the girls, and a third for the boys—a kitchen, a living room, and a dining room. The family piano stood against the wall in the dining room. Baths were accomplished using a washtub in the kitchen filled with hot water from the cook stove, and the water for drinking and bathing was carried to the house in buckets from a well located on the other side of the campus. Eventually plumbing was added, but even the youngest daughter remembered the kerosene lamps and buckets of water. One very important consideration for this African-American couple made this home very special and overshadowed its physical shortcomings—the environment. The entire campus area was protected and safe for both the adults and the children, the neighbors were helpful, friendly, and educated—similar to themselves, and the school for the children, the college laboratory school, was equal to the best available for African Americans living in the south.

In 2010, James' youngest daughter Marian Floredia Wilson Turner, then 91 years of age, reminisced about her childhood:

> The house where I lived was just a stone's throw from the elementary school where I attended. All I had to do was just run out the door. I could be there in five minutes, and, so, I used to go in the mornings. I always hated that I lived so close to the school that I couldn't bring my lunch, because all the kids brought their

Figure 8-5. The Wilson home ca. 1922. James sits on the swing, his four children—Hester, James, Karl, and Marian, in descending age and size—are grouped on the right, and an older neighbor boy, Frank Adair, stands on the left. James Jr. holds a drumstick; Marian may be holding a trumpet.

lunches, but I went home for lunch and came back. It was a happy time. I knew all my classmates, and the teachers were really like family. You could never do anything out of line, [for if you did] you would get home quicker than you could get there. But it was a happy time. I remember going from elementary school through the sixth grade in what was a three-room school house.[6]

A year later Marian added more about her father and mother:

Well, he had a very even disposition, and if he had to speak to you about anything, you just felt awful that he had to do it. He never raised his voice. My mother was the one to carry the big stick. . . . We went on picnics. . . . My mother did all of that [prepare the food]. . . . [We went] up on campus, some nice, quiet, shady place. . . .

I was taught the piano by a woman named Miss Hopkins,

---

[6]Recorded interview with Marian F. W. Turner, September 20, 2010.

and she wore a wig, and when she played on the piano the wig would turn. We'd sit there and wait for it. She was wonderful.⁷

Marian Wilson Turner's memories of her childhood were fond, and they confirm what James' diary suggests. As pressures from the college for credentials and academic success rose, James turned ever more dearly to the Bible as part of his personal and professional identity. Even by this early date in the Buchanan years he had read the Good Book from cover to cover several times over. Marian remembers that "he didn't read it [the Bible] to me, but I know I read the Bible more because of him, because he read his Bible every day."⁸ At Normal James enjoyed debating the meaning and interpretation of passages with friends, faculty, and students, so it was natural for him to seek an increased leadership role in both the Sunday School activities and the formal Bible classes at the college. During this period President Buchanan appointed him Superintendent of Sunday School for the college, and Buchanan also allowed him to develop and teach a college course that would prepare A. & M. students to become teachers of Sunday School classes after graduation.

In the 1919 photo below, Figure 8-7, the male students of A. & M. are now wearing their military uniforms, a result of World War I and the development of Reserve Officers' Training Corps units at state-supported, land grant colleges.⁹ As the United States began to get involved in the war in Europe, officers from the United States Army Infantry were sent to land grant colleges to organize a Students' Army Training Corps (S. A. T. C.). After this first step was taken, A. & M., in 1918, requested and received permission to organize a unit of the Reserve Officers' Training Corps (R. O. T. C.) on campus. The practice of male students wearing their military uniforms to classes continued for several years after the war.

In addition to the regular, non-music-teaching responsibilities he had undertaken, Bible Training and Sunday School Teacher

---

⁷Recorded interview with Marian F. W. Turner, March 1, 2011.
⁸*Ibid.*
⁹The Army Reserved Officers' Training Corps (ROTC) began when President Wilson signed the National Defense Act of 1916. http://www.cadetcommand.army.mil/history.aspx (accessed 9/28/2014).

Figure 8-6. 1915 Bible Training Class, 27 students, 18 men and 9 women. Wilson sits front and center.[10]

Figure 8-7. 1919 Sunday School Teachers' Training Class. Wilson stands at the upper left, Bible in hand.[11]

[10]Morrison, *History*, p. 141.
[11]*The Normalite 1919: Annual of Agricultural and Mechanical College*, Vol. 3 (Normal, AL: [College Print Shop, 1919]), p. 81

Figure 8-8. Y. M. C. A. Cabinet, Alabama A. & M., 1919. Wilson is seated in the center.[12]

Training Classes, James also deepened his participation in elective religious organizations at A. & M. by becoming a faculty sponsor for the Young Men's Christian Association activities on campus.

Even though he added these new responsibilities, Wilson continued all his various musical activities—band, chorus, Minstrelnola Club, solo recitals, composing music, writing arrangements, and more. James became an incredibly busy and an almost omnipresent campus figure. Wilson's college band, which was all male at that time, then became the R. O. T. C. Band as well. All the male students at Normal below the collegiate level were required to take a three-hour per week course in Military Science and Tactics as part of the S. A. T. C., and all the male college students were required to take two years of R. O. T. C. Those successfully completing the first two years could elect to take two additional years of R. O. T. C. as juniors and seniors. So, in addition to all the previous college functions in which the band participated, Wilson now inserted regular outdoor parade drills into his schedule as the band now led the student troops back and forth across the athletic field.

[12]*The Normalite 1919*, p. 79.

Figure 8-9. The R. O. T. C. Band. Wilson, trumpet in hand and hatless, stands top, center.[13]

Figure 8-10. A. & M. Commercial Orchestra of 1919. In addition to Wilson on trumpet, there are one cornet, two trombones, two clarinets, a violin, a viola, and a piano. Ida Councill Buchanan sits at the piano.[14]

[13]*The Normalite 1919*, p. 72.
[14]*The Normalite 1919*, p. 102.

THE BUCHANAN YEARS: 1910—1920

A. & M. College Band Concert

First Baptist Church

Tuesday evening, February 18, 1913

JAS. H. WILSON, Conductor   MISS WILLIE DISMUKE, Soloist
H. W. BLACK   } Readers
MISS SUSAN T. WHITFIELD

PROGRAM

OPENING SELECTION	Rink
MARCH — "Nebuchadnezza"	Stevenson
READING — "Lias" *H. W. BLACK*	Dunbar
LULLABY — "Kentucky Babe"	Buck
CORNET SOLO — "Jesus Lover of My Soul" *MISS WILLIE MAE DISMUKE*	
MELODY	Band
READING — "The Sign of the Cross" *MISS SUSAN T. WHITFIELD*	Wilson Barrett
INDIAN — "Red Bird"	
CONCERT WALTZ	
MARCH — "My Old Kentucky Home"	Foster
FINALE	The Star Spangled Banner

—Taps—

Agricultural and Mechanical College
Normal, Alabama

Program

Band and Minstrelnola Club

JAMES H. WILSON, Conductor
H. W. BLACK, Reader

Thursday, Jan. 1st, '14, 7 P. M.

MARCH The Normal Students	Wilson
SONG The Torpedo and the Whale	Audran
TRUMPET SOLO (a) Scintilita	Perkins
(b) Believe me if all those endearing charms	
Prof. J. H. Wilson	
READING In the Morning *Mr. H. W. Black*	Dunbar
REVERIE In Silent Thought	Morrison
CHORUS All Through the Night	Owens
FINALE My Spanish Rose	Anon

Students' Social

Figure 8-11. Two sample programs from concerts during the Buchanan years.

One should note that most of these same band musicians would also have led hymns in chapel services, played a number or two for programs such as rhetoricals, Founder's Day, commencement, and virtually all public affairs. James would have had to have been present, too, without fail, to conduct rehearsals, lead the students in concert, and play occasional solos himself. To top off this formidable workload he even took charge of the school's commercial orchestra. And who was the band's pianist? Ida Councill Buchanan. See Figure 8-10, above.

Through 1916 Wilson's official listing of responsibilities in the college bulletin remained the same—Band Director, Vocal Music, and English branches, but in 1917 Wilson's appointment at A. & M. changed. No documents nor any living witnesses have surfaced to explain how James managed to work his way into the business office, but the job he began that year, university bookkeeper, would become for him the first rung up the administrative ladder. From this post he would slowly progress to Secretary of Faculty, Financial Secretary, and, just a few years before his retirement, University Treasurer, the first African-American to hold this position at A. & M.

As soon as he acquired responsibilities as the college bookkeeper, James Hembray Wilson occupied the office adjacent to the president's office, and in this cubicle he eventually became responsible for handling all the monies of the college. He collected

Figure 8-12. King's Counting House. [James H. Wilson, bookkeeper, at work in his office, 1919.][15]

[15]*The Normalite 1919*, p. 94.

Figure 8-13. The 1919 A. & M. baseball team with two batboys, probably James, Jr. and Karl. Wilson stands at the back wearing a derby hat.[16]

fees, paid bills, made bank deposits in Huntsville, and became accountable for all the financial records of Alabama A. & M. as well. In the 1919 college yearbook, the student editor jokingly captioned the picture of Wilson standing and calculating in his office, "King's Counting House."

As if all these activities did not keep Wilson busy enough, he also coached the baseball team. His career unfolded in an era of small colleges, black and white, when adaptability and multiple competencies were not just prized but necessary attributes for faculty and staff.

Much less is known about the activities of James' wife Exeline during this period, but she, too, must have been a formidable young woman. In addition to bearing and raising four children during these years, she was appointed laundress of the college in 1913, a

---

[16]*The Normalite 1919*, p. 98.

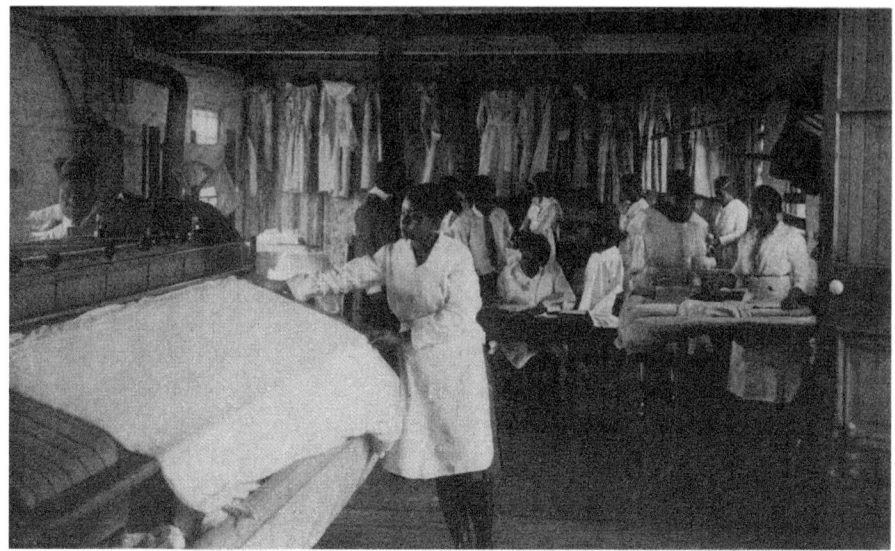

Figure 8-14. The Laundry at Alabama A. & M.[17]

staff position in which she oversaw the work of the students who ran the commercial machines of the laundry. The laundry was also a classroom, and its activities were part of the Female Industries program of the college. As this industrial program functioned, it received, washed, pressed, and repaired the laundry of faculty and students alike. Here Exeline would supervise and teach young women students and an occasional man who hoped to find gainful employment after college in one of the few commercial fields open to African-American women and men at that time. She taught these students how to do their work and manage their business affairs, such as record keeping and ordering supplies.

Exeline's employment at A. & M. was not continuous for all the years between 1910 and 1920, as four pregnancies intervened, but we have evidence of her occupation as laundress during the 1913-1914 academic year, and we also know that she was appointed Superintendent of Female Industries, a prestigious faculty and administrative position, for two academic years, 1917-1918 and 1918-1919.[18]

---

[17]*The Normalite 1919*, p. 54.
[18]Bradford, "A. & M. Music Faculty," [typescript].

Where James was able to construct a busy and secure life at Alabama A. & M. College, President Walter S. Buchanan was not. Buchanan's accomplishments as President were not trivial: he was able to upgrade the faculty, construct several much-needed buildings for instruction and residential living, contribute to the infrastructure with books for the library, improve the plumbing on campus, add modern steam power to generate electricity and drive the commercial machinery, and present to the outer world through speeches and newspaper reports the many successes of the college and its graduates. Unfortunately, he never was able to balance the budget with sufficient revenues to match the spending his vision for the college required. To a certain extent he became a victim of the war years, a period of declining state and federal support; to a greater extent he never learned to spend within his means.

The second factor in the high rate of faculty turnover was centered in the inability of the College to receive state funds as scheduled in order to pay salaries on time. The available minutes of the Board of Commissioners show that from 1913 to 1920 fourteen bank notes were negotiated with the W. R. Rison Banking Company payable by Walter S. Buchanan, being executed by him for Alabama A&M College for Negroes. During this time President Buchanan was responsible for paying off contractual notes for the amount of $93,100.

This kind of financial stress placed a burden on the President while at the same time causing apprehensiveness among the faculty about the College's ability to meet its payroll obligation.[19]

One should realize that in 1920 $93,000.00 was an enormous sum of money. Still, the deficiency was certainly not the result of Buchanan's lack of effort in fundraising. He had successfully garnered two large donations to the college from Virginia McCormick, daughter and heir of inventor Cyrus McCormick, of $19,000 for a domestic science building and $10,000 for a campus hospital. With student labor these buildings, and more, were constructed and put into service while he was in office, but he was never able to convince the state to increase its share of A. &

---

[19]Morrison, *History*, p. 100.

M.'s support. For example, in June of 1914, President Buchanan delivered a thorough, reasonable, and carefully argued proposal to the Governor of Alabama, the Honorable Emmet O'Neal, requesting a portion of the federal funds allotted to the state of Alabama by the new Smith-Lever Act, a United States congressional bill intended to provide financial support for agricultural extension work by land grant colleges. He argued that, based on the population of agricultural workers employed in the state, the black colleges should receive 30% of the funds and that the white A. & M. school at Auburn should be given 70%.[20] Governor O'Neal appointed a committee of seven men, all Caucasian, to review the proposals from the various African-American schools in Alabama and make a recommendation. They did and recommended that Tuskegee and Normal be the only black schools to receive funds, 30% of the state grant, 15% to each institution. The committee's recommendation was ignored, and the decision makers awarded all the monies to the all-white college at Auburn. History can judge the institutionalized racism of these political leaders, whose decision tolled the death knell for Buchanan's career at Alabama A. & M. Though it would not defeat the college, it did defeat the man.

At this point Buchanan had become desperate for money to operate his college. When he took the job in 1909 the college was only receiving $15,000 per year from the state and federal governments combined, and even then that was $5,000 per year less than the annual expenses required to run the institution.[21] Because he made serious attempts to upgrade Alabama A. & M., all of which were expensive, most notably construction and salaries, Buchanan had run up an insurmountable debt for the college in the service of his commission as its president and his dreams to move the college forward. Institutional debt was his undoing. The faculty lost confidence in him as did the trustees. The Treasurer of the State Board of Commissioners wrote to the Governor of Alabama about the college's financial dilemma, the banks refused further loans, the state issued warrants [IOU's]

---

[20]The entire proposal may be found in Morrison, *History*, pp. 104-122.
[21]Morrison, *History*, p. 98.

instead of negotiable instruments during the war years, and, in 1919, the state reduced the standing of the institution from college to that of a junior college, and the name of his school was changed to the State Agricultural and Mechanical Institute for Negroes. This change was a bitter pill for President Buchanan to swallow. Quickly thereafter, student enrollment declined, too, for few African-Americans had the financial resources to send their children to college, and A. & M. would no longer be able to offer a four-year bachelor's degree..

    Only one student was awarded a bachelor's degree from the Academic Department at the 1920 Commencement, Thomas Elmore from Nicholasville, Kentucky, a young man brought to A. & M. by Wilson. He was the son of Ollie Elmore of Elmore's Cyclone Band, the same hometown band that Wilson directed a decade ago. All the other students commencing that day received diplomas or certificates. As a result of these circumstances, Buchanan lost hope and submitted his resignation. After a campus farewell program for him and his wife, Ida, he left Normal for good after the May commencement exercises, taking his family to Pittsburgh, Pennsylvania, where he planned to serve as the business manager of an African-American magazine, *The Competitor*, published in that city. James no longer had a friend in court. Ida Councill Buchanan was gone.

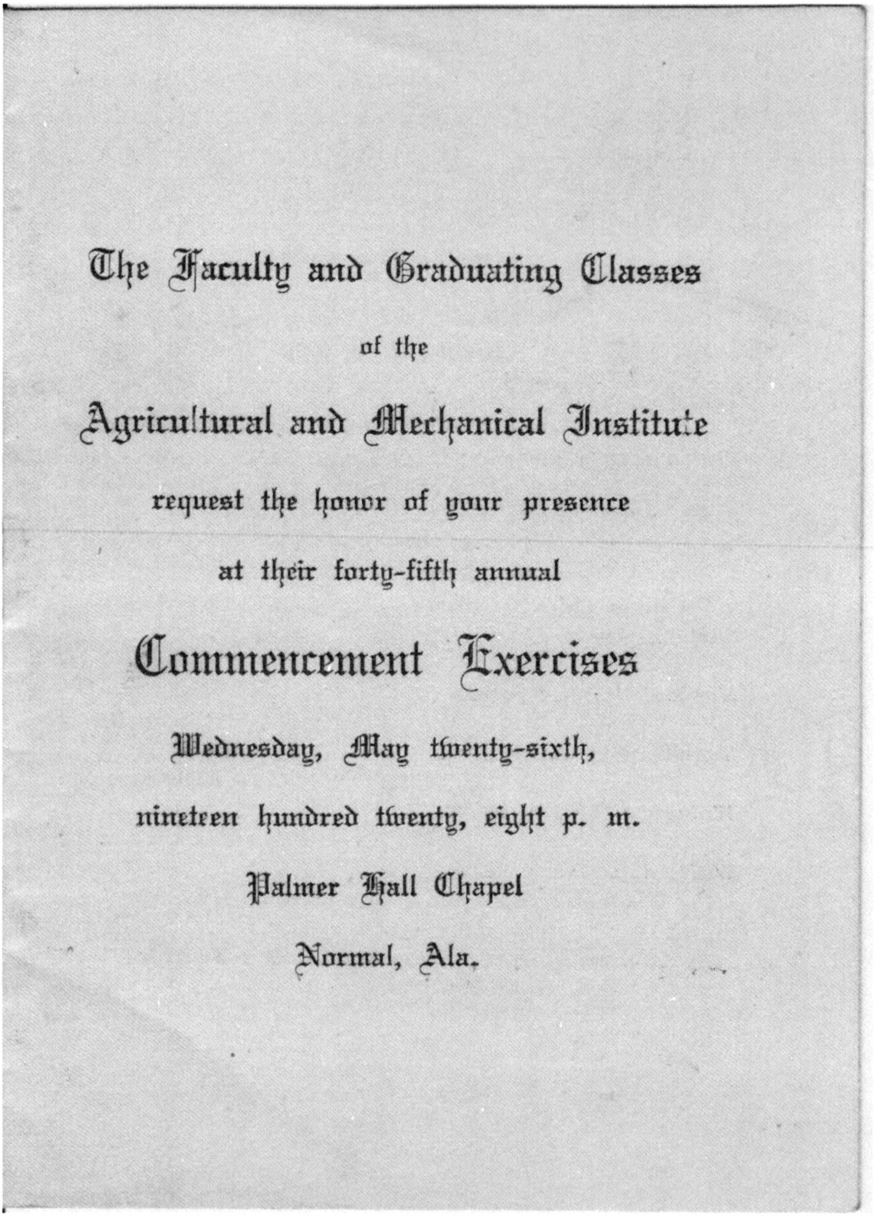

The Faculty and Graduating Classes

of the

Agricultural and Mechanical Institute

request the honor of your presence

at their forty-fifth annual

Commencement Exercises

Wednesday, May twenty-sixth,

nineteen hundred twenty, eight p. m.

Palmer Hall Chapel

Normal, Ala.

Figure 8-15. Cover of the 1920 Commencement Exercises program, May 26, 1920

CHAPTER NINE

New Presidents and a Reshaped Identity: the 1920s

James was not upset to learn that Theophilus R. Parker had been chosen by the State Board of Commissioners to replace Walter Buchanan after the Board accepted Buchanan's resignation in 1920, for Professor Parker, now Acting President Parker, had served for one year as Dean of the Alabama A. & M. Institute. Wilson knew the man well, for his office was adjacent to both President Buchanan's and the Dean's. During his first year at A. & M., Parker had proven his merit as both an administrator and a teacher.

Parker's appointment was viewed by James' colleagues as a vote of confidence in the faculty's ability to keep the institution operating successfully into the future. The reduction in grade to junior college was, they hoped, a temporary setback, just another obstacle to those used to frequent roadblocks placed in their way. Most but not all of the faculty laid the blame for the Institute's problems at the feet of their former president, who, in their opinion, was unable to live up to the standard of their revered founder, William Hooper Councill. A former student, now a professor of history and civics, Thomas M. Elmore, recounted the experience five years later:

> In 1920, when all seemed well to the student body due to their high expectation of returning in the fall to a New Normal based on the University Plan, they were greatly disappointed to be informed that the name of our Alma Mater had already been changed by state authorities [to] A. & M. Institute and that "Little Daddy Buchanan" had resigned to become editor in chief of a Brand New Magazine, The Competitor, in the smoky city of Pittsburgh, Pa. . . . it was rumored that the state officials were planning to close our Alma mater due to such a heavy indebtedness. . . . until an optimistic "Big Daddy" in the person of our own President

Parker shouldered the burden in 1921 and after a short period of two years the debt of $40,000.00 or more was liquidated.[1]

Wilson, like many of his colleagues, was comforted by the state's choice of one of their own to lead the enterprise, and he was prepared to work diligently at Parker's side to help the man succeed.[2]

On a personal level for Wilson, the fact that Parker had served as a missionary to Liberia for seven years before coming to Normal fit well into James' own plans for Christian missionary work among the students of A. & M. Up to this time Wilson had primarily been "preaching to the choir," that is, most of his endeavors had been offered to the convinced, the converted, and the committed—those who regularly, willingly, and without complaint presented themselves in church, Sunday school, Y. M. C. A. meetings, or Sunday School Teacher Training class. In 1922, James was ready to test unexplored waters by immersing himself into a new realm of outreach—publication. If he were to communicate with people who did not otherwise come to him, he would have to develop a means of sharing his religious views with a more distant public.

To start this endeavor he submitted an article to a popular African-American journal, *The Half-Century Magazine*. Unlike the brief comments he may (or may not) have written earlier for the Indianapolis *Freeman*, he now contributed a signed essay and became fully responsible for its contents. *The Half-Century Magazine*, which appeared bi-monthly at this time, advertised:

> . . . to act as a medium of expression for various ideas and opinions of Colored people of every class. That, we believe, is the only way to get acquainted with every condition and phase of Colored life in America and render necessary assistance. . . . we invite our readers to send in articles on social, religious or political conditions pertaining to the race whether they agree with the editor's views or not."[3]

---

[1] *The Normal Index*, v. 11 (April-May, 1925), p. 67.

[2] Parker's six years in office are summarized in Morrison, *History of Alabama Agricultural and Mechanical University: 1875-1992*, pp. 149-161. Elmore's statement, abbreviated here, is reproduced in Figure 9-3, below.

[3] *The Half-Century Magazine*, v. 13, n. 1 (Chicago, IL: Half-Century Pub. Co, July-August, 1922), p. 9.

James responded to the journal's invitation with a one-page, 1,300 word essay, "The Church and Dancing." Stimulated to action by an earlier article in the journal with the same title but with which he had major reservations, he took his stand in writing against what he viewed to be misinterpretations of the Bible's teachings about dance.[4]

In 1922 dance was entering American popular life in a way and at a rate never before experienced in the United States. This decade in America was appropriately labeled the "Roaring Twenties" by virtue of a new metropolitan life style, the explosion of night clubs and dance halls, the rapid distribution and later prohibition of alcohol, the energetic flapper dances such as the Lindy Hop along with its attendant wardrobe, the new social dances of two-step, fox trot and sexy tango, and more, much of it related to the aftermath of World War I and the return of American soldiers quickly transformed from boys to men in Europe. The 1920s were part of the "Jazz Age"—new music, new dances, and a new morality. Young people, white as well as black, were losing interest in their churches, and though Wilson acknowledged the problem in his article—"Some churches are now introducing dancing as a means of holding the young people"—he perceived sin in social dancing and virtue in modesty and restraint. He was ready to argue with those churches and their leaders. In his view their proffered solution to poor attendance would create an even greater problem for the churches and their congregations, one that far overshadowed the immediate concern of dwindling membership.

He wrote:

> .... I am speaking in defense of the Bible, the Book of Books, the book that is profitable for teaching, for reproof, for correction, for

---

[4]The earlier article by Jean Voltaire Smith, "The Church and Dancing," *The Half-Century Magazine*, v. 12, n. 2 (Chicago, IL: Half-Century Pub. Co, February, 1922), pp. 9 & 19, is critical of African-American preachers of the time and suggests they are more concerned about contributions to their church than they are about the welfare of their parishioners, especially the young. Smith concludes:

> We admit that the art has been abused by many, but .... Dancing in the home, or under proper chaperonage in public places of a respectable sort, is a pleasant, innocent amusement.

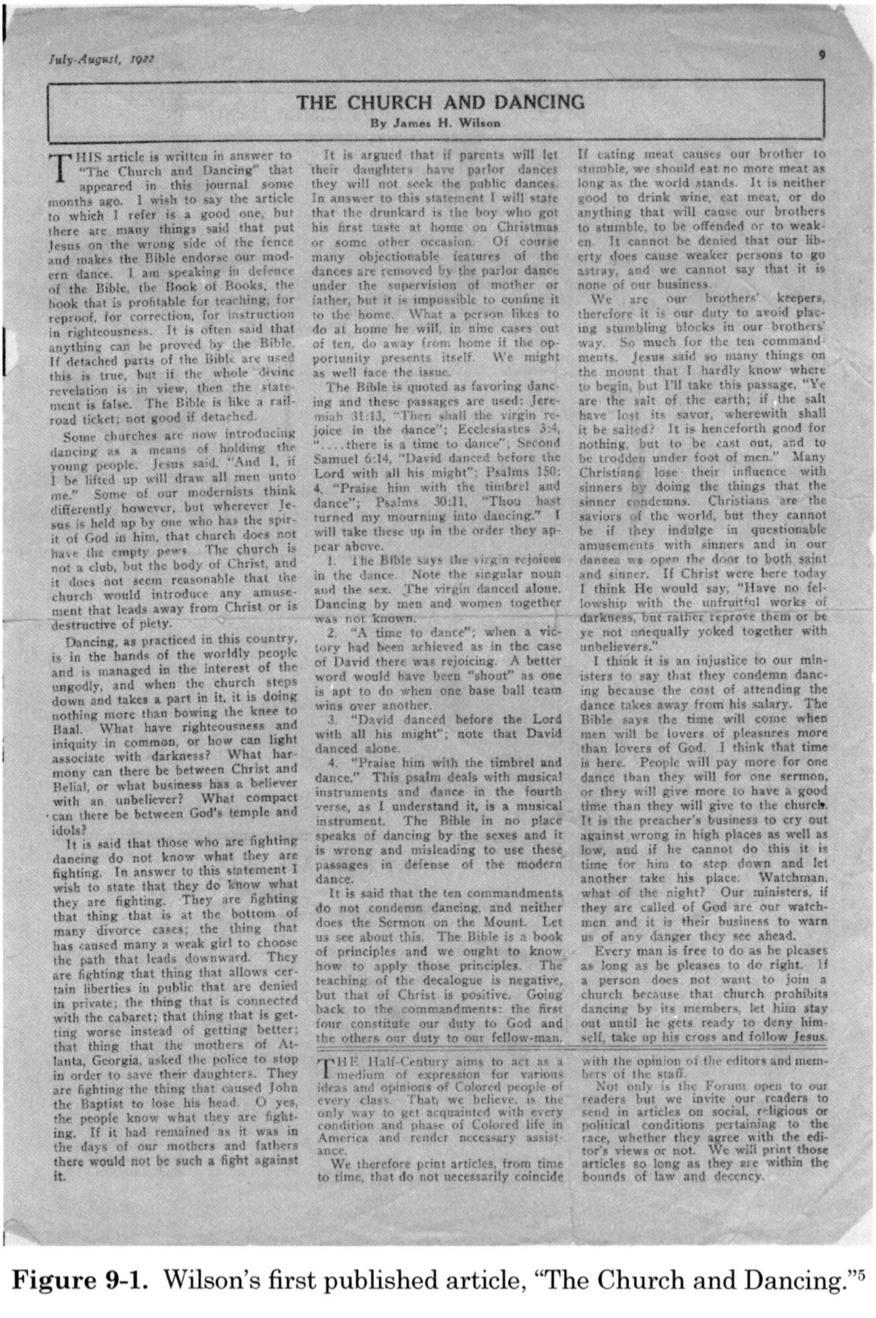

July-August, 1922 9

THE CHURCH AND DANCING

By James H. Wilson

THIS article is written in answer to "The Church and Dancing" that appeared in this journal some months ago. I wish to say the article to which I refer is a good one, but there are many things said that put Jesus on the wrong side of the fence and makes the Bible endorse our modern dance. I am speaking in defence of the Bible, the Book of Books, the book that is profitable for teaching, for reproof, for correction, for instruction in righteousness. It is often said that anything can be proved by the Bible. If detached parts of the Bible are used this is true, but if the whole divine revelation is in view, then the statement is false. The Bible is like a railroad ticket; not good if detached.

Some churches are now introducing dancing as a means of holding the young people. Jesus said, "And I, if I be lifted up will draw all men unto me." Some of our modernists think differently however, but wherever Jesus is held up by one who has the spirit of God in him, that church does not have the empty pews. The church is not a club, but the body of Christ, and it does not seem reasonable that the church would introduce any amusement that leads away from Christ or is destructive of piety.

Dancing, as practiced in this country, is in the hands of the worldly people and is managed in the interest of the ungodly, and when the church steps down and takes a part in it, it is doing nothing more than bowing the knee to Baal. What have righteousness and iniquity in common, or how can light associate with darkness? What harmony can there be between Christ and Belial, or what business has a believer with an unbeliever? What compact can there be between God's temple and idols?

It is said that those who are fighting dancing do not know what they are fighting. In answer to this statement I wish to state that they do know what they are fighting. They are fighting that thing that is at the bottom of many divorce cases; the thing that has caused many a weak girl to choose the path that leads downward. They are fighting that thing that allows certain liberties in public that are denied in private; the thing that is connected with the cabaret; that thing that is getting worse instead of getting better; that thing that the mothers of Atlanta, Georgia, asked the police to stop in order to save their daughters. They are fighting the thing that caused John the Baptist to lose his head. O yes, the people know what they are fighting. If it had remained as it was in the days of our mothers and fathers there would not be such a fight against it.

It is argued that if parents will let their daughters have parlor dances they will not seek the public dances. In answer to this statement I will state that the drunkard is the boy who got his first taste at home on Christmas or some other occasion. Of course many objectionable features of the dances are removed by the parlor dance under the supervision of mother or father, but it is impossible to confine it to the home. What a person likes to do at home he will, in nine cases out of ten, do away from home if the opportunity presents itself. We might as well face the issue.

The Bible is quoted as favoring dancing and these passages are used: Jeremiah 31:13, "Then shall the virgin rejoice in the dance"; Ecclesiastes 3:4, "....there is a time to dance"; Second Samuel 6:14, "David danced before the Lord with all his might"; Psalms 150:4, "Praise him with the timbrel and dance"; Psalms 30:11, "Thou hast turned my mourning into dancing." I will take these up in the order they appear above.

1. The Bible says the virgin rejoices in the dance. Note the singular noun and the sex. The virgin danced alone. Dancing by men and women together was not known.

2. "A time to dance"; when a victory had been achieved as in the case of David there was rejoicing. A better word would have been "shout" as one is apt to do when one base ball team wins over another.

3. "David danced before the Lord with all his might"; note that David danced alone.

4. "Praise him with the timbrel and dance." This psalm deals with musical instruments and dance in the fourth verse, as I understand it, is a musical instrument. The Bible in no place speaks of dancing by the sexes and it is wrong and misleading to use these passages in defense of the modern dance.

It is said that the ten commandments do not condemn dancing, and neither does the Sermon on the Mount. Let us see about this. The Bible is a book of principles and we ought to know how to apply those principles. The teaching of the decalogue is negative, but that of Christ is positive. Going back to the commandments: the first four constitute our duty to God and the others our duty to our fellow-man. If eating meat causes our brother to stumble, we should eat no more meat as long as the world stands. It is neither good to drink wine, eat meat, or do anything that will cause our brothers to stumble, to be offended or to weaken. It cannot be denied that our liberty does cause weaker persons to go astray, and we cannot say that it is none of our business.

We are our brothers' keepers, therefore it is our duty to avoid placing stumbling blocks in our brothers' way. So much for the ten commandments. Jesus said so many things on the mount that I hardly know where to begin, but I'll take this passage, "Ye are the salt of the earth; if the salt have lost its savor, wherewith shall it be salted? It is henceforth good for nothing, but to be cast out, and to be trodden under foot of men." Many Christians lose their influence with sinners by doing the things that the sinner condemns. Christians are the saviors of the world, but they cannot be if they indulge in questionable amusements with sinners and in our dances we open the door to both saint and sinner. If Christ were here today I think He would say, "Have no fellowship with the unfruitful works of darkness, but rather reprove them or be ye not unequally yoked together with unbelievers."

I think it is an injustice to our ministers to say that they condemn dancing because the cost of attending the dance takes away from his salary. The Bible says the time will come when men will be lovers of pleasures more than lovers of God. I think that time is here. People will pay more for one dance than they will for one sermon, or they will give more to have a good time than they will give to the church. It is the preacher's business to cry out against wrong in high places as well as low, and if he cannot do this it is time for him to step down and let another take his place. Watchman, what of the night? Our ministers, if they are called of God are our watchmen and it is their business to warn us of any danger they see ahead.

Every man is free to do as he pleases as long as he pleases to do right. If a person does not want to join a church because that church prohibits dancing by its members, let him stay out until he gets ready to deny himself, take up his cross and follow Jesus.

THE Half-Century aims to act as a medium of expression for various ideas and opinions of Colored people of every class. That, we believe, is the only way to get acquainted with every condition and phase of Colored life in America and render necessary assistance.

We therefore print articles, from time to time, that do not necessarily coincide with the opinion of the editors and members of the staff.

Not only is the Forum open to our readers but we invite our readers to send in articles on social, religious or political conditions pertaining to the race, whether they agree with the editor's views or not. We will print those articles so long as they are within the bounds of law and decency.

Figure 9-1. Wilson's first published article, "The Church and Dancing."[5]

[5]James H. Wilson, "The Church and Dancing," *The Half-Century Magazine*, v. 13, n. 1 (Chicago, IL: Half-Century Pub. Co, July-August, 1922), p. 9.

instruction in righteousness. It is often said that anything can be proved by the Bible. If detached parts of the Bible are used this is true, but if the whole divine revelation is in view, then the statement is false.

He made no bones about what he planned to do in his essay. In his introductory statement he identified his authority, the Bible, and only suggested his own credentials, a thorough familiarity with the entire contents of the Bible. He warned his readers:

> Dancing, as practiced in this country, is in the hands of the worldly people and is managed in the interest of the ungodly, and when the church steps down and takes a part in it, it is doing nothing more than bowing a knee to Baal.

A vehement accusation, indeed, for he was comparing those churches that would use social dancing to attract the young back into their midst to the encampment of the Israelites when Moses returned to his people from Mount Sinai with the Ten Commandments inscribed on the tablets of stone and found them dancing before a false idol:

> And it came to pass, as soon as he came nigh unto the camp, that he saw the calf, and the dancing: and Moses' anger waxed hot, and he cast the tables out of his hands, and brake them beneath the mount.[6]

What stronger condemnation could Wilson have made of those church leaders who would allow dancing inside their own temples? What could have triggered so emotional an outburst from a former minstrel musician who willingly played musical accompaniment in support of dancing on the stage? Something touched a nerve, and it would seem that he alluded to it when he wrote:

> It is said that those who are fighting dancing do not know what they are fighting. In answer to this statement I wish to state that they do know what they are fighting. They are fighting that thing that is at the bottom of many divorce cases; the thing that has caused many a weak girl to choose the path that leads downward. They are fighting that thing that allows certain

---

[6]Exodus 32:19.

liberties in public that are denied in private; the thing that is connected with the cabaret; . . . they are fighting the thing that caused John the Baptist to lose his head.

Apparently he was feeling the anguish of his separation and divorce from Georgia when he wrote, "that thing that is at the bottom of many divorce cases; the thing that has caused many a weak girl to choose the path that leads downward." Had Georgia enjoyed dancing with others in her loneliness as he traveled about the country with his minstrel shows? We do not know, but we might remember that the majority of society in America at the time of his marriage and divorce held double standards for men and women—men could vote, women could not; men could aspire to any profession; women could work as teachers and maids but when married should be housewives and mothers; men could socialize with whomever they pleased; good girls and married women could not. Wilson was a product of his time and environment, and his response to this particular issue was to declare that everyone must do away with all mixed-gender, social dancing. In all fairness to the man we might add to these observations that in his youth he, like others of his generation, held to this double standard, but in his growing maturity, he found a solution to this problem in his Bible that applied equally to men as well as women. In future years he would soften his stance on this issue, but at this time his stand was absolute.

In this article Wilson used a method of argument that he repeated many times in his future essays. This approach becomes quickly apparent as one reads further into the body of this brief composition—first an exposition of his thesis, then a display of the relevant Bible passages, next an analysis and synthesis of their contents, and finally a personal conclusion based on logical reasoning and the authority of the holy scripture. He is careful not to claim authority for himself. His authority is the Bible, King James edition, a book he carried everywhere and read cover-to-cover more than once. Although Wilson was not a Bible scholar in the modern sense of a man or woman trained in Aramaic, Hebrew, Greek, and Latin, and who studies ancient documents and compares variants among them, he was a Bible scholar in the eyes of his African-American contemporaries, a man who had read all of the Bible, thought deeply about its meaning, was able to quote chapter and verse, and both learned and taught through critical discussions with his students and peers.

Having stated his thesis, he listed Jeremiah 31:13, Ecclesiastes 3:4, Second Samuel 6:14, Psalm 150:4, and Psalm 30:11.[7] In none of these passages did Wilson find support for men and women dancing together. "The Bible in no place speaks of dancing by the sexes and it is wrong and misleading to use these passages in defense of the modern dance." He went on to argue that the omission of dancing from the Ten Commandments, ten rules for moral living, does not indicate God's approval of everything not mentioned. Also he referenced Christ's Sermon on the Mount before he summarized, "Christians are the saviors of the world, but they cannot be if they indulge in questionable amusements with sinners, and in our dances we open the door to both saint and sinner." His conclusion, designed to lead his reader to his own firmly fixed belief, follows logically from his evidence and argument:

> Every man is free to do as he pleases as long as he pleases to do right. If a person does not want to join a church because that church prohibits dancing by its members, let him stay out until he gets ready to deny himself, take up his cross and follow Jesus.[8]

In this manner, Wilson established his pattern for reaching out through the written word, and after this first attempt he would use his essays to communicate primarily with students. In the coming years we see him composing sermons and homilies, the one to instruct and the other to increase hope. This vision of Wilson's resulted in a series of short essays, usually of one page or less, and in each he dealt with subjects touching on daily living and moral responsibility. In each he knew he must admonish his readers to follow the guidance of the Bible. And he knew exactly where he could effectively publish

---

[7] In addition to the five Bible passages listed in Wilson's article: Jeremiah 31:13; Ecclesiastes 3:4; 2nd Samuel 6:14; Psalms 150:4; and Psalms 30:11, one might also examine: Exodus 15:20; Job 21:11-12; Judges 11:34, 21:21 & 23; Isaiah 13:21; Psalms 149:3; Lamentations 5:14-15; 1st Samuel 18:6, 30:16; 2nd Samuel 6:14; 1st Chronicles 15:29; Matthew 11:17; Mark 6:22; and Luke 7:32, 15:25. They would all seem to be consistent with Wilson's argument.

[8] All Wilson quotations are from James H. Wilson, "The Church and Dancing," *The Half Century Magazine*, Figure 9-1, above.

Figure 9-2. Cover, *The Normal Index*, February, 1927.

NORMAL AND RELIGION
By JAMES H. WILSON

THE TWO FRUIT CAKES
Galatians 5:20, 21, 22

In this lesson we have two kinds of fruits given us. I shall call one the Christians' fruit cake and the other the Devil's fruit cake. In the Devil's fruit cake we have fornication, uncleanness and lasciviousness. These sins lead to the destruction of the body and soul. We are told that our bodies are the temples of God and such should be kept in a healthy condition. We also have enmities, strife, jealousies, wrath, factions, divisions parties. The Devil is satisfied when he can divide the people of God. Every time a new denomination or cult is organized he laughs in his sleeve. When denominations wrangle and fight over doctrines etc, the Devil is satisfied for he knows when we are arguing over this and that form of a practice we are neglecting the sinner. Any movement for the union of the church displeases the devil and he immediately begins to block it and he does not use his own to do it either. Envying, drunkeness and revellings, also come in as a part of the Devil's fruit cake. Envy is one of his most dangerous ingredients. Drunkenness is one of his best ingredients for when one is drunk he will do most any thing the Devil wants him to do. Revellings effect our health and character. So much for the Devil's fruit cake.

But the fruit of the spirit is love, for God so loved; God is love. By this shall all men know you are my deciples if you love one another. Peace - Blessed are the peacemakers for they shall be called the children of God. Longsuffering, kindness goodness, faithfulness, meekness, self control. The Christian's fruit cake is made up of the very best fruit that can be obtained. Now which shall it be: Death, the Devil's fruit cake, or life, the Christian's fruit cake?

REMINISCENCES
READ AT THE FIFTIETH ANNIVERSARY
By THOMAS M. ELMORE, '20

On this the twenty-seventh of April in the Year of our Lord, one thousand nine hundred and twenty-five, we have begun the celebration of our Alma Mater's 50th. Anniversary. It pleases us to know that she has been a worthy foster mother to thousands of graduates and ex-students of several states and that she has been as a pillow of cloud by day and a pillow of fire by night in directing them to the highest callings in the world of professions, industry and thrift. Thus in her general roll call she can boast of the following aggressive Alumni: W. H. Trenholm, President; State Normal Institute, Montgomery Alabama; Ira R. Bryant, Secretary of the A. M. E. Publishing Company, Nashville, Tennessee; J. H. McConico, National Grand Auditor of the Mosaics Templars of America; S. B. Elliot Supreme Grand Master of the Mosaic Templars, Oscar W. Adams, Editor of the Birmingham Reporter; W. T. Woods, Principal of Councill School, Ensley, Alabama; George W. Haines, Secretary of the Federation of the Churches of Christ; H. C. Hopkins, Principal of the Public Schools, Anniston Alabama; G. W. Scott, Principal of School at Pratt City; M. H. Griffin, President Elect of Alabama State Teachers' Association; E. Z. Mathews, Principal of Sheffield High School; Dr. C F. Nalls, Birmingham; Hazel Terrel, Pastor St. John's A. M. E. Church, Montgomery; H. W. Black; Cashier Fraternity Bank, Memphis, Tenn.; Willam Fennoy, Contractor and Builder, St. Louis, Mo.; Mrs. Ida Councill Buchanan, Musician, Pittsburgh, Pa.; Mrs. Clara Frieson Moore, Prima-dona, Chicago, Ill. Dr. E. A. Harris, Huntsville, Alabama.

Among the early reminiscences, imformation has come to us concerning a very distinguished gentleman in the person of Prof. R. L. Hyde. On one bright May morning in 1891 when our Alma Mater was being moved from the historic city of Huntsville to the most beautiful spot in the Tennessee Valley, the said gentleman had honor of bringing President Councill's suit case and being relieved of the luggage in front of the Library quoted the seal of Alabama, "Here We Rest." It is reported that this courageous Alumnus hung around Normal so long that they had to give him a diploma in order to get rid of him. At our last hearing Professor Hyde was principal of the Bowling Green Academy in the Blue Grass State.

Again we are reminded of the founder's devotion to our Alma Mater, the esteem which he held among men of honor and the sacrifice which he made for his race until his death in 1909. During the period at which time our Alma Mater was in moaning due to loss of its noble founder, there appeared on the campus a gentleman small in statue but who gave all evidence of being interested in Normal as well as in one who loved it so dearly. Within three months, the said gentleman was married to the accomplished daughter of the late President Councill and became his worthy successor to begin the new administration in the following fall. He was looked upon by students as "Little Daddy Buchanan" and was styled by one of the Trustees as "The Boy President" due to his youthful age. He delighted in helping worthy students and will ever be remembered for the inspirational lectures rendered at the Sunday evening Vesper. It was during the early part of his administration that with the assistance of student labor two new buildings were erected — The Virginia McCormick Hospital and the William Hooper Councill Domestic Science Building.

Near the latter part of President Buchanan's administration a very peculiar incident occured at the college barn, when three well known Normalites — J. Pompey Thomas, James Watson, and Sylvester Russell — were engaged in conversation concerning a rumor that the name of our Alma Mater was to be changed from A. and M. College to A. and M. Institute; Old Bess the campus mule, who had helped to move our Alma Mater from Huntsville to Normal, is reported to have overheard the conversation and dropped dead two years before her 30th birthday.

In 1920, when all seemed well to the student body due to their high expectation of returning in the fall to a New Normal based on the University Plan, they were greatly disappointed to be informed that the name of our Alma Mater had already been changed by state authorities from A. and M. Institute and that "Little Daddy Buchanan" had resigned to become editor in chief of a Brand New Magazine, The Competitor, in the smoky city of Pittsburgh, Pa.

This indeed seem to be one of the most unsettled periods at Normal, Our Alma Mater was heavily in debt and a man of far-sighted vision plus the patience of a Job was needed to fill the vacancy as president.

It was at this time that one of our most faithful graduates in the person of Mr. R. B. Prentice, who had been around Normal for ten or more consecutive years and who was serving the institution as chief cook, is reported to have lost weight when it was rumored that the state officials were planning to close our Alma Mater due to such a heavy indebtedness. we were again informed that he did not begin to regain his weight until an optimistic "Big Daddy" in the person of our own president Parker shouldered the burden in 1921 and after a short period of two years the debt of $40,000.00 or more was liquidated.

After fifty years of actual endeavor by these three great administrators we have come to witness on this occasion one of the biggest efforts ever attempted for the maintenance of a larger, better and a more attractive Normal.

J. F. Drake Memorial Library Archives

Figure 9-3. Wilson's article, "The Two Fruit Cakes," in *The Normal Index*, April-May, 1925.

his ideas, a medium popular with the student body of Alabama A. & M. Institute, the campus magazine, *The Normal Index*. He gave his regular column a title, "Normal and Religion."

Most of Wilson's printed essays are emotionally charged, and when he addressed students in *The Normal Index* he nearly always delivered a message that concluded with a choice. In "Two Fruit Cakes," based on Paul's Epistle to the Galatians 5: 20-22, and published in April, 1925, he offered his readers one, only one, piece of fruit cake for desert. They were free to select either the Devil's recipe, filled with "envying, drunkenness and revellings" or Christ's cake, full of the fruit of the spirit—love, peace, longsuffering, kindness, goodness, faithfulness, meekness and self-control. He concluded:

> The Christian's fruit cake is made up of the very best fruit that can be obtained. Now which shall it be: Death, the Devil's fruit cake, or Life, the Christian's fruit cake?[9]

Wilson wrote on many topics—missionary work in "The Harvest and Laborers"; the importance of working together in ""Getting Back on the Job"; guarding against evil in "Watch Your Step"; every day is holy in "The Day the Lord Made"; and an unusual and brave attempt to convince his readers in 1928 that "Black is Beautiful." In his article, "Whiter Than Snow," Wilson began his essay by quoting Psalm 51:7, "Purge me with hyssop, and I shall be clean: wash me, and I shall be whiter than snow." He informed his readers that "This is the only passage in the Bible that mentions anything whiter than snow. All the others have white as snow." He fearlessly tells his readers, and in 1928 a Black man in the South had much to fear,

> I have always objected to Negroes singing the song, "Whiter than Snow" for many reasons. . . . 1st. I do not see how anything can be whiter than snow. . . . 2nd. We as a race have too long been taught to think in terms of white so much so that certain weak minded ones of my race have tried to get out of the race into the other race. . . . Our boys and girls ought to be taught that black is as much the standard as white and we cannot teach them that if

---

[9]*The Normal Index*, v. 11 (April-May, 1925), p. 67.

we sing "Wash me and I shall be whiter than Snow" for the idea that most of us get of heaven is that we are all going to be white when we get there.[10]

There is in this work a maturity of thought and a dedication to racial equality that is most unusual in the United States during the 1920s. In New York there may have been a Harlem Renaissance, but in Huntsville, Alabama, black students from A. & M. were allowed to go to town only with permission, with a chaperone, and only on one designated day a week. At the age of 47 when he wrote "Whiter than Snow," James H. Wilson began to use his Bible in a manner that could have brought repercussions upon himself and his family, and he did not shrink from his task. Though the readership of *The Normal Index* was primarily the campus population of students, faculty, and staff, it was a public document that surely met the eyes of politicians and trustees. This writing, "Whiter Than Snow," not only reflects the author's bravery but his commitment to the all-important mission—elevate the race, provide African-Americans the tools for advancement, show his people a road to happiness, fulfillment, and eventually heaven. To do so, he used the language of race, whiteness in particular, to undo itself. Whiteness as a potentially racialized metaphor gives way to the higher racially universal state of being "pure in heart." He concluded his article with these words:

> We should not strive to be whiter than snow or even white, but we should pray to be pure in heart, for the pure in heart shall see God.

Although none of Wilson's oral presentations in church or Sunday school survive, it would seem fair to assume that this mild-mannered, soft-spoken man addressed his listeners in the same homely boldness with which he approached his readers. He would describe an issue he felt was weighing heavily on himself and his brothers and sisters. With this topic in mind he would go on to explain how various Bible passages dealt with it, and he would offer no easy solutions. He then would conclude by presenting

---

[10]*The Normal Index*, v. 14 (March, 1928), p. 65.

JAMES H. WILSON

Instructor in Vocal Music; Bandmaster; Secretary to the Dean; Graduate, Cincinnati High School.

Figure 9-4. Alabama A. & M. Institute 1923 *Bulletin* photo with Wilson's appointment as an Officer of the Administration.

his listeners a choice—do what you please and follow the easy or popular path that will eventually lead to damnation, or take up your cross and struggle to make this world better for yourself, your race, and all mankind. If you choose this right path you may not make it easier for yourself in this life, but "the pure in heart shall see God." His challenge put the ethical onus back on the individual to choose well without compromising on a clear and rigorous moral framework.

During this same decade, James' many responsibilities

increased rather than leveled off or diminished. In 1923, in addition to his faculty appointment as bandmaster, and his staff appointment as bookkeeper, he became one of the Institute's four Officers of Administration—Secretary of Faculty.[11] As part of the Executive Committee he worked on policy with President Parker, Dean M. L. Kiser, and Supervisor of Female Industries Dora W. Adair.

He continued his bookkeeping responsibilities and his classroom teaching, but when he saw a need at the Institute he did his best to help alleviate the problem. For example, James' campus concert schedule had always remained crowded, but as the need to attract students increased, he took his band on tour and also played solo trumpet recitals off campus as a representative of the junior college. By the mid-1920s the student population had fallen to little more than the bare minimum necessary to keep the Institute functioning. At the May 26, 1927, commencement exercises, only six candidates graduated from Normal, three men and three women. Wilson knew music could be used as an effective recruiting tool, for army bands played to attract volunteers and minstrel bands played and marched to bring in the paying audience. His response to A. & M.'s enrollment problems was to go on the road again throughout Alabama and tell his listeners why they or their children should seek to improve their lives by furthering their education at the Alabama Agricultural and Mechanical Institute. His belief in the cause of higher education for African-Americans, bolstered by his solid Christian convictions, transformed this man from just another good teacher in the preparatory school and college into a musical evangelist for Alabama A. & M.

His host, often an African-American church, would advertise the "free" musical event, and at these concerts James would take the opportunity to tell his audience about the merits of A. & M., speak about the value of a diploma or certificate, answer questions about cost, housing, and other concerns. The programs, printed in advance at A. & M, were passed out to all who came, and they were a souvenir of the concert the audience could take home. In no preserved recital or concert program is James ever listed

---

[11]Rev. Dr. Henry Bradford, Jr., "A. & M. Music Faculty," [typescript with manuscript additions].

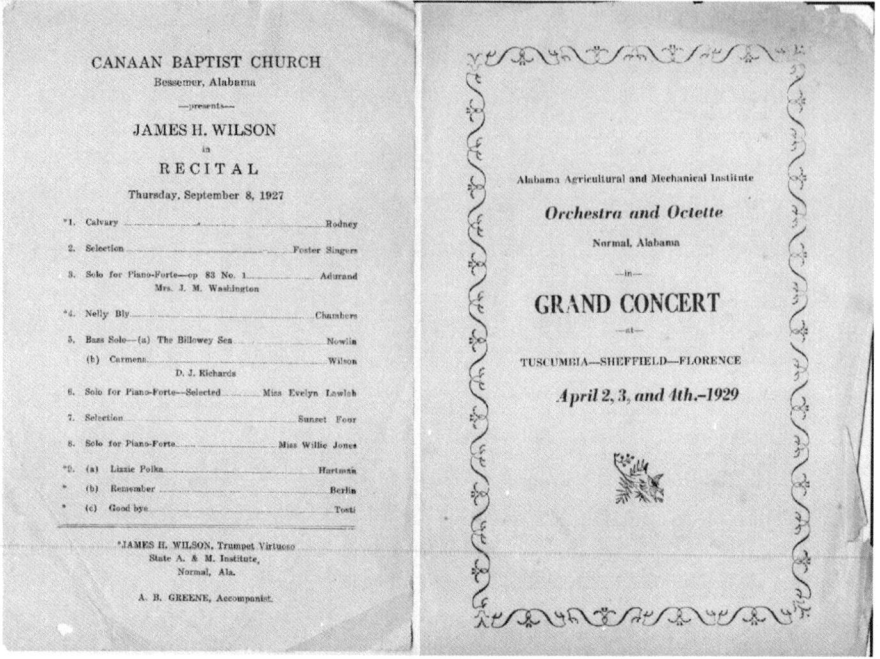

Figure 9-5. Programs performed off-campus. Trumpet recital in Bessemer, Alabama, and Orchestra and Octette concerts repeated in Tuscumbia, Sheffield, and Florence, Alabama.

without his Alabama A. & M. affiliation. He no longer presented himself as an independent concert artist; he was by this time the distinguished music Professor from A. & M. or the virtuoso cornet and trumpet soloist from Normal. He always entertained with three missions—perform well, recruit students, and integrate music into his evangelical Christian outreach. His September, 1927, concert at Canaan Baptist Church in Bessemer, Alabama, opens with "Calvary" by Paul Rodney. Offered as a trumpet solo with accompaniment, the text, by Henry Vaughan, was still popular and generally known. The words focus on the saddest day in Christian history and offer words of hope to those who suffer:

> The pilgrims throng thro' the city gates
> While the night is falling fast;
> They go to watch on Calvary's hill
> Ere the twilight hours are past;

> Though dark be the way, with eyes of faith,
> They gaze on His Cross above;
> And, Lo! from each heart, the shadows depart,
> As they list to His words of love . . . .
> > "Rest, rest to the weary, Peace, peace to the soul;
> > Tho' life may be dreary, Earth is not thy goal. . . ."[12]

Such a text would be especially poignant and meaningful to African Americans of Alabama, who in that day suffered much in a racially repressive atmosphere. Wilson's Bible and Wilson's trumpet both brought messages of hope, purpose, and fulfillment.

It is interesting to note that about this time James and Exeline took on more responsibilities at home as well. James' aging father, Jacob, was going blind, and he became unable to support himself or continue living alone, so James caught the train at Normal station, rode it to Nicholasville, gathered up his father, and brought him back to A. & M. to live with his family of six. Rather than see Granddaddy Wilson as a burden, James' entire family welcomed Jacob into their home and into their lives. Daughter Marian, spoke about her days with her grandfather:

> Oh, he was wonderful. He taught me everything. He came to live with us because he was losing his eyesight. He taught me to read, and just so much about life. He came to live with us because he was going blind, but he took me everywhere. People used to worry because I was just a child, and I would take him everywhere that I went. And if I would explore on a ledge, I would take him. He never fell or anything like that, but that was terrible. I didn't realize it, of course. I treated him like he was a sighted person. . . . [He told me about] life and his travels. He was a musician and he went on to a band, and I don't remember too much about it. I only know what he told me.[13]

The Wilsons' parental care extended to Exeline's mother as well when James and Exeline later brought Elizabeth Litton Polk to their home from Nashville.

---

[12]Rodney, Paul and Henry Vaughan, "Calvary" (1895). Connecticut College, *Historic Sheet Music Collection*. Paper 37. http://digitalcommons.conncoll.edu/sheetmusic/37 [accessed December 8, 2012].

[13]Interview with Marian F. W. Turner, March 1, 2011.

Figure 9-6. Snapshot of Jacob, left, sitting on the Wilson porch step, conversing with friend and neighbor, Thomas Elmore (circa 1925).

[My grandmother] on my mother's side, she lived in Nashville, and I know we would go for a visit every year. Her name was Lizzy, Lizzy Litton. I remember going on a train to visit her.... After her health was failing she came to live with us. That was nice....[14]

And what a musical household Lizzy would have been able to enjoy:

[My sister, Hester] played piano. [We played duets.] My older brother [James] played trumpet, and my brother next to me [Karl] played drums. And there was a summer I remember, they always had a summer school, they had a program, "Thirty Minutes With The Wilsons." And we all did something and did numbers together. My sister and I played duets and solos.... My older brother and my dad played duets.[15]

All the while, money must have been a serious concern.

[14]*Ibid.*

Feeding, clothing, and educating four children was expensive; adding a dependent parent was a problem. Even before Jacob came to live with the Wilsons, James saw an opportunity to earn additional money from an outside source, the United States Government. When the postmaster job at Normal fell vacant in 1919, James, even though he was employed full-time by the college, applied for and was awarded the position of Postmaster. This created two problems for the man: justifying a second salary and finding the time to do the additional work. Typically his ingenuity found one solution to both problems at once. Exeline would run the post office. Since the U. S. Government did not employ women in the Postal Service in 1919, he became Postmaster in name and she served as Postmistress in fact.[16] His vote for women's rights was almost certainly driven by financial necessity more than principle, but with Exeline's help he remained the Postmaster at A. & M. from 1919 to 1942.[17] Both James and Exeline were kept busy wearing many hats and performing many chores. At the very least, Exeline was a full-time homemaker, part-time Postmistress, and occasional teacher. Their youngest daughter, Marian, had happy memories of the post office, too, for on occasion her mother gave her Special Delivery letters to carry to the addressees on campus, and she got to keep the tip for herself.

Where James Hembray Wilson's busy and rewarding life during the 1920s was yielding much fruit, the even busier life of his boss, President Theophilus R. Parker, ran awry. Although he repaid the $40,000.00 debt he inherited from Buchanan when he assumed office two years earlier, he found it impossible to keep the college

---

[15] *Ibid.*

[16] There were some earlier exceptions, but they were rare. The Smithsonian National Postal Museum informs us:

> The Civil War opened career opportunities to women serving unofficially in the postal system in small numbers. With the men fighting at the front, women were hired to temporarily fill in the vacancies. They were also employed out of "charity for those whose husbands or sons had been their sole support."

http://www.postalmuseum.si.edu/womenhistory/women_history/history_19century.html (accessed February 11, 2013). However, married women, officially, were banned from employment in the postal service until after 1921, and women were not allowed to carry mail in Chicago until 1944!

[17] *Notable Kentucky African Americans Database*, "Postal Service" (University of Kentucky Libraries), http://www.uky.edu/Libraries/NKAA/subject.php?sub_id=80 (accessed November 12, 2011).

from falling into debt again. The Alabama State Agricultural and Mechanical Institute had no endowment, and Parker had no "back up money" to keep the operation solvent. To fulfill the mission of the Junior College and build toward a fully reinstated four-year college, he felt he had to maintain quality programs led by qualified faculty, and their salaries plus the campus expenses cost more than he was allotted or could raise from outside sources. To achieve his goals he overspent, and it was his undoing. Richard David Morrison sympathetically explains:

> Special efforts were made during this period to support each division of the College as well as possible, in spite of a reported deficit in the budget each year. These deficits were not caused by poor management, but rather because the budgets were too restricted for the support of a properly organized approved educational institution whose mission was in tune with the needs of the people.
>
> For example, in 1925 the Department of Nurse Training was well organized, housed and thoroughly equipped in the Virginia McCormick Hospital Building, which was provided by the McCormick family. This training facility served a dual purpose of providing health care for the sick in a hospital and training professional nurses. This important department was forced to close because of the lack of financial support. The modern equipment in the operating room was moved to the hospital in Huntsville, Alabama. There is no reason [given nor any record] available that shows during this time that Negroes were admitted to that hospital for an operation.[18]

The bitterness of Morrison's final statement certainly must have been felt personally by African-Americans on campus who became ill and needed medical treatment. Matters came to a head two years later. Again Morrison reports:

> Serious difficulties arose during President Parker's tenure because the administration failed to limit state supported expenses to the $15,000 annual budget. Part of this dilemma was brought on because of a decline in enrollment and the

---

[18]Morrison, *History of Alabama Agricultural and Mechanical University: 1875-1992*, p. 153.

recession after World War I. Another contributing factor was the administrator's refusal to reduce or delete programs or courses. Their situation became so critical in 1927 that it was thought by the local community that the school was on the verge of being closed.[19]

The Alabama State Legislature's Recess Committee on Education visited A. & M. on May 5, 1927, a sizable group of five state senators and eight representatives, and they brought with them the county superintendent of education plus six additional political figures including trustee David A. Grayson. These men were fed and entertained by the Institute, and they visited classes, inspected facilities, and listened to a prepared message from President Parker. Quickly the committee reported its dissatisfaction with the administration of the Institute to the State Board of Education, and about one month later President Parker read an article in the *Montgomery Journal* that revealed he had been replaced as President of the State A. & M. Institute by Professor Drake, Dean of the College at Alabama State College in Montgomery, Alabama, effective July 1, 1927. One can only imagine the turmoil on campus as word of these events spread from mouth to ear. Parker and his wife left Normal immediately after commencement, and President Drake and his wife arrived before the opening of classes in September. Little did anyone know that President Joseph Fanning Drake was the answer to their prayers, and little did James Hembray Wilson foresee that he would work by Drake's side until his own retirement some two and one-half decades later. Certainly he would never have imagined that one day he would be painted into a historic mural in the Joseph Fanning Drake Library on his campus standing beside this man, the person whom most of his colleagues believed was coming to Normal, Alabama, to shut down the school and close its doors forever.

And no one was more surprised to have been offered the job at Alabama A. & M. than Professor Joseph Fanning Drake. Richard Morrison dramatically recounts the sequence of events that took

---

[19]*Ibid.*, p. 155.

Figure 9-7. A. & M.'s fourth president, Joseph Fanning Drake.

place in May and June of 1927:

> This appointment came as a complete surprise to Professor Drake. Mrs. Drake has often related her vivid recollection of a telephone call, received by her husband, one Sunday morning, late in May

1927 from State Superintendent of Education, Dr. John W. Abercrombie. In this telephone conversation, Dr. Abercrombie stated that, "We have decided that we want you to be President of the College for Negroes at Normal, Alabama—think about it and talk it over with your wife. The next meeting of the Board is on June 15, 1927; let me have your answer before that date. We are dissatisfied with the administration of that school. If you do not go we will close it—the power is in our hands to close it."

Before Professor Drake had time to respond, the *Montgomery Journal* announced, in a headline, "Professor Drake Appointed President of A&M Institute to Replace Parker." The State Board commented to Professor Drake that, "We did it this way so that you could not back out. We have observed your work, both at the college and state levels—you are the man we want to be President up there."[20]

Although one might fairly interpret these circumstances as one more example of powerful white politicians and appointees manipulating a competent but powerless black man, thus depriving him of his rights to freedom of choice in this matter, it would only be fair to credit these decision makers with reasonably good intentions in their show of force. Had Drake, for any reason—health, home, family, or whatever—decided to say "no," they would have had ample excuse, or justification, to close the Institute, and such a move would have had profound negative implications on the African-American citizens of Alabama in the long run. It would appear that in its power play, the State had confidence in Drake and wanted him to succeed.

After Professor Drake and his wife arrived on campus and moved into the President's residence, the State made elaborate preparations to introduce him to the faculty and students and smooth out this very difficult transition in leadership. A formal program of welcome, almost an inauguration ceremony, took place in the Institute's chapel on September 28, 1927. State and local officials dispelled the notion that in appointing Drake there was any intent to close the college. One of the men who had been a member of the State Board of Commissioners since 1903, attorney David A.

---

[20]Morrison, *History of Alabama Agricultural and Mechanical University: 1875-1992*, p. 162.

Figure 9-8. David A. Grayson, State Board of Commissioners, member since 1903.

Grayson, a man who had actively participated in overseeing the college through the terms of all the former presidents—Councill, Buchanan, and Parker, had the honor of introducing the new president of Alabama Agricultural and Mechanical Institute, Joseph Fanning Drake.

Grayson began by recounting Drake's birth and schooling in Alabama, service in the Army, graduate study at the University of Chicago and Columbia University, and experience in education as both teacher and administrator. He continued with these words:

The foregoing shows that President Drake, though a young man, gives promise of being quite as great a leader of his people as was the illustrious William Hooper Councill, who gave the land on which the buildings, some $300,000 in value, stand, together with nearly all the buildings—except those given by Mr. Carnegie and Miss Virginia McCormick. The state has contributed nothing towards buying the land nor has it furnished a nail, plank, or brick in erecting the buildings. Councill knew he was giving his "all" into the keeping of the white people of Alabama. Councill died a poor man.

The local white officials of the Institute are just now succeeding in getting the state officials to appreciate the importance of the sacred trust conferred on the State of Alabama by Councill, a former slave. The State Board of Education has every assurance with absolutely no feelings of doubt that they have succeeded in picking the very best man in the country to achieve the ambitions of the late William Hooper Councill and to carry to a successful conclusion the new and big program for the Institute, made possible by recent legislative enactments.[21]

These words of assurance and encouragement by a familiar local white leader who actively took part in the supervision of A. & M. for almost three decades smoothed the way and paved the path for the Institute's new leader, President Joseph Fanning Drake. Grayson was the key watchdog of Alabama A. & M., the white man who served as Treasurer of A. & M. during the years previous to Wilson's appointment, the chairman of Madison County's Democratic Party committee, and a member, real or ex officio, of every state appointed review or presidential search committee. No white man in Alabama knew more about Alabama A. & M. or had greater influence relating to its governance than David Allison Grayson.[22]

Though no one could have predicted at that moment what Drake's future would provide, this young leader would remain in office and serve his academic community from 1927 to 1962, three and one-half decades as President of the College. One of the first wise decisions

---

[21]*Ibid.*, p. 165.

[22]Unrelated to this narrative but interesting: David Grayson played on the University of Alabama's first varsity football team, and in 2012, 141 years after his birth and 65 years after his death, was elected into the Huntsville-Madison County Athletic Hall of Fame. See Mark McCarter, "Huntsville Hall of Fame:

made by this gifted leader was to retain the services of his financial secretary and continue Wilson's active participation in the Institute's executive committee meetings where he served as secretary.

Wilson's role in the Institute's business affairs increased almost immediately after Drake assumed office. In the spring of that academic year Wilson received a brief unsigned memo, possibly from President Drake or Professor R. A. Carter, outlining some of his responsibilities:

April 21, 1928

To: James H. Wilson

[Re:] A survey of the land grant colleges by the Federal Government

We cooperate.

    1. Committee includes Chairman R. A. Carter, Director of Instruction

    2. Institutional control, finance, physical plant; Mr. James H. Wilson,

    Bookkeeper, Financial Secretary.

    3. Internal organization and administration, staff problem; Mr. R. A. Carter. . . .

We trust that you will give your earnest and sincere thought to this information in order that you might be in a position to discuss intelligently when representatives come.[23]

Wilson was clearly more than a bookkeeper. He was now the ranking officer, beneath the President, for institutional control and the physical plant of the Institute, including maintenance; and he was also in charge of the efficient and accurate handling of the

---

David Grayson was on Alabama's first football team, 120 years ago," *Huntsville Times* [http://www.al.com/sports/index.ssf/2012/04/huntsville_hall_of_fame_david.html, accessed December 10, 2012.]

[23]University Archives, Joseph Fanning Drake Library, "Miscellaneous Correspondence," Folder "W,", transcribed by Professor Louis Auld, October 25, 2011.

school's monies including the work of purchasing agent. After their visit we can assume the auditors filed a favorable report based on their inspection of the college, for no further mention of this government survey or notations of deficiencies appears in the records. James ran a tight financial ship. We can see this when he had occasion to write this note to Professor Carter while supervising student accounts:

[Undated, but contemporary with the above memo.]

Director Carter:

Please do not enroll Henry . . . until his fees are paid. He has permission to go on with his classes but all marks are to be retained until fees are paid.

Yours truly,

James H. Wilson

Bookkeeper[24]

Along with his responsibilities, Wilson also had an important level of authority as well. And one may measure the importance of Wilson's position at this particular time in the history of the institution by remembering that the future of the Alabama A. & M. Institute, its very existence, depended on the astute management of resources, the absolute need to keep expenditures within the institution's annual budget. By handling the college's money and by serving as the college purchasing agent, Wilson shared this burden with President Drake, and the two of them, working together, turned Parker's disaster into Drake's triumph.

During Drake's first and second years at A. & M., he and Wilson received monthly salaries of $225.00 and $125.00, respectively. The college's financial records, in Wilson's hand, record all the salaries for the Institute's full-time and part-time employees as well as the variety of payments to vendors, students, and miscellaneous extras. The ledgers record a continuous monthly payment in these same amounts from August of 1928 through September of 1932

---

[24]*Ibid.*

Figure 9-9. Detail of mural painting in the Joseph Fanning Drake Memorial Library. Wilson stands immediately behind President Drake, upper left.

for these two men, a run of four years without change for either.[25] After the collapse of the financial markets in 1929, the United States entered its most severe depression in history. The salary payments remained steady for a while, but by 1932, the Institute again ran into serious financial trouble, as did nearly every other person and institution in the United States. In October, 1932, no one at A. & M. received any salary. A month later, in November, salaries resumed, but at a new level, and everyone's salary had been modestly reduced. President Drake's had been lowered to $200.00 per month and Financial Secretary Wilson's to $110.00, and this level of payment continued for almost a year, through September of 1933. The available resources, however, were still less than the college's needs. Drake responded to the dilemma differently from

---

[25]University Archives, Joseph Fanning Drake Library, "Disbursement Voucher Register, 1928-1940," notes taken by Frank Tirro, October 26, 2011.

his two immediate predecessors in office, Buchanan and Parker. He decided that everyone must share the college's burden equally, and once again salaries were reduced, each person at A. & M. this time taking a drastic percentage cut. There was no favoritism shown, and salaries were paid with the money that was in hand. In October and November, once again, no one received any salary. In December, Drake only took home $125.00 and Wilson received but $80.00, slightly more than half of what they were making six years earlier. These salary levels continued for another year until, in December of 1934, the school was finally able to inch up the figure to $160.00 for the President and $90.00 per month for his Financial Secretary. These two men and their colleagues kept the limping Institute alive, and they accomplished their mission because all the men and women of Alabama A. & M. truly believed in the goals and purpose of their college to lift up those young people in their charge—socially, vocationally, intellectually, and morally. By the 1930s James Hembray Wilson had established beyond all doubt about his credentials and academic training that he was not a peripheral figure in this academic community; he was a leader and a fully accredited member fighting in the trenches alongside his comrades in the midst of their battle for survival.

Figure 10-1. Alabama A. & M. Institute Band, 1933.[1]

[1]Morrison, History of Alabama Agricultural and Mechanical University: 1875-1992, p. 259.

CHAPTER TEN

The Omnipresent Professor: 1930—1941

Once the faculty and students settled down after the big shakeup of 1927, the first few years of the Drake administration seemed to move along smoothly. However, the stock market crash of 1929 bode poorly for the future of the Institute, and, consequently, for Wilson as well.[2] In 1930 James' oldest child, Hester, turned eighteen and was ready for college, and the elder son, James, Jr., was just two years behind his sister. Wilson knew college costs for two would draw heavily upon his financial resources, and he also realized he would turn fifty years of age come December. He was no longer a young man, and his years show clearly in a photograph with the 1933 Alabama A. & M. band (Figure 10-1, opposite). In the lower right-hand corner one can see a distinguished but elderly gentleman holding a trumpet pictured alongside a group of definitely younger musicians.

When Wilson thought about his future, he became increasingly aware that his youngest child, Marian, was only eleven, and would be needing tuition money for college even after his 60th birthday. Where would sufficient resources come from, and how had the years passed so quickly? After all, life expectancy at birth for all American males in 1930 was fifty-eight years, and only forty-seven years for African-American men.[3] James had already passed that benchmark. And he also worried about his job. Even though all the students referred to him as "Professor Wilson," he knew it was a courtesy and not a reality. He had never received a professorial appointment at A. & M. He was, in fact, a member of the staff, a bookkeeper promoted to financial

---

[2]After the calamitous selloffs in the U. S. stock market in October of 1929, the market took forty years, until November 3, 1954, to recover to the September 3, 1929, high— all of the 1930s, all of the 1940s, including the World War II years, the postwar years, and into the first years of the Korean conflict.

secretary who served as bandmaster and Superintendent of the Sunday School. If truth be told, he felt blessed to be allowed to teach the Sunday School Teacher Preparation class and an occasional Bible class. As time progressed it became ever more apparent to him, especially when he participated in the Executive Committee meetings, that President Drake was being forced to upgrade his faculty as well as the programs and facilities in order to reinstate the institution to its former four-year college status. Drake was constantly searching for highly qualified African-American men and women with advanced degrees, and James could only boast a high school diploma. He had a family to support, and he could afford neither the time nor the money to enroll in college. It was not pleasant for him to admit that a black man his age was hardly in a position to earn a college degree, even less likely to be able to add a master's degree or a doctorate to a baccalaureate. He struggled for a solution.

These somewhat grim thoughts sent Wilson back to his Bible for guidance and hope, and this process not only inspired him to continue writing articles for the *Normal Index* that he hoped would provide assurance and direction for the next generation of African Americans now enrolled as students at Normal, but it also triggered a possible solution to usefully further his own education without leaving home and sacrificing his job. Sometime during these years he enrolled in the correspondence course division of the Moody Bible School of Chicago.[4] Exactly when he did this and how long the process took him is not certain, but he satisfactorily completed the required distance learning program and earned for himself a diploma from the Moody Bible School.[5] Actually, a

---

[3]"Life Expectancy at Birth by Race and Sex, 1930-2010" (http://www.infoplease.com/ipa/A0005148.html), accessed September 16, 2012. Source of Data: National Center for Health Statistics, National Vital Statistics Reports (http://www.cdc.gov/nchs/).

[4]The Moody Bible Institute was a pioneer in distance learning. It organized a Moody Evening School in 1903 to train lay workers, and it began its Moody Bible Institute Radio Broadcasts in 1925. (http://www.moodyministries.net/crp_MainPage.aspx?id=58239) accessed September 16, 2012.

[5]*Who's Who in Colored America*, eds. G. James Fleming and Christian E. Burckel, 7th ed. (Yonkers-on-Hudson, NY, Christian E. Burckel & Assoc., 1950), p.565. His enrollment was confirmed at the James Hembray Wilson Alabama State Black Archives Research Center and Museum, Normal, Alabama. Browne [no first

correspondence course was a brilliant solution for the practical problems of this homemade Bible scholar and teacher of Bible students and Sunday School teachers. Upon the completion of his curriculum of study he sought out and asked assistance from the Rev. Homer C. Lyman, D.D., of the International Sunday School Association. This distinguished man was the Superintendent of Sunday School Work in all Black Colleges in the South. Almost two decades earlier, in July of 1913, this influential Caucasian religious leader spoke in Zurich, Switzerland, of his efforts and experiences in the struggle to further African-American religious education and African-American education in general.

TEN MILLION NEGROES' RELIGIOUS EDUCATION

> I count it a privilege of my life to speak in behalf of ten million negroes in America. . . . My years of labor for the negroes have given me an insight into their nature, and a confidence in their ability and character. . . . Have the negroes the desire and capacity for education? They have 2,800 public schools, 30,000 teachers, and a million and a quarter pupils, 260 colleges, industrial and boarding schools of higher grade. They have 23,000 ministers and 30,000 church buildings. . . . Is not the real secret of this marvelous progress the direct result of personal contact with consecrated men of God, the pioneer missionary teachers?[6]

---

name given], "The Man Himself," *The State A. & M. Campus Journal* [1938], p. 3, reports:

> This is the story of a man who has become an institution himself. For 35 years he has been a part of A. and M., serving under all four of its presidents. . . . He is an authority on the Bible and will not hesitate to give his advice freely. He can take his trumpet and play it so sweetly that it takes your breath away. . . . He took a correspondence course from the Bryant-Stratton College in Chicago and received a diploma. His refusal to spend one year's residence on the campus prevented his getting a degree. When the book-keeper resigned he accepted the position."

Being unable to confirm Wilson's enrollment and diploma through the registrar's office at either Moody or Bryant-Stratton for lack of a social security number for Wilson, I have chosen to follow the evidence of Wilson's submission to *Who's Who in Colored America*.

[6]Homer C. Lyman, "Ten Million Negroes' Religious Education", in *World-Wide Sunday-School Work: The Official Report of the World's Seventh Sunday-School Convention, held in Zurich, Switzerland, July 8-15, 1913*, ed. by Charles Gallaudet Trumbull (London and New York City: The World's Sunday-School Association, [1913]), pp. 449f.

Clearly Dr. Lyman was a man who could help James achieve his own personal goals of furthering African-American religious education, and with his support and President Drake's approval, James became the first person at Alabama A. & M. to offer and teach a correspondence course, Sunday School Teacher Training. It was a perfect match. One can see in this move that in addition to Wilson's astounding energy and dedication of purpose, he possessed entrepreneurial skills that were truly remarkable. This correspondence course was one more layer in the dike that protected his security at Normal, and it was just one more example of James' ability to rise above seemingly insurmountable difficulties and succeed.

During the 1930s, little by little and step by step, James H. Wilson became one of the most active and familiar personalities on campus, a living example and an inspiration to the students of A. & M. Wilson participated fully in the activities of the Young Men's and the Young Women's Christian Associations on campus, the Y.M.C.A. and Y.W.C.A. In 1930 James had been elected Honorary President of the Y.M.C.A., and he simultaneously functioned as the Faculty Advisor for the Y.W.C.A. A student and his future son-in-law, Charles Orr, became president of the campus organization that year and served as editor of the *Y.M.C.A. Hand Book*.

In the 1930-1931 issue of the *Y.M.C.A. Hand Book*, Wilson wrote an article expressing his belief in the need for a program of character building in higher education, and the Y.M.C.A. and the Y.W.C.A. were two means toward this end.

Our Religious Organizations

At Normal we are busy trying to prepare our young men and women to be leaders. . . . We cultivate the head and in our trade schools the hand. Why should the heart, the most important part of the individual, be neglected?

Most of our criminals are young men. . . . A good many of them are educated young men. . . . Something has been left out of their training. Their hearts have been neglected.

Yes, we believe in our religious organizations as an important factor in character education. . . .

THE OMNIPRESENT PROFESSOR: 1930—1941

It may appear a little old fashion to go back to the family altar but if this old fashion institution is going to redeem our youth I for one vote for the re-establishing of it.[7]

Because of his unstinting labor with these organizations, the campus Y. M. C. A. dedicated the first volume of their semi-annual publication to Professor Wilson the following year.

In this dedicatory issue he once again delivered a message of need and urgency.

Figure 10-2. Wilson's personal copy of an Alabama A. & M. Institute *Y.M.C.A. Hand Book*.

The Sunday School in the past was a place where children were taught by incompetent teachers. The school was poorly conducted by officers who had not studied organization or methods. . . .

The one-room school has given place to the well equipped Sunday School building with its trained teachers, specialists and officers. Teachers who not only know their Bibles, but are well trained in the arts and sciences as well. Teachers who make special preparation for each lesson and each student.[8]

One can see here that Wilson had clear ideas about what needed to be accomplished, and he actively proselytized and made his presence and ideas known on campus. He worked hand in hand with President Drake, and he had the President's complete support in this effort.

---

[7]Alabama A. & M. College, *Y. M. C. A. Hand Book*, v.2, n. 2 (Normal, AL: Alabama A. & M. College, [1931]), p. 30.

[8]Alabama A. & M. College, *Y. M. C. A. Hand Book*, v.3, n. 1 (Normal, AL: Alabama A. & M. College, [1932]), pp. 16 and 47.

Figure 10-3. Wilson and his Sunday School Teacher Training Class.

To understand President Drake's work better, and to measure the progress of the institution during these years, we might note that beginning in 1927, the year of Drake's appointment, the A. & M. faculty numbered but twenty-four men and women, and only one person on his faculty possessed a Master's degree. By 1942, one year after the institution regained its four-year, college-degree-granting status, President Drake could boast a faculty of 52 members who had earned one Ph.D. and twelve master's degrees.[9] During these years of severe financial depression, war in Europe, and eventual American entrance into a world conflict that again sapped young men from the student rosters, Drake's most serious problem at Normal continued to be adequate funding, and Wilson's prudent advice, careful financial records,

---

[9]Morrison, *History of Alabama Agricultural and Mechanical University: 1875-1992*, p. 205.

Figure 10-4. *Y.M.C.A. Hand Book*, 1931-1932, page 5.

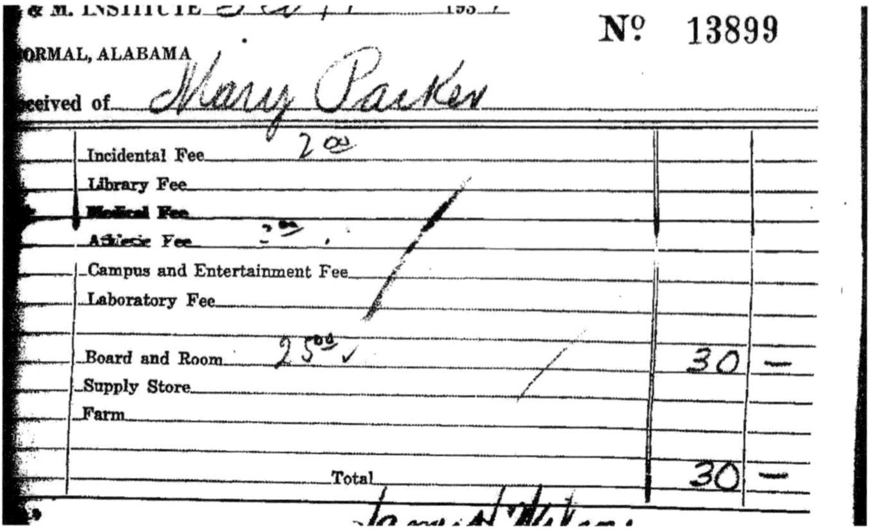

No 13899

ORMAL, ALABAMA

ceived of Mary Parker

Incidental Fee 2 00		
Library Fee		
Medical Fee		
Athletic Fee 2 00		
Campus and Entertainment Fee		
Laboratory Fee		
Board and Room 25 00	30	—
Supply Store		
Farm		
Total	30	—

Figure 10-5. Carbon copy of receipt given to student Mary Parker, signed by Wilson.

cautious money management, and tight-fisted spending helped enable Drake, during these extreme depression years, to succeed where his two predecessors had failed in better times. Wilson accounted for the Institute's receipts and expenditures in small detail. To see an example of this process, we might view the carbon copy of a mid-year student receipt, that of Mary Parker, a high-school junior from Owens Cross Roads, a small town about twenty miles southeast of Normal, Alabama.[10]

Attention to detail, of course, is the hallmark of a good financial manager, and when Mary Parker came to Wilson's office in February, 1937, to make payment on her school expenses, the receipt given her listed $2.00 for some incidental fee, $2.00 collected for an athletic fee, a quick slash for the standard $1.00 laboratory fee, and $25.00 toward board and room for a total payment at that time of $30.00. Because student financial resources differed widely at A. & M., board and room collections varied considerably.

[10]*Alabama State A. & M. Institute Bulletin: Catalogue Edition 1936-1937*, v. 18, n. 14 (August, 1937), p. 73.

6 STATE AGRICULTURAL AND MECHANICAL INSTITUTE

OFFICERS OF ADMINISTRATION

JOSEPH F. DRAKE, A. B., A. M. ....President
JAMES H. WILSON ....Financial Secretary
OLIVIA E. DUNLOP, B. S. ....Secretary to the President
ROBERT A. CARTER, A. B., M. S. ....Dean
GEORGE O. McCALEP, A. B., A. M. ....Principal of the High School
SIMON A. HALEY, B. S., M. S. ....Director of Agriculture
ADDIE M. BUTLER, B. S. ....College Home Economics
INA A. BOLTON, A. B., A. M. ....Girls' Counselor
JAMES L. BRAY ....Dean of Men

OFFICERS OF INSTRUCTION

JOSEPH F. DRAKE, A. B., A. M. ....President
    Talladega College; Columbia University
    Graduate Work, Cornell University

ROBERT A. CARTER, A. B., M. S. ....Dean and Science
    Talladega College; University of Michigan

SIMON A. HALEY, B. S., M. S. ....Director of Agriculture
    A. and T. College; Cornell University

GEORGE O. McCALEP, A. B., A. M. .... Science,
    High School Principal
    University of Kansas

**HENRIETTA J. CARTER, A. B., A. M. ...Mathematics and Physics
    Talladega College; University of Michigan

INA A. BOLTON, A. B., A. M. ....Freshman English
    Washburn College; University of Kansas

RUTH P. BINFORD, A. B., A. M. .... Mathematics
    Howard University; Columbia University

NATHAN A. LANGFORD, A. B., A. M. .... Social Science
    Talladega College; Ohio State University

*EDWIN H. BAYLISS, B. S., A. M.....Social Science and Mathematics
    Prairie View State College; State University of Iowa

HARRIET J. TERRY, A. B. ....English
    Howard University; Year of Graduate Work, Columbia University

ERNEST F. HAMILTON, A. B. .... Biology
    Indiana State Teachers College;
    Graduate Work, Indiana State Teachers College.

Figure 10-6. State A. & M. Institute *Bulletin,* August, 1937, p. 6.

On two adjacent days, February 11th and 12th, six consecutive receipts confirmed $10.00, $6.50, $30.00, $3.00, $6.50, and $50.00 for board and room. However, the $1.00 laboratory fee was always collected, indicating, one might presume, that instructional costs had to be paid in order for a student to attend class, while board and room charges might be worked out with some form of financial arrangement, perhaps student labor.

In a real way, during these years Wilson moved up to second in command of the Institute, not in academic matters, of course, but in administration. We see this in the listing of the faculty and staff in the yearly bulletins. Names in the various categories were not listed alphabetically until there were a group of equals. In the category, "Officers of Administration," Wilson is now always listed second, just below "Joseph F. Drake, A. B., A. M................President."

It is interesting to observe that Wilson also had been given a certain level of authority in academic matters stemming from financial control, for he was able to inform professors that particular students may or may not be allowed into their classes if their payments were in arrears.

The following letter (Figure 10-7), addressed to Professor Nathan A. Langford, Professor of Social Science at A. & M., illustrates Wilson's license to exclude. Unfortunately, it also hides his humanity. In fact, he cared very much for many students with their own individual needs. Several former students interviewed have repeated the same message of kindness, understanding, and support. Ella Byrd McCain, a woman who served as librarian at A. & M. for forty-six years said:

> When I graduated from high school, my father told me I couldn't go to college. My brother went to Tuskegee, and my sister to A. & M., but there wasn't enough money for me. I wrote to Mr. Wilson, and he took me under his arm. He found work for me in the library, and also in the canteen, and he told Dean Carter I was a good, hard-working person who would succeed. I stayed every summer and worked. He was an architect for my life, and his goodness was amazing. He was a god.[11]

[11] Phone interview while visiting Alabama A. & M. University, October 25, 2011.

JAMES H. WILSON
NORMAL, ALABAMA

January 9, 1939

Mr Langford ;

I am away c for a few hours on business. Please see that President Drake gets this report.

I am having several students to come in this morning and they must carry a note from me signed by me before entering their classes.

There will be others to follow as soon as I can get to it. We must see that all persons who owe make some kind of adjustment before we can carry them any longer.

Since I am away they shall have to wait until I return to enter class. Some of these should go home.

Yours truly,
James H. Wilson

P S Make arrangements for band concert at Oakwood either Thursday or Saturday. I prefer Saturday night. The Sabbath is over at 6:00 o'clock. Call Frazier.

Figure 10-7. Letter to Professor Langford, January 9, 1939.

In spite of financial hardship, Wilson made it possible for Ella Byrd McCain to successfully complete her Bachelor of Science Degree in Home Economics in May of 1945.

The postscript of Wilson's letter to Langford is interesting, too, perhaps even amusing. Though his bandmaster position had by now become totally adjunct to his administrative post as Financial Secretary, Wilson continued to direct the band and was referred to on campus as "Professor Wilson, Director of the Band." Regardless of his other responsibilities, the band remained very close to his heart, and though very busy, he continued to direct concerts on and away from campus frequently. Oakwood College, now Oakwood University, is a Historically Black Seventh-Day Adventist institution in Huntsville, Alabama, about seven or eight miles southwest of Alabama A. & M. We see in this addendum to Langford's letter that Wilson intended to play a concert for Oakwood on their campus and preferred Saturday to Thursday. Anticipating an immediate "no" to Saturday from the Adventists, who celebrate their Sabbath on Saturday rather than Sunday, he reminded Langford that their Sabbath ends at 6:00 p.m. on Saturday and that an evening concert would not violate their beliefs. Perhaps "Frazier" is the band's contact at the sister institution. Finally, this letter also illustrates that Professor Langford was serving as Wilson's assistant. There are four imperatives and only one receives a "Please": "Please see that President Drake gets this report." "... they must carry a note from me ...." "Make arrangements for band concert at Oakwood...." "Call Frazier."

Finance was one key aspect of James H. Wilson's life, but music, religion and family stood tall as equals. Long before the above letter was written, in March of 1930, Wilson took the band to Oakwood Junior College where he not only conducted but was the composer of the third number on the program, "Silas Green" march. Then he also performed a trumpet solo, "Russia" by Thomas Alexandrovich de Hartmann, and he saw to it that his oldest daughter, Hester, had an opportunity to accompany him on piano. At the Athletic Convocation held in October of that same year, all present sang three songs: "The Alumni Song," "A. and M. Forever," and "A. and M. College," and our Mr. Wilson directed the

THE OMNIPRESENT PROFESSOR: 1930—1941

Figure 10-8. Financial Secretary Wilson seated in his office with account books, ledger sheets, and typewriter.

band and led the singing. During these years he seems to have been everywhere doing everything. For example, he was actively involved in the Ben Macato Club, the first sorority on campus. Earlier, in 1928, a few female students approached him to ask his opinion about the wisdom of starting a social sorority that emphasized culture, morality, and social grace. He encouraged them, and when they returned to ask if he had any suggestions for a distinctive name for their proposed campus club, he offered, "The Ben Macato Club," because *"ben marcato"* in Italian means "well marked," and certainly the young ladies chosen for membership in this new sorority should be well marked by their upbringing, education, Christian beliefs, and social grace. It is almost certain Wilson had learned this musical phrase in rehearsal under an Italian conductor, and the immigrant's broad sounding "a" and quick-rolling "r" transformed *marcato* into "mah-cah-to" in his limited Italian vocabulary.

In April of 1931 the Ben Macato Club presented an "American Indian Operetta" for the campus community. Their musical skit employed six characters, and as would be expected, all are women: the queen, her sister, her three children—Fudgee, Wudgee, and Pudgee, and an old squaw. In the program Wilson is listed as "Organizer," and for the chorus of eight students, two of whom are men, Wilson's elder daughter, Hester, served as accompanist. The home-made script tells the following story:

SYNOPSIS

Once each year the maidens of the Wanta Tribe repair to a secluded spot to celebrate the Feast of the Red Corn, the one finding the Red Ear has her wish granted. This year the old Squaw tells the maidens the four winds have whispered to her that no wish will be granted, but the Queen, whose King has disappeared, entreats old squaw that the four winds will grant a wish and return her King.[12]

Such was the innocent script from which one would be hard pressed to find a moral or religious message, but we must remember that the Ben Macato Club was first and foremost a social sorority, an organization in which a group of friendly young women met and passed time together. One might extrapolate a little evidence from this program that James H. Wilson was, in his mature years, beginning to soften his hard-line stand on strict, conservative interpretations of Bible passages as spelled out in his first published article, "The Church and Dancing." Not only are two men included in the small chorus of "well marked women," but the back cover of his copy of the program has the pencil additions of four musical numbers offered on the program that evening, the second of which is a waltz, a social dance intended for a man and woman dancing together. His involvement in this program is certain, not just from the listing of his name as "organizer" but also from the pencil annotations in his own block print, where we can read that the fourth number on the program, "Maggie," is for "Brass Quartette." No one else on campus would have supervised

---

[12]Program booklet, Friday, April 24, 1931, Bibb Graves Hall, 8:00 p.m.

or directed a brass quartet on that campus but James H. Wilson, Sr. He ruled the roost in brass territory.

Wilson was close to his children. When he made a business trip to Norton, Virginia, in 1934, he bought a picture postcard depicting "Rough Waters in a Mountain Stream." He addressed it to his two youngest, "Karl T[almadge] & Bunk Wilson," using a nickname he invented for Marian Floredia. He wrote on this penny post card with its one-cent commemorative stamp celebrating Fort Dearborn and the Chicago Century of Progress:

Norton, Va.
May 10, 1934

> Daddy is thinking of you and am wondering if you are helping mamma all you can. Be real good and if mamma doesn't have any thing against you I'll give you something
> from
> Daddy

As James' children grew older and achieved some real competence in musical performance, he began to enjoy performing with them for campus audiences. Along with their musical lessons taken with their various campus teachers, including himself, they played recitals sponsored by their teachers. James got the idea to show them off all together and first scheduled a concert during the summer session for a program entitled "Wilson's Ensemble."

The ensemble consisted of all his children: James, Jr. on trumpet; Hester and Marian on piano; Karl on drums; plus six other musicians—five students playing two violins, two clarinets, and trumpet as well as James' friend from Nicholasville, Professor Thomas Elmore, on saxophone. Wilson, of course, conducted, and he also arranged the opening number, the refrain of "Universal March" by E. DeLamater, in an interesting way for this non-standard ensemble. The first chorus was played by two trumpets unaccompanied, and Wilson's son, James, Jr., played second trumpet. The next chorus was scored for two pianos and two violins, and President Drake's son, Harold, played second violin. The third chorus used both pianists, the two violins, both clarinets and the saxophone, and the fourth and final chorus was scored

WITH TRUMPET AND BIBLE

Figure 10-9 Front and back of Picture Postcard from James H. Wilson to Karl and Marian.

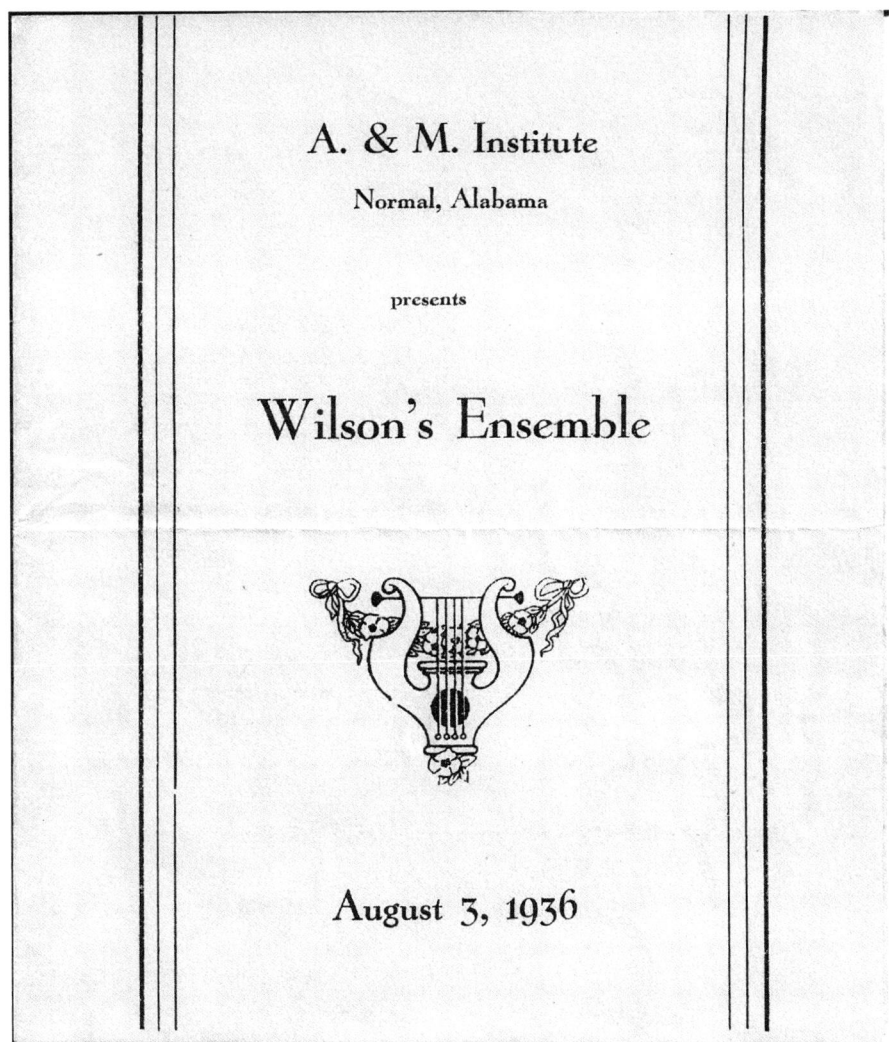

Figure 10-10. Program cover, Wilson's Ensemble, 1936.

for all. In this closing number, James' youngest son Karl at last joined in on drums. On one number, "The World is Waiting for the Sunrise," James picked up his trumpet and played a duet with his son, James, Jr. This long-lasting popular song, first published in 1919 by Gene Lockhart and Ernest Seitz, carried a message of hope that James surely felt at this point in his life:

Figure 10-11. Thirty Minutes with the Wilsons, July 27, 1938.

> Dear one, the world is waiting for the sunrise,
> Every rose is covered with dew.
> And while the world is waiting for the sunrise....

The success of this first family concert spurred Wilson to try a similar venture again the following summer, but this time in a slightly altered format, "Thirty Minutes with the Wilsons." These popular family concerts, intended as entertainment for the students and faculty during the summer term, continued for the remainder of the decade while James' children were still living at home. Though popularly received, no one enjoyed these programs more than the proud father.

And we can see that the listeners enjoyed the music as well. An anonymous writer reviewed the July 27th concert for the August, 1938, issue of *The Normal Index* and wrote:

MUSIC WITH THE WILSONS

> Prof. James H. Wilson is well known throughout the nation for his musical ability. His musical capacity has obviously been transferred to his children for each possesses an unusual musical ability. We had the pleasure of hearing the Wilson family in a thirty minutes program Wednesday . . . at the regular chapel exercises. Our hearts were thrilled by the quartets, duets, and solos rendered . . . . Everyone enjoyed each rendition. This fact was evident as each number was followed by hearty applause.[13]

James never let go of his solo career, but he never again pursued it as an independent professional. He played recitals on and away from campus frequently, but always as a representative of the Institute. A typical recital program might include other faculty performers, both to accompany but also to solo, as can be seen on this campus recital program from January of 1937. He was accompanied by Mrs. Lula Hopkins-Randall. Mrs. Hopkins-Randall must have had great skill in order to perform movements from the Liszt *Rhapsodie Hongroise*, a difficult recital piece. His colleague, Edward Johnson, sang Massenet and Tchaikovsky but also included two works by a contemporary African-American composer, J. Rosamond Johnson, a pianist, composer, and singer working in New York and a leading member of the Harlem Renaissance.[14]

---

[13]*The Normal Index* (August, 1938), p. 3.

[14]J. Rosamond Johnson is best known as the composer of "Lift Every Voice and Sing," a hymn popularly known in the United States as "The Black National Anthem." His brother, James Weldon Johnson contributed the lyrics. The music and words are available at: http://www.hymnary.org/hymn/UMH/519.

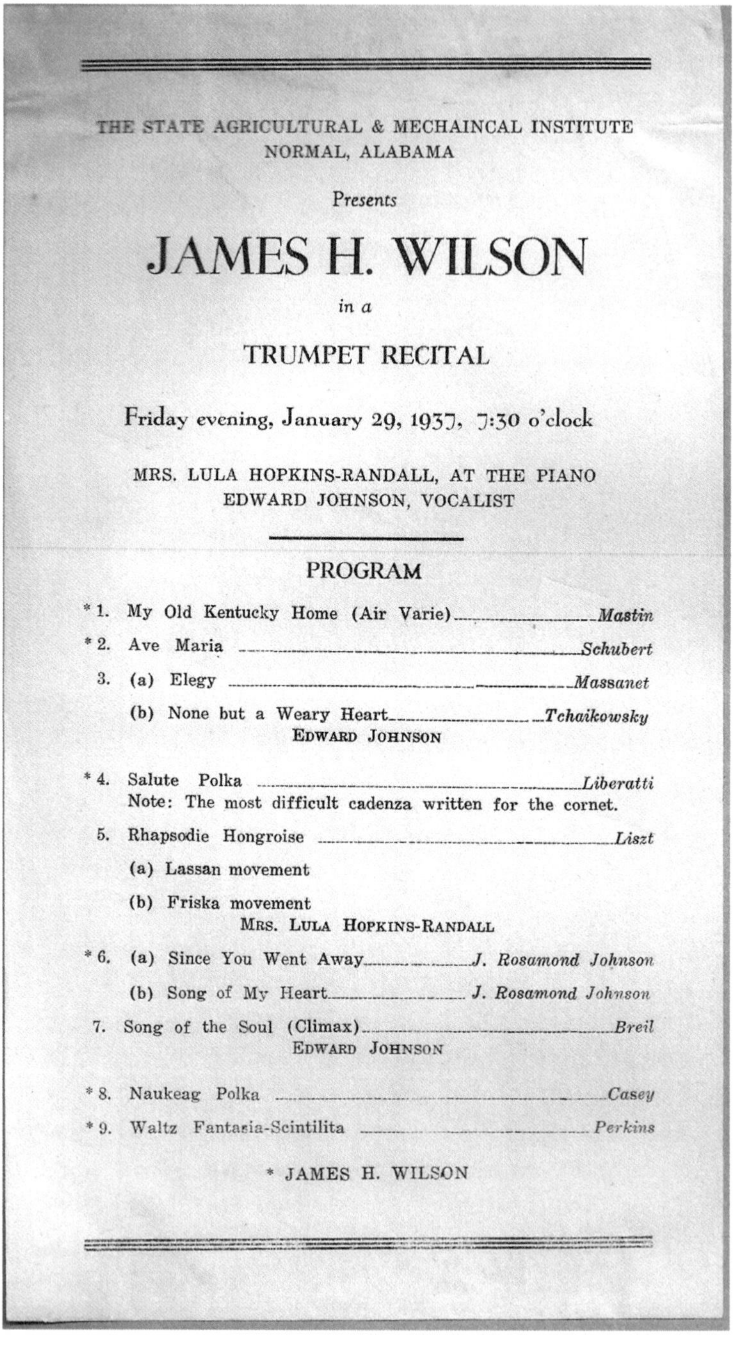

THE STATE AGRICULTURAL & MECHAINCAL INSTITUTE
NORMAL, ALABAMA

Presents

JAMES H. WILSON

in a

TRUMPET RECITAL

Friday evening, January 29, 1937, 7:30 o'clock

MRS. LULA HOPKINS-RANDALL, AT THE PIANO
EDWARD JOHNSON, VOCALIST

PROGRAM

* 1. My Old Kentucky Home (Air Varie) .... *Mastin*

* 2. Ave Maria .... *Schubert*

3. (a) Elegy .... *Massanet*

    (b) None but a Weary Heart .... *Tchaikowsky*
        EDWARD JOHNSON

* 4. Salute Polka .... *Liberatti*
    Note: The most difficult cadenza written for the cornet.

5. Rhapsodie Hongroise .... *Liszt*

    (a) Lassan movement

    (b) Friska movement
        MRS. LULA HOPKINS-RANDALL

* 6. (a) Since You Went Away .... *J. Rosamond Johnson*

    (b) Song of My Heart .... *J. Rosamond Johnson*

7. Song of the Soul (Climax) .... *Breil*
    EDWARD JOHNSON

* 8. Naukeag Polka .... *Casey*

* 9. Waltz Fantasia-Scintilita .... *Perkins*

* JAMES H. WILSON

Figure 10-12. Wilson recital program, January 29, 1937.

The program was varied—popular songs and dance settings, brief European classical pieces, and two numbers by a black composer. It is interesting to note that Wilson pointed out that "Salute Polka" contained "The most difficult cadenza written for the cornet." He was proud of his virtuosity and was not the least bit embarrassed to point it out to his audience. There may even have been a hint of vanity expressed in this announcement, too, just as one may have sensed some earlier when looking at the photographs displaying his sartorial elegance. James was a confident man with a strong sense of self-worth.

Sometime during the late 1930s Wilson accepted another responsibility, that of Associate Editor of the monthly journal, *The Normal Index*. How much time this involved is not known, for he shared responsibility with other colleagues, but one must remember that in addition to his appointment as Financial Secretary, he was the Superintendant of Sunday School, bandmaster, postmaster, sponsor of the Ben Macato Club, involved in the Y.M.C.A., faculty advisor of the Y.W.C.A., teacher of a correspondence course and a Sunday School Teacher course and a Bible class, author of religious articles, recitalist, and father and husband. Granted, he did not pursue each activity full time on every day, week and month, but being a good family man, with the help of his remarkable wife, was indeed a 24/7 responsibility he never shirked.

James youngest, Marian, had to delay entering college because of financial constraints, but she completed her two-year junior college program at A. & M. and received her diploma in Teacher Training at the May, 1939, commencement exercises. Having decided to pursue an undergraduate degree, she applied and was admitted to Virginia State College. During her college years, both her mother and her father wrote constantly—her mother about friends, relatives, and events:

Tuesday Nite 1/23/40

Dear Marian:

It is still snowing. I mean it is *deep*. We had to have [Mr.] Strong make a path for us. You had better come & get us, before the snow covers us all up . . . . The School children are having a big time Snow-balling & making Snow-men. Mr. Kendricks' In-laws' home burned Sunday. Well I hope this old house doesn't catch fire. . . .

Wednesday A.M. 1/24/40 P.S.

Well I woke up with a terrible neuralghis (misspelled I know). And it is still snowing. . . .

 Be sweet

  Mother[15]

Although James did not write as frequently as Marian's mother, a number of letters are preserved and they illustrate this father's care, approval, and willingness to help. One noticeable difference is that all of his were typed; all of hers were handwritten.

His first letter, little more than a note, was sent shortly after Marian's first semester began:

Hello Bunks:

Just a a line to let you know we are thinking of you. Every time we sit down to eat we think about the dishes and you. Well I am champene [sic] now. I beat your mother [in cards] last night 5 to 4.

We had band practice Monday and yesterday. I believe we are going to have a good band. I have about ~~thwenty~~ twenty-eight members. Little Glover isn't so hot – He'll learn however.

Well this is just a line. When you write tell us every thing and how you like and what you are doing. Don't work yourself to death now.

 DADDIE[16]

---

[15]Letter to Miss Marian F. Wilson from Mrs. Jas. H. Wilson, mailed January 24, 1940.

[16]Letter to Miss Marian Floredia Wilson from James H. Wilson, mailed September 21, 1939.

The Omnipresent Professor: 1930—1941

In a very interesting letter written during Marian's second semester we see that James' manner of fatherhood did not include demanding strict obedience to him, even in religion. Apparently, once the children reached a certain age, they were given the freedom to make their own decisions, in this case whether or not to be baptized. Also, there is some evidence that Wilson was struggling with the social issue of "Separate but [un]Equal":

Normal, Alabama

February 22, 1940

Dear Bunks

Virginia State College for Negroes only

You must pardon me for not answering your very interesting letter. I was glad to hear you say you made a profession of faith. I hope you will present yourself to some minister for baptism.[17] Good for you. I was very much pleased with your marks. I didn't expect a high grade in math, but you must be improving. We received Karl's grades and he is on probation this quarter. I hope he will pull up.... The Sunday School is moving on smoothly. The attendance is about 130. I am to be in Decatur [Alabama]Sunday to speak at the Presbyterian church at the morning service.... I am glad you saw Karl again. Write him and try to encourage to do better in his grades. You know what to write. Don't make him mad. Tell him you understand that he made fair marks.... I am glad you are well and doing so well. We speak of you every day. Your mother said if she hadn't heard from you she was coming up there and get you (SMILE) Be a good girl as usual.

DADDIE[18]

This letter provides us a glimpse of this father's love and concern for his children, even after they have left the nest. It tells a little of the success of his Sunday School program, and it reflects

---

[17] Apparently Marian had refused the more normal practice of professing her faith around age seven or eight and had waited until she was twenty years old. Most unusual for a member of a Baptist family whose father was so involved in religious teaching!

[18] Letter to Miss Marian F. Wilson from James H. Wilson, mailed February 23, 1940.

a little of his relationship with Karl. Like the Journal of 1908, these personal writings tell us much about the man's interaction with those he loves. On the envelope for this letter he typed:

>Miss Marian F Wilson
>
>Virginia State College

but on the letter itself, hidden from outside eyes, we find:

>Dear Bunks
>
>Virginia State College for Negroes only

In 1940, in Alabama and Virginia, he would have been risking serious repercussions for himself, his daughter, and perhaps all of his family were he to complain publicly about segregation and the imposition of Jim Crow laws on public facilities. James was a careful man, and this private but physically produced and visible statement comes as a genuine surprise. It may seem a little thing today, but it was no minor offense in the *de jure* segregated south of that era. The Ku Klux Klan was ever vigilant in Alabama.

In a letter sent at the beginning of Marian's second year at Virginia State, he writes of Marian's scholarship application, James, Jr.'s job application, and Exeline's letter with money.

>September 30, 1940
>
>Dear Marian;
>
>We received your letter with the scholarship blank. You will have to fill out where it asks for information about your expenditure for the past year.
>
>I appreciate your willingness to help. I hope you will do good work and make an impression. You can never tell what this will mean to you in the future. You must have made a wonderful impression last year for Mr. Singleton to recommend you.
>
>... James had a telegram from ~~Flodi~~ Florida asking him to send in his application [for a job] to Ft Pierce which is at the other end of the world.

... Your mother is sending you the money you asked for. Be a good girl.

DADDIE[19]

One of the more amusing communications sent to his daughter was mailed two months later, and it contained only seven words: "BUSY : HAVEN'T TIME TO WRITE   DAD."[20] Finally, in one more of the sixteen preserved letters James mailed to Marian when she was a student at Virginia State College, we learn for the first time that he is beginning to suffer health problems.

JAMES H. WILSON, SR.

NORMAL, ALABAMA

July 15, 1941

Dear Bunks ;

I was glad to get your letter . . . and thought I would write you. I note that you were very much concerned about me and that you are praying for me. I appreciate that very much.

Your daddy has been sick. I was all run down and had the malaria again. I lost four pounds in less than a week.

I am much better now and ready to go back to work this week and I am going to let your mother rest. She needs it. She has been suffering with neuritis. She has been to the doctor twice.

. . . . I haven't played this summer. I had a tooth put in front and find it hard to play. I've got to learn how to play on this tooth.

Karl and James are a great help to your mother. Karl washes the dishes and works in the post office and drives occasionally. James works around the yard keeping the grass cut and doing whatever he sees what is to be done.

---

[19]Letter to Mrs [stet] Marian Floredia Wilson from James H. Wilson, mail September 30, 1940.
[20]Letter to Miss Marian Floredia Wilson from Office of the Financial Secretary, mailed November 30, 1940.

.... I must close now.... Continue to be a good girl   for

  - Daddy - [21]

We do not know where or when James contracted malaria. This letter gives the first mention of this illness in the documents preserved. James was not a large man and throughout his life he remained quite thin. Losing four pounds in one week meant losing a noticeable percentage of his total body weight, an indication of the severity of the attack. Additionally, the loss of a front tooth for a high-brass player deserves special comment. A cornetist or trumpeter controls pitch, volume, and tone by vibrating the lips which are pressed against the front teeth by the mouthpiece of the instrument. Whether Wilson's tooth replacement was an implant, which would be highly unlikely for a black man in 1941,[22] or a dental bridge with its fastening wires, the loss and replacement of a front tooth would be a shattering experience to any professional musician whose career depended on embouchure control. For many non-musicians the loss of a front tooth might seem nothing more than a cosmetic issue, but for a master trumpet player it would usually spell the end of a career. Once again we see James meeting a serious challenge and saying, "I've got to learn how to play on this tooth." In so many ways this man's spirit is indomitable.

Not many months later, on December 7, 1941, the Japanese bombed Pearl Harbor, the United States joined the allies and entered into World War II, and James commenced his final decade of service at the Alabama A. & M. Institute.

CHAPTER ELEVEN

The War and Post-War Years: 1941-1951

The social and intellectual climate at Normal showed signs of change as the war in Europe began to affect concerned citizens in the United States. On campus in 1940 the second-year junior-college students presented a program on "Negroes in the Arts." Up to this time the curriculum and the public programs of A. & M. may have included a work or two by African-American artists, but the meat and potatoes of the "serious" repertoire in the old days was Shakespeare, Wordsworth, and Longfellow or Bach, Schubert, and Rossini, masters of the Western European classical tradition.[1] This time the evening program in Bibb Graves Auditorium was dedicated to the theme, "The Negro is a contributor to America." In the printed program one finds the quotation of a now famous poem by Langston Hughes, poet laureate of the Harlem Renaissance, a beautiful and complicated work. The poem both praises and criticizes the country he loves, and these black Alabama students, in the midst of the racism and prejudice that surrounded the protective environment of their Alabama A. & M. campus, found the need to proclaim these defiant words in print in their program:

---

[1] As if in confirmation of this statement, the program of the Institute's Commencement Exercises that year, May 27, 1940, included four musical numbers on the program: a processional— "War March of the Priests" by German composer Felix Mendelssohn; a brass ensemble number—an arrangement of "In the Gloaming" by English composer Annie Fortescue Harrison; an anthem— "Inflammatus" from the *Stabat Mater* by Gioachino Rossini; and an anonymous spiritual—"Fare You Well."

> I am the darker brother
> They send me to the kitchen when company comes.
> But I laugh and eat well, and grow strong
> Tomorrow I'll sit at the table when company comes.
> And no body will dare say to me eat in the kitchen then.
>
> —Langston Hughes.[2]

Remarkably, this poem, "I, too, sing America," was not published until 1945, five years after this evening's presentation at Normal and almost two decades before the Civil Rights Movement became powerful in the late 1950s and 1960s. How the A. & M. students received a copy of the work or what correspondence or interaction they may have had with Hughes is not known, but it seems clear that this moment signaled the birth of a new intellectual climate on campus that seems to have few, if any, noteworthy precedents in the years before. On the cover of the program Wilson wrote in pencil, "Rotten." Whether this referred to the quality of the evening's performance or was actually his opinion of the ideas presented is difficult to determine. We know he was more than aware of racial injustice and that he was outspoken in his efforts to help lift up his people, but it seems that the core of his belief lay not in defiance and open anger but in bettering oneself and demonstrating merit and accomplishment. The Christian message of love not hate was the path he proclaimed, even though the racial hatred and segregation in the south touched close to home. As Christ taught his followers:

---

[2]Hughes' poem as printed in the student program differs from the final version published by Hughes in 1945. Clearly influenced by Walt Whitman's "One's-Self I sing" and "I hear America singing," the published version reads:

> I, too, sing America.
>
> I am the darker brother.
> They send me to eat in the kitchen
> When company comes,
> But I laugh,
> And eat well,
> And grow strong.
>
> Tomorrow,
> I'll be at the table
> When company comes

> Nobody'll dare
> Say to me,
> "Eat in the kitchen,"
> Then.
>
> Besides,
> They'll see how beautiful I am
> And be ashamed--
>
> I, too, am America.

Figure 11-1. Sophomore Class Night Program, "Negroes In the Arts."

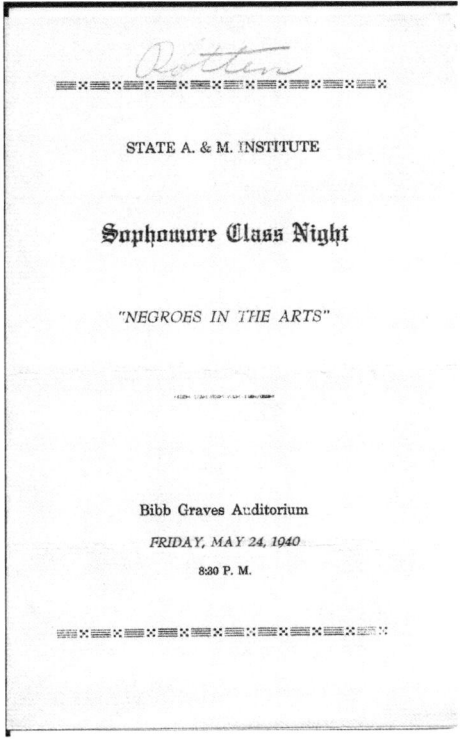

But I say unto you, Love your enemies, bless them that curse you, do good to them that hate you, and pray for them that despitefully use you, and persecute you;
[Matthew 5:44]

It is indeed possible he approved of neither the evening's performance nor the subsurface anger expressed in some of the evening program's content.

Wilson's musical activities remained lively at the beginning of this decade, but as his health became more fragile, he started to use student assistants, and for the first time some were listed on the programs—Wallace Huff, Chief Musician; Lucius Daniels, Principle Musician; Richmond Belle, Librarian; Phillip Cooper and Annie Ruth DeVaughn, Librarians.[3] It may have been partly the result of changing times in college band music as well, for when Wilson began his tenure at A. & M., his bands would number fifteen to twenty players at most, including boys from the grade school and high school. The November 15, 1940, concert program showed thirty-six musicians on the roster, all college students and at least two of these were women—Annie Ruth DeVaughn, horn, and Urtha Pearson, trombone. They and a few other women are shown in the band photo (Figure 11-2), including a woman majorette or baton twirler. Times were changing indeed,

---

[3]Programs, Band Concerts, April 25 and November 15, 1940, and continuing.

ALABAMA A. & M. COLLEGE BAND - NORMAL

Figure 11-2. The Modern A. & M. Band. New uniforms, more members, women musicians, and a majorette.

but vestiges of the past show as well. In the same photo, Urtha Pearson, the trombonist, was wearing high heels, a precarious article of clothing for a member of the marching band. Perhaps it was just window dressing for the photo session, but most likely not.

President Drake had been granted permission in 1939 to add a third year to the Junior College program, and he was likewise allowed in 1940 to add a fourth year to complete the undergraduate curriculum. A short time later the Institute became once more the Alabama Agricultural and Mechanical College, but in the meantime it was the Institute that awarded college degrees again at the 1941 baccalaureate.[4]

During this same period the United States Congress passed a compulsory Selective Military Service Act, and President Drake was appointed the chief registering officer for Normal, Alabama. On October 16, 1940, one-hundred-fifty students and faculty between the ages of twenty-one and thirty-five registered for the draft.[5] When

---

[4]Morrison, *History of Alabama Agricultural and Mechanical University*, p. 188.
[5] "150 Register on Conscription Day," *The Collegiate Digest*, v. 6, n.2 (October 19, 1940), p. 1.

reporters asked students what they thought of the draft, responses varied, of course, but one young coed's reply to an interviewer made clear the campus's awareness of the impending war:

> The United States should be preparing for war because most of the European countries are at war and it seems as though the United States will be drawn into war soon. The army should be well trained and the United States should still be preparing to have a sufficient number of men and war supplies to have a strong army and navy.
>
> Doris Mae Mitchell[6]

Students had, and expressed, opinions about other matters as well. New issues were beginning to surface in the 1940s that had been repressed or ignored in the past. We have already noted the new interest in a greater emphasis on African-American artists, in women entering domains formerly restricted to men only, and on more attention to world affairs. Then, for the first time, open criticism of the importance allotted to religion and compulsory attendance at religious services and events bubbled up. An unsigned article, "The Role of Religion in College Life," was published in *The Normal Index* in 1940. It was almost certainly the work of the Reverend Henry Bradford, chaplain of the college.

In it he wrote:

> The role played by religion in college life is generally thought to be influenced by the nature of the college, its history as well as by influences affecting its founding and early development....
>
> The founder of the State Agricultural & Mechanical Institute, and its president for 35 years was an ordained minister, a devout churchman, and a believer in the value of religion as a part of the educational process. Though the school became a State institution soon after its founding, during the 65 years of its history, emphasis upon religion and religious activities has been comparable to that found in many of the church colleges....

---

[6]"Student Comment," *The Collegiate Digest*, v. 6, n.2 (October 19, 1940), p. 2.

Figure 11-3. The Rev. Dr. Henry Bradford, Jr., Chaplain of Alabama A. & M. Institute and College.

Out of a total enrollment of 533 students, only 27 do not claim church membership, with 309 belonging to the Baptist denomination and 142 divided among three branches of Methodism. . . .

. . . . Evidences of indifference toward the program merely reflect the growing tendency of the general community within recent years to discredit religion. On the campus the influence of the increasing skepticism of youth and the attitudes of some workers toward the program are contributing factors to the apparent lag. . . .

Wherever we have heard rumblings in the camp with reference to too much religion or too many religious exercises, we have often discovered that the objections were not based on feeling that the sharing of such experiences had no contribution to make to the student's own personal growth, but rather upon a feeling influenced by some contact that participation in religion programs was not the collegiate thing to do in this modern age of educational liberalism.[7]

All of these signs of change at the newly restored four-year degree-granting college had a direct impact on the professional and personal life of James Hembray Wilson, Superintendent of the Sunday School, sponsor of the campus Y.M.C.A. and Y.W.C.A. groups, director of a military style band that had, for decades, been a bastion of male exclusivity. Then, at the age of sixty years and with a noticeably weakening body, he began his final years of service to the institution he loved, the college that had given him so much—his wife, a home and family, security, education for his children, meaningful work, respect and prestige—so much, indeed. How would he meet the new challenges? In some ways, "Head on!"; in other instances we see a moderation of his views and a slowing down as he neared retirement.

James' Sunday School activities, both chapel and class, slowed not at all. His 1941 Sunday School Teacher Training Class of nineteen students not only met regularly but staged a dramatic production for the students, *The Story of Ruth*.[8] Here, as with his band, Wilson was beginning to master the arts of asking for help and delegating authority. Miss Placidia E. Thigpen, Dean of Women, directed the play while his colleague in music, Samuel W. Hill, the choir director and college organist, provided or supervised most of the music. Likewise, when a new swing orchestra emerged on campus, Wilson did not assume the leadership of the group himself as was his custom in the past for all instrumental ensembles. Instead, he left it in the hands of a student, "Lil Henry"

---

[7] [Rev. Dr. Henry Bradford, Jr.], "The Role of Religion in College Life, *The Normal Index*, v. 22, n. 2 (February, 1940), pp. 3 and 10. The style of writing of this article shows definitely that this is not the work of Wilson. Since the author claims to represent "the religious tradition of the institution," I have assumed it must be the Chaplain or the President. Were it the latter, surely his name would have appeared as author.
[8] Program of the Sunday School Teacher Training Class, *The Story of Ruth*, presented in Bibb Graves Auditorium, March 23, 1941.

WITH TRUMPET AND BIBLE

Figure 11-4. Invitation booklet to the 65th Commencement Exercises, cover.

MR. THOMAS M. ELMORE

We, the class of 1941, dedicate this invitation to Mr. Thomas M. Elmore in recognition of his devoted service to A. and M. Institute.

Figure 11-5. Dedication page of 1941 Commencement Exercises Invitation Booklet.

Glover, who also wrote the arrangements for the dance band.[9] And notice, it was a *dance* band in the current swing style that was functioning on campus. However, James' regular trumpet recitals and occasional solos in church and elsewhere continued apace as he began to overcome the problems associated with his tooth extraction and replacement bridge.

May of 1941 brought a triumphant celebration to the Normal campus on the occasion of the sixty-sixth annual commencement exercises. Once again the Institute was able to award four-year college degrees after many years of junior college status. Wilson could not help but be pleased to see that his longtime friend, student, and colleague from Nicholasville, Professor Thomas Elmore, received the dedication of the commencement invitation booklet.

Of course James was doubly pleased to find himself the dedicatee of the 1941 *Bulldog*, the college yearbook of the graduating class, and he bought an extra copy, signed it, and sent it to his daughter Marian.

The dedication reads:

> To our dear Financial Secretary who has labored so diligently for A. & M. Institute for nearly two score years; a natural businessman; a musician by avocation; a loyal and true Normalite; a person respected by all his associates; do we, the members of the class of 1941, humbly dedicate this volume.

The love and respect these graduating seniors held for "Professor" Wilson is truly remarkable. "To our dear Financial Secretary." This is the man that takes money from the students! It is amazing that these men and women who were about to receive college degrees earned from a well-educated and experienced faculty might be humbled by this high school graduate. They recognized, one way or another, that Wilson was truly an extraordinary human being.

---

[9]*The State A. & M. Campus Journal*, v. 7, n. 3 (February 15, 1941), p. 2. Trumpeter Henry Bernard Glover, after graduating from Alabama A. & M. in 1943, went on to become a successful music recording business executive, working with Lucky Millinder, Sonny Stitt, Sarah Vaughan, and Dinah Washington among many others.

Figure 11-6. Dedication page of the 1941 *Bulldog*.

Over the years, James Hembray Wilson maintained a long-lasting and long-distance friendship with W. C. Handy. The world-famous composer and trumpet soloist periodically received invitations to campus for concerts of his music or to address the students. On every visit he made a point of spending time with his old friend and minstrel colleague, James H. Wilson. Marian, Wilson's youngest child, remembered, when in her 90s:

The War and Post-War Years: 1941-1951

He [Handy] must have come there [to Normal] for concerts. I think that was the reason why he was there. Of course, he and my father knew each other very well, and I remember that when he used to come onto campus he was very anxious to see my father. And he would . . . [pause, chuckle, and restart] We had two dogs, and the dogs would not let anybody come to the house. The dogs would stop them some distance away. And I remember him coming to the house and him calling to my father because the dogs were after him.[10]

On the Founder's Day program of 1945, W. C. Handy delivered the Founder's Day Address. In the following photograph we see James sitting in the background at the far end of the stage and Handy, standing behind a small podium, speaking into two microphones, one for amplification and one for recording. Two members of the State Commission are seated on stage behind Handy, and behind these two men are pictured a few student members of the band. In the foreground we view two unidentified women, one in a patterned dress and one in white. James, in suit and bow tie, leans forward, turns his head to the right, and listens intently. Handy was a well-educated man and a fluent speaker, and in this photo, standing in his tuxedo, he uses his hands expressively, almost as if conducting a musical ensemble. He clearly is speaking either from memory or extemporaneously, for he would never be able to read his notes from the knee-high table top set up as a podium.

Although James and Handy maintained a correspondence that lasted over many years, only eight letters from Handy to Wilson have been preserved. These date from June of 1942 to March of 1953, an interesting period in the lives of both men. All of Handy's letters carry cordial and respectful messages to his old friend. In June of 1942 Handy responded to a letter written to him by James:

My dear Friend Wilson:

I have your letter before me, and now I can tell you why it has been so long since I wrote.

---

[10]Interview with Marian F. Wilson Turner, September 20, 2010.

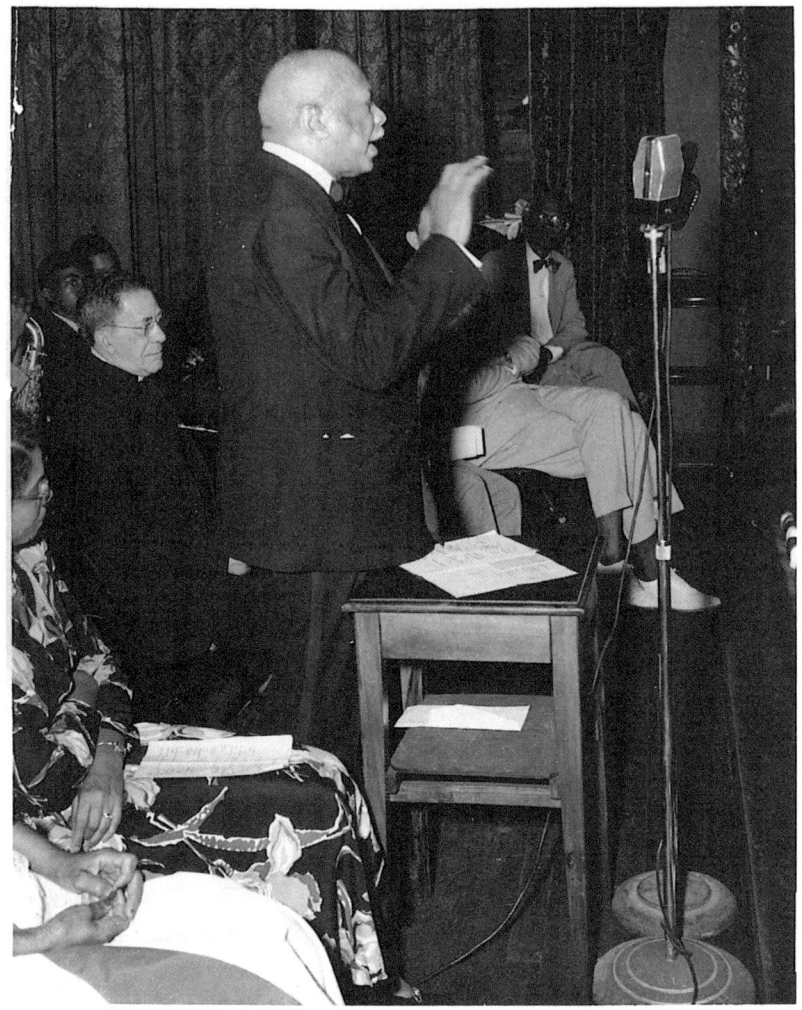

Figure 11-7. "Father of the Blues" W. C. Handy speaking at Alabama A. & M. Wilson looks on, far right

Some of your friends had me to intercede for you on Hobby Lobby Program with Dave Elman,[11] to come to New York to give a specimen of your fine trumpet playing. . . .

---

[11]Hobby Lobby was a popular radio show hosted by Dave Elman. People were invited to present their own unusual hobby to a studio audience and lobby for more attention to that particular hobby.

THE WAR AND POST-WAR YEARS: 1941-1951

This first of the preserved letters is presented in reproduction in its entirety below:

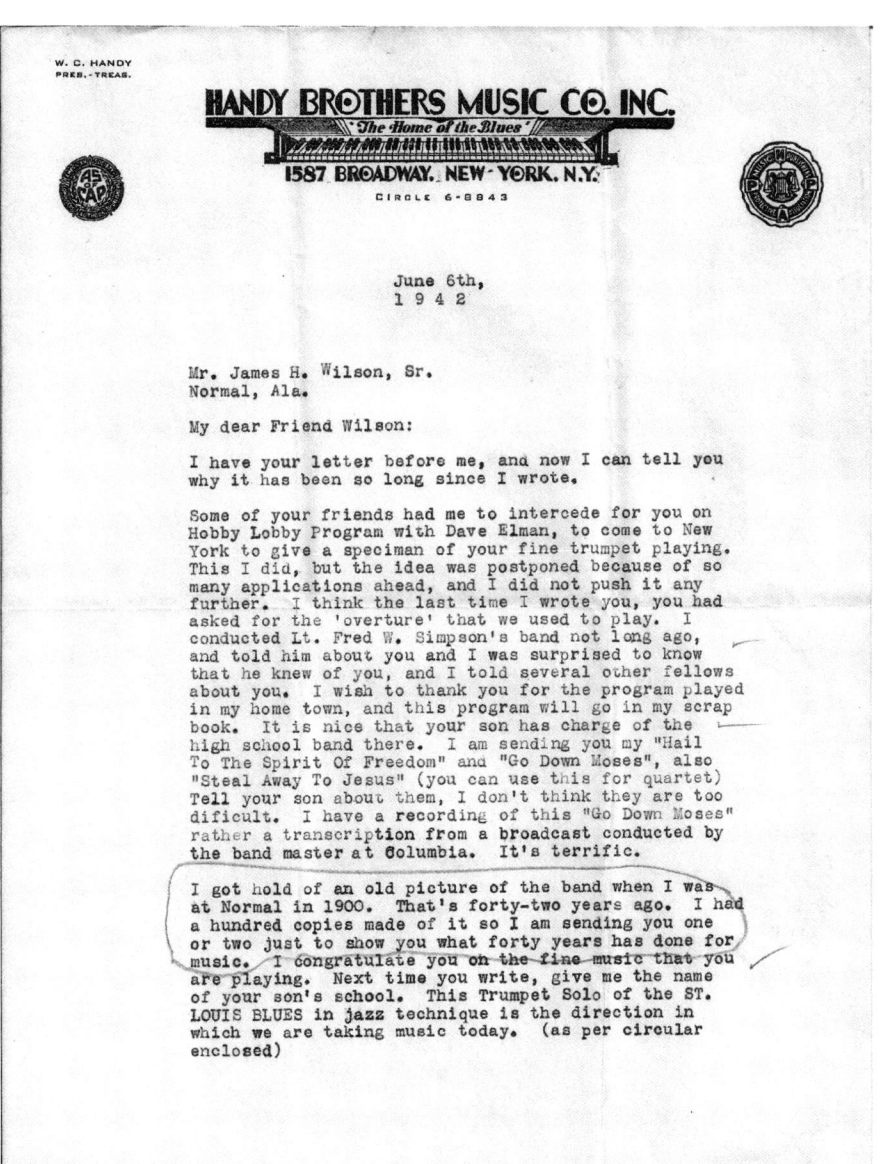

Figure 11-8. Letter from W. C. Handy to James H. Wilson, June 6, 1942, page 1

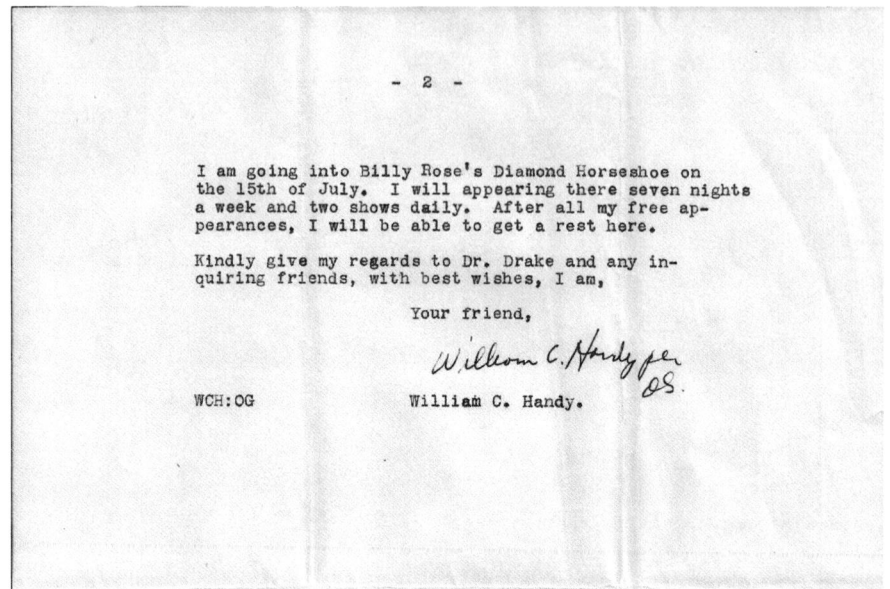

Figure 11-9. Letter from W. C. Handy to James H. Wilson, June 6, 1942, page 2.

The circular referred to in the letter advertises Handy's publication of Leonard Sues' arrangement of Handy's "Saint Louis Blues," and the reverse side shows a sample of the music for piano and trumpet. Just above the photo of the trumpet player a small rectangle displays a patriotic flag presenting thirteen stars and a vigilant colonial minuteman. The text reads: "*Pledge Your Support.* BUY WAR SAVINGS BONDS AND STAMPS." During World War II the government encouraged Americans to buy war bonds to help support the war effort. A bond purchased for $18.75 could be redeemed in ten years for $25.00. Children were encouraged to buy savings stamps in smaller amounts and to paste them into booklets which, when full, could be redeemed at the post office for a paid-up war bond. Handy, in publishing and distributing his advertisement, was also performing a patriotic duty.

The letter also refers to a 1900 photograph of Handy with his A. & M. band, and someone, perhaps Wilson, circled this passage in the letter in pencil. Wilson owned a copy of the 1900 band photograph, and it is used for illustration in the Prologue, Figure P-1.

The War and Post-War Years: 1941-1951

Handy wrote again in August of that year to report that he was playing "two shows a night at the Diamond Horseshoe, including Sunday nights."[12] In this letter he responds to a comment Wilson made about A. & M. in an earlier letter and offers understanding and advice:

> I can understand how you feel about losing your best players as they leave school [for the army and navy] but imagine you should have grown used to it by this time. It is strange how one can adapt himself to certain conditions. When I had a professional band I couldn't stand for trivial mistakes or a note out of tune and it would get on my nerves and disturb me mentally, and yet when teaching beginners the most outlandish noises didn't disturb me as long as they were making some sort of progress.

In the same letter he explained his own method of letter writing—he dictates and signs. In this case it is a daughter who was taking the dictation and typing the letter.

In July of 1943 Handy wrote Wilson again, and we can feel the closeness of their friendship as Handy unloads about overworking himself. He was still playing with the Billy Rose show, but then it had been taken on the road. He wrote, "Have been working about sixteen to eighteen hours a day, and you know that is too much. It has dulled my mind and made it almost impossible for me to think clearly." Indeed, the load was too much for the 70-year-old "Father of the Blues," and in December of 1943 Handy wrote his Alabama friend to tell him, "... the doctors have ordered me to discontinue business and correspondence. I was two weeks in the hospital without knowing what happened or where I was."[13] Handy had suffered a fall off a subway platform in New York City, and though he did not say it in his letter, Wilson's old friend had been partially blinded. A few months later Julius J. Adams, a reporter for the *New York Amsterdam-News*, wrote of his visit to Handy's home for an interview and reported that the composer's "... sight is not so

---

[12]Letter from W. C. Handy to James H. Wilson, Sr., August 12, 1942. The Diamond Horseshoe was a famous New York nightclub owned by impresario Billy Rose.
[13]Letter from W. C. Handy to James H. Wilson, Sr., December 13, 1943.

Figure 11-10. (2 pages) Circular enclosed in Handy's letter to Wilson.

The War and Post-War Years: 1941-1951

good and he has to feel his way about, but he is most cheerful."[14]

The overwork and illness of Handy may have started Wilson scrutinizing his own situation He had already resigned his government job as campus postmaster effective June 30, 1942,[15] but since Exeline had run the shop in his stead, that resignation had little effect on his daily activities. Then, around 1945, he approached President Drake to explain that he felt it was time for a younger man to take over his responsibilities as Director of the band. One might well imagine the enormity of that decision. James continued directing for another academic year while Drake searched for his replacement, and in September of 1947, the opening issue of *The Normal Index* for the Fall Semester announced:

Full-Time Bandmaster Named

For the first time in its history, the State A. & M. Institute has a full time bandmaster this year. He is Mr. W[ilton]. V. Robertson, formerly a teacher in the Birmingham public schools and was, during the war, a member of the USA AF [Air Force] Band.

Already since Mr. Robertson came to the campus in July, a large number of musical instruments have been purchased. . . .

In addition to the purchase of instruments, the school has purchased a repertory of classic, semi-classic and popular music for use of the prospective band.[16]

The following year, 1948-1949, Wilson took over the band once again when "Mr. Robertson, the band director for the 1947-1948 academic year, failed to return the following year."[17] The tired and ailing 67-year-old Wilson would never abandon his beloved college or band in a time of need, but now he was replacing a full-time director, and the concerts, games, and additional programs away from campus had started to become a heavy burden. He was beginning to show signs of wear. No wonder!

---

[14]Julius J. Adams, "Movie Of The Life Of 'Father Of The Blues' Suggested," *New York Amsterdam-News*, (May 6, 1944.

[15]Oscar Smith, "U. S. Post Office Completes 31 Years on College Campus," *The Normal Index Supplement*, v. 30, New Series (May 1, 1948), p. 4.

[16]*The Normal Index*, v. 30, n. 1 (September, 1947), p. 5.

[17]"W. C. Handy Once Directed A. & M. Band," *The Normal Index*, v. 32, n.4 (December 1949), p. 6.

THE WAR AND POST-WAR YEARS: 1941-1951

College Band Gives Concert On And Off Campus

When the bandmaster failed to return last fall after summer vacation, Mr. J. H. Wilson, a veteran hand at directing bands of high caliber. . . .

At a recent performance at Oakwood College, the following program was rendered:

>March United......................J. H. Wilson
>
>Poet and Peasant..................Suppe
>
>Wedding of the Winds...........Hall
>
>My Old Kentucky Home.... .....Dalby
>
>American Patrol...................Meacham
>
>Princess of India..................King
>
>Roberteen Polka..................J. H. Wilson
>
>Il Trovatore........................Arr. Hayes
>
>The Lost Chord................... Sullivan
>
>March, Americans We........... Fillmore
>
>Retreat
>
>Our National Anthem
>
>Taps[18]

This article is interesting because it implies much about Wilson's situation—the band, which was close to James' heart, and A. & M. in general. That his replacement as band director failed to return in the fall confirms the difficulty Drake had to face with every attempt to hire qualified faculty and keep them on the roster. The school, then as now, constantly had to deal with inadequate funds, and the pool of qualified, degree-bearing African-Americans was insufficient to supply the many academic positions available to them across the country.[19] When James was allowed to resign his

---

[18]*The Normal Index*, v. 31, n. 1 (September, 1948), p. 13.

position as bandmaster after the 1947 spring commencement, he was kept on as "consultant" for the band, an unpaid responsibility, a listing that lasted until his retirement in 1951. So now, the tired and ageing man not only shouldered all the band responsibilities, but its membership was as large as it had ever been. At the end of the above article we find a listing of all the college band members who played at that first concert of the season, and there were thirty men and eight women, and these names did not include the drum majors or baton twirlers who marched at the football games or homecoming parade through the streets of Huntsville. Directing the band had become a more complicated responsibility.

The program, too, indicates not only that Wilson was still composing and arranging pieces for the band—Roberteen Polka is a new concert number, but last year's purchases of music for Mr. Robertson added a few pieces that had not been programmed by Wilson in the past. The "American Patrol" march by Frank W. Meacham, although composed long before, became an American radio and recording hit during World War II when it was arranged by Jerry Gray for Glenn Miller's swing orchestra. "The Lost Chord" by Sir Arthur Sullivan is another number of enduring popularity that Wilson had not seen fit to program before. But once again we discover a "classic" concert band favorite, Franz von Suppé's romantic *Poet and Peasant* Overture. In 1948, with a more sizable band and more experienced players than when he began work at A. & M. forty years earlier, he could program these light-classic warhorses and give a respectable public performance. He surely enjoyed this work, but it was wearing him down.

President Drake found a satisfactory replacement for Wilson in the next academic year, Mr. Jonathan Ford, and the college was very pleased with Ford's work. But once again, the new man did not see A. & M. as a long-term commitment, and he left after two years, in 1951, the year of James H. Wilson's retirement. While Jonathan Ford watched over Wilson's band, other matters of particular significance to Wilson took place at the end of this decade.

---

[19]Morrison, *History of Alabama Agricultural and Mechanical University*, pp. 199ff.

Figure 11-11. W. C. Handy, Benefit Concert Program Cover.

Wilson's friend, W. C. Handy agreed to sponsor and attend a benefit concert in his own hometown of Florence, Alabama, and he invited James to join the program as a featured soloist.

The proceeds of the concert were to go to the building fund of the parish named in honor of Blessed Martin de Porres, the patron saint[20] of mixed race people, a man especially revered by African-American Catholics. On the program that Sunday afternoon, the Mayor of Florence spoke and the manager of the Florence Chamber of Commerce presented Handy with a gift from the city. James, accompanied by his friend, the Rev. Henry Bradford, played two numbers on his trumpet, a ballad composed by British violinist Teresa del Riego in 1901, "O Dry Those Tears," and another lyrical solo by Italian/British composer Sir Francesco Tosti, composed in 1880, "Good-Bye!"

The two old friends, Wilson and Handy, once again shared a concert program. In a strangely similar manner to their relationship in minstrel days when one conducted and the other performed, that particular Sunday saw one speak and the other play. Why no works of Handy were performed that day by anyone on the program remains a mystery, especially for such an occasion in the composer's hometown, the city that today offers tourists a visit to the log cabin that is the W. C. Handy Home and Museum. As for Wilson, he loved the romantic ballads of the late 19th- and early 20th-centuries, and he may never have given a second thought to the possibility that he might be doing his friend an injustice by choosing Tosti rather than Handy.

The end of this decade was good for Wilson both on the job and at home. His children were now grown and succeeding. The oldest, Hester, earned her Master's Degree from Columbia University while her husband, Charles Orr, pursued his Ph.D. from the same institution. James, Jr. was an instructor of printing at the Hampton Institute in Virginia, and Karl, after serving his tour of duty with the army, found employment as a coils tester at the Western Electric Company in Baltimore.

---

[20]Canonized in 1962.

Program

Prelude	No Love Like Thine
	Arranged by Edwards

Burrell High School Brass Sextette
Mrs. Alma Robinson, Directress

Star Spangled Banner	Audience
Invocation	Father Isidore, O. S. B.

Pastor Blessed Martin de Porres Parish
Florence, Ala.

The Lord's Prayer	Malotte

Miss Ernestyne Whiteside
Accompanist—Miss Doris M. Watkins

Welcome Address	Hon. E. F. Yeilding

Mayor of Florence

Ave Maria	Schubert, Bach-Gounod
Agnus Dei	Bizet

Miss Ernestyne Whiteside

O Dry Those Tears
Tosti's Goodbye

Mr. James H. Wilson
Accompanist—Mr. Henry Bradford
Alabama A. & M. College

Let Us Break Bread Together	Miss Rubye Doss
Italian Street Song	Miss Wendolyn Wallace
Ritual Fire Dance	De Salla
Country Gardens	Grainger

Mr. Henry Bradford

Selections	Mrs. Nell Bradford
Introduction of Mr. W. C. Handy	Mr. James Wilson
Contribution	Mr. W. C. Handy
Presentation of Gift	Mr. C. H. Jackson

Manager of Florence Chamber of Commerce

God Bless America	Audience

Figure 11-12. W. C. Handy, Benefit Concert Program, June 12, 1949.

Figure 11-13. Karl Wilson at Camp Ellis, Illinois.

Figure 11-14. Marian and John Turner, 1948.

The youngest, Marian, worked as Secretary to the President of Atlanta University, and in 1947 announced her engagement to John Brister Turner, a graduate of Morehouse College and a former Tuskegee Airman. One day, Turner would distinguish himself in the field of social work as editor-in-chief of the 1977 edition of the *Encyclopedia of Social Work* and as Dean of the School of Social Work at the University of North Carolina. All in all James and Exeline had much to enjoy in their family.

At work, two significant events in the life of Wilson occurred on campus before James' retirement. In 1947 he was promoted to Treasurer of Alabama Agricultural and Mechanical College,[21] and in 1951, the year of his retirement, the college saw fit to celebrate a James H. Wilson Appreciation Day, the first of its kind and perhaps the last. The promotion was more than honorary, indeed more than just a change in title. It was not just an honor bestowed on a faithful and elderly associate, for along with the promotion, another man, Leander Patton, was hired to replace Wilson and serve the college as Financial Secretary. Never before had Wilson been given a paid employee to help him in his work. And if, as the first African American

---

[21]Fleming and Burckel, *Who's Who in Colored America*, p. 565.

Figure 11-15. Treasurer Wilson and Financial Secretary Patton at work in the business office, 1950.

to carry the designation "Treasurer" at A. & M., he had even greater control of the money of the college in this southern state where real control of the college funds had been carefully overseen by Caucasian eyes, this change would note an historic event. The bookkeeper and the financial secretary kept records, receipted monies received, and paid expenditures from allocated funds. By definition, the treasurer was the person in charge of the treasury, the person *in charge* of the college's money. This financial power may have been more fiction than fact in Alabama in 1947, but times were changing, and he was participating fully in an important event of the day.

In 1950 as the college celebrated its 75th anniversary, the members of the A. & M. Alumni Association published a booklet filled with pictures of familiar campus scenes. One of the photographs showed Treasurer Wilson in his office with Financial Secretary Patton near at hand working at his desk.

Beneath the identifying caption the alumni editor wrote:

Figure 11-16. Souvenir Booklet, Founder's Day Celebration with Wilson's annotation on the cover.

This is a familiar scene to all Alumni and students of the College, for all persons matriculating at the Alabama A. and M. College must deal with the business office personnel. Mr. Wilson and Mr. Patton work hard to keep financial records, accounts, and reports up to date. "Efficiency" is the word that explains their activities.[22]

---

[22]John Thomas, ed., *The Heritage 1950* (Normal, AL: Education Club of the Alabama Agricultural and Mechanical College, 1950), p.25.

Seven Faculty Members Have Served 25 Years or Longer

Recognition is given here to the seven faculty members of the Alabama A. & M. College who have given 25 years or more of service as teacher or associate of the college family.

Mr. James H. Wilson
This year Mr. Wilson is rounding out 46 years of service at the college.

Had it been possible for Mr. James H. Wilson to have 4 more years on the staff before this celebration of the Seventy-Fifth Anniversary of the Alabama A. & M. College, he should have been entitled to a double portion of the recognition accorded those ending 25 years of service at the college, for then he would have rounded out exactly 50 years as a man of many responsibilities. He breaks a record in tenure, nevertheless, for he is the only member on the college staff who has served under all four presidents of the college.

Something would seem amiss at Normal should the student's eye run through the faculty pages of the school catalog and not find there the name, J. H. Wilson, or go to the business office window, to Sunday School, to the band room, or walk down the street and not see the little wafer of a man with the searching look in the eye, the black goatee, the little grin, and hear the hissing chuckle of friendliness.

There's something about music and Bible that entrances Mr. Wilson, and he cannot let go of either. When he was very young he acquired the ambition to teach music in a college, but he also wanted to give service in religious areas. He has been a student of Bible, therefore, since youth and in more recent years he studied theology for a time and took a course in Bible science from the Moody Bible School of Chicago.

As to becoming a teacher of music in a college, his dream

19

Figure 11-17. Wilson's recognition in the Founder's Day booklet for years of service.

THE WAR AND POST-WAR YEARS: 1941-1951

The College celebrated the seventy-fifth anniversary of its founding for five days in May of 1950. Various events and exhibits took place during the formal observance of this historic occasion: a play on May 3rd, an educational conference during the day and a musical concert in the evening of the 5th, and a Founder's Commemoration Exercise on Sunday, the 7th. A souvenir program booklet was prepared and printed by the college, and in it seven faculty members were singled out for having served the college for twenty-five or more years. James, of course, was first on the list.

Wilson wrote on the cover, "See inside   J H W, Sr." Obviously he was pleased with something and sent this copy to his daughter, Marian. On page 19 we see what he wanted to share with her (Figure 11-17, above).

In spite of a few noticeable health problems, these were good times for James Hembray Wilson. As a much loved and respected father figure of his academic community, he was, in these years, receiving public recognition for decades of service to his college. Most importantly, his family was healthy, happy, and growing, and he, at last, had reached the moment when he was about to enter retirement and be able to enjoy the fruits of his labor. In the spring of 1951, at the end of his final academic year of full-time employment at A. & M., Wilson received an unprecedented honor from his beloved institution. President Drake declared that May 21, 1951, would be "James H. Wilson Appreciation Day." Wheels were set into motion to prepare a convocation for this campus icon. Committees were appointed, letters of invitation mailed to family and alumni, and speakers chosen to tell his story and say, "Thank you."

The minutes of the Special Committee appointed for this event reveal that the first committee immediately appointed five subcommittees to help them with the work: one for the program, another for student participation, a third for finance, one more for gift selection, and, finally, a fifth on decoration. At least two dozen campus committee members became involved in this single event to pay tribute to one of their own. Invitations were sent to the honoree and his wife, every member of his family, the Ministers' Union, his pastor and the members of his church, Oakwood College, and to other organizations with which he was associated. They

> ALABAMA AGRICULTURAL AND MECHANICAL COLLEGE
> NORMAL, ALABAMA
>
> Minutes of the Special Committee
> in connection with
> THE JAMES H. WILSON APPRECIATION DAY, MAY 21, 1951
>
> The Special Committee met in the President's Office Tuesday afternoon, May 8, 1951 at 4:30 o'clock to discuss plans for a special convocation in honor of Mr. James H. Wilson. It was stated that this special convocation will be held in the new auditorium-gymnasium on May 21, 1951.
>
> The following phases of the program were discussed:
>
> a. The type of program to be presented - (nature of program)
> b. The type of expression the faculty would like to make
> c. Student participation
> d. Alumni contribution
> e. The Citation: How should it be worded?
>
> The Committee on Selection of a gift for the faculty suggested that a gift of sterling silver would be most appropriate. A sterling silver pitcher with goblets was suggested. It was estimated that a contribution of $3.50 from each faculty and staff member would cover the cost of this gift. The faculty is to be notified by letter concerning this convocation and the amount of contribution.
>
> An invitation will be sent to Mr. and Mrs. Wilson requesting their presence on this occasion. Invitations will also be sent to each member of his family, The Ministers' Union, his Pastor and his church, Oakwood College, and other organizations with which he is very closely affiliated.
>
> The following planning committees were appointed:
>
> 1. Program Committee: Mr. Henry Bradford, Chairman   Mrs. Bradford
>   Mr. W. H. Hollins   Mr. Kendrick
>   Dean R. A. Carter   Mr. R. H. Lee
>
> 2. Student Participation:
>   (to meet and elect   Dr. E. H. Wallace, Chairman
>   the Chairman)   Mr. W. T. Bush, Co-Chairman
>   Mrs. Bulls   Mr. J. Ford
>   Mr. Browder   Miss P. E. Thigpen
>   Mr. J. L. Bray   Miss M. A. Smith
>   Mr. J. P. Cochran
>   Including Class Presidents: Mr. Edward Oliver, Senior Class
>   Mr. Bush, Junior Class
>   Mr. Jack Bonham, Sophomore Class
>   Mr. Charles W. Sanders, Freshman Class
>
> 3. Finance Committee: Mr. L. R. Patton, Chairman
>   Mr. T. M. Elmore
>   Mrs. N. L. Bradford
>
> 4. Committee on Gift Selection: Dean R. A. Carter, Chairman
>   Mrs. M. Chambers   Mr. Henry Bradford
>   Mrs. A. K. Hobson   Mr. R. H. Lee
>
> 5. Committee on Decoration: Mr. Thomas Morris, Chairman; Mrs. M.
>   Mrs. Mary Chambers

Figure 11-18. Minutes of the Special Committee, James H. Wilson Appreciation Day.

also decided that the convocation would be held in the recently constructed auditorium-gymnasium. It would seem that these colleagues, working on even one more committee than usual, were not resentful but enthusiastic.

THE WAR AND POST-WAR YEARS: 1941-1951

Figure 11-19. Souvenir Cover for James H. Wilson Appreciation Day Program.

A handsome program was printed, and a special souvenir cover for the honoree and his family was produced as well. When the program was finalized there was music aplenty. The organ played, the audience sang, the college choir performed, and the band presented two numbers. Jonathan Ford, the band director selected

Figure 11-20. Program Cover, James H. Wilson Appreciation Day Convocation.

a composition by Wilson for the first, "Bugle Call" march, and for the second, Ford composed a work himself to show his own personal respect for his predecessor, "Ode to J. H." The president of the college spoke, and a student led the responsive reading, Matthew 5: 33-48, which included the verse quoted earlier in this chapter:

> "But I say unto you, Love your enemies, bless them that curse you, do good to them that hate you, and pray for them that despitefully use you, and persecute you;
> [Matthew 5:44]

The student chosen to lead the reading was the son of Wilson's closest friend at Normal, Thomas Elmore, who was himself the son of Ollie Elmore, the manager of Elmore's Cyclone Band of Nicholasville, Kentucky, the hometown band that Wilson directed over forty years earlier. How carefully the committee crafted this ceremony of institutional and personal thanks!

Mr. James L. Bray, Dean of Men, delivered the address for the occasion, and in it he reflected philosophically on the nature of friendship, human nature, and physical nature, and informed his audience:

> We are told that James H. Wilson came to Normal with a Bible in one hand and a trumpet in the other. With these instruments of good cheer he has labored continuously in the field of social-relations – teaching Christian ideals and making music, the kind that softens the hearts of those who hear. Surely, the soul of the man is attuned to the vision of REALITY.[23]

On this outstanding occasion, all of James' family attended. In his and Exeline's living room in the new faculty housing unit, his children and two grandchildren gathered before the piano for a family portrait (Figure 11-22, below).

James heart was filled with the many outpourings of love and respect, and now, for the first time in his seventy years, he was looking forward to a moment of rest and reflection. Wishful thinking! It never happened.

---

[23]James L. Bray, "James H. Wilson – The Man," [Full text of address presented by Dean J. L. Bray], *The Normal Index*, New Series, vols. 33-4, nos. 1-4 (March 1951-December 1952), pp. 21ff.

Program

ACADEMIC PROCESSION

ORGAN PRELUDE   Dr. Elsie Hill Wallace

HYMN

    Leaning on the Everlasting Arms   *Showalter*
                    Audience

> What a fellowship, what a joy divine,
> Leaning on the Everlasting Arms!
> What a blessedness, what a peace is mine,
> Leaning on the Everlasting Arms!
>
> *Refrain*
> Leaning, leaning, safe and secure from all alarms;
> Leaning on Jesus, leaning on Jesus
> Leaning on the Everlasting Arms.
>
> Oh, how sweet to walk in this pilgrim way,
> Leaning on the Everlasting Arms!
> Oh, how bright the path grows from day to day,
> Leaning on the Everlasting Arms!
>
> What have I to dread, what have I to fear,
> Leaning on the Everlasting Arms!
> I have blessed peace with my Lord so near,
> Leaning on the Everlasting Arms.

RESPONSIVE READING   Mr. T. M. Elmore
                                                    College Business Office Assistant

Matt. 5:33-48

Leader: Again, ye have heard that it hath been said by them of old time, Thou shalt not forswear thyself, but shalt perform unto the Lord thine oaths;
Audience: But I say unto you, Swear not at all; neither by heaven; for it is God's throne:
Leader: Nor by the earth; for it is his footstool: neither by Jerusalem; for it is the city of the great King.
Audience: Neither shalt thou swear by thy head, because thou canst not make one hair white or black.
Leader: But let your communication be, Yea, yea; Nay, nay: for whatsoever is more than these cometh of evil.
Audience: Ye hath heard that it hath been said, an eye for an eye, and a tooth for a tooth.
Leader: But I say unto you, That ye resist not evil: but whosoever shall smite thee on thy right cheek, turn to him the other also.
Audience: And if any man will sue thee at the law, and take away thy coat, let him have thy cloke also.
Leader: And whosoever shall compel thee to go a mile, go with him twain.
Audience: Give to him that asketh thee, and from him that would borrow of thee turn not thou away.
Leader: Ye have heard that it hath been said, Thou shalt love thy neighbour, and hate thine enemy.
Audience: But I say unto you, Love your enemies, bless them that curse you, do good to them that hate you, and pray for them which despitefully use you, and persecute you;
Leader: That ye may be the children of your Father which is in heaven: for he maketh his sun to rise on evil and on the good, and sendeth rain on the just and on the unjust.
Audience: For if ye love them which love you, what reward have ye? Do not even the publicans the same?
Leader: And if ye salute your brethren only, what do ye more *than others?* Do not even the publicans so?
Audience: Be ye therefore perfect, even as your Father which is in heaven is perfect.

Figure 11-21. (2 pages) Convocation Program, James H. Wilson Appreciation Day.

THE WAR AND POST-WAR YEARS: 1941-1951

INVOCATION　　　　　　　　　　　THE REVEREND HENRY BRADFORD JR.
　　　　　　　　　　　　　　　　　　　　　　　　　College Chaplain

MUSIC
　　BATTLE HYMN OF THE REPUBLIC　　　　　　　　　*Key*
　　　　　　THE COLLEGE CHOIR
　　　　NELL LANE BRADFORD, *Director*

THE OCCASION　　　　　　　　　　　　　　DR. J. F. DRAKE
　　　　　　　　　　　　　　　　　　　　　　President of the College

MUSIC
　　BUGLE CALL　　　　　　　　　　　　　　*James H. Wilson*
　　　　　　THE COLLEGE BAND
　　　　JONATHAN FORD, *Director*

INTRODUCTION OF SPEAKER　　　　　MRS. HARRIETT J. TERRY
　　　　　　　　　　　　　　　　　　　College Instructor of English

ADDRESS　　　　　　　　　　　　　　　MR. JAMES L. BRAY
　　　　　　　　　　　　　　　　　　　　　　Dean of Men

SPECIAL MUSIC
　　ODE TO J. H.　　　　　　　　　　　　　*Jonathan Ford*
　　　　　　THE COLLEGE BAND

EXPRESSIONS AND PRESENTATIONS

THE ALMA MATER
　　A. & M. COLLEGE, MOTHER DEAR　　　　　　　*J. F. Drake*

　　　　A. & M. College, mother dear
　　　　Rich in heritage divine
　　　　Bless'd by the life of Council Trenholm
　　　　Who gave her all that thou might'st shine.

　　　　　　Chorus
　　　　A. & M. College, bless to thy name
　　　　Long live thy fame, long live thy fame.

　　　　Many thy brave and loyal sons
　　　　Sent from thy shrine on Normal's Hill
　　　　Filled with a zeal, her tasks well done
　　　　Anxious thy mandates to fulfill.

　　　　Long may you live to bless the world
　　　　For right and justice take a stand
　　　　As from your lofty heights you view
　　　　Your children's work throughout the land.

Figure 11-22. The Wilson Family, 1951. Exeline and James are seated on the piano bench. James, Jr. stands at the left. Proceeding to the right one sees Hester Wilson Orr; granddaughter Marian Elizabeth Turner; her mother, Marian Wilson Turner; Karl Wilson; and his son, James Hembray Wilson, III.

CHAPTER TWELVE

Coming Full Circle

After Alabama Agricultural and Mechanical College held its May, 1951, commencement exercises, James and Exeline walked out of the auditorium knowing that they could relax at home, enjoy the family, and think of how they might travel together and enjoy life in retirement. James hardly had a chance to catch his breath before the college drafted him to direct the band once again. Jonathan Ford resigned the post after the 1951 commencement, having served but two years, and his replacement, Phillip Cooper, only lasted half that long. President Drake cried out to his old friend for help while he tried to mend the tear in the faculty fabric. James would never refuse this good man. He began preparing the college band for the football season, and he readied his concert band for a program in the chapel at Christmas time. *The Normal Index* reported:

Professor J. H. Wilson Directs Band
In First Chapel Concert of School Year

The Alabama A. & M. College band, under the direction of Mr. J. H. Wilson, presented a pre-Christmas concert in the college chapel, Friday, December 12 [1951].

Numbers played were: . . . .

All numbers on the program were arranged by Mr. Wilson.

The band consists of the following musicians: . . . .[1]

[6 trumpets, 2 horns, 5 trombones, 1 baritone horn, 1 bass, 4 clarinets, 5 saxophones, 5 drums and cymbals, and 1 bell lyre. The total equals 30 players, approximately the number seen in the photo below, Figure 12-1.]

---

[1]*The Normal Index,* New Series, vols. 33-34, nos. 1-4 (March 1951-December 1952), p. 2.

Figure 12-1. A gray-haired James H. Wilson leads a pep band from the bleachers of the athletic field on "The Hill."

Ford's replacement, Phillip Cooper, must have performed his duties unsatisfactorily, for in an undated letter from Wilson to his daughter, Marian Turner, James explained:

Dear Bunks;

Just a line to enclose this program on which I played Friday night. I was encored.

The band goes to Oakwood Saturday evening. I think we have our hands on a man for next year. They have done well this year. I practically had to make this band. . . .

I am doing well. I think my health is much better. I am getting my latest march in shape for publication. A white man in Nashville promised to see what can be done about it. I'll let you know how I come out. Wish me luck. Kiss Angel Pie [granddaughter Marian Elizabeth] and give my love to John [husband John Turner].

Your Dad[2]

[2] Undated letter but certainly written circa 1952-53, after granddaughter's birth and before grandson's birth. The circumstances of health and condition of band could only refer to this academic year.

It is sad to learn that Wilson felt he had to remake the band, for it had been doing so well under the direction of Jonathan Ford. Of course it is good to hear the seventy-plus man say I am doing well, but he qualifies his evaluation with "I think my health is much better." He is not certain.

In retirement James seems to have had the desire to leave something tangible behind. He had composed many works for band, and for the first time in his life he actively sought publication. James first turned to his old friend, W. C. Handy. In fact, Handy had come to James in July of 1951 to request that Wilson have his band try Handy's latest number, "The Big Stick Blues March."[3] Wilson did as his friend requested and wrote Handy a letter in December of that year, requesting that Handy consider James' march, "United," for publication by Handy's New York publishing business. Handy acknowledged receipt but said it would be impossible for him to work on it until after the first of the year, since his assistant, Charles L. Cooke, was busy scoring a new production of the Noble Sissle and Eubie Blake musical, *Shuffle Along*. Apparently Wilson had included no score, only the parts, for Handy wrote again in January to say that Cooke was back in the office and had been set to work scoring Wilson's music. There would have to be a delay again until the score was finished.[4] However, he promised publication in the January letter, "When we receive the score, we will send contracts for publication." Unfortunately, luck ran out for Wilson. In November, Handy wrote again, "Because of my blindness . . . [and because Dr. Cooke] got tied up in writing shows . . . that is the cause of my failure to publish it as I had planned. So today I am sending [back] the original parts of your March UNITED."[5]

Apparently Wilson wrote again to Handy in late 1952 or early 1953 to confide some of his concerns about being called back at his age to direct the A. & M. band once again. Handy responded in March to console his friend and tell him about his own activities and concerns.

---

[3]Letter to James H. Wilson from R. Hayes Strider, writing for W. C. Handy, dated July 3, 1951.
[4]Letter to James H. Wilson from W. C. Handy, dated January 11th, 1952.
[5]Letter to James H. Wilson from W. C. Handy, dated November 28th, 1952.

Figure 12-2. Letter from W. C. Handy to James H. Wilson, November 28, 1952.

In the post script we see that once again Wilson had to face the disappointment of having a work, "Kentucky Blue Grass" march, rejected by the Handy Brothers Music Co., Inc. (Figure 12-4, below).

In the undated but contemporary letter to "Bunks," above, Wilson informed Marian about his "latest" march. Since the works sent to Handy were written some years before, it is good to learn that the man was still composing. Matching this information, from letters James wrote to Handy and to his daughter, Marian, with details found in the last *Normal Index* article mentioned, that reported he had arranged all the music for the chapel Christmas concert, we can see that composition, orchestration, and publication were serious issues with him in retirement. Although many of his orchestrations were caused by necessity, to adjust music for beginning players or unbalanced ensembles, this is certainly not the case with those he would have considered fit for publication. The first clarinet part of the "Silas Greene March," with its tricky rhythms, repeated articulations, and rapid scalar passages was not conceived for beginners (Figure 12-5).

The E♭ Cornet part of "United," the march sent to W. C. Handy, has a two-octave drop between adjacent notes with but a short rest separating the upper and lower notes between measures 3 and 4. Also the three measures before the 1st ending of the second strain are extremely difficult. One does not hand that part to a novice cornetist (Figure 12-6).

The Solo Cornet part of the "Alabama A and M College March" (Figure 12-7) likewise requires a skillful musician to accomplish the ornamented octave-run up to high B♭ and back down, seen at the beginning of the number. When opportunity presented itself, that is, when Wilson had skillful professional or college musicians, his requirements for performance were uncompromising.

If one were to criticize these compositions with respect to creativity, one might say that Wilson's music was old fashioned. But that would be a narrow and unsympathetic view. The craftsmanship is excellent, even though the music rings with the sound of the past, a reminder of the heyday of marching and concert bands when James stood at the pinnacle of his profession. But as late as the 1950s, the

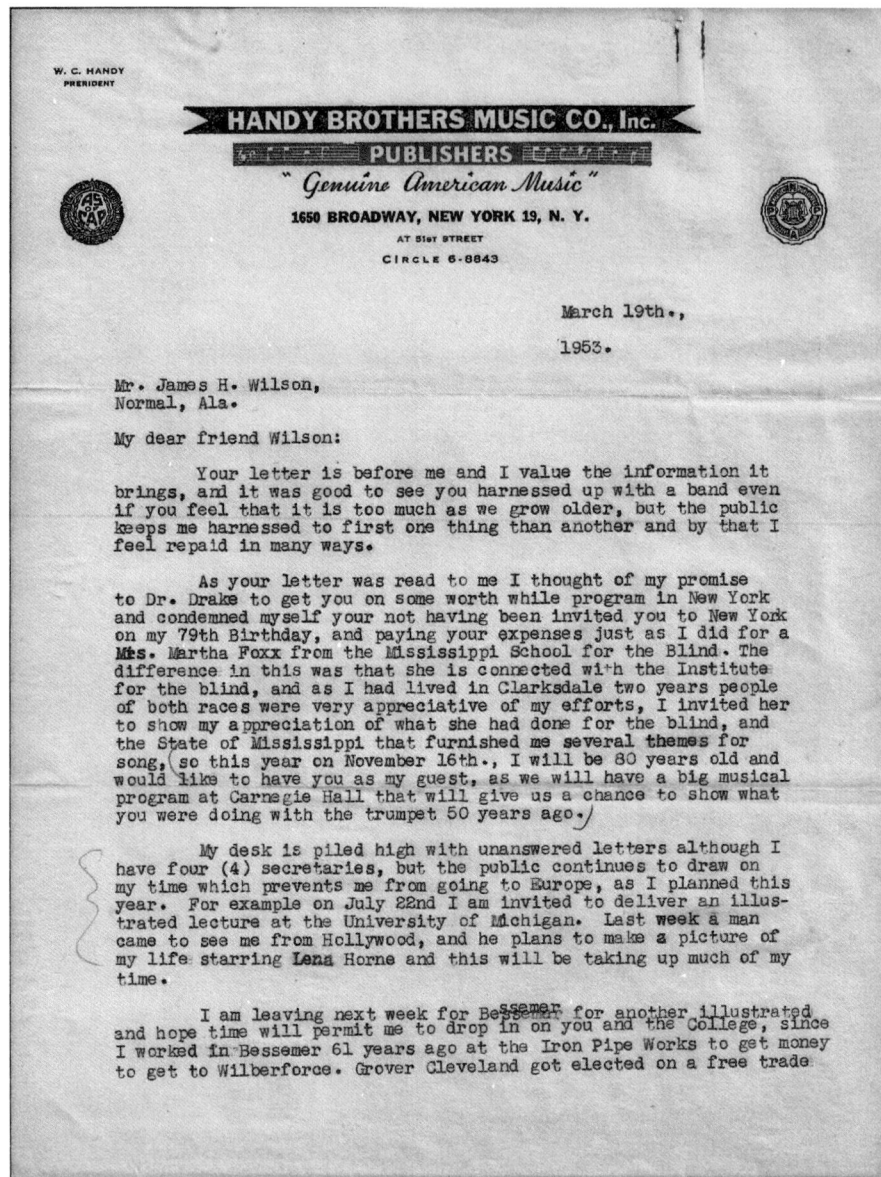

Figure 12-3. Letter from W. C. Handy to James H. Wilson, March 19, 1953, page 1.

Mr. James H. Wilson.   March 19th., 1953.

policy. England could ship ore to Bessemer cheaper than we could mine it and everything closed down and I left Bessemer with 20 cents in my pocket and a quartet for the Chicago World Fair, and the quartet went on the blink, the Fair was postponed and I didn't get to Wilberforce, so keep this under your hat, I have talked in every University and College for our people but today haven't seen Wilberforce, which confer a Doctor of Music degree on me. When I was a school boy in Florence, Ala., the old McGuffey Fifth Reader had a lesson that I never forgot, quote "Never brag of the fish you didn't catch" so when I've got it in the bag, you will know about it.

Monday I am to appear at the Madison Square Garden for the NAACP and of course will be trumpeting the ST. LOUIS BLUES. You may be able to hear us on Radio or see us on TV.

I have been up four nights until two o'clock, then drive 18 miles to Tuckahoe making me late at the office and depending on others to find your manuscript which they are doing.

I was at the Urban League where there were 1800 guests at the Waldorf Astoria, where my birthday dinner was given and the other night was at the W.C.Handy Foundation for the Blind meeting, another night at the Forest Neighborhood House Dinner, over radio on WHOM, and will be at the Freedom House luncheon at the Town Hall Club, where I will set on the Speakers Stand to hear Dr. Bunche in his report on India.

So this letter goes forward and we won't stop until we get your namuscript to you.

By the way Mrs. Herman G. Clayborne of Birmingham, Ala. is our guest until we leave for Bessemer, when she will leave with us to go back to Birmingham.

Since dictating this I find that I can't leave here until the 31st., of March for Birmingham and by the time I take care of rehearsals, etc. it will be too late to come to Normal and because of engagements of April 5th.6th & 7th, I must return much to my regret.

Will write you further when we find your manuscript.

Best regards to you and the entire Institution, I am

                               Your friend,

WCH:abb   W.C.Handy

P. S. We have just come across your "KENTUCKY BLUE GRASS" in our pending file, and are mailing it out at once to you. First Class Mail.

Figure 12-4. Letter from W. C. Handy to James H. Wilson, March 19, 1953, page 2.

Figure 12-5. "Silas Green March," Clarinet I, by James H. Wilson.

years of James retirement, the same band sound was still popular, and Paul Lavalle's Band of America enjoyed great success with its weekly radio broadcasts. Likewise, this style of composition for band was functional, and therefore had an enormous market. It was the regular sound that led marching feet in the military and precision drills at half time on the athletic field. James, in his retirement, was not outmoded. Neither was he worn out.

And along with his band responsibilities and compositional interests, he continued to play solo pieces in recital and on band programs, an amazing feat for a septuagenarian trumpet player. But he was getting tired, and we can feel him heave a sigh of relief when he tells his daughter in one of his "Dear Bunks" letters, "I think we [President Drake and he] have our hands on a man for next year." Unfortunately, he and Drake will once again find disappointment as one bandmaster after another comes for one or two years and then departs to work elsewhere. In the ensuing years

Figure 12-6. "United," a March, E♭ Cornet, by James H. Wilson.

Figure 12-7. The "Alabama A and M College March," Solo Cornet, by James H. Wilson.

there was a succession of short-term band director appointments at A. & M., and it was a long time coming before a dedicated and capable man replaced Wilson for the long haul.[6]

Toward the end of James' year as recalled bandmaster, the Alabama State Teachers Association held their seventh Annual Meeting in Tullibody Auditorium of Alabama State College in Montgomery. Two programs of music were offered the attendees, and on March 27, 1953, Wilson played a trumpet solo, a "Fantasia on Tramp, Tramp, Tramp" for the gathered assembly. Written by Edwin Franko Goldman, the fantasia and variations on a popular song from the World War I years, was a defying piece of music, and Wilson, at seventy-two, was still willing to challenge himself and learn additional solo repertoire. Furthermore, he performed well. In his own personal copy of the program he typed, "Encore." The listeners were pleased and impressed.

Later that year, the college band played a concert as part of the Founder's Week Observances. James arranged a humorous number to open the program, "He Didn't Know But One Tune," a simple take-off on a popular ditty, and he programmed one of his own new compositions, the "Alabama A. & M. College March," amidst works by Sousa, Sibelius, and McDowell. He was working hard, having fun, and viewing the light at the end of the tunnel. Only one more month to commencement! And when the summer arrived, things did quiet down somewhat for this gentle, old man.

James' single continuing responsibility at the college was the Sunday School. He remained director of the program, and in late 1954, he and his friend, the Rev. Henry Bradford, Jr., published a four-page Christian newsletter, *The Glad Tidings*. On Wilson's personal copy James typed "Volume 1 December 1954 Number 1." Apparently the omission was an oversight by these fledgling editors. They clearly intended this project to continue and become a regular campus publication. In this first issue Wilson contributed a brief article, "Putting Old Wine In New Bottles . . . .", an exhortation asking the readers to abandon the old Sunday School of the past, "a place where children were taught by incompetent teachers. . . .

[6]Rev. Dr. Henry Bradford, Jr., "A. & M. Music Faculty," [typescript with manuscript additions]

conducted by officers who had not studied organization or methods." He tells them,

> The one room school has given place to the well equipped Sunday School building with its trained teachers, specialists and officers Teachers who not only know their Bibles, but are well trained in the arts and sciences as well. Teachers who make special preparation for each lesson and each student. We dare not put old wine into new bottles lest the bottles be broken.[7]

Wilson may have been an old man, but he had lost none of his evangelical fire. In the next issue of *The Glad Tidings* he contributed no article, but his name was listed on the front page as "Director of Sunday School." On the same page we learn that Mrs. James H. Wilson was teaching the Sunday School Teacher Training Class. He retired and she replaced her husband in that faculty assignment![8] In January of 1956, under the heading "NORMAL and RELIGION," the same heading he used for his *Normal Index* articles, James again contributed a full-page, two-column article, "'The Little Foxes' Song of Solomon 2:15," and the evangelical fire flared up once again. He explained that in this Bible passage the foxes creep into the vineyards and eat the roots of the grapevines, destroying the crop. He likens the hyphen ["-"] to a little fox and brings his lesson right into mainstream 20th-century America:

> The late President Woodrow Wilson said and I quote, "There are many hyphens left in America – for my part I think the un-American thing is the hyphen." End of quotation. Any movement that is calculated to strike at our American way of life is dangerous. We call it un-American. Just that small mark we call hyphen makes it subversive. What is all the noise we hear over the radio and in the newspapers? [Senator Joseph McCarthy and fears of Communist subversion.][9] .... This little hyphen is carried

---

[7] *The Glad Tidings*, v. 1, n. 1 (December 1954), p. 1.
[8] *The Glad Tidings*, v. 1, n. 2 (January 1955), p. 1.
[9] Not to be confused with the House Committee on Un-American Activities. McCarthy was a senator and not a representative. He chaired the Senate Permanent Subcommittee on Investigations.

over into Christendom. We are known as Baptist-Christians, Methodist-Christians, Presbyterian-Christians, etc. This little hyphen makes us narrow, bigoted, mean and obnoxious. This little fox makes it hard for Christians to work together for the salvation of the world.[10]

And in this last phrase we might measure the scope of James' Christian ambitions—Save the World. This son of a slave, this trumpet playing, high school graduate wanted to work in harmony with all Christians and save the world. The little foxes were working against him, and so, unfortunately, was Father Time. He and Exeline were nearing their final years.

Exeline had served as instructor of the Sunday School Teacher Training Class for only one year before she started to suffer some serious health problems. Marian Turner, her daughter then living in Cleveland, brought her mother to the Cleveland Clinic for diagnosis, and the reporting doctor sent Exeline a letter informing her that her heart muscle showed signs of strain (enlarged slightly on the left), her blood pressure was 270/144, and her fasting blood sugar was elevated to 120. Standards have become even more stringent in recent years, but even then the doctor recommended she avoid overexertion, follow a strict diet to avoid diabetes, and take several medications for various other issues.[11] The A. & M. Wilsons were both deteriorating physically.

Would James slow down? Not if he could help it. In December of that year, eight days before his seventy-fourth birthday, Wilson took his trumpet from its case to join the program of the Christmas Musical Event in the campus gymnasium-auditorium. The organ played, the college choir and the men's glee club sang, two vocal soloists contributed musical numbers, and a professor of speech and English from Oakwood College read, "The Way of the Wise." With more than 1,200 music lovers in attendance, James played Schubert's "Ave Maria" for the offertory.[12] Three

---

[10]*The Glad Tidings*, v. 2, n. 1 (January 1956), p. 1.
[11]Letter to Mrs. James H. Wilson, Sr. from Richard N. Westcott, M.D., dated September 26, 1955.
[12]*Alabama A. & M. College News*, v. 4, nos. 11-12 (November-December, 1955), p. 1.

Figure 12-8. At an outdoor gathering, the elderly James H. Wilson stands ready to perform with his trumpet.

months later he, accompanied by the Reverend and Mrs. Henry Bradford, traveled to Birmingham, Alabama, to play a public recital. Both Henry and Nell Lane Bradford were accomplished pianists, and she also served on the A. & M. faculty as director of the college choir. Their interesting program was divided into five groups: Wilson, Mrs. Bradford, Mr. Bradford, Wilson, and Mrs. Bradford. The music selected by these three musicians ranged from "My Old Kentucky Home" to Johannes Brahms, Eric Satie, and Spirituals.[13] The Bradfords were young; Wilson was not. Regardless, the invincible old man went back to Normal and coached a trombone quintet[14] for a band program directed by his latest replacement, Thomas V. Dawson, an excellent musician and competent bandmaster.

At the beginning of the next academic year, September of 1956, Wilson published his most lengthy article in *The Glad Tidings*. In "Three Men – Three Philosophies," Wilson describes three people—a robber, a Levite, and a Samaritan—and entreats his readers to beware the philosophies of the first two. Instead,

---

[13]*Alabama A. & M. College News,* v. 5, n. 3 (March, 1956), p. 3.
[14]Program, The College Band, Thomas V. Dawson, Conductor, March 20, 1956.

they should adhere to the example of "The good Samaritan [who] does not know race, creed or religion. If a person needs help it is our indispensable duty to help him."[15] The familiar story from Luke 10:30-37 has been used countless times to exhort young people to do the right thing, but Wilson surprises us when he refers, in 1956, to a bombing in Birmingham a few years earlier, because the infamous bombing in Birmingham of the 16th Street Baptist Church where four young girls were killed did not take place until 1963.[16] Wilson told his readers:

> A few years ago a member of our group's home was bombed in Birmingham, and members of the other group [who] were up in arms about it demanded that something be done about it. I think something was done about it. These were the good Samaritans. I believe that there are still some Samaritans all over the south land of ours.
>
> Young people, as you go through this world, are you going to be a robber, beating and cheating your way; taking undue advantage of the weak; wrecking men's lives or are you going to be a Levite – passing people up because you are selfish, or are you going to be a good Samaritan? Don't beat them up; don't pass them up; but lift them up.[17]

That "member of our group" hit close to home, yet Wilson's faith and idealism carried him beyond the immediate distress of the situation and let him warn his readers:

> Young men and women are told that an open mind means to banish all previous views and find their orientation in a new and independent world of thought which usually turns out to be some brand of rationalism that rejects miracles and modifies the authority of the Scriptures.

---

[15]"Three Men – Three Philosophies," *The Glad Tidings*, v. 2, nos. 7-8 (September 1956), pp. 1f.

[16]An informative website relating the history of the 1963 bombing and the civil rights actions that followed in the aftermath of the tragic event may be viewed at: http://www.english.illinois.edu/maps/poets/m_r/randall/birmingham.htm (accessed October 7, 2012).

[17]"Three Men – Three Philosophies," *The Glad Tidings*, v. 2, nos. 7-8 (September 1956), p. 2.

The Glad Tidings

Published monthly by the A. and M. College Church and Sunday School in the interest of the college family.

VOLUME II   NORMAL, ALABAMA - SEPTEMBER, 1956   NUMBER 7 - 8

MINISTRY OF THE CHAPEL

Henry Bradford, Jr. .... Chaplain
James H. Wilson .... Director of Sunday School
Nell L. Bradford .... Director of the Choir
~~Barthonia S. White~~ .... Organist

SCHEDULE OF SERVICES

Sunday School .... 9:30 a. m.
Morning Worship .... 11:00 a. m.
Sunday Vespers .... 7:00 p. m.
Bible Training Class
     each Tuesday Evening .... 7:00 p. m.

He Answers Prayer

God answers prayer; sometimes, when hearts are weak,

He gives the very gifts believers seek.

But often faith must learn a deeper rest,

And trust God's silence when He does not Speak;

For He whose Name is Love will send the best.

Stars may burn out, nor mountain walls endure,

But God is true, His promises are sure

For those who seek.

Sunday School Items

Guest speakers and teachers for July and August: Dr. O. B. Edwards, Dean Oakwood College and Elder E. E. Rogers, Professor of languages Oakwood College.

Sunday School and Church Items

Normal, a pioneer in religious education is giving a four year Bible Training Course beginning this year.

Mr. Harrison Lee, Misses Joyce Pulley and Lucy Nell Green are new additions to the Sunday School faculty.

The enrollment for September is 226 with an average attendance of 165.

Three Men - Three Philosophies

JAMES H. WILSON

A certain man went down from Jerusalem to Jericho and fell among thieves which stripped him of his raiments and wounded him and departed and left him half dead. Thieves and robbers are all around us; men who rob us of everything we have. In religion we are often robbed of everything we have learned at home from father and mother. Young men and women are told that an open mind means to banish all previous views and find their orientation in a new and independent world of thought which usually turns out to be some brand of rationalism that rejects miracles and modifies the authority of the Scriptures. It is an awful thing to wreck a young person's faith by our modernistic teaching and preaching. More harm than good is done by such teaching or preaching for it sometimes leaves a person dazed or like the man on the Jericho - half dead.

If a person wants to believe in the miracles or the virgin birth, why disturb that faith. In college we meet some professors and students with peculiar views on religion, morals and sex. If one is not strong he will go back home with less than he brought to college. You will leave Jerusalem to Jericho and they will strip you of your child-like faith, your good name and morals and leave you a pitiable sight. The philosophy of these people is, "What's yours is mine if I can get it," and believe me they usually get what they want. I have heard of instances where a girl must give all she has in order to get a good grade. Here is your thief who strips you and leaves you half dead.

We are told in the Bible that the glory of a woman is her hair. I like to think that the glory of the woman is her virtue and modesty. If she loses these then she has lost everything. There are certain land marks which we should observe as we travel this road to Jericho. Sometimes we call them guide posts. We see these as we travel the highways. I like to think that these signs are put there for me. Some of these are very familiar to motorists: Curve ahead, drive slowly; slippery road when wet, drive cautiously; caution, men working ahead; speed limit, fifteen miles an hour. These are no good if not observed. In one of the Psalms I read, "For thy name's sake lead and guide me." Young people remember the land marks of your father and mother. They know the way and can point out the pitfalls to you. Better listen to them.

They may be old and maybe they cannot read as well as you, but they have something that you should have and that is good common sense. I heard a song some years ago where a circus manager wanted a young lad to lead a lion around and the answer goes something like this, "I ain't seen inside of a school and can't spell dog or cat, but I'm not going to lead a lion around 'cause I got good common sense." Common sense is the

Figure 12-9. Wilson's last published article, "Three Men – Three Philosophies."

He was not about to have any of these modern ideas subvert his beliefs or change the message of his life. The Bible was James Hembray Wilson's guide and his authority, and he professed that young men and women must come to grips with Scripture, study and debate the meaning of these holy words to understand them better, and then pursue a life in accordance with these values.

Age was now about to have its way. In October of 1957 James underwent cataract surgery to his right eye.[18] Three months later, in January of 1958, he wrote to "Bunks" to inform his daughter that, "Your mother will have her teeth in next week and then I can take her out to every thing."[19] In the letter he enclosed a financial statement listing his income and expenditures for one full year, and from the statement we see clearly that he and Exeline were not wealthy and were living very frugally. To help them, the college apparently decided to allow the couple to live out their final years in faculty housing, rent free, for he also wrote, "Not having to pay rent helps out considerably."

```
                    Marian
                            THE WILSONS
                            FINANCIAL STATEMENT    1956-1957
                            Beginning August 1, 1956 ending July 30, 1957

        EXPENDITURES
                                                    INCOME
        FOOD---------------------$ 739.25
        wife  WIFE--------------   285.00
        INSURANCE---------------   275.47           Retirement benefits   $ 2070.48
        FUEL--------------------   164.89           Social Security         250.60
        HOUSEHOLD --------------   155.58           Recitals                 50.00
        DOCTOR & MEDICINES------   119.10           From James            * 250.60 *
        CLOTHING----------------   107.84           Making out income
        CAR EXPENSE-------------   104.53             forms for teachers     15.00
        DRIVER------------------    68.10           Other                   209.08  #
        LAUNDRY & CLEANING------    66.53
        RECREATION & AMUSEMENT--    62.45           TOTAL INCOME          $ 2893.66
        CHURCH -----------------    60.25
        SAVINGS-----------------    17.50           *  Half of this amount given your
          SUBSCRIPTIONS---------    45.20              mother
        PAYMENT FOR LABOR ------    24.56           #  Received some of this for instruction
        POSTAGE-----------------    14.37              on the trumpet
        MISCELLANEOUS ITEMS-----    59.27

        TOTAL      ----------- $ 2399.69
```

Figure 12-10. Wilson's personal accounting of income and expenditures, August 1, 1956, to July 31, 1957.

---

[18]Bill from Dr. J. D. Moorman, Medical Arts Building, Huntsville, Alabama, dated October 8, 1957. The second cataract was removed in 1960 (letter to Mrs. Marian W Turner, mailed September 16, 1960.)

[19]Letter from James H Wilson to Mrs. Marian W Turner, mailed January 22, 1958.

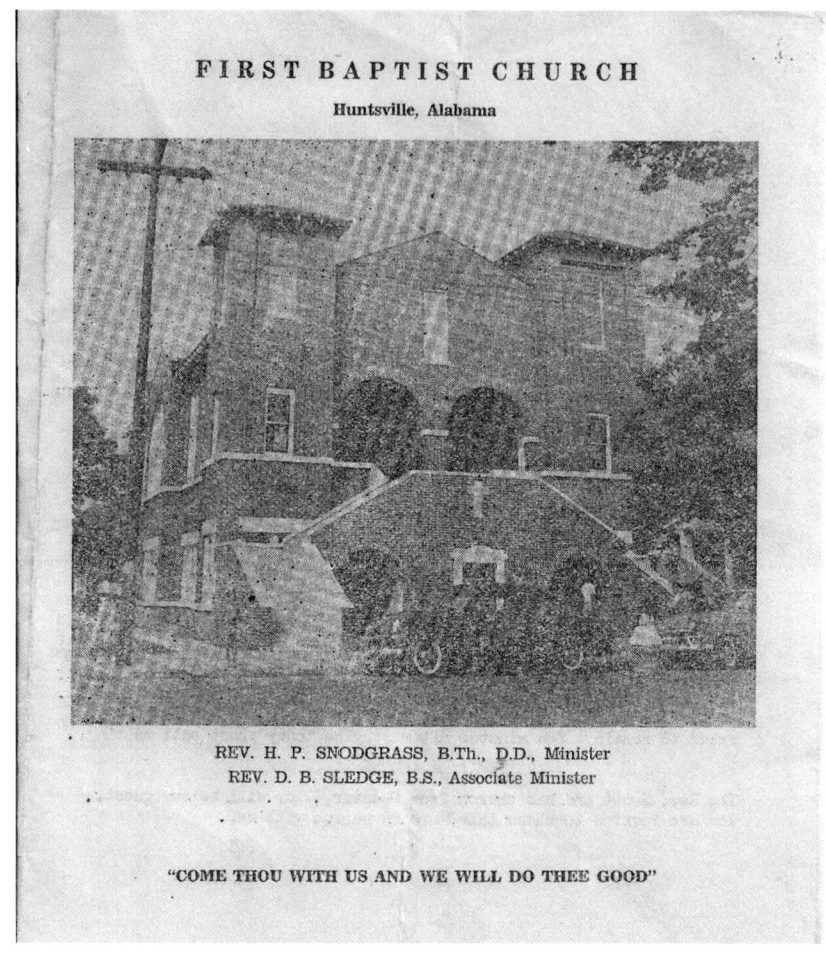

Figure 12-11. Cover, Program for Sunday Worship from Wilson's church, December 20, 1960.

Unbelievably, in February of 1959, the 79-year-old trumpeter joined a soprano and her accompanist, Katherine J. Patterson and Malcolm J. Breda, for a Sunday evening recital in Bibb Graves Auditorium.[20] And one day after his 80th birthday, James was still listed on the back of the First Baptist Church's Sunday Worship Program as one of the Deacons of the church. In his handwriting on that same page we discover something new, a brief

---

[20]Program for An Hour of Music (February 15, 1959).

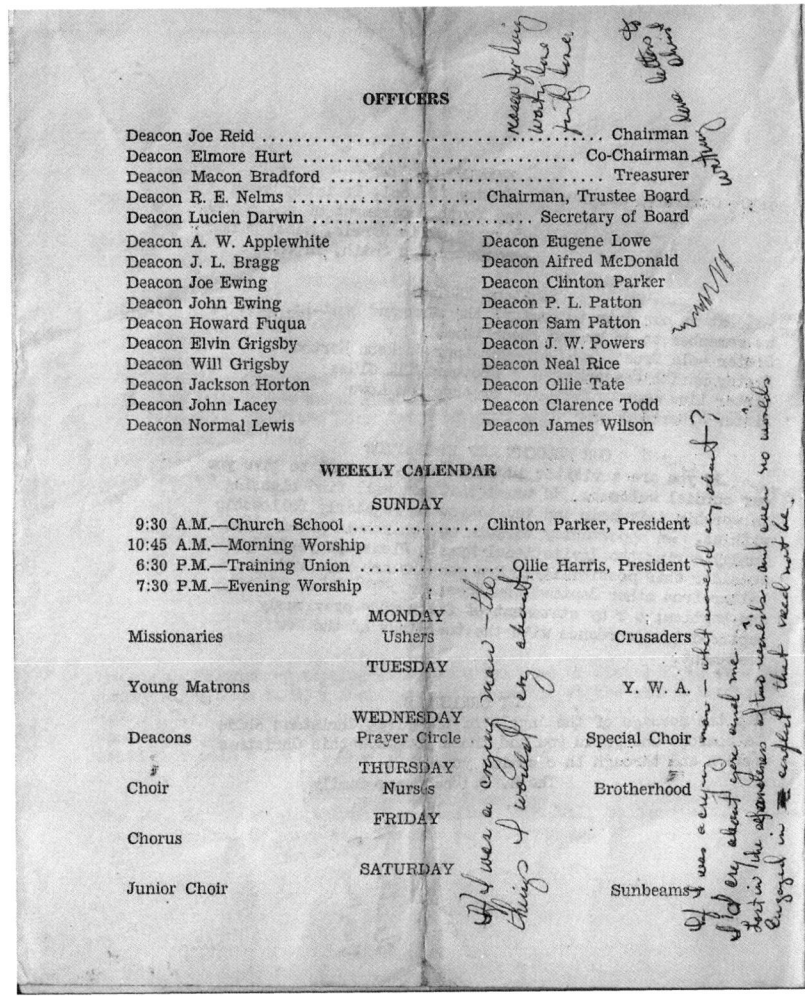

Figure 12-12. Back page of December 20, 1960, worship service. Poem and listing as Deacon of the church.

poem accompanied by some related thoughts. The style is almost identical to a blues lyric:

> If I was a crying man—the things I would cry about.
> If I was a crying man—what would I cry about?
> I'd cry about you and me . . .
> Lost in the separateness of two worlds . . . and even no worlds
> Engaged in conflict that need not be.

Figure 12-13. James Hembray Wilson and Exeline Elizabeth Polk Wilson rest here.

Was he contemplating death, his own and Exeline's? Two worlds, the living and the dead? Or was he thinking of something entirely different, perhaps the current events in Alabama, of racial struggle, the worlds of black and white? With nothing like this poem ever discovered before, it remains a surprising mystery. To the right of this poem we see a nib-clearing scribble and then,

>   writing love letters to Christ

What is the relationship of these words to the poem? And above these five words, we also can read in the margin,

>   reason for living
>   wanting love
>   finding love

During these last few years James did think seriously about death. In September of 1960 he wrote Marian again, and after thanking her for coming to Normal to help, he writes:

> Let us all hope and pray that your mother will soon be her old self again. It is a fine thing that she has you children to look after her welfare.
>
> She deserves everything that we all can do for her for she is a very fine and good person. When my time comes to go I can go with the satisfaction that she will be in good hands.
>
> Again accept our appreciation for your coming to the rescue. Love from both of us to all of you.

DADDY

James Hembray Wilson was indeed a complex man. He had lived a full and fruitful life, and on October 2, 1961, he left this world for the next. Exeline, who was ten years his junior, joined him only eight months later.[21] Inseparable in life, and inseparable in death. They were laid side by side in the Brandontown Cemetery of Huntsville, Alabama.

James' memorial service at the college took place in Bibb Graves auditorium on the 6th of October, and, appropriately, the college band played to accompany the procession of pallbearers, honorary pallbearers, and flower bearers as they carried and filed after the casket to the front of the auditorium. As these thirty-eight men and women solemnly walked down the aisle, the band, directed, by Thomas Dawson, performed "They That Sow In Tears," a work composed years before by W. C. Handy but dedicated to his friend, Professor Wilson, just two months before his own death.[22] Among the honorary pallbearers walked two of James' revered friends, President Drake and Professor Thomas Elmore. The college choir sang an anthem, and another dear friend, the Rev. Dr. Henry Bradford, Jr., read the scripture. James' enjoyed life,

---

[21]Exeline's immediate cause of death was heart failure, but the Death Registration Notice, June 20, 1962, also indicates cancer, an "Obstructive Carcinoma of the Sigmoid Colon."

[22]James Hembray Wilson Memorial Service Program, October 6, 1961.

Figure 12-14. The James Hembray Wilson State Black Archives Research Center and Museum.

Figure 12-15. The James H. Wilson Building, beneath the left broadcasting tower, crowns the campus buildings.

Figure 12-16. Patricia Ford, Director of the State Black Archives Research Center and Museum, stands before an oil portrait of James Hembray Wilson.

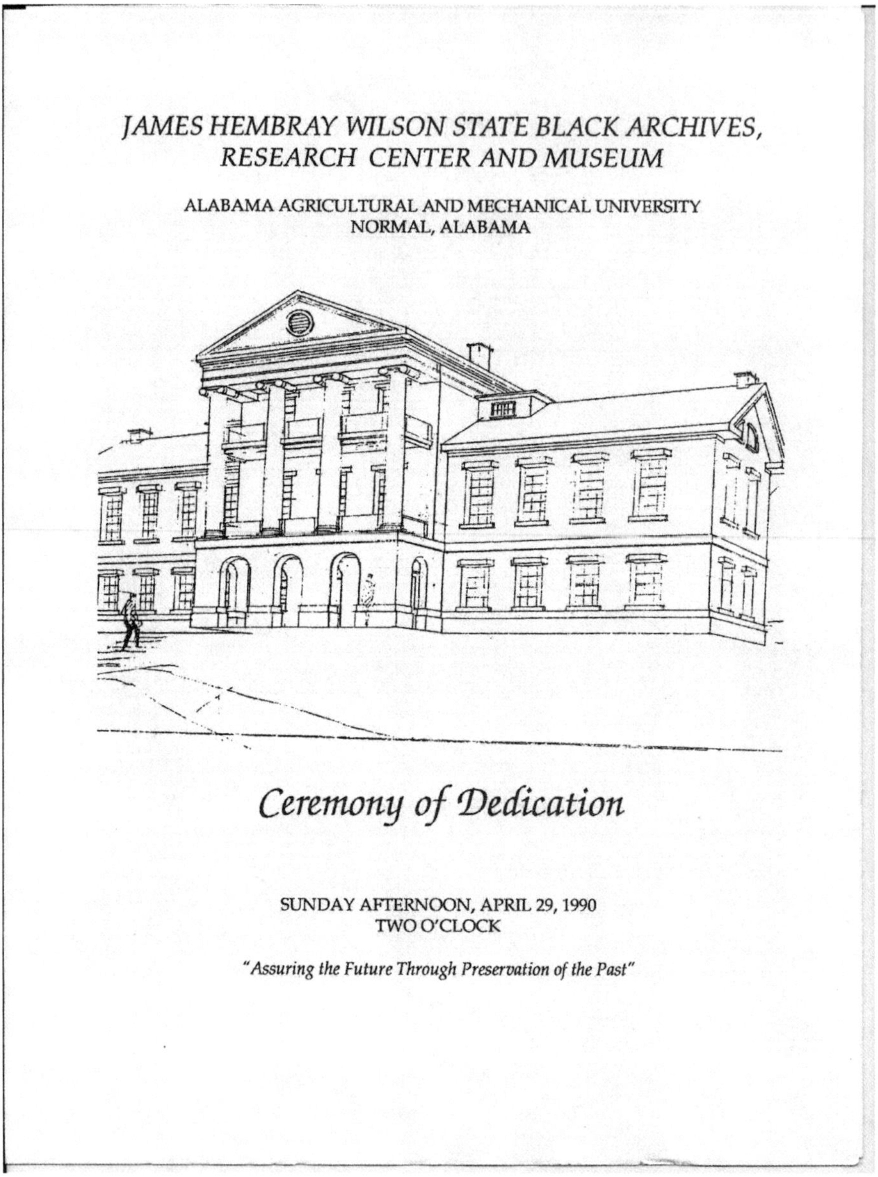

JAMES HEMBRAY WILSON STATE BLACK ARCHIVES, RESEARCH CENTER AND MUSEUM

ALABAMA AGRICULTURAL AND MECHANICAL UNIVERSITY
NORMAL, ALABAMA

Ceremony of Dedication

SUNDAY AFTERNOON, APRIL 29, 1990
TWO O'CLOCK

"Assuring the Future Through Preservation of the Past"

Figure 12-17. Program cover, Ceremony of Dedication, James Hembray Wilson State Black Archives Research Center and Museum.

Ceremony of Dedication

Dr. Carl Harris Marbury, *Presiding*

PRELUDE..Instrumental Ensemble
Arthur Wesley, *Conductor*

HYMN–"Our God, Our Help"..Watts

Our God, our help in ages past,
Our hope for years to come,
Our shelter from the stormy blast,
And our eternal home!

Time, like an ever rolling stream
Bears all its sons away;
They fly, forgotten, as a dream
Dies at the opening day.

Our God, our help in ages past,
Our hope for years to come,
Be Thou our guide while life shall last,
And our eternal home.

LITANY..Dr. Henry Bradford, Jr.
Pastor
Church Street Cumberland Presbyterian Church

MUSIC–"Cantante Domino"..Hans Leo Hassler
UNIVERSITY CHOIR
Richard Tucker, *Director*

THE LEGACY OF JAMES HEMBRAY WILSON.......................Mrs. Hester W. Orr
Daughter
Durham, North Carolina

Mr. Henry Glover
Arranger, Composer, Producer, Performer (Retired)
St. Albans, Long Island, New York

MUSIC–"Ride The Chariot"..Henry Smith
UNIVERSITY CHOIR

UNVEILING OF THE PORTRAIT OF JAMES HEMBRAY WILSON, SR.
Dr. Carl Harris Marbury

INSTRUMENTAL SOLO–"His Eye Is On The Sparrow".............................Martin
George Upshaw, *Trumpet*

BENEDICTION..Dr. Henry Bradford, Jr.

Tour of the James Hembray Wilson State Black Archives, Research Center and Museum

Reception

Figure 12-18. Ceremony of Dedication Program, Dr. Carl Harris Marbury, President of the College, presiding.

and his funeral service, lovingly planned, with all his family and campus friends in attendance, would have brought him joy, too.

One might think that the story of James Hembray Wilson would end here, after his death, funeral, and interment, but it does not. In a way his memory created a living presence on campus for many years. Wilson's friend, President Joseph Fanning Drake, the fourth president of Alabama Agricultural and Mechanical College, resigned at the end of the 1961-1962 academic year, and a young Richard Morrison, Ph.D., replaced Drake and served twenty-two years. He, in turn, was replaced by Douglas Covington, Ph.D., but this man left unexpectedly in 1987 after only three years in office. The surprised State Education Commission selected a former A. & M. student who had known Professor Wilson in the 1950s, Carl Marbury, Ph.D., to step in as Interim President for two years, and then, in 1989, he became President of the College-now-become-a-University and served two additional years in that post. During his first years in office, Marbury began an ambitious program of construction and renovation, and he remembered:

> The state approved the location of an Alabama Black History Museum on campus, and one of the buildings, the old Domestic Science Building, was being renovated and had been chosen to house the collection. Since the money for renovation was not being donated by a private person or family, we had an opportunity to name the building and dedicate it ourselves. I appointed a faculty committee and asked them to draw up a list and consider those persons they thought worthy of this honor and to submit their names to me. After much deliberation the committee recommended James Hembray Wilson, and I approved their selection.[23]

The family was told, plans were made, and a date in February, 1990, during the University's Black History Month was chosen for a dedication ceremony. When it became clear the renovations would not be completed in time the date was moved to April. An oil portrait to hang in the lobby of the building had been commissioned, and, once again, James Hembray Wilson was honored by the

---

[23]Telephone interview with President Emeritus Carl Marbury, October 27, 2011.

University that provided him the means to pursue his creative and meaningful life.

At the Ceremony of Dedication, President Marbury unveiled the Portrait, James' daughter, Hester, spoke of his legacy, and his friend, Dr. Henry Bradford, Jr., now Pastor of the Church Street Cumberland Presbyterian Church, led the litany of dedication. At the sixth invocation he said:

> To the perpetual memory of James Hembray Wilson, Sr. who wrought good works on Normal's Hill in days gone by, as a tribute to his musical genius, his Christian gentility, his biblical scholarship, his business and managerial acumen, and his abiding influence on those who knew him;

And the audience responded:

> We dedicate this edifice.

Appendix One

James H. Wilson Journal
January 1—June 30, 1908

This transcription of James Hembray Wilson's Journal attempts to reproduce the manuscript with typescript as accurately as possible, preserving Wilson's orthography, abbreviations, spellings and misspellings, so that the reader might get a sense of reading an unedited original document. The booklet used by Wilson is small (3 ⅝" x 5 ¾") and leather-bound, and the acid content of the cheap paper is gradually browning and decaying the paper. The pages are lined for writing, and the guide lines run the short dimension of the page, the width and not the length. Hence, reproducing the page in type, line by line, would waste most of the right side of the page. By using double columns, this problem is solved but it destroys the sense of smallness and tidiness that is projected from the original. Wilson writes in ink, and both his printing and script are clear and neat. Erasures are not possible, and some false starts are crossed out.

The lines which were printed in the booklet before sale were probably inserted with the intention of selling the booklet for use as a personal financial record. Ruled with blue horizontal lines and three red vertical lines—the single red line on the left leaves space for a date; the two vertical red lines on the right mark spaces for dollars and cents. The left of these latter two is actually a vertical double-line that separates the item-entry-space from the cost. Wilson basically ignored these vertical lines and wrote over them, and he did not number his pages. On the manuscript I have numbered them lightly in pencil in the lower right hand corners, and these page numbers appear in this transcription in brackets. All other comments in brackets [ ] are mine, too, not Wilson's.

APPENDIX ONE

Figure A1. Leather Cover of James H. Wilson Journal.

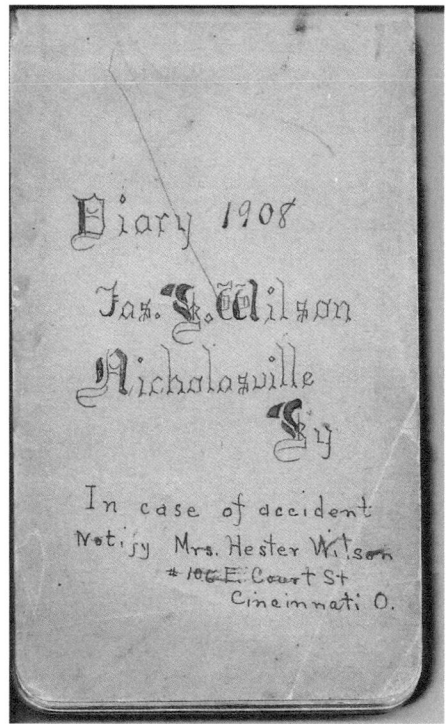

Figure A2. Wilson Journal, flyleaf, recto.

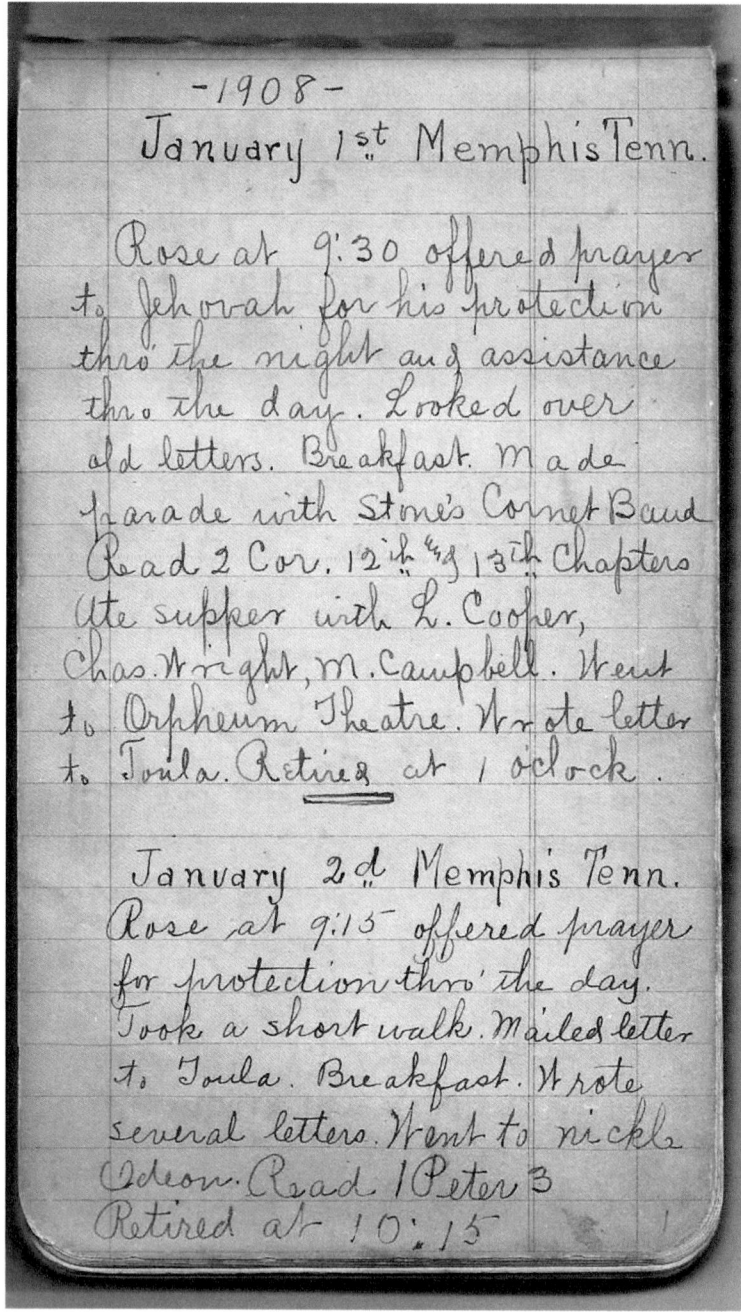

Figure A3. Wilson Journal, page 1, January 1 and 2, 1908.

APPENDIX ONE

[inside front cover]
    OK/ 10¢

    1819—1919

[flyleaf, recto]
    Diary 1908
    Jas. H. Wilson
    Nicholasville
        Ky

    In case of accident
    Notify Mrs. Hester Wilson
    #106 E. Court St.
    Cincinnati O.

    1928
    1908
    ———
       20

[p.1]

    -1908-
January 1st Memphis Tenn.

Rose at 9:30 offered prayer
to Jehovah for his protection
thro the night and assistance
thro' the day. Looked over
old letters. Breakfast. Made
parade with Stone's Cornet Band
Read 2 Cor. 12th and 13th Chapters
Ate supper with L. Cooper,
Chas. Wright, M. Campbell. Went
to Orpheum Theatre. Wrote letter
to Toula. Retire at 1 o'clock.

———

January 2d Memphis Tenn.
Rose at 9:15 offered prayer
for protection thro' the day.
Took a short walk. Mailed letter
to Toula. Breakfast. Wrote
several letters. Went to nickle
Odeon. Read 1 Peter 3

Retired at 10:15

[p. 2]
Memphis Tenn. Jan 3d
Rose at 8:50 Offered prayer.
Read 2 Peter 2d & 3d Chapters
Wrote to sister Goines. Breakfast.
Sent off telegrams for Mme
Kersands. Bathed. Wrote Toula
Began an arrangement on
Melody in F. Walked out in
town. Retired at 11:18

———

Memphis Tenn. Jan. 4th
Rose at 9:35 Offered prayer
Breakfast. Read 1 Tim. 1
Wrote Daisy and Toula also letter
of importance for Mme Kersands.
Worked on arrangement.
Read Matt. 1st and 2d Chapters
Finished arrangement of
Medley ["Melody" above] in F.
Retired at 8:50

[p.3]
Memphis Tenn. Jan. 5th
Rose at 8:35
Read Rom. 1st Chapter
Breakfast.
Attended morning service
at Avery Chapel. A.M.E.
Sermon very good. Dr. Porter.
Text Isa. 35: 8-10
Choir very good. Baptism
Dinner. Attended night
services at Metropolitan Baptist
Church. Services good.
Sermon by Eld. Price fair
Text Gal. 5:22 Choir fair.
Nice church. Large congregation
Rev. Searcy Pastor.
Retired at 10:50

[p.4]

Memphis Tenn. Jan. 6th
Rose at 9 Offered prayer.
Read Rom. 2 Breakfast.
Made parade. Wrote a few
letters. Played for benefit
at Church's Auditorium.
Retired at 1:30

———

Memphis Tenn. Jan. 7th
Rose at 10. Offered prayer.
Read Rom. 3ᵈ Breakfast
Wrote letter to Toula.
Walked up town. Went
to Orpheum Theatre.
Retired at 10:52

———

Memphis Tenn Jan. 8th
Rose at 9:30. Offered prayer.
Read Rom. 4 Breakfast
Shaved. Walked out in
[p. 5]
town and purchased a
box of shoe polish at a
negro shoe store. Wrote
several letters.
Retired at 10:35

———

En route Memphis Tenn
to Clarksdale Miss Jan 9
Rose at 9:35 Breakfast
Read Rom. 5:
Arrived in Clarksdale at
one o'clock. Wrote a
few notes. Took a short
walk with Lloyd Cooper.
Retired at 11:40

———

Clarksdale Miss. Jan. 10
Rose at 9:05. Breakfast.
Read Rom. 6 : 7 Chapters
Parade Wrote several
letters. Concert. Show

Rainy day. Retired at 11:20

[p. 6]

Clarksdale Miss. Jan 11
Rose at 9:40 Read Rom. 8
Offered prayer. Breakfast.
Parade. Wrote letter to T___
Concert and show.
Retired at 11:45

———

Greenville Miss Jan. 12
Rose at 11:00 Offered
prayer. Breakfast. Read
a newspaper. Wrote a letter.
Read Rom. 9:10:11:12:13.
Attended services at
Star of Bethlehem Baptist Church
Pastor read Ps. 95 [95 in pencil,
same hand]
Covenant Meeting in which
I took a part. Small congre-
gation. Fair church.
Rev. Lindsay Pastor.
Retired at 11:00

———

[p. 7]
Greenville Miss. Jan. 13
Rose at 9 Offered prayer
Read Rom. 14:15:16
Arranged notes in route
book. Concert. Show
Retired at 11:15

———

Enroute Greenville
to Grenada Jan 14
Rose at 9:45 Offered prayer
Breakfast. Wrote letter P___
Read 1 Cor. 1:2:3 Shaved
Parad. Concert. Show.
Arrived in Grenada 5 o'clock
Retired at 11:20

APPENDIX ONE

Winona Miss. Jan. 15
Rose at 9 Offered prayer.
Read 1 Cor 4
Parade. Wrote letter to T____
Dinner first meal of
[p. 8]
the day. Quite an accident
with the car in which Mme
Kersands and L. D. Henderson
were hurt. Dishes broken. Stove
broken. Breakfast lost. Card to
Ga___ Concert. Show
Mrs. McMahon
visited us from Chi Retired at
11:45

―――

Durant Miss. Jan 16
Rose at 10 Offered prayer
Breakfast. Read 1 Cor. 5
Parade. Wrote letter of import-
-ance for Mme Kersands
Studied a few chapters of the
Bible. Concert. Show. Cold day
Retired at 10:45

―――

Jackson Miss. Jan. 17
Rose at 8:30 Offered
prayer. Breakfast. Parade

[p.9]
Went with Lloyd Cooper to
purchase a watch. Letter to
T____ Read 1 Cor. 6
Shave. Hair cut. Concert. Show
Took supper at restuarant
Most equipped negro restaurant
and bakery ever saw. seen
[correction probably other hand]
Retired at 12:30

―

Yazoo City Miss Jan 18

Rose at 9:15 Offered
prayer. Breakfast. Went to
P. O. and received 8 letters
2 postals. Parade. Received
a handsome present from T____
Wrote T____ Read 1 Cor 7:
8: 9: Concert. Show.
Retired at 11:30

[p. 10]
Yazoo City Miss. Jan 19
Rose at 9:45 Offered
prayer. Breakfast. Read
I Cor 10
Left Yazoo City at 10:10
en route for Canton
Arrived at Canton at 2
Wrote a letter of importance for
Mme Kersands. Wrote to T___
*Attended services at Mt.
Zion Baptist Church
Congregation large. Nice
church. Text Gal. 6: 7-8
Sermon good by Rev. Adams
Choir poor.
Rev. R. Simms pastor
Sister Covington B. Y. P. W.
organizer addressed church
Retired at 11:45
-- -- -- --
*Pencil annotation in left margin:
"Ga."

[p.11]
  Canton Miss. Jan 20
Rose at 8:45 Offered prayer
Read I Cor II Breakfast
Parade. Wrote letters to T____
M. E. Smalley & Sister Goines
Bought vest and shirt
Concert. Show. Retired at 11:20

―――

Ackerman Miss. Jan 21
Rose at 9:50 Offered prayer
Breakfast. Read I Cor. 12
Wrote several letters of im-

portance. Did not leave
the car all day. Left
Ackerman en route for
Storksville at 6:30 P.M.
Read a book. Retired at 8:30

Storksville Miss. Jan 22
Rose at 8:30 Offered prayer
Read I Cor. 13-14 chapters.
Breakfast. Paraded to
[p. 12]
the A. and M. College of Mississippi. Over 900 students.
Wrote a few letters. Concert.
Show. Retired at 11:35

West Point Miss. Jan 23
Rose at 9:25 Offered
prayer Breakfast.
Read I Cor. 15 Parade
Letters of introduction to
Daisy and Toula. Concert.
Show. Very cold day.
Retired at 11:45

West Point Miss Jan 24
Rose at 8:55 Offered
prayer. Read I Cor. 16
Shaved   Breakfast
Left West Point en route for
Aberdeen at 10 A. M.

[p. 13]
arrived at Aberdeen 10:45
Parade led band alone.
Foot race between Harry Toney
Harry Conway. Wrote to T____
Concert. Show. Retired at 11:05

Amory Miss. Jan 25
Rose at 8:50 Offered prayer Read 2 Cor. 1 Breakfast. Wrote several letters

for David D. Smith
(important) Wrote Eld. Dicker[-]
son and Mrs. C. B. Graves
Sent souvenir card to T____
Concert. Show. Retired at 11.

Tupelo Miss Jan. 26
Rose at 9:50 Offered prayer. Read 2 Cor. 2
Breakfast.
Went in company with
David Smith to Rising
[p. 14]
Star Baptist Sunday School.
Addressed the same taking for as
a foundation of remarks
John 2: 14, 18, 19 verses
Remained to services
Text Rev. 2: 10
Sermon good. Congregation small and small
church. Rev. Hall pastor
Left Tupelo en route
for Corinth Miss. at
5:50 Arrived in Corinth
at 7:30 Went in company with Mme. Kersands
to the St. Marks* Baptist Church
too
late to hear sermon.
Congregation small.
Retired at 9:05
-- -- -- --
*"St. Marks" inserted above.

[p.15]
Corinth Miss. Jan. 27
Rose at 8:30 Offered
prayer. Read 2 Cor. 3
4: 5:   Breakfast.
Read letters from Ga. T____
M. E. Smally, W. S. Baily, Minnie
Johnson. Wrote to T____
Ga. Prof W. H. Councill

APPENDIX ONE

Minnie J. Visited Mrs. Mayfield. Concert. Show Retired at 11:50

Corinth Miss Jan 28
Rose at 8:15 Met Chas Hunter of St. Louis Breakfast. Left Corinth at 8:40 en route to Boon[e]ville Arrived at Boon[e]ville 9:20 Parade. Letters to Mrs. Archer and Prof W. H. Councill
for Mme Kersands
[p.16] Town reported to be very bad but was treated very nicely. Concert. Played exclusively to white audience. Read Ps. 75 Retired at 10:50

Booneville Miss. Jan 29
Rose at 8:10 Offered prayer. Read 2 2 Cor. 6:7 Letter to T____ and M. E. Smalley. Breakfast. Left Boon[e]ville en route for Tupelo at 10:45 Arrived in Tupelo at 11:30 Parade Letter to T____ B. T. Concert Show Retired at 10:40

[p.17]

Tupelo Miss Jan. 30
en route to Corinth.
Rose at 8 Offered prayer. Read 2 Cor 7:8: John. 8 Rev. 20 Breakfast. Arrived in Corinth at 10 oclock Left Corinth at 12 M. en route to Sheffield

Ala. arrived Sheffield at 2:30 Paraded to Florence and Tuscumbia on car. Cold day Met Wm Reynolds a Normalite. Concert Show Retired at 10:50

[p. 18]
Jan 31
Courtland Ala
Rose at 9:50 Offered prayer. Read 2 Cor 9. Para Breakfast Rained all day. Parade. Wrote T____ Annabel. Read a book. Concert Show. Retired at 12:25

Courtland Ala. Feb. 1
Rose at 8:50 Offered prayer. Read 2 Cor 10:11 Left Courtland en route for Decatur at 10:30 arrived at Decatur 11:30 Parade. Wrote T____ Visited Dr. Steers Infirmary and residence at invitation of Miss Ross, my ex student. Very cold day.
[p. 19]
Concert. Show Retired 11:15

Decatur Ala. Feb. 2
Rose at 8:30 Offered prayer. Read Gal. 1 Ecc. 3:5:12: Matt. 1:5: 1 Sam. 28 Left Decatur at 4:20 P.M. en route for Scottsboro. Arrived 7:05 Took a birds eye view of Normal.(A. and M. College) while en route. Attended services at Baptist Church

291

Text Eze. Sermon
poor. Church small.
Congregation small.
Very cold day. Retired 9:40.

[p. 20]
Scottsboro Ala. Feb. 3
Rose at 9:00 Offered
prayer. Breakfast.
Parade. Wrote T____ and
several others
Read Gal. 2 Concert.
Show. Beautiful day
Retired. 10:50

———

Scottsboro Ala Feb 4
Rose at 7:35 Offered
prayer. Left Scottsboro at
7:35 en route for
Chattanooga Tenn. ar-
rived at Chatt. 10. Paid
Mr. and Mrs. John Pitts a
visit and dined.
Left Chattanooga at
3:00 en route for
Dalton Ga. arrived
[p. 21]
Dalton at 4:30 Parade
Received a package
from N. O. also letter from
T____ Concert. Show
Read Gal 3: 4: 5
Eph. 1
Retired at 11:35

———

Dalton Ga. Feb. 5
Rose at 9 Offered pray-
er. Read Eph. 2 Break-
fast. Left Dalton at 10.
11:30 arrived Rome
Rainy day. Beautiful
city. Wrote T____ G____ [Toula
and Georgia]
Harry Prampin a letter

for Mme Kersands
Concert. Show. Retired 11:45
[p.22]
Rome Ga. Jan Feb. 6
Rose at 8:50 Offered
prayer. Breakfast.
Read Eph. 3 En route
to Atlanta arrived
Atlanta at 10:30 Parade
Wrote T____ Prof. W. H. Councill
Beautiful day. Concert
Show. Ate supper at
restaurant with Lloyd
Cooper. Sat in smoking
room of the Terminal
Station conversing.
Retired at 1:45

———

Atlanta Ga. Feb. 7
Rose at 9 Offered prayer
Read Eph 4 Breakfast.
Shaved. Parade. Paid
Rev. M. C. Manning A.M., DD.
[p. 23]
a visit and took dinner.
Spent a most pleasant
afternoon at his residence.
Treated very hospitibly [sic]
Concert. Show. Beauti-
ful day. Somewhat
warm. Letter to T____
Retired at 12:30.

———

Atlanta Ga. Feb. 8
Rose at 9:50 Offered
prayer. Breakfast. Drop-
ped a few postals.
Parade. Wrote G____ [Georgia]
Dined with W. Ellis
Porter. Spent a pleasant
evening with him. Con-
cert Show. Read Eph. 5
Retired at 12:25

[p. 24]
Atlanta en route to Chattanooga Feb. 9 Rose at
11:25 Read Eph. 6
Phil. 1:2:3 Breakfast.
Arrived Chattanooga at
1:15 Spent the day
and night with Mr and
Mrs. Jn o. Pitts Rained
the entire day. Wrote T____
Retired at 11:25

———

Chattanooga Tenn. Feb 10
Rose at 8:30 Breakfast.
Read Phil. 4
Rainy day. Took a
short walk. Read poetry
Retired at 11:05

———

Chattanooga Tenn. Feb 11
Rose at 3:50 Walked
[p. 25]
to the Central Sheds.
Breakfast. Wrote Prof.
W. H. Councill of Ala.
Walked to P. O. and sent
a few postals. Went from
there to Mr. and Mrs. Jn o
Pitts and had dinner.
Wrote T____ Read Col. 1
Walked to town and
purchased paper and
souvenir cards. Read
and wrote poetry
Retired at 10

———

Chattanooga Tenn. Feb. 12
Rose at 8:45 Breakfast
Wrote Mme. Kersands
Read Col. 2 Read and
wrote poetry. Visited
with Mr. Jn o Pitts G. W.
Franklin the leading
undertaker of the city
[p. 26]
Met Miss Nettie Olden
formly [sic] of Orpheus Jubilee
Singers who favored us
with a solo. Miss Mamie
Olden, Miss Lee, Mrs.
Franklin, Mable Franklin
Miss Meyers. Mr. Franklin
and daughter entertained
with cornet and piano.
Visited the James Build-
-ing the highest building
in Chatt., East Side
Phamacy [sic], Y. M. C. A.
met Prof. L. W. Henderson
of Howard High School
R. C. Hawkins letter carrier
Sec. Johnson. Messrs
Bryson and Morris.
Returned Home
Retired 11:20

[p. 27]
Chattanooga Tenn.
Offered prayer. Feb. 13
Rose at 8:45 Breakfast
Did a little writing
Went to P. O. from
there to the central
sheds from there to
the Bijou Theatre to
see "The Boy Detective."
Visited J. D. Fagala
Undertaking Establish-
ment. Met J. F. Trimble
undertaker, Misses Lillian
Pulliman and Stamfis [?first
letter?]
Wrote T. Sent a valentine
to Bertha Staunton Gettysburg
Pa.
Read a few poems
Read Col. 3:4: 1 Thess. 1
Rainy day. Retired 10:55

[p. 28]
Chattanooga   Feb 14
Rose at 7:40 offered prayer
Read 1 Thess. 2. Breakfast
Went to P. O. Parade. Very
long indeed. Wrote T____
Sent a Valentine to T____
Rained the whole day long.
Concert. Show. R Met
Miss Johnson teacher at
A. and M. College Normal Ala.
Retired 11:50

Chattanooga   Feb. 15
Rose at 8:(10) Offered pray-
-er. Played a few select-
-ion[s] on the piano for my
own amusement. Breakfast.
Read 1 Thess. 3 Went to
P. O. from there to Hippo
drume [sic]. Parade. Matinee
[p. 29]
Went home in company
with Mrs. Pitts and Williams
Wrote T____ Concert. Show
Went to David Smith's
residence from there to
East Side Pharmacy and
had a glass of soda with
Mr. Jn o Pitts from there
to Mr. Pitts['] and bade
family goodbye. To
the car   retired at 1:15

En route Feb. 16 from
Chattanooga to Nashville
Rose at 10:25 Offered
prayer. Breakfast Read
1 Thess 4:5
Arrived Nashville
6:35 Attended services
at Fair view Baptist
Church. Text   John 7:46
Sermon poor   Church*

-- -- -- -- --
*Scribble in left margin "1020"[?]

[p. 30]
neat. Congregation
large. Company Roy
Johnson. Retired 10:20

Nashville Tenn. Feb 17
Rose at 8:30 Breakfast.
Read 2 Thess. 1:2:3:
En route from Nash-
ville to Princeton Ky.
arrived Princeton
12:30 Parade Wrote
Prof. W. H. Councill, M. E.
Smally and Maggie L
Freeman. Dropped a
few postals. Wrote letter
of importance for
Manzie Campbell. Con-
cert. Show.
Retired. 11 oclock

[p. 31]
Morganfield Ky
                    Feb 18
Rose at 10 Offered
prayer. Breakfast.
Shaved. Bought a
pair of shoes. Pa-
rade. Wrote D____
T____   Rainy day.
Concert. Show.
Read Ps. 1: 2:
Retired at 11:30

Morganfield Ky. Feb 19
Rose at 9 Offered prayer.
Read 1 Tim.2:3:
Left Morganfield at
9:50 en route for Evansville Ind.
Arr.
Evansville at 11:30

Appendix One

and greeted with an
abundance of snow
[p. 32]
Parade. Purchased
a pair of shoes. Wrote
Jno. Pitts of Chatt. and A____
Worked on an arrange-
ment for Jas. Lacy. Con-
cert. Show. Retired 11:00

Qwensboro Ky. Feb. 20
Rose at 9 Offered prayer.
Read 1 Tim. 4 Parade.
Met Mis Hayden of Rock-
port Ind. Spent a few
pleasant hours with
her. Met Mrs. McCarter,
L Steward, N. Samuels
S. Price, Mrs. Jackson,
of Owensboro Mrs. Jackson
of Rockport Ind. Looked
for a restaurant but in
vain. Plenty of mud
[p.33]
Ate supper at Mrs.
Samuels. Accompanied
Miss Hayden to the opera
house. Concert. Show.
Retired at 11:30

Evansville Ind Feb. 21
Rose at 9 Offered prayer.
Breakfast. Went to depot
to see about getting train
for Lexington. Read 1 Tim. 5
Packed up. Hair cut.
Bade the boys good
bye. left Evansville
at 2:15 en route for
Louisville Ky. Purchased
two books to read. News
agent tried to [blank]
me into trading rings
but was too shrewed

for him. Arrived
Louisville at 7:30
[p. 34]
Took a cab for Mr. Neigh-
bors the photograper; not
finding him at the studio
went to Mrs. Mollie Gray
to spend the night.
Went to restuarant [sic] and
had lunch. Read a
book entitled "The Devil
of today" Retired 10:30

Louisville Ky. Feb. 22
Rose at 6:25 Went to
Tenth St. Depot. Read
1 Tim 6 Left Louisville
en route for Lexington at
7:35 A. M. Arrived Lexington
at 11:50 Went to Campbell's
Restaurant [sic] for dinner.
Met Wm Fields. Went to
Neighbors. Spent the
[p. 35]
Afternoon with Mrs.
Hawthorne. Accompanied
Mrs. H____ to Mrs. Dennis
to give a music lesson.* Had
my baggage transferred [sic]
to C. S. depot. Paid a [Cincinnati
Southern]
short visit to Mrs. Mills.
Left Lexington en route
for Nicholasville at 6:50
arr. 7:30 Had lunch.
Attended supper given
by the B.Y.P.W. and
candy pulling given
by members of my father[']s
club of Christian Church.
Retired at 12.

Nicholasville Ky. Feb 23
Rose at 8:30 Arranged
toilet. Breakfast. Attended

Sunday School at
Baptist Church. Very nice
-- -- -- --
*"lesson" inserted above line.

[p. 36]
school. Addressed the
same. Remained to
morning service.
Text John   Sermon
by John Fisher D.D. good
Congregation small. Choir
poor. Accompanied Mrs.
M. E. Smalley home for
dinner. Attended evening
services at the Christian
Church. Text 1 Cor 16: 2
Sermon by Eld Morrison
of A. M. E. Church   good.
Congregation large. Choir
fair. Rally in which my
father was a contestant.
Had lunch at home.
Attended B. Y. P. U.
services very good. Addressed
the same. Remained

[p. 37]
to evening services and
assisted the choir by presiding at
the organ.
Text Matt 25: 24 by
Jno. Fisher D.D.   fair
choir good. Congregation
small. Went to the Christian Church to hear
the result of rally. My
father was the winner.
Stopped by a restaurant
and had a piece of pie.
Wrote T____ retired at
11:50

———

Nicholasville Ky. Feb 24
Rose at 8:30 Breakfast

Read 2 Tim 1   Wrote
G____   Made the following visits Mr. D. S.
Waide, Accompanied
by Mrs M. E. Smalley.
visited Elders Fisher

[p. 38]
Dickerson and Morrison,
my aunt Maggie,
Cousin Rosie, Jallie[?]
Chatwell, Public School.
Katherine Hutchison,
Jno. Smith, Supper.
Bath. Attended supper
given by the A. M. E.
Church. Treated Mrs.
Smalley, Elliott Jackson.
Dora   Went to
depot. Left Nicholasville en route for
Huntsville Ala. at
10:45   Arrived Chattanooga at 5:15
Feb. 25
Went to David P Smith
and had breakfast.
Left Chattanooga

[p. 39]
at 10:30 en route for
Fearns Ala. Arrived at 2:10 Went
immediately
to President's office and
met a few of the teachers.
Accompanied by Miss
C. King went to dining
hall and had dinner.
Met Mr. Griffin the commandant who treated
me very hospitably.
Attended devotional exercises. Heard address
by Miss Patrick. Introduced
to student body and
made a few remarks.

APPENDIX ONE

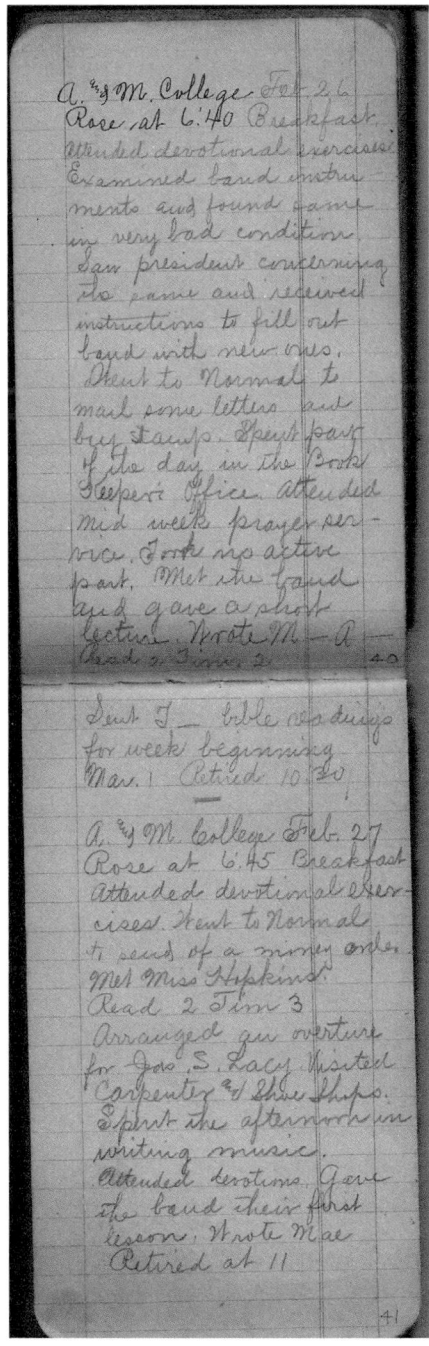

Figure A4. Wilson Journal, page 41, February 26 and 27, 1908.

Visited the judge and had
coco [sic] cola and peanuts on
Mr. Griffin. Wrote T____
retired 10:40

[p. 40]
A. and M. College* Feb 26
Rose at 6:40 Breakfast.
Attended devotional exercises.
Examined band instruments and found same
in very bad condition.
Saw president concerning
the same and received
instructions to fill out
band with new ones.
Went to Normal to
mail some letters and
buy stamps. Spent part
of the day in the Book
Keeper's Office. Attended
mid week prayer service. Took no active
part. Met the band
and gave a short
lecture. Wrote M____ A____
Read 2 Tim. 2
-- -- -- --
*Here and elsewhere there is
evidence of Wilson having reread
and gone over his notes. It is clear
on this page, that where he wrote
originally in pencil he rewrote over
some of the text in ink [or possibly
filled in blank spaces, but I do not
think so]. The first three lines of
page 40 read as follows: [**boldface**
= ink; black = pencil]
A. and M. College Feb. 26
Rose at 6:40 Breakfast.
Attended devotional exercises.

[p. 41]
Sent T____ bible readings
for week beginning
Mar. 1 Retired 10:30

———

A. and M. College Feb. 27
Rose at 6:45 Breakfast
Attended devotional exercises. Went to Normal
to send of[f] a money order.
Met Miss Hopkins.
Read 2 Tim 3
Arranged qu overture
for Jas. S. Lacy. Visited
Carpenter and Shoe Shops.
Spent the afternoon in
writing music.
Attended devotions. Gave
the band their first
lesson. Wrote Mae
Retired at 11

[p. 42]
A. and M. College Feb 28
Rose at 6:55 Breakfast
Attended devotional
exercises. Read 2 Tim 4
Wrote T____
Heard lectures in chapel
by Dr. Williams of
Huntsville. Visited Miss
Johnson. Went to
Normal. Attended
devotions. Students
Meeting Subject Have
I a plan in life etc
Trained glee Club
for Adelphia Society.
Retired at 11

———

A. and M. College Feb 29
Rose at 6:55 Shaved
Breakfast. Trained
glee club. Arranged
[p. 43]
music for band
Spent an hour in
training the band.

APPENDIX ONE

Sent a letter C. F. Geiger
& Co ordering band
instruments. Went to
Normal to see two
teachers off. Visited
Prof. Hopkins & family
Trained Glee Club. Attended devotions. Trained
Glee Club. Met Miss
Councill who had been
away visiting. Wrote T____
Carrie Kendricks Bathed.
Retired at 11

___

A. and M. College March 1
Rose at 6:30 Breakfast.
Attended Y. M. C. A.
meeting and took a
part in discussion
[p. 44]
from Dan. 1:-8 Subject
Stand up for the right.
Good meeting. Read
Titus   Attended
morning services in
chapel. Text Rom 8:13
Sermon good. Eld. Ramsey
chaplain. Choir very
good. Wrote G____ A. H. ____
K. H. Went to Sunday
School. Large attendance
Taught Senior Class of
Boys. Supper. Accompanied Mrs. King and
Miss Wright to their
hall. Attended Sun____
Evening Meeting in
the chapter [chapel?] Chaplain
read Rom 12
Meeting good. Wrote letters
Retired at 10:30
[p. 45]
A. and M. College M'ch 2
Rose at 6:30 Breakfast.
Chapel for devotions.

Visited Misses Johnson's
and Gibson's room.
Appeared before Junior
and 2^d Normal classes
for penmanship.
Rehearsed Mrs Johnson'
Class for rhetorical.
Trained glee club.
Retired at 11

___

A. M. College May [?]

[p. 46]
[blank]

[p. 47]
A and M. College Mch. 5
Rose at 6:30 Breakfast
Chapel. Trained Misses
Gibson's and Johnson's
classes for rhetorical.
Trained a class of
girls for concert. Glee
Club. Chapel. Wrote
Ga. Teachers' meeting
Discussion "What affect* will
imagration [sic] have on the
negro?" Ably discussed
by Mr. Lowery, Rev.
Ramsey and Prof. Hopkins.
Chapel to assist Miss
Johnson's class for
rhetorical. Read Heb. 3
Retired 10:40

___

A. and M. College Mch. 6
Rose at 6:45 Breakfast
Chapel. Visited Mrs.
[p. 48]
King's room. Very interesting class. Assisted Miss
Johnson in her class
rhetoricals. Class did
not do so well. Played

299

a solo for the Adelphia
Society (Ave Maria)
Program good. Met
Mrs Hanna and Miss
Asher of Decatur Ala.
Retired at 9

A. and M. College Mch 7
Rose at 6:30 breakfast.
Witnessed military drill
by students   also fire
drill. Band rehearsal.
Played a game of ball.
First of the season.
Chapel. Prayed. Band

[p. 49]
rehearsal. Wrote T____
arranged several
pieces of music.
Read Heb. 3 Retired 12:55

A. and M. College Mch 8
Rose at 6:45 Breakfast.
Lead [sic] Y. M. C. A. and
Y. W. C. A. in a joint
meeting. Read for
scripture lesson Heb. 13
Address by J. B. Pickett.
good. Inspected Chase
and Langston's Hall.
Morning services. Scripture
lesson 2 Peter 3 by Rev.
Ramsey. Sermon by
Mr. Johnson of senior
college class. Text 2 Pet. 3:18
Subject Christian Develope-[sic]
ment. Fair. Sunday
School. Largely attended

[p. 50]
My class was the banner
class. Col. 30 cts. Visited
Miss Johnson. Evening

program in Chapel.
Play solo "Tram   [?Traumerei?}
Prof. Hopkins addressed
school from subject
"Self Control" Excellent
indeed. Program good.
Wrote Sister Goines,
M. E. Smalley. Retired
at

A. and M. College Mch. 9
Rose at 6:30 Break-
fast. Usual work with
classes, glee club and band
Retired at 11

A. and M. College Mch 10
Rose at 6:15 Breakfast.
Usual work
[p. 51]
Heard address by Miss
Gibson subject "What
science has done for
the home." Excellent.
Retired at 11

A. and M. College Mch 11
Rose at 6:40 Breakfast.
Chapel. Usual work.
Prayer services. Took
a part. Assisted Miss
Johnson with Junior choir
and Miss Gibson's class
Started a letter to T____
Retired at 11:30

A. and M. College Mch 12
Rose at 6:45 Breakfast
Chapel. Usual work,
Band played for Pres.

Councill. Student's [sic]
Social. Arranged Music
[p. 52]
Retired at 11

———

A. and M. C. Mch 13
Rose at 6:45 Break-
fast. Usual duties.
[in left margin:] Wrote T____
Played for Second
Prep. Rhetoricals. Very
good. Retired at 11

———

A. M. C. Mch. 14
Rose at 6:40 Breakfast.
Went to Huntsville
Met Delia Donigan.
Purchased some things
for Mrs. King. Left Hunts-
ville at 1:40 en route
for Normal. Visited Mrs.
King. Chapel. Retired at 11

———

A. M. C. Mch 15
[p. 53]
Rose at 6:20 Breakfast.
Y.M.C.A. Subject
Put not your trust in
the material things
of this life. Matt 6:

———

A. M. C. Mch 16
Morning services.
Text 1 Cor 3:11
Sermon very good by
Rev. Ramsey. Had
visitors from Hunts-
ville.. Sunday School.
My class was the banner
class. Sunday Night
services. The Junior
Choir rendered a pleas-
ing program.
Retired at 10

———

[p. 54]
A.M.C. Mch. 16
Rose at 6 Band rehearsal
Breakfast. Chapel.
Mrs King's class.
Band rehearsal at
four. Chapel.
Band rehearsal.
Retired at 11

———

A.M.C. Mch 17
Rose at 6:40 Breakfast
Chapel. Usual duties.
[in left margin:] Letter to T____
Band concert at four.
Chapel. Band rehearsal
Retired at 11—

———

A.M.C. Mch 18
Rose at 6:50 Breakfast.
Chapel. Usual duties.
Reheared Sextette for
[p. 55]
Pebody L, S. Wrote T____
Pitched hose shoes.
Supper. Rehearsed
girls in Chapel.
Led prayer meeting
Read for lesson
1 John 4. Twelve per-
[in left margin:] Wrote several
letters
sons took an active
part. Band rehearsal
Retired at 11

———

A.M.C. Mch 19
Rose at 6:30 Breakfast.
Chapel. Rehearsed sextette.
Mrs. King[']s Class.

Wrote several letters.
Band played in Chapel.
Had visitors. Dr. Mc
Kinney Ex president
of Alabama Academy
Dr. William of Huntsville
[p. 66]
Band rehearsal.
pitched horse shoes.
Rehearsed Miss King's class
Teachers meeting.
Pebody L. S.
Read
Retired at
———

A.M.C. Mch 20
Rose at 7 Breakfast.
Chapel. Wrote Rev. D. P. Jones
Schaved. Rehearsed Glee
Club. Girls. Played a
solo for Pebody L. S.
Started a letter to T____
Retired at 10:45
———

A.M.C. Mch 21
Rose at 7 Breakfast.
Finished letter t[o] T____
Began an arrangement
for band band on Song
[p. 57]
by Mac Dowell. Pitched
[To A Wild Rose ??]
a few games of horse shoe
Chapel for rehearsal.
Mrs. King's Class. Rehearsed
Minstrel Nola Club. Played
for Mrs. King[']s Rhetoricals.
Very good. Arranged
a piece of music for
a brass quartette. Studied
S. S. lesson. Read Heb. 4
Retired at 11
———

A. M. C. Mch. 22
Rose at 7 Breakfast.
Went to Y.M.C.A. heard
addressed [sic] by Prof. Archer
Morning service Text
Joshua
Sermon good. Sunday
School. Reviewed Lesson
2. Visited Mrs. King.
Chapel for devotions
[p. 58]
Spent evening meal pleasantly
in Prof. Hopkin's office.
Wrote T____ Wrote letters
of introduction to Mrs. King in
T_____ Retired at 11
———

A. M. C. Mch 23
Rose at 6:50 Breakfast.
Chapel. Usual duties
Arranged music
in the afternoon. Pitched
horse shoes. Read
Heb 5: 6: 7:
Retired at 11
———

A. M. C. Mch 24
Rose at 6:40 Bre
Shaved. Breakfast.
Chapel. Usual duties.
Band rehearsal at
[p.59]
4 o'clock. Played
horse shoes. Wrote
Gergia [sic], Laura Pram [difficult
to read last name]
pin.
       Retired at 11:15.
———

A. M. C. March 25
Rose at 6:30 Breakfast
Usual duties. Pitched
horse shoes. Attended

APPENDIX ONE

prayer services. The
meeting very interest
-ing. Retired at 11

A. M. C. Mch 26
Rose at 6:30 Breakfast
Chapel. Usual duties.
Had band picture
made. Rehearsed
a chorus. (mix)
Attended round
[p. 60]
table. Read
Heb. 8
Retired at 11:10

A. M. C. Mch 27
Rose at 6:40 Breakfast.
Usual duties. Industrial
parade. Band played.
Very shabby indeed.
Wrote T____ Retired 11:20

A. M. C. Mch 28
Rose at 6:45 Breakfast.
Arranged Miss
Hopkins' Lullaby for
band. Band rehearsal.
Rehearsed chorus.
Attended banquet given
by Fred. Douglas[sic]
Debating Society Quite
[p. 61]
a swell afair [sic].
Read Heb. 9
Retired at 12:45

A. and M. College Mch 29
Rose at 8:30 Chapel
for choir rehearsal.
Missed breakfast for the first
time also Y.M.C.A.

Morning services.
Dr. McKinney ex presi-
-dent of Central Alabama
Academy preached
Text 2 Kings 9:24
Sermon good. Dinner.
Began an arrangement
on Arrah Wanna.
[in left margin:] Read Heb. 10
Sunday School. Dr. Mc
Kinney reviewed school.
Supper. Chapel for evening
services. No special pro-
[p. 61]
-gram rendered. Time
spent in singing
Jubilee Hymns. Very
inspiring. Retired at 10:30

A. M. C. March 30
Rose at 6:30 Breakfast
Chapel. Usual duties.
Arranged a piece of
music. Signed pay
roll Read Heb. 11
Attended supper
given by second
yr. Normal Class
Band rehearsal
Retired at

A. M. C. March 31
Rose at 6:45 Breakfast
chapel. Normal duties.
Taught bible in third
prep. class. Band
[p. 63]
rehearsal. Read
Heb. 12 and 13 chapters.
Chapel. Retired 10

A. and M. C. Apr. 1
Rose at 6:50 Breakfast

303

Chapel. Shaved. Arrang
-ed a piece of music.
Went to Normal to mail
letters Read James 1: 2:
3 Chapters. Band concert
at four oclock at Carnegie
Library. Played in dining
hall at five oclock.
Prayer services. Band rehearsal. Retired at 11:45

———

[p. 63, near bottom]
A. M. C. Apr 2 '08
Rose at 7:00 Breakfast.
Chapel. Wrote E. M. Pitts
and Gertrude Jones.
Penmanship in Junior and
[p. 64]
second yr. classes. Rehearsed
chorus. Teachers. meeting.
Band concert at Carnegie
Library at 6 oclock
Retired at
Read James 4
Retired at 11:10

———

A. M. C. Apr. 3
Rose at 7:00 Breakfast
Chapel. Wrote T____
Miss Freeman. Witnessed
Junior Normal rhetoricals.
Read James 5
Witnessed Delcarte enter-
-tainment. Very good.
Arranged program.
Retired at

———

[p. 65]
A. M. C. Apr. 4
Rose at 6:50 Breakfast
Arranged music
Band rehearsal.
Read 1 Peter 1

Studied S. S. Lesson
Played practice game
of ball. Second game
of season. Attended
reception given in
honor of Dr. Archer
Dean of college depart-
ment and valevictorian [sic]
of class '08 Meharry College.
Band played
Retired at 11:50

———

A. M. C. Apr. 5
Rose at 7:00 Breakfast.
Chapel for morning
services. W. S. Pittman
preached. Text Col. 3:1
[p. 66]
Sunday School. Program
in which I rendered a
solo. Read 1 Peter 2
Retired at 9

———

A. M. C. Apr. 6
Rose at 7 Breakfast.
Sent notices to Hon. Grayson,
Messrs Hunt and Mayhew
and Miss McCormick
Huntsville. Arranged a
piece of music. Re-
hearsed Second yr. class.
Rehearsed girls of chorus.
Band rehearsal at 4 o'clock.
Led the line to Chapel.
Rehearsed entire program
in the chapel. Wrote
T____. Wrote several
copies for penmanship
Read 1 Peter 4
Retired at 1:10
[p. 67]
A. M. C. Apr. 7
Rose at 7 o'clock Breakfast
Chapel. Rehearsed band.

APPENDIX ONE

Rehearsed cornet solo
Read 1 Peter 5
Wrote M___ A___ and
Mary Garrett. Retired 11

———

A. M. C. Apr. 8
Rose at 7
Breakfast. Chapel
Usual duties
Band rehearsal.
Read 2 Peter 1: 2
Band and Choruses
Retired 11 oclock

———

A. M. C. Apr. 9
Rose at 7 oclock.
Breakfast. Chapel. Usual
duties. Rehearsed with
Mrs. Archer's May Pole
Wrote Hon. Hunt and
Mayhew of Huntsville
Ala. Wrote music.
Rehearsed cornet solo
Band & chorus.
Read 2 Peter 3
Retired at

———

A. M. C. Apr. 10 '08
Rose at 6:50 Chapel
Taught 2^d prep. class
for Mrs. King. Arranged
for concert. Industrial
parade. Band concert.
Largely attended. The
affair a grand one.
Program nicely rendered.
~~Retired at~~
Read ~~2~~ 1 Jno 1
Retired at

———

[p. 69]

A. M. C. Apr. 11 '08
Rose at 7:00 Breakfast.
Attended Y.M.C.A.
Morning services.
Eld. Leak of Oak Wood
School preached.
Text 1 Cor. 13: 13
Excellent sermon.
Eld. Berry & Prof Henry
from Oak Wood were dn[??]
present. Sunday School

[p. 70]
Eld Berry addressed
school. Prof. Henry gave
a selection on the piano.
Good. Had quite a tete
a tete with a number
of girls. Chapel for
evening program.
Band played three selections.
Wrote T____ Retired at 10

———

A. M. C. Apr. 13
Rose at 7:00 Breakfast
Chapel. class in penmanship.
Went to Huntsville.
Sent G____ $1700
Band played in chapel
~~Retired at 11~~
Read 1 Jn o. 3
Retired at 11

———

[p. 71]
A. M. C. Apr. 14
Rose at 7:00 Breakfast.
Chapel. Classes in pen-
manship. Band went
to Mc Cormick[']s and
rendered some choice
selections. Serenaded
the Oak Wood School.
Arrived at Normal
at 2:30 A.M.

Retired at 3:00

———

A. M. C. Apr. 15
Rose at 7:00 Breakfast
Chapel. Visited Misses
Johnson's & King's classes.
Penmanship.
Read 1 John. 4: 5:
Band played. Chapel.
Several boys reprimanded
and four expelled
[p. 72]
from the institution
for breaking in[to] a store
and stealing goods. Two
were members of the
band.
Retired at 9:50

———

A. M. C. Apr. 16
Rose at 7:00 Breakfast
Chapel. Rehearsed
Second Normal Class
for their rhetoricals. Reorganized band. Pen-
manship. Visitors from
Oak Wood School.
Eld. Leak preached
Text Rev. 22: 3
Subject the soul. Argument
was without substantial
foundation. Solo by
one of the young ladies
of Oak Wood.

[p, 73]
Teachers' Meeting.
Read 2 John 3 John
Jude. Retired
Wrote T____ Retired 12:30

———

A. M. C. Apr. 17
Rose at 7:10 Breakfast

Chapel. Second Nor-
mal class rhetoricals.
Very good.
Read Rev. 1
Students meeting in
chapel. Very good.
Choir rehearsal. Wrote T____
Retired at 10

———

A. M. C. Apr. 18
Rose at 7 Breakfast
Wrote several letters.
Read Rev. 2: 3:
Rainy day. Chapel
for decoration.
[p. 74]
Supper. Chapel for
devotions. Attended
Annual Banquet of the
Adelphic L. [Literary] Society
Quite a nice affair.
Rev. Chas. Stewart acted as
master of ceremonies.
Accompanied Miss Mar-
Gu[e]rite Thompson to
table and hall. Started a
letter to Toula
Retired at 12:30

———

A. M. C. Apr. 19
Rose at 7. Breakfast.
Y.M.C.A. Rev. Chas.
Stewart addressed same
on subject "Man's abuse
to himself." Morning
service. Rev. Chas. Stewart
preached. Text Matt 28: 6
[p. 75]
Sermon excellent.
Finished letter to T____
Sunday School. Visited
Prof Hopkins & family.
Chapel. Program render-
-ed by Junior Choir.

Rev. Ramsey delivered
an address Subject
Christ our benefactor
Act. 10
Read Rev: 4: 5:
Retired at 10

———

A. M. C. Apr. 20
Rose at 6:30 Breakfast
Chapel. Rehearsed 1st
Normal Class.
Read Rev. 6
Retired at 11

[p. 76]
A. M. C. Apr. 21
Rose at 6:30 Breakfast.
Chapel. Rehearsed
1st Normal Class for
class rhetoricals. Taught
Mrs. King['s] Class. Rehearsed
or rather called rehearsal
for chorus. Serenaded
Mrs. Hamilton and President
Councill. Read Rev. 7: 8
Wrote several letters
Retired at 11

———

A. M. C. Apr. 22
Rose at 7 Breakfast.
Chapel. Rehearsed
1st Normal Class for
class rhetoricals. Arr-
ranged some music.
Rehearsed 1st Normal
class Read Rev. 9: 10
Retired at 11

[p. 77]
A. M. C. Apr. 23
Rose at 7 Breakfast.
Chapel. Rehearsed
1st Yr. class. Penman-
ship in Junior & second

Yr. classes. Chapel
Rehearsed 1st yr. class.
Wrote T____
Read Rev. 11
Retired at

———

A. M. C. Apr. 24
Rose at 7 Breakfast
Chapel. Rehearsed
Senior Normal Class
Visited 2d prep. and
Junior Normal Classes
Witnessed program
in latter room.
Chapel. Phyllis
Wheatley L. S. rendered
[p. 78]
a pleasing program
Played Solo
Read Rev. 12
Wrote T____
Retired at 10:40

———

A. M. C. Apr. 25
Rose at 7 Breakfast.
Pitched horse shoes.
Wrote papa. Read
Rev. 13 Chapel for de-
votions. Choir practice.
Retired at 10

———

A. M. C. Apr. 26
Rose at 7 Breakfast.
Y.M.C.A. led meeting
subject Man's obedience
to God's Law. Rom.
Morning services.
Rev. Ramsey preached
[p. 79]
Sermon good
Text Rom. 8: 28
Wrote T____ studied S. S.
lesson. Sunday School.

Chapel for devotions
Chaplain Ramsey
read Matt 7.
Read Rev. 14: 15
Retired at 9:30

———

A. M. C. Apr. 27
Rose at 7:10 Breakfast
Chapel. Rehearsed senior
class on class song.
Penmanship in 2nd yr.
and Junior classes.
Wrote T____. Read
Rev. 16. Rehearsed
senior class. Wrote
B____ P____ Fisk W____
Retired at 9:55

———

[p. 80]
A. M. C. Apr. 28
Rose at 6:45
Breakfast. Chapel.
Rehearsed Seniors on
class song. Wrote
Mrs. Smith of Chattanooga.
Read Rev. 17: 18
Band rehearsal
Retired at 10
[in right margin:]
lecture by
Mrs. Hamilton,
　　good

———

A. M. C. Apr. 29
Rose at 6:30 Breakfast.
Chapel. Rehearsed
seniors on class songs.
Penmanship.
Read Rev. 19: 20:
Began packing up
Retired   10:50

———

A. M. C. Apr. 30
Rose at 6:50
Breakfast.
[p. 81]
Chapel. Rehearsed
senior class. Visited
Miss Johnson and
Mrs. King rooms.
Penmanship. Began
an arrangement on
Narcissus for band.
Read Rev. 21: 22:
Rehearsed Octett of
senior class. Accompa-
-nied Miss Crockett to
her hall. Retired at
9:50

———

A. M. C. May 1
Rose at 6:00 Chapel
for early morning prayer
service. Breakfast.
Inserted a quotation in
Miss Crockett['s] tablet.
Read Matt. 1
Wrote T____ Worked

[p. 82]
on arrangement.
Celebration of the
33^{d} anniversary of
the institution.
Program in chapel at
11 oclock. Interesting.
Supper. Program at
7 oclock. Band
played. Chorus rendered
two selection[s].
Played Palms.
Address by Prof. Sterling
of Sheffield Ala.
One of the first gradu-
-ates of the school.
Wrote T____
Retired at 10:10

Appendix One

A. M. C. May 2
Rose at 8:50 Finished
letter to T____ went to
Normal. Read
Matt 2: 3:
[p.83]
Dinner. Umpired a
game of ball. Wrote
T____
Retired at

A. M. C. May 3
Rose at 6:50 Breakfast.
Y.M.C.A. M, Hardy
Griffin led. Sister
Broughton lectured.
Morning service
Sister Broughton
spoke from the subject
The conquest of righteous-
-ness. Very good. Sun-
day School. Outing
after S. S. Chapel for
evening program.
Chorus sang two num-
-bers. Mr. Haines read
Job 28: as a lesson
Played "Palms'

[p. 84]
Address by Mr. Haines
Gen Sec. of Y. M. C. A.
Very good.
Read Matt 4
Retired at 10:

A. M. C. May 4
Rose at 6:50 Chapel
Breakfast. Chapel.
Visited Mrs. King Miss
Johnson and Miss Hender-
-son's rooms. Penman-
-ship in 2^d yr. and
Junior classes.
Y.M.C.A. Rehearsal
of senior class song.
Lecture by Mr. Haines.
Invited to Mrs. King.
Read Matt 5
Retired 9:25

[p. 85]
A. M. C. May 5
Rose at 7
Breakfast. Chapel
Penmanship.
Read Matt. 6
Rehearsal.
Retired at 9:45

A. M. C. May 6
Rose at 7 Breakfast
Chapel. Penmanship.
Wrote several letters
Studied S. S. Lesson
Read Matt. 7
Chapel for prayer
service. Meeting good.
Retired at 9:30

A. M. C. May 7
Rose at 6:45 Breakfast
Chapel. Penmanship.
Read Matt 8: 9: 10
[p. 86]
Retired at 10

A. M. C. May 8
Rose at 7 Breakfast
Chapel. Penmanship.
Read Matt. 11: 12
Rehearsed senior class
Retired at

309

A. M. C. May 9
Rose at 6:30
Breakfast. Pitched
several games of
horse shoes. Rehearsed
senior class.
Retired at 9:30

———

A. M. C. May 10
Rose at 6:40 Breakfast.
Y.M.C.A. subject
The Christian's call to
duty. Led by J. E. Ford.

[p. 87]
Morning service
Sermon by W. J. Wilson
of class '08 Text Heb. 12: 1
Subject The Christian
Race. Studied S. S. lesson.
Read Matt. 13
Attended Odd Fellows
services at Fearns
Chapel for evening
devotions. Prof Archer.
address[ed] assembly.
Retired at 9:30

———

A. M. C. May 11
Rose at 6:45 Breakfst
Chapel. Rehearsed
Senior class. Went to
Normal and mailed
letter to Toula and
others. Penmanship
in which the time
was taken in talking

[p. 88]
to Juniors about the
conduct of some of the
male members of class.
Instruction given in
2nd Yr. class on pen-
manship. Read Matt. 14
rehearsed seniors
Retired at 9:30

———

A. M. C. May 12
Rose at 6:50 Breakfast.
Chapel. Address by
Dr. L. R. King an evangel
-ist of Jackson Miss.
Very good. Introduced
by Dr. Williams pastor
of A. M. E. Church
Hunt[s]ville Ala.
Read Matt 15
Rehearsed seniors.
Retired at 9:30

[p. 89]
A. M. C. May 13
Rose at 6:50 Breakfast
Chapel. Rehearsed
seniors.   Read
Matt 16: 17   Rehearsed
Glee and minstrelnola
clubs. Prayer services.
Good in deed.
Retired at 9:30

———

A. M. C. May 14
Rose at 6:50 Breakfast.
Chapel. Rehearsed with
choir. Rehearsed seniors.
Penmanship in 2^d
Yr. class. Began
taking inventory of halls etc.
Teachers'
meeting. Wrote T____
Read Matt 18
Retired 10:30

[p. 90]
A. M. C. May 15

APPENDIX ONE

Rose at 6:50 Breakfast.
Chapel. Rehearsed seniors
Went to Huntsville. Company
Wm Tate. Hair cut. Shave.
Addressed 79 invitations
Wrote 75 visiting cards for
students. Choir rehearsal.
Rehearsed Minstrelnola Club.
Read Matt. 19
Retired at 11:35

———

A. and M. College May 16
Rose at 700 Breakfast.
Palmer Hall. Wrote several
visiting cards for senior
girls. Rehearsed senior
class and glee club.
Read Matt. 20
Christian Recorder Received
basket of fruit from
First Normal Class as

[p. 91]
a token of their appreciation of my services rendered
them. Retired at 10:30

———

A. M. C. May 17
Rose at 6:30 Breakfast.
Attended joint meeting
of Y.M.C.A. and Y.W.C.A.
presided at organ.
Choir rehearsal. Morning
service Sermon by
Chaplain Ramsey
Text Titus 2: 11-12
Subject :Christian practices'
Sunday School. Class
interesting. Read
Matt. 21. Did not attend
night services.
Retired at 9

[p. 92]

A. M. C. May 18
Rose at 6:50 Breakfast.
Chapel. Senior Class
rehearsal. Read
Matt 22. Visited
Mrs. King's room. Heard
class in spelling.
Rehearsed senior class.
Wrote a few quotations
in a bible belonging
to Miss Clark of class '08
Chapel for devotions.
Rehea[r]sed Senior class.
Gll Glee and Minstrel[-]
nola clubs. Tedious
job. Mark penman-
ship papers.
Retired 10:30

———

A. M. College May 19
Rose at 7 Breakfast
Chapel for devotions

[p. 93]
Choir rehearsal. Assisted
Mrs. King in her exami-
nation. Read Matt. 23.
Address by Mr. Wilson
of Jamaica
Rehearsed seniors and
glee club. Retired at 10

———

A. M. C. May 20
Rose at 7:10 Missed
breakfast. Chapel for
devotions. Went to
Normal. Dinner
Rehearsed octette of
Senior Class. Arranged
Foilet. Led prayer
meeting Read for
lesson Gal.
Meeting good. Last
one of the year.

311

Rehearsed Senior Class
and Glee Club. Read

[p. 94]
Matt 24 Retired at 10:30

___

A. M. College May 21
Rose at 6:50 Breakfast
Chapel for devotions.
Choir rehearsal. Rehearsed
Octtett [sic] of Senior class.
Cut out letters for Miss Johnson
assisted by Miss Gus Clarke.
Went to Huntsville and
purchased four books
for the following persons
as presents. A. Gus Clark,
Mollie Ardis, Mary Single-
ton and Sara Bright. All
members of class'08.
Rehearsed cornet solo with
Miss Bramlet. Read
Matt 25 Retired at 11:45

[p. 95]
A. and M. College May 22
Rose at 7. Breakfast.
Chapel for devotions
Rehearsed seniors. Re-
hearsed cornet solo. Wrote
several cards. Sent present
to Mollie Ardis. Chapel
for senior graduating
exercises. Eleven graduated.
Excellent. speaking from
Mattie Owens. Address to
class by Prof. Hopkins
prin. of Normal depart-
ment. Read Matt 26
Retired at

___

A. M. College May 23
Rose at 7 Breakfast.
Rehearsal of Minstrel-
nola club. Went to
Normal. to Chapel

[p. 96]
for devotions and ad-
dress to literary. Prof.
W. R. Wood of Decatur
Ala. delivered address
to literary societies.
Good. Program rendered
good. Minstrelnola Club
sang two selections.
Excellent. Presided at
organ for devotions. Of-
fered prayer. Directed
club. Read Matt. 27
Retired

___

A. and M. College May 24
A day long to be
remembered. Rose at
7 Breakfast. Met Dr.
C. H. Parrish. Sat at same
table. After breakfast
showed him over the
grounds. Choir Rehearsal

[p. 97]
Baccalaureate sermon
by Dr. Chas. H. Parrish A.M. ["D"
under "A"]
Text John 7: 17 Subject
Obedience. Excellent
Music Superb. Sunday
School at 3. Address
by Rev.   Brooks
pastor St. John A.M.E.
Church Huntsville Ala.
Subject :Love" Excellent.
Chapel at night for
religious societies.
Fine lecture by
Dr. C. H. Parrish on the
Holy Land. Instructive.

Glee Club sang two
selections. Read Matt 28
Retired at

[p.98]
A. and M. College May 25
Rose at 6:50
Industrial Graduating
Exercises. Glee and Minstrel[-]
nola clubs sang. Rev.
Williams Huntsville Ala
delivered the address.
Rehearsed Octttett [sic] of
senior class. Graduat.
ing exercises of senior
normal and ~~col~~ college
classes twenty five
in all. 2 received degree
of B. S. Rev. Williams
of Huntsville delivered
the address. Good.
~~Pp~~ played solo.
Read Luke 1
Retired at 12:50

———

A. and M. College May 26
Rose at 6:30 Breakfast
[p. 99]
Chapel. Sang several
jubilee hymns. Went to
Normal to see some
of the students. Gradu-
ates reception. Escorted
Miss Hazel Tatnall of
class '08 to table. Minstrel
nola club sang two
songs. Chapel for
~~din~~ devotions. Ad-
-dresses by Mr. J. A.
Wilson of class '07
Mr. Jas. Bailey '06
Miss Delanare Asher
and Dr. Councill. Con.
versed with Miss Augusta
Clark of class '08

Read Luke 2
Retired at

[p. 100]
A. and M. College
                May 27
Rose at 5   breakfast.
Chapel for farewell
meeting with students
Offered closing prayer.
Went to Fearns with stu-
dent body. Went as far
as Huntsville. Purchased
ticket for Morton Smith.
Bought some collars.
Went to Fearns to see
some more off.
Supper. Devotions and
prayer meeting.
Began packing up.
Read Luke 3
Retired at 11

[p. 101]
A. and M. College May 28
Rose at 9 oclock. Break-
fast. Went with inventory
committee to take in-
ventory of buildings etc
Hard job. Went to de-
votions. Dr. Archer made
a short talk on tabricalosus
[tuberculosis??]
Read Luke 4
Wrote Gus Clarke 4 [II?]
Retired at

———

A. and M. College May 29
Rose at 7 o'clock
Breakfast. Went to Nor-
mal. Finished work
on inventory committee.
Read Mark 1
Sent several programs
Attended teachers meeting

Finished packing up
[p. 102]
Retired at

———

A. M. C. May 30
Rose at 7 Breakfast.
Wrote out report of
band. Visited or rather
paid Miss Roten a
call. Visited the
Hopkins Family. Went to
devotions. Read Mark 2: 3
Wrote T____ and others
Retired at 10:30

———

A. M. College May 31
Rose at 8 oclock.
Breakfast. Morning ser-
vice Text
Sermon by Rev. Ramsey.
Wrote Daisy. Read
Mark 4 Went to devo-
tions at 7 oclock. Met
at Mrs. King and had
[p. 103]
quite a nice time
Retired at

———

A. and M. College June
Rose at 6 Breakfast.
Last meal at the school
Went to Normal and ex-
pressed grip home.
Bade teachers good
bye. Bought a type
writer. Went to Huntsville
and purchased a ticket
for Chattanooga Tenn.
Had lunch with Mr.
Griffin. Left C Huntsville
en route for Chattanoo-
ga at 5:15 Arrived
destination at 9:05

Went to Mr. and Mrs. David
Smith. Played a few
selections on cornet
and piano.
[p. 104]
Read Mark 5
Retired at 11

———

Chattanooga Tenn
June 2
Rose at 8 Played
a few pieces on the
piano. Breakfast.
Went to town a[nd] purchased
a pr. of shoes and other
things. Sent off a
few souvenir cards.
Wrote L. W. Went in
company with Mrs.
Smith to visit Mr. Jno
Pitts. Met Miss Barnett
Read Mark 6
Retired at 11

———

Chattanooga June 3
Rose at 8 Played
[p. 105]
a few selections on
piano. Breakfast.
Visited Scotts and West[-]
brooks black smith
shop. also visited
Mrs. Pitts. Read Mark 7
Retired at

———

Chattanooga June 4
Rose at 8 Played a
few selections on piano.
Packed up. Breakfast.
Left Chattanooga at 11
oclock en route for
Somerset. Arrived desti[-]
nation at 4:10 P.M.

Went to Rev. W. H. Williams
Attended prayer meeting
at First Baptist Church.
Read Mark 8
Retired at 11

[p. 106]
Somerset Ky. June 5
Rose at 6 oclock. Break-
fast. Wrote Mrs. Smith.
Went to P.O. Visited Mr.
Kyle Barber Shop. Paid
Bessie Miller of Lancaster
a call. Read Mark 9.
Practice a little on the
cornet. Read a few interest[-]
ing debates. Spent day
most pleasantly. Attended
prayer services.
Read
Retired at 11

Somerset Ky. June 6
Rose at 5:55 Breakfast.
Wrote T____ went to P.O.
Read Mark 10 Also
Pendleton's theory on the
intermediate state of
the dead

[p. 107]
Practice or rather played
a few selections on the cornet.
Attended church
meeting at 1st Baptist
Church. Left Chatt
Somerset at 4:10 en route
for Nicholasville Arr.
Nicholasville at 6 Had
supper at Mrs. Elmore.
Retired at 12

Nicholasville June 7
Rose at 6 Breakfast.
Sunday School. Talked
from chart. Morning
service. Presided at
organ. Rev. Tull preached
Text
Dined with Mrs. Smalley
K of P sermon at Bap. Ch.
Sermon by E. U Hantham D.D.
Text 1 Cor 13
Sermon excellent

[p. 108]
Played cornet solo.
Addressed B.Y.P.U.
Remained to evening
services. Rev. Tull
preached. Text Jno.
Retired at 10:30

Nicholasville June 8
Rose at six. Breakfast
Visited sister Dickerson
Left Nich. at 2:36 en
route for Lex. arr. des-
tination at 3:00
Met Eld. A. U. Davis and
Dr. Timblake Visited
Mrs. Buckner, Hawthorne
Neighbors, Turner Supper
at Campbells Res[t]aurant
Retired at 11

Lexington Ky June 9
[p. 109]
Rose at 10:30 Din-
ner first meal. Visited
ACousin Amanda Weltraus.
Neighbors. Purchased some
music. Read Mark 10
11: 12: 13: 14: 15: 16
Met Celia Cissell also Mrs.
Tatman. Visited Glendora
Gill Retired at 12

Lexington Ky. [June] 10
Rose at 8:20 Visited
Celia Cissel. Missed trained
Breakfast at Campbells
Dinner at Mrs. Mattie
Tatman. Spent day most
pleasantly at Mrs. Tatman['s.]
Met Maune Porter. Read
Luke 5 Left Lex. at
6:45 for home. Choir
practice. Retired at 10
Wrote several letters

[p. 110]
Nicholasville June 11
Rose at six. Break-
fast. P. O. Practice
cornet and type. Visited
Mrs. Richard and played
a few songs
on cornet
also Rairy family
Brooks. Read Luke 6
Retired at 12

———

Nicholasville June 12
Rose at 6:30 Breakfast
Began an arrangement
on "Largo" Studied S. S.
lesson. Visited Eld. Dickerson
Read Luke 7
Retired 11

———

Nicholasville June 13
Rose at 6 Breakfast
Went to Lexington.
Hair cut and shave
[p. 111]
Visited Mrs. Tatman.
Met Cousin Hannah Rus-
sel. Went to Union Depot.
Met Miss Gay. also
Mack of Versailles. Went
to Union Station met

Beulah Price direct
from Fisk. also Hamilton
Read Luke 8 Left
Lex. in company with
Miss Price at 6:45 for
Nicholasville. Visited
Mrs. Smalley. Retired 11

———

Nicholasville June 14
Rose at 6:45
Breakfast. S.S. Taught
1st B. Class. Explained
chart Remained to
morning services. Presided
at organ. cornet) Dr. Bailey
of Jefferson Ind. preached

[p. 112]
Text
Sermon good. Dinner.
Attend Good Samaritan
services at B. C.
Sermon by Rev. Morrison
of the A. M. E. Church.
excellent.
Text Luke
B.Y.P.U. Evening
services. Presided at
organ. Dr. Bailey
preached
Text 133 Ps. 1
Sermon good.
Read Luke Retired 11

———

Nicholasville June 15
Rose at 6:35 Breakfast.
Wrote T____ Visited
Rev. Bailey. Met Lulu
Lyons Sallie. Went to
[p. 113]
Lexington. Read
Luke 9 Band rehearsal.
Retired at 11:30

Lexington June 16
Rose at 12:05 Dinner
first meal. Visited
Glendora Gills. Supper
Visited Dr. and Mrs.
Hawthorne. Read
Luke 10 Wrote T____
wrote several cards.
Retired at 10:30

Lexington June 17 [corrections to
date, this day and the next two]
Rose at 10:25
Dinner first meal
Visited Mr. Tatman
Read Luke 11
Wrote one part to a piece
of music. Hamilton's
for supper. Band

[p. 114]
rehearsal. Retired 11

Lexington June 18
Rose at 7:40 Breakfast. Left Lex. for
Nich. arrived home
at 10:10 Went to
Camp Nelson. Visited
Miss Clays and played
a few selections on
piano. Read Luke 12
Retired at 12

Camp Nelson Ky. June 19
Rose at 8 Wrote
Mrs. Smith. Breakfast.
Visited the Jevis family
Thos Fry. Practice
a little on cornet.
Paid a short visit to
Mrs. Price. Retired 12

[p. 115]
Camp Nelson June 20
Rose at 8:30
Read Luke 13:14:15
Left Camp Nelson in
company with Mr. Pnc- [??]
Miss Cora Clay. Visited
Mrs. Jno. Pitts and Lyons.
Retired at 12

Nicholasville June 21
Rose at 7 Invited
Mrs. Lucy Clark for breakfast. S. S. Morning
service Dr. Bailey
preached. Sermon
good. Text Matt
Evening servi— Sermon
good by Dr. Bailey
Text Prov. 22
B.Y.P.U acted as
M. C. election of
officers.

[p. 116] [pp. 116-120, handwriting
switches style from formal to
informal, pencil to pen, careful
to careless, script to printing—
strange!]
Evening serv— Dr
Bailey preached
Text Isa.
Sermon good.
Wrote T____ M____ A.
Jas Lacy
Retired at 12:15

Nicholasville [June] 22
Rose at 6:15 Went to
Lexington in co. with
Rev. Jones & Bailey.

Breakfast. Attended
ministers & deacons
meeting. Visited several
places etc Literary So. Pleasant
green [in right margin—pleasant
green is a location]
[in left margin:] Band rehearsal
Retired at 12

———

Lex. 23 June
Rose at 9
Dinner first meal.

[p. 117]
Went to depot to
meet delegates from
Nich. Took supper
at Mrs. Cook.
Band rehearsal
Retired at 12

———

Lex. June 24
Rose at 9
Dinner. Went to
Pleasant green
to rehearse etc
Band rehearsal
Retired at

———

Lex. June 25
Rose at 8
Type wrote several
songs for Mrs. Buckner [Bucknes?, Buckne?]
Played for funeral
Left Lex. at six en
route for Paris. Arr
destination at 7:20
[p. 118]
gave concert on
street. Had a pleasant
time at Miss
Freemans.

Retired at 12

———

Paris Ky. June 26
Rose at six
Breakfast. Played
a few pieces at
depot. left Paris
for Frankfort at
9 Played for O. F.
picnic. Met Genyelar [gamelon?]
band. Dedication of
OF building. Met
the grand governess.
and several others.
Lulu Waide. Left Fran
kfort at 12 Arr—
Paris at 2:20
Retired at 3

[p. 119]
Paris Ky June 27
Rose at 6[:]30
left Paris at 7 oc
for Lexington
Arrived Lex. at 8
Breakfast. Went to
Hon [???] T____ also
Union Station met
deligates from Mr. Stal—
left Lexington for
Nicholasville at 8:50
[in left margin:] Read Luke 16-17-18
Retired at 12

———

Nicholasville June 28
Rose at 7:00
Breakfast. S.S.
Reviewed Shool [School?]
Morning services
Eld. Britton Preached
Sermon Text Eph.
Good Fair. Evening
services at A.M.E.

[p. 120]
Church. Dr. Bailey
preached   Text Phil
Sermon good
B.Y.P.U.
Evening services
Dr. Bailey preached
Job 14   Good
Read Luke 19
Wrote T____
Retired
Nicholasville June 29
Rose at 7 Breakfast
Arranged music
greater part of day
Retired 11
Nicholasville June 30
Rose at 7 Breakfast

Arranged music
Paid a few visits.
Retired at
[in left margin:] Offered prayer
Mr. Martin

[back flyleaf]
clay   July 1
Rose at 6 Breakfast
Mi_____
Left Nich—7 for
Lex.—
[bottom half of back flyleaf torn off]

[reverse of back flyleaf is blank]

[inside back cover is blank]

Appendix 2

James H. Wilson Band and Tour Booklet [1908]

Unbound. Same size and character as James H. Wilson Journal, except there are no covers.

[flyleaf, recto]
[An orange, printed sticker is pasted or glued onto the page. It is oval shaped, and it resembles a Victorian mirror outlined in ribbons with two floral designs at left and right, top. The oval mirror-shaped frame is wider than it is tall, and printed in the center of the frame, in the same color maroon ink as the frame, one finds:]

Jas. H. Wilson
Nicholasville, Ky.

[flyleaf, verso]

Kersands
Minstrels.
Season. 1907-08

Hamilton's Band

=1=

Jas. H. Wilson	Director
Denis J. Cook	Cornet
S. H. Conley	Cornet
C. Wilson	Clarinet
Geo. Guin	Clarinet
Thos. Fry	Horn
Wm. Helm	Horn
H. S. Hamilton	Horn
E. L. Miller	Trombone
Chas. Weir	Baritone
W. L. Fields	Tuba

Al. Johnson	Tuba
Frank Tatman	S. Drum
Geo. Washington	B. Drum

Summer 1906
Lexington Ky.

Cook's Peerless Concer[t]
-Band-

=2=

Jas. H. Wilson	Director
Thadius	Solo Cornet
D. J. Cooks	First "
Thos. Stevens	Clarinet
Vertner Tandy	Clarinet
Henry Boulder	1st Horn
Wm. Helm	2d Horn
Smith Sanford	3d Horn
H. S. Hamilton	4th Horn
Harrey Winchester	Bariton [sic]

320

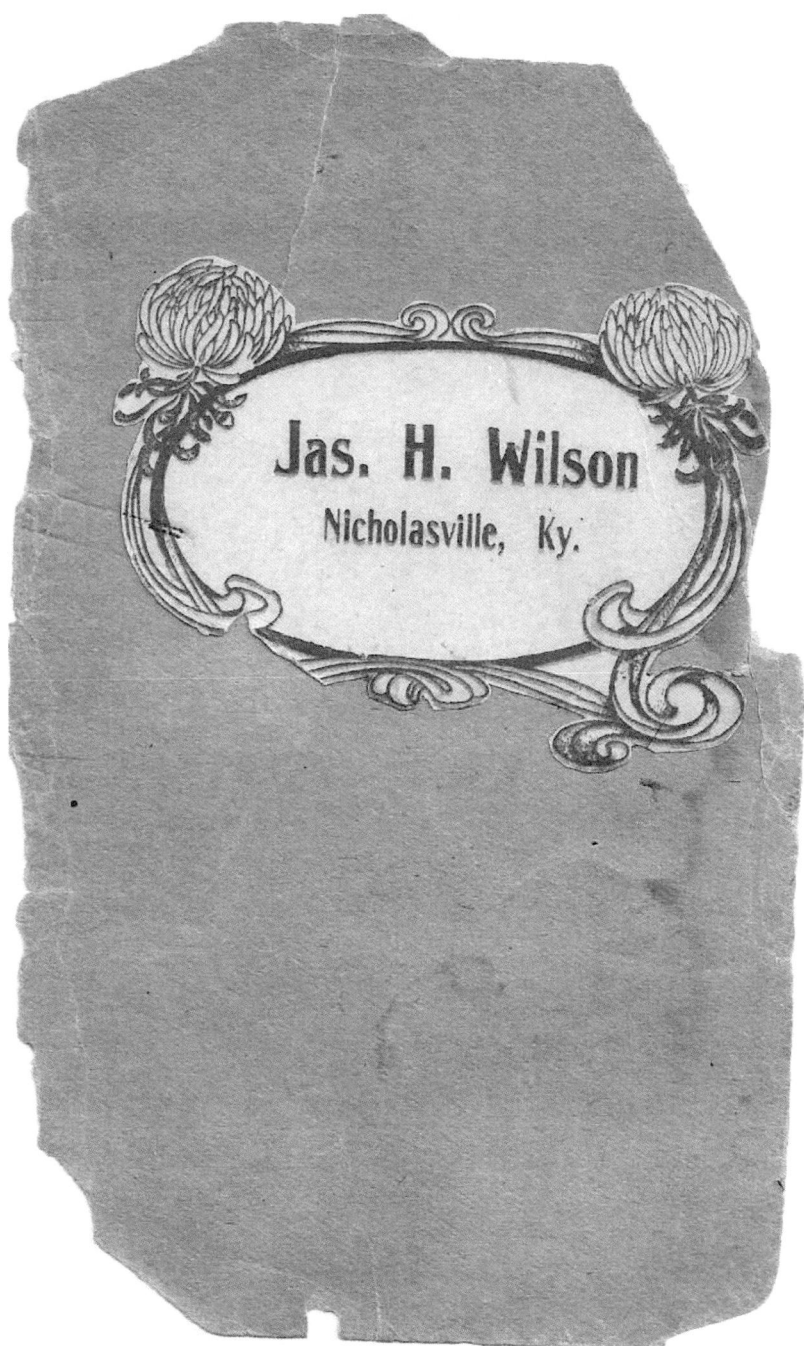

Figure A5. Flyleaf, recto. James H. Wilson Band and Tour Booklet.

Figure A6. Flyleaf, verso. Lettering in Wilson's hand, ink.

APPENDIX TWO

Cal. Miller	Trombone	B. S. Gaten	Clarinet
Sid. Hamilton	Trombone	Chas. T. Watts	First Horn
W. Coons	Trombone	Benj. W. Lee	Second
Al. Johnson	Tuba	W. A. Law	Trombone
Wm. Jackson [sic]	Bass	Chas. S. Crossen	Trombone
		W. Cal Miller	Trombone
		Walter Watkins	Baritone
		Lloyd Cooper	Tuba
		Skip Farrel	S. Drum
		J. A. Watts	Cymbals
		Jakie Smith	B. Drum

Lexington Ky.
[1902-1903]

Hamilton's Band

=3=

[" >" means a pencil checkmark precedes the name.]

Jas. H. Wilson	Director
Hugh Swift	Solo Cornet
Jas. Johnson	First "
Cornelius Wilson	Clarinet
Geo. Guin	Clarinet
Saml. Simpson	1st Horn
Wm. Helm	2d Horn
H. S. Hamilton	3d Horn
E. L. Miller	Trombone
Geo. Johnson	Trombone
W. Coons	Trombone
Chas. Weir	Baritone
W. L. Fields	Tuba
Al. Johnson	Tuba
Ed. Brown	S. Drum
Frank Tatman	B. Drum

Billy Kersand's Minstrel
1906-1907

Lacy's Orchester [sic]

=5=

Jas. S. Lacy	Leader
W. Cal. Miller	2d Violin
Chas. T. Watts	viola
B. S. Gaten	Clarinet
Walter Watkins	Sax
Jas. H. Wilson	Cornet
Chas. S. Crossen	Trombone
Lloyd Cooper	Bass
Skip Farrel	Traps

Billy Kersand's Minstrel
Season 1906-1907

=6=

[blank other than page number];

Elmore's Cyclone
-Band-

=7=

Jas. H. Wilson	Director
Ed. Overstreet	Cornet

Summer 1907
Lexington Ky.

Lacy's Challenge Band

=4=

Jas. S. Lacy	Director
Jas. H. Wilson	Solo Cornet
P. M. Logan	Solo Cornet
C. Johnson	First "

323

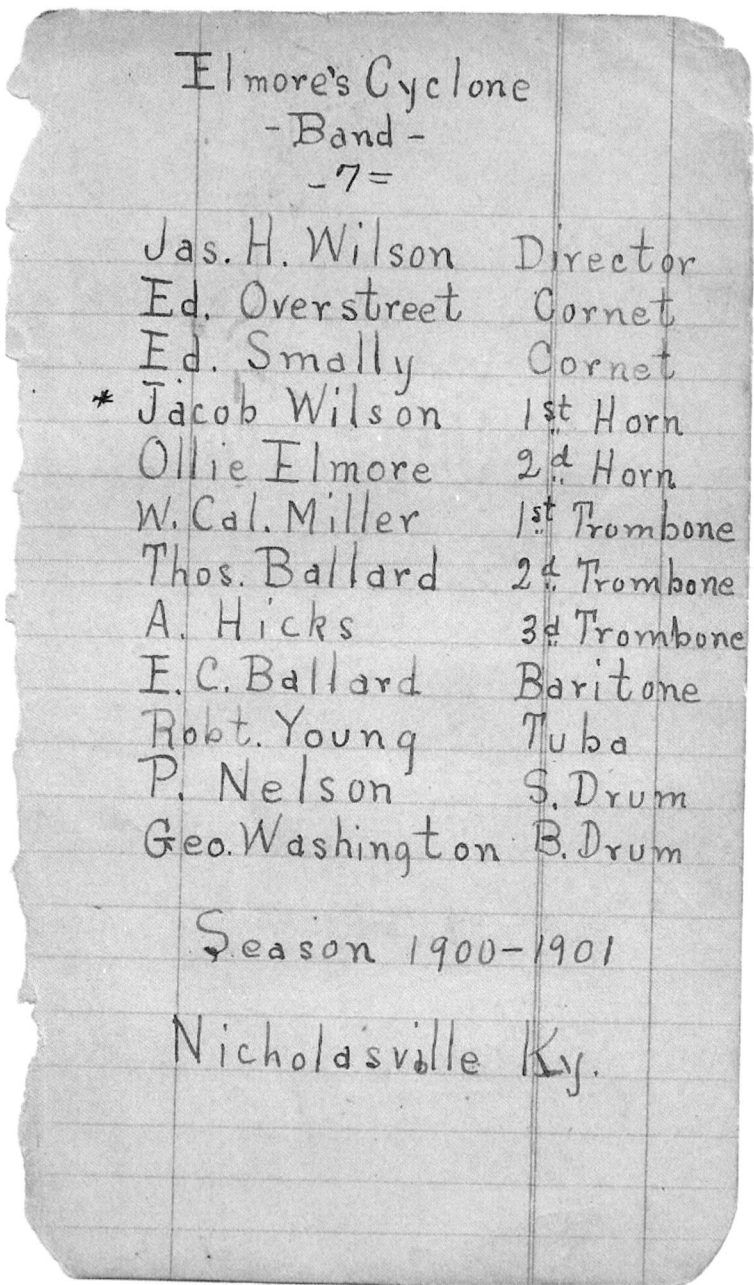

Figure A7. Roster, Elmore's Cyclone Band.

Appendix Two

Ed. Smally	Cornet
*Jacob Wilson	1st Horn
[father and band manager]	
Ollie Elmore	2d Horn
[father of Thomas Elmore]	
W. Cal. Miller	1st Trombone
Thos. Ballard	2d Trombone
A. Hicks	3d Trombone
E. C. Ballard	Baritone
Robt. Young	Tuba
P. Nelson	S. Drum
Geo. Washington	B. Drum

Season 1900-1901
Nicholasville Ky.

[The asterisk does not look original. The ink does not match the remainder.]

=8=

[p. 8 blank]

D   [Probably a false start (the leader's name)]

=9=

Dan Desdunes Stewart.	LeaderJno.
Geo. Bryant	2nd Violin
	Piano
Jas. Tucker	Bass
L. Teo	Clarinet
Chas. Hunter	Flute
Harry Prampin	Cornet
[>] Jas. H. Wilson	Trombone
Laura Prampin	Traps

Nashville Students
Season 1899-1900

=10=

[p. 10 blank]

Housley's Orchestra

=11=

G. W. Houseley
C. T. Watts
Henry Graves
Jas. H. Wilson
Lloyd Cooper
Emmit Mason
B. A. Houseley

Season 1901-02

=12=

[p. 12 blank]

Johnson's Superb Band

=13=

Jas. H. Wilson	Director
Rich. Taylor	Solo Cornet
Jas. Tevis	First "
Thos. Fry	First Horn
Walter Leavel	Second "
Roy Bright	Third "
E. L. Miller	Trombone
Chas. Williams	Trombone
Robt. Williams	Trombone
Burritt Tribble	Baritone
Al. Johnson	Tuba
Robt. Steel	S. Drum
Chas. Clay Jr.	B. Drum

Camp Nelson Ky.

=14=

[p. 14 blank]

Cyclone Band

=15=

Jas. H. Wilson
Nathan Wilkins
Wm. Hopkins

J. Singleton
Arthur Isler
B. Covington
Fred. Campbell
Chas. Wilson
Chas. Wright
M. Campbell
Jack Alex
Wm. Grant

Allen's Minstrels

Season

=16=
[p. 16 blank]

-Route-
-1907-

=17=

September -	Illinois
2	Chicago Heights
3	Danville
4	Decatur
5-6-7	E. St. Louis
8	Sedalia Mo
	Kansas
8	Leavenworth
10-11	St. Joseph Mo
12-13	Topeka
14	Lawrence

=18=
[p. 18 blank]

=19=-

September -	Kansas
15	Leavenworth
16	Ottawa
17	Emporia
18	Wichita
19	Winfield
20-21	Coffeyville
22	Independence
23	Oswego
24	Columbus
25	Pittsburg

=20=
[p. 20 blank]

=21=

September -	Missouri
26	Joplin
27	Springfield
28	Fort Smith Ark
	Indian Territory
30	Muskogee
October	
	Muskogee
1	Tulsa
2	Sapulpa
	Chandler
4	King Fisher

=21=
[p. 21 blank]

=23=

October	Oklahoma
5	Enid
6	Guthrie
7-8	Oklahoma City
9	Pauls Valley Ind. Ter.
10	Shawnee
	Okla.
11	Ardmore Ind Ter.
	Texas
12	Sherman
14	Gainesville
15	Bonham
16	Denison

Appendix Two

	=24=	16	San Marcos
[p. 24 blank]		18	La Grange
		19	Port Arthur
	=25=	=30=	
October	Texas	[p. 30 blank]	
17	Paris		
18	McKinney	=31=	
19	Greenville	November — Louisiana	
21-22	Ft. Worth	20	Lake Charles
23	Terrell	21	Jennings
24	Dallas	22	New Iberia
25	Denton	23	Crowley
26	Waxahatchie	24	Washington
28	Corsicana	25	Opelousas
29	Hillsboro	26	Jenerette
		27	Franklin
	=26=	28	Thibodaux
[p. 26 blank		29	Morgan City
		30	Houma
	=27=		=32=
October	Texas	[p. 32 blank]	
30	West		
31	Cleburne		=33=
November		December — Louisiana	
1	Waco	1-7	New Orleans
2	McGregor	8	Donaldsonville
4	Marlin	9	Plaquemine
5	Bryan	10	Baton Rouge
6	Calvert		Mississippi
7	Austin	11	Port Gibson
8	Taylor	12	Vicksburg
9	Brenham	13	Monroe La.
		14	Pine Bluff
	=28=	16	Hot Springs
[p. 28 blank]		17-18	Little Rock
		19	Newport
	=29=		=34=
November — Texas	[p. 34 blank]		
11	Houston		
12	Galveston		=35=-
13	Victoria	December	
14-15	San Antonio	20	Poplar Bluff Mo.
		21	Cairo Ill.

	Tennessee
23	Jackson
24-5	Memphis
26-31	Memphis

January – 1908 - Tennessee
7   Memphis

	Mississippi
10-11	Clarksdale
13	Greenville
14	Grenada

=36=
[p. 36 blank]

=37=
January	Mississippi
15	Winona
16	Durant
17	Jackson
18	Yazoo City
20	Canton
21	Ackerman
22	Starkville
23	West Point
24	Aberdeen
25	Amory

=38=
[p. 38 blank]

=39=
January
Mississippi
27	Corinth
28	Booneville
29	Tupelo

Alabama
30	Sheffield
31	Courtland

	February
1	Decatur
3	Scottsboro

	Georgia
4	Decatur
5	Rome
6-7-8	Atlanta

=40=
[p. 40 blank]

=41=
February	Tennessee
14-15	Chattanooga

	Kentucky
17	Princeton
18	Morganfield
19	Evansville Ind
20	Qwensboro [sic]
21	Evansville Ind

-to-
Home Sweet Home
[Nicholasville, KY]
stopping at Louisville
and Lexington Ky.
Fare $6.50

[page 42]

[in pencil—different hand]

Maggie   25
         20

[End of James H. Wilson Band
and Tour Booklet. All the leaves
are loose, unbound, and in
fraying condition.]

Appendix 3

Known Compositions and Arrangements by James H. Wilson

A. Chronological List by Earliest Known Reference

Title	Date	Genre
Drag Lotz	1906	Ragtime
Shame Lotz	1906	Ragtime
Reveille	1906	Band, March
Bugle Call, The	1907	Band
Gloomorian	1907	Orch., Minstrel
Melody in F (A. Rubinstein, Op.3, No.1)	1908	Band Arangement
Arrah Wanna (J. Drislanee) & T. Mors	1908	Band Arrangement
Miss Hopkins' Lullaby	1908	Band Arrangement
Narcissus [probably Ethelbert] Nevin	1908	Band Arrangement
Foilet [?]	1908	[Band] Arrangement
Adelphicites	1912	Band
Alabama	1912	Band Arrangement
Nannie Bell	1912	Band
Alpha, The	1912	Band Grad.
Duet for Two Horns	1913	Two Horns
Normal Students, The	1914	Band
Comet, The	1914	Band
Normal Students March	1914	Band
Floredia	1922	Trumpet & Piano
Victor (March)	1922	Band
Carmena	1927	Vocal Solo (Bass)
Walso (March)	1928	Orchestra
Silas Green (March)	1930	Band
Drakesonian March, The	1934	Orchestra

Title	Date	Genre
Governor's March, The	1934	Orchestra
Kentucky Blue Grass (March)	1940	Band
Our President (March)	1940	Band
Roberteen Polka	1948	Roberteen
Polka (arrangement)	1949	Cornet Solo w. Band
Alabama A. & M. March	1953	Band
Novelty "Playing With The Scales"	1953	Band

B. Alphabetical List by Title

Title	Date	Genre
Adelphicites	1912	Band
Alabama	1912	Band Arrangement
Alabama A. & M. March	1953	Band
Alpha, The	1912	Band
Arrah Wanna (J. Drislane & T. Morse)	1908	Band Arrangement
Bugle Call, The	1907	Band
Carmena	1927	Vocal Solo (Bass)
Comet, The	1914	Band
Drag Lotz	1906	Ragtime
Drakesonian March, The	1934	Orchestra
Duet for Two Horns	1913	Two Horns
Floredia	1922	Trumpet & Piano
Foilet [?]	1908	[Band] Arrangement
Gloomorian	1907	Orch., Minstrel
Governor's March, The	1934	Orchestra
Kentucky Blue Grass (March)	1940	Band
Largo [probably G. F. Handel]	1908	[Band] Arrangement
Melody in F (A. Rubinstein, Op.3, No. 1)	1908	Band Arrangement
Miss Hopkins' Lullaby	1908	Band Arrangement
Nannie Bell	1912	Band
Narcissus [probably Ethelbert Nevin]	1908	Band Arrangement
Normal Students, The	1914	Band
Normal Students March	1914	Band
Novelty "Playing With The Scales"	1953	Band

APPENDIX 3

Title	Date	Genre
Our President (March)	1940	Band
Reveille	1906	Band, March
Roberteen Polka	1948	Band
Roberteen Polka (arrangement)	1949	Cornet Solo w. Band
Shame Lotz	1906	Ragtime
Silas Green (March)	1930	Band
United	1906	March
Victor (March)	1922	Band
Walso (March)	1928	Orchestra

List of Illustrations

Frontispiece. A photographic portrait of James Hembray Wilson (1880-1961), circa 1908. ii

Prologue
Fig. P1. W. C. Handy and the Alabama A. & M. Band, ca. 1900. viii
Fig. P2. James H. Wilson with the Alabama A. & M. ROTC band in 1919. ix

Chapter 1
Fig. 1-1. Jessamine County Court House, Nicholasville, Kentucky 2
Fig. 1-2. South Main Street, Nicholasville, Kentucky. 3
Fig. 1-3. 1850 Slave Schedule, Jessamine County, Kentucky. 6
Fig. 1-4. Marriage Certificate, Jacob Wilson and Hester Monroe. 7
Fig. 1-5. An older period home in Hervey Town in Nicholasville, Kentucky. 8
Fig. 1-6. Map of Nicholasville, Kentucky, in 1877. 9
Fig. 1-7. Colored Christian Church, Nicholasville, Kentucky. 14
Fig. 1-8. Bethel Methodist Church [formerly Bethel A. M. E. Church]. 15
Fig. 1-9. The early "Colored Baptist Church" in Hervey Town, Nicholasville. 16
Fig. 1-10. Map, Nicholasville, Kentucky, to Cincinnati, Ohio 19

Chapter 2
Fig. 2-1. A vintage building, East Court Street, Cincinnati, Ohio. 20
Fig. 2-2. A vintage five-storey building across from 106 East Court Street. 23
Fig. 2-3. Lithograph poster advertising Jacob Litt's *In Old Kentucky*, ca. 1893 26
Fig. 2-4. Lithograph poster advertising Al. W. Martin's *Uncle Tom's Cabin* 29
Fig. 2-5. Buffalo Soldiers Band on parade. 32
Fig. 2-6. 9th Cavalry Trumpet Corps with soloist James H. Wilson. 32
Fig, 2-7. 9th Cavalry Trumpet Corps, detail. 33
Fig. 2-8. Minstrel Festival Announcement in the *Indianapolis Freeman*, 1889. 34

List of Illustrations

Fig. 2-9. Georgia Minstrels announcement in the *Anaconda Standard*, 1901.   41

Fig. 2-10. James H. Wilson, cornet, with trombonist Earl Miller.   42

Chapter 3
Fig. 3-1. Cuban Military Band, Spanish-American War, 1898.   46
Fig. 3-2. Header of Wilson Concert Tour Program.   49
Fig. 3-3. *Bulletin*, Alabama State Normal and Industrial School for Negroes   53
Fig. 3-4. The "Old Mountain Spring," Normal, Alabama.   54
Fig. 3-5. Alabama A. & M.'s founder, William Hooper Councill.   58
Fig. 3-6. The *Indianapolis Freeman*, January 2, 1904.   61
Fig. 3-7. Map, Nicholasville, Kentucky, to Normal [Huntsville], Alabama.   62

Chapter 4
Fig. 4-1. Advertisement for Musicians, People's Band of Columbus, Ohio.   64
Fig. 4-2. Hamilton's Military Band, circa 1905.   67
Fig. 4-3. Poster for Callender's Georgia Minstrels with Billy Kersands [1870s].   67
Fig. 4-4. Map of Wilson's Railroad Tour with Kersands Minstrels, 1907-1908.   75

Chapter 5
Fig. 5-1. James H. Wilson Journal. Flyleaf.   76
Fig. 5-2 An unidentified photograph from Wilson's personal collection. [Toula?]   82
Fig. 5-3. James H. Wilson Journal. Cover.   84
Fig. 5-4. James H. Wilson Journal. Flyleaf.   85
Fig. 5-5. James H. Wilson Journal. Entries for January 1st and 2nd, 1908.   86
Fig. 5-6. Wilson and his minstrel show colleague, Manzy Campbell.   96
Fig. 5-7. A photographic portrait of James H. Wilson, circa 1908.   98

Chapter 6
Fig. 6-1. Program cover, Commencement Exercises, Senior Prep. Class, 1909.   100
Fig. 6-2. Program, Commencement Exercises, Senior Preparatory   108

　　　　　　　Class, 1909.
Fig. 6-3. "Arrah Wanna" by J. Drislane and T. Morse.　　　　109
Fig. 6-4. "Arrah Wanna: An Irish Indian Matrimonial Venture"　110
Fig. 6-5. Hamilton's Military Band. Lexington, Ky. Jas. H.　　118
　　　　　Wilson, Director.
Fig. 6-6. Hamilton's Military Band in Camp, 1908.　　　　　119

Chapter 7
Fig. 7-1. The Alabama A. & M. campus [circa 1938].　　　　122
Fig. 7-2. Advertisement for the agricultural program,　　　 124
　　　　　[circa 1930].
Fig. 7-3. The Mechanical Arts Building, A. & M. Brochure　 124
　　　　　[circa 1930].
Fig. 7-4. Letter from Henrietta M. Archer to H. Hopkins,　 126
　　　　　September 18, 1908.
Fig. 7-5. Letter from Henry E. Archer to H. Hopkins,　　　 127
　　　　　September 24, 1908.
Fig. 7-6. An oil portrait of the young Exeline Polk Wilson.　129
Fig. 7-7. Postcard from James Wilson to Exeline Polk.　　　130
Fig. 7-8. Message side of card from James to Exeline,　　　131
　　　　　March 5, 1909.
Fig. 7-9. A. & M.'s second president, Walter Solomon Buchanan.　135
Fig. 7-10. "If Life Be a Dream" by Burleigh and Stanton [1904].　136
Fig. 7-11. Vocal and Piano Recital, September 17, 1909.　　137
Fig. 7-12. Vocal and Instrumental Recital Program,　　　　 139
　　　　　October 1, 1909.
Fig. 7-13. 1910 U. S. Census, Madison Cty., Alabama,　　　 140
　　　　　Meridianville Precinct 11.
Fig. 7-14. James H. Wilson's certificate of divorce from Georgia　141
　　　　　Wilson.

Chapter 8
Fig. 8-1. Cover, program of A. & M. Industrial Department　147
　　　　　Graduation, 1912.
Fig. 8-2. Program of the Commencement Exercises, Industrial　148
　　　　　Dpt., 1912.
Fig. 8-3. A snapshot of James, Jr. and Hester outside their home,　152
　　　　　circa 1917.
Fig. 8-4. A studio portrait of James, Jr., aged 2 years and　152
　　　　　4 months.

List of Illustrations

Fig. 8-5. The Wilson home, ca. 1922.	154
Fig. 8-6. 1915 Bible Training Class.	156
Fig. 8-7. 1919 Sunday School Teachers' Training Class.	156
Fig. 8-8. Y. M. C. A. *Cabinet*, Alabama A. & M., 1919.	157
Fig. 8-9. The R. O. T. C. Band.	158
Fig. 8-10. A. & M. Commercial Orchestra of 1919.	158
Fig. 8-11. Two sample programs from concerts during the Buchanan years.	159
Fig. 8-12. King's Counting House. James H. Wilson at work in his office, 1919.	160
Fig. 8-13. The 1919 A. & M. baseball team.	161
Fig. 8-14. The Laundry at Alabama A. & M.	162
Fig. 8-15. Cover of the 1920 Commencement Exercises program, May 26, 1920.	166

Chapter 9

Fig. 9-1. Wilson's first published article, "The Church and Dancing."	170
Fig. 9-2. Cover, *The Normal Index*, February, 1927.	174
Fig. 9-3. Wilson's article, "The Two Fruit Cakes," 1925.	175
Fig. 9-4. 1923 A. & M. Institute Bulletin. Wilson, Secretary to the Dean.	178
Fig. 9-5. Off-campus recital programs.	180
Fig. 9-6. Jacob Wilson with Thomas Elmore, circa 1925.	182
Fig. 9-7. A. & M.'s fourth president, Joseph Fanning Drake.	186
Fig. 9-8. David A. Grayson, State Board of Commissioners	188
Fig. 9-9. Detail of mural painting in Joseph Fanning Drake Memorial Library.	192

Chapter 10

Fig. 10-1. Alabama A. & M. Institute Band, 1933.	194
Fig. 10-2. Alabama A. & M. Institute Y. M. C. A. *Hand Book*.	199
Fig. 10-3. Wilson and his Sunday School Teacher Training Class.	200
Fig. 10-4. Y. M. C. A. *Hand Book*, 1931-1932, page 5.	201
Fig. 10-5. Receipt given to student Mary Parker, signed by Wilson.	202
Fig. 10-6. State A. & M. Institute *Bulletin*, August, 1937, page 6.	203
Fig. 10-7. Letter to Professor Langford, January 9, 1939.	205

Fig. 10-8. Financial Secretary Wilson, seated in his office with account books. 207
Fig. 10-9. Front and back of Picture Postcard from Wilson to Karl and Marian. 210
Fig. 10-10. Program cover, Wilson's Ensemble, 1936. 211
Fig. 10-11. Thirty Minutes with the Wilsons, July 27, 1938. 212
Fig. 10-12. Wilson Recital Program, January 29, 1937. 214

Chapter 11

Fig. 11-1. Sophomore Class Night Program, "Negroes In The Arts." 223
Fig. 11-2. The Modern A. & M. Band. 224
Fig. 11-3. The Rev. Dr. Henry Bradford, Jr., Chaplain. 226
Fig. 11-4. Invitation Booklet to the 65th Commencement Exercises, cover. 228
Fig. 11-5. Dedication page of 1941 Commencement Exercises Invitation. 228
Fig. 11-6. Dedication page of the 1941 *Bulldog*. 230
Fig. 11-7. "Father of the Blues" W. C. Handy speaking at Alabama A. & M. 232
Fig. 11-8. Letter from W. C. Handy to James H. Wilson, June 6, 1942, page 1. 233
Fig. 11-9. Letter from W. C. Handy to James H. Wilson, June 6, 1942, page 2. 234
Fig. 11-10. Circular enclosed in Handy's letter to Wilson. 236, 237
Fig. 11-11. W. C. Handy, Benefit Concert Program Cover. 241
Fig. 11-12. W. C. Handy, Benefit Concert Program, June 12, 1949. 243
Fig. 11-13. Karl Wilson at Camp Ellis, Illinois. 244
Fig. 11-14. Marian and John Turner, 1948. 245
Fig. 11-15. Treasurer Wilson and Financial Secretary Patton at work, 1950. 246
Fig. 11-16. Souvenir Booklet, Founder's Day Celebration, Wilson's annotation. 247
Fig. 11-17. Wilson's recognition in the Founder's Day booklet. 248
Fig. 11-18. Minutes of Special Committee, James H. Wilson Appreciation Day. 250
Fig. 11-19. Souvenir Cover for James H. Wilson Appreciation Day Program. 251

LIST OF ILLUSTRATIONS

Fig. 11-20. Program Cover, James H. Wilson Appreciation Day Convocation. 252
Fig. 11-21. Convocation Program, James H. Wilson Appreciation Day. 254, 255
Fig. 11-22. The Wilson Family, 1951. 256

Chapter 12

Fig. 12-1. A gray-haired James H. Wilson leads a pep band from the bleachers. 258
Fig. 12-2. Letter from W. C. Handy to James H. Wilson, November 28, 1952. 260
Fig. 12-3. Letter from W. C. Handy to James H. Wilson, March 19, 1953, p. 1. 262
Fig. 12-4. Letter from W. C. Handy to James H. Wilson, March 19, 1953, p. 2. 263
Fig. 12-5. "Silas Green March," Clarinet 1, by James H. Wilson. 264
Fig. 12-6. "United," E♭ Cornet, a march by James H. Wilson. 265
Fig. 12-7. The "Alabama A. & M. College March," Cornet, by James H. Wilson. 266
Fig. 12-8. The elderly James H. Wilson, ready to perform with his trumpet. 270
Fig. 12-9. Wilson's last published article, "Three Men — Three Philosophies." 272
Fig. 12-10. Wilson's personal accounting of income and expenditures. 273
Fig. 12-11. Cover, Program for Sunday Worship at Wilson's church. 274
Fig. 12-12. Wilson poem and listing as Deacon of the church. 275
Fig. 12-13. James Hembray Wilson and Exeline Elizabeth Polk Wilson rest here. 276
Fig. 12-14. The J. H. Wilson State Black Archives Research Center and Museum. 278
Fig. 12-15. The James H. Wilson Building crowns the campus buildings. 278
Fig. 12-16. Patricia Ford, Director of State Archives, before the Wilson portrait. 279
Fig. 12-17. Program, Ceremony of Dedication, Wilson State Black 280

Archives.
Fig. 12-18. Ceremony of Dedication Program, President Marbury presiding. 281

Appendix I
Fig. A-1. Leather Cover of James H. Wilson Journal. 285
Fig. A-2. Wilson Journal Flyleaf. 285
Fig. A-3. Wilson Journal, page 1, January 1 and 2, 1908. 286
Fig. A-4. Wilson Journal, page 41, February 26 and 27, 1908. 297

Appendix II
Fig. A-5. Flyleaf, recto, James H. Wilson Band and Tour Booklet. 321
Fig. A-6. Flyleaf, verso, Lettering in Wilson's Hand. 322
Fig. A-7. Roster, Elmore's Cyclone Band. 324

Acknowledgements

This book would never have seen the light of day except for the generosity of my dear friends, Marian Wilson Turner, and her husband, John Brister Turner, the William Rand Kenan Jr. Professor of Social Work at the University of North Carolina. Their first of many gifts to me related to this project was Marian's father's trumpet and baton, and I have in turn given them to the Yale University Collection of Musical Instruments. In addition to the trumpet they also gave me a box of memorabilia including photographs, concert programs, magazine articles, and more that had once been collected and saved by Marian's father, James Hembray Wilson. Several years later, Marian's daughter, Marian Turner Hopkins, discovered among her mother's possessions her grandfather's only surviving daily journal that itemized activities from January through June, 1908. That, too, was given me, and with this pocket-sized notebook in my custody, my work began in earnest. There could never have been a biography of this fascinating man without the enthusiastic and repeated help of these three dear friends.

Good books and artful jazz are necessarily collaborative efforts. When the soloist and the rhythm section are not carefully listening and working together, responding to cues, building upon the contributions of each participating musician, their collective music cannot rise above the mediocre. This book is like an ensemble performance, because many talented and dedicated individuals contributed their best efforts to make my narrative coherent, honest, and interesting. Where there are faults and shortcomings, the blame is surely mine. Where there is life and inspiration in the writing, the credit must be shared among many talented individuals working toward a common goal, that of revealing the life and times of James Hembray Wilson. I gratefully acknowledge the contributions of those who helped with the research, and the list begins with Andrew Hugine, Jr., Ph.D., the President of Alabama A. & M. University. He approved my visit to the A. & M. Campus and cleared the way for me to explore the university archives at both the J. F. Drake Memorial Learning Resources Center and the Alabama State Black Archives Research Center and Museum housed in James H. Wilson Hall. To help search these repositories, my friend and colleague, Louis E. Auld, Ph.D., Professor Emeritus of Central Connecticut State University, accompanied me to Normal, Alabama, and doubled the effectiveness of my visit by combing through documents with me and allowing me time to interview people living in the vicinity who had known Wilson as students, friends, and colleagues. Gary Bush, MSLS, M.Ed., the acting Director and Head of Public and Information Services at the Drake Memorial Learning Resources Center, as well as Prudence Bryant, Reference and Information Services Supervisor, Carla Clift, Interim University Archivist, and Patricia Ford, Director of the Alabama Black Archives and Research Museum, all went out of their way to be accommodating. As I worked in the library archive, Michelle Baker, a Graduate Assistant in the Library was especially helpful. She not only retrieved requested material, but she scoured the archive for other items that might be of interest. I am sincerely grateful to all these fine people for their expertise, enthusiasm, and willingness to share.

While in Normal, the Rev. Dr. Henry Bradford, Jr. and his wife, Nell Lane Bradford, both of whom were musical colleagues of James Hembray Wilson, welcomed me into their home, spoke of the old days, and retrieved photos and documents for my use. Glenda E. Gill, Ph.D., Professor Emerita of Drama at Michigan Technological University, was most cordial and supportive. She grew up on campus when her father replaced Wilson as Postmaster at Normal. Together, all of these fascinating people of A. & M. not only led me to useful evidence, but they helped flesh out the human environment of the college in a way that archival documents cannot.

Several colleagues at Yale assisted me as well in my various researches. Suzanne Eggleston Lovejoy, then the Interim Music Librarian of the University, and Remi Castonguay, the Public Services Projects Librarian in the Gilmore Music Library, were more than useful in teaching this old paper-and-ink researcher how to access great stores of electronic data, such as census documents, African American newspaper archives, and photograph collections. Two other Yale librarians, Julie Linden, Librarian for Political Science, International Affairs, and Government Information, and Dianne Kaplan, Head of Public Services, Manuscripts and Archives, were vital in offering me practical advice about how to overcome barriers encountered in my archival searches. Without all this expert help I am certain I could never have laid hands on all the materials I needed to examine.

Three close friends from Durham, North Carolina, went on a "treasure hunt" in Chapel Hill to see if they might find the lost journals of Wilson, and though those particular gems eluded them I must thank Marie Hammond, Kathy Register, and J. Samuel Hammond for a box of correspondence that is priceless in its own way. Later, Sam Hammond went far beyond the call of duty and volunteered not only to construct my index for this book but also to read the text critically and perform copy-editor service. My daughter-in-law, Misty Gale Anderson, Ph. D., Professor of English and Adjunct Professor of Theatre at the University of Tennessee, holder of the D. Allen Carroll Chair of Teaching, and Editor of the scholarly journal, *Restoration*, read an early version of my manuscript and also offered advice. Clearly this book is a collaborative venture.

When I visited Kentucky to explore Wilson's birthplace and surroundings, Dr. Linda A. Lear, M.D., of Nicholasville, Kentucky, was then the President of the Jessamine County Historical Society, and she sent me to a meeting where I met Ernestine M. Hamm. Without their help Wilson's "Old Kentucky Home" would in many ways still remain a mystery to me. Dorice Caise Brown, Deputy Clerk of the County Court, kindly guided me through the Jessamine County Court House Archives, directed me to Hervey Town, and commented about the old railroad connections. As you can see, many hands were actively helping me write this book every step of the way. Railroad history is the specialty of Jerry Pitts, a friend in Albuquerque, New Mexico, and he helped me explain aspects of routes, tracks, connections, equipment, and more that at first were quite puzzling. Jerry's wife, Virginia, is a genealogy buff, and she introduced me to some of the blessings and shortcomings of Ancestry.Com.

When finally I completed a reasonably polished draft of this book, my long-time friend and a distinguished literary agent,

Don Gastwirth, responded with passionate enthusiasm. Both he and my editor, Bob Kessler, Managing Editor of Pendragon Press, immediately sensed how this story opens a window into an important but little known period of African American life in the South, a time of interesting and robust musical, social, and intellectual activity. John Graziano, the Series Editor for American Music and Musicians at Pendragon, and Caterina Lindig, the Office Manager of the Press, have both contributed much. I am truly incapable of adequately expressing my gratitude to all these wonderful people.

As I researched this book, I made several trips to North Carolina, Ohio, Kentucky, Alabama, Illinois, and elsewhere to build a narrative based on evidence. These trips were both expensive and time consuming, and without the willing support of my lovely wife, Charlene, this book would forever have remained but a pipe dream. While we were in Italy she read early drafts of the first chapters, and when we returned home she never complained when I left her alone for a business trip. She encouraged me in all my efforts and truly believed in the importance of this project. *Cara mia, ti amo!*

Brief Recommended Reading List

This book is based on primary documents and interviews that are all cited in the footnotes. Scholars will be able to track them down in research libraries, civic archives, and on the web, but the general reader will most likely not be interested in pursuing them beyond what is presented in this biography of James H. Wilson. On the other hand, that same reader might enjoy learning more about some of the subjects touched upon in this volume, and the following books and articles should all be readily available. I have enjoyed them all and can recommend them to the reader without reservation.

Abbott, Lynn and Doug Seroff, *Out of Sight: The Rise of African American Popular Music, 1889-1895* (Jackson, MS: University Press of Mississippi, 2002).

Abbott, Lynn and Doug Seroff, *Ragged But Right: Black Traveling Shows, "Coon Songs," and the Dark Pathway to Blues and Jazz* (Jackson, MS: University Press of Mississippi, 2007).

Cannon, Frank Robert, Jr., *Bethel Methodist Church, Jessamine County, Kentucky . . . 1838-1996* (Nicholasville, KY: [author], 1996).

Cimbala, Paul Alan, "Fortunate Bondsmen: Black 'Musicianers' in the Antebellum Southern United States" (unpublished Master's thesis, Emory University, 1977).

Dunnigan, Alice Allison, *The Fascinating Story of Black Kentuckians* (Washington, D.C.: Associated Publishers, 1982).

Evans, David, "Handy, W. C.," in *Grove Music Online. Oxford Music Online,* http://www.oxfordmusiconline.com/subscriber/article/grove/music/12322 (accessed June 1, 2011).

Fleming, G. James and Christian E. Burckel, eds. *Who's Who in Colored America*, 7th ed. (New York: Who's Who in Colored America Corp, 1950),

Floyd, Samuel A., *Black Music Biography: an Annotated Bibliography* (White Plains, NY: Kraus International Publications, 1987).

Floyd, Samuel A., ed., *Black Music in the Harlem Renaissance: a Collection of Essays* (New York: Greenwood Press, 1990).

Floyd, Samuel A., *Black Music in the United States: an Annotated Bibliography of Selected Reference and Research Materials* (Millwood, NY: Kraus International Publications, 1983).

Franklin, John Hope, compiler, *Three Negro Classics*: *Up from Slavery* / Booker T. Washington. *The Souls of Black Folk* / William E.B. Dubois. *The Autobiography of an Ex-Colored Man* / James Weldon Johnson ; with an Introduction by John Hope Franklin (New York: Avon Books, 1965).

Handy Brothers Music Co., Inc., *Catalog of Music from the House of Handy* (New York: House of Handy, 1948).

Handy, W. C. (William Christopher), *Father of the Blues: An Autobiography*. Ed. Arna Bontemps. Forward by Abbe Niles. (New York: Da Capo Press, 1985).

Handy, W. C. and Eileen Southern, "Letters from W. C. Handy to William Grant Still," in *The Black Perspective in Music*, v. 7, n. 2 (Autumn, 1979), pp. 199-234.

Kenrick, John, "A History of the Musical Minstrel Shows" (http://www.musicals101.com/minstrel.htm, accessed February 3, 2012).

Kernodle, Tammy Lynn, "'Anything you are shows up in your music': Mary Lou Williams and the Sanctification of Jazz" (Ph.D. dissertation, Ohio State University, 1997).

Kernodle, Tammy Lynn, *Soul on Soul: The Life and Music of Mary Lou Williams* (Boston: Northeastern University Press, 2004).

Merritt, Russell, "Nickelodeon Theaters, 1905-1914: Building an audience for the movies," *The American Film Industry*, ed. Tino Balio (Madison, WI: University of Wisconsin Press, 1976), pp. 83ff.

Morrison, Richard David, *History of Alabama Agricultural and Mechanical University: 1875-1992* (Huntsville, AL: Liberal Arts Press, 1994).

Oakley, Giles, *The Devil's Music: A History of the Blues* (London: British Broadcasting Corporation, 1976)

Rhodes, Stephen L., *A History of the Wind Band*, http://www.lipscomb.edu/windbandhistory/index.htm (accessed April 23, 2012).

Southern, Eileen, *African-American Traditions in Song, Sermon, Tale, and Dance, 1600s-1920: an Annotated Bibliography of Literature, Collections, and Artworks* (New York: Greenwood Press, 1990).

Southern, Eileen, *The Music of Black Americans: A History* (New York: W. W. Norton & Co., 1997).

Southern, Eileen, ed., *Readings in Black American Music* (New York: W. W. Norton, 1983).

Toll, Robert C., *Blacking Up: The Minstrel Show in Nineteenth-Century America* (New York: Oxford University Press, 1974).

Williams, Lawrence H., *The Charles H. Parrishes: Pioneers in African-American Religion and Education, 1880-1989* (Lewiston, NY: Edwin Mellon Press, 2002).

Young, Bennett H., *A History of Jessamine County, Kentucky, from its Earliest Settlement to 1898* (Lexington, KY: Courier-Journal Job Printing Co., 1898).

Locations and Acknowledgements for Illustrations

Figure No.

P1.	Wikimedia Commons, http://commons.wikimedia.org/wiki/File:WCHandy_ w_A%26M_College_band_1900.jpg [public domain]
P2.	James Hembray Wilson's personal collection. *The Normalite 1919*, v. 3 (Normal, AL: Alabama Agricultural and Mechanical College, 1919), p.72. [public domain]
1-1, 1-2	Frank Tirro photograph.
1-3.	1850 Slave Schedule, Jessamine County, Kentucky [public domain]
1-4.	Jessamine County Court House, Marriages-Colored [public domain]
1-5.	Frank Tirro photograph
1-6.	[D. G.] Beers & Company, *Atlas of Bourbon, Clark, Fayette, Jessamine, and Woodford Counties, Ky* (Philadelphia, D. G. Beers & Co., 1877, image 22. [public domain]
1-7.	Bennett Henderson Young, *A History of Jessamine County, Kentucky, from Its Earliest Settlement to 1898*. S. M. Duncan, associate author. (Louisville, Ky: Courier-journal job printing co., 1898), p. 192. [public domain]
1-8.	Frank Tirro photograph.
1-9.	Young, *History of Jessamine County, op. cit.*, p. 186. [public domain]
1-10.	Courtesy of the Yale University Library Map Department.
2-1. 2-2.	Frank Tirro photograph.
2-3.	Library of Congress, http://www.loc.gov/pictures/item/var1993000086/PP/ [public domain]
2-4.	Library of Congress, http://www.loc.gov/pictures/item/var1994001233/PP/ [public domain]
2-5.	Courtesy of Alabama A&M University Archives, Alabama A&M University.
2-6. 2-7.	James Hembray Wilson's personal collection.

LOCATIONS AND ACKNOWLEDGEMENTS FOR ILLUSTRATIONS

2-8.	*The Freeman*, v. 12. Issue 36 (Indianapolis, IN: September 23, 1899), p. 5. [public domain]
2-9.	*The Anaconda Standard*, v. 12, n. 181 (Anaconda, MT: March 10, 1901), p. 9. [public domain]
2-10, 3-1, & 3-2.	James Hembray Wilson's personal collection.
3-3.	William Hooper Councill, *Normal, Alabama, or Information about the State Normal and Industrial School for Negroes* (Montgomery, AL: Roemer Printing Co., [1896]), p. 3. [public domain]
3-4.	James Hembray Wilson's personal collection. *The Normalite 1919*, v. 3 (Normal, AL: Alabama Agricultural and Mechanical College, 1919), p. 102. [public domain]
3-5.	James Hembray Wilson's personal collection. *The Normalite 1919*, v. 3 (Normal, AL: Alabama Agricultural and Mechanical College, 1919), p. 2. [public domain]
3-7.	James Hembray Wilson's personal collection. [public domain]
3-8.	Courtesy of the Yale University Library Map Department.
4-1.	*The Freeman*, v. 15. Issue 20 (Indianapolis, IN: May 17, 1902), p. 5. [public domain]
4-2.	James Hembray Wilson's personal collection.
4-3.	Wikipedia, "Billy Kersands," http://en.wikipedia.org/wiki/Billy_Kersands [public domain]
4-4.	Google Earth, destinations inserted by author into United States map.
5-1 to 6-2.	James Hembray Wilson's personal collection.
6-3 & 6-4.	Courtesy of the Duke University Libraries, digital collections. Used with permission.
6-5 to 6-6.	James Hembray Wilson's personal collection.
7-1 to 7-5.	Courtesy of Alabama A&M University Archives, Alabama A&M University.
7-6.	Frank Tirro photograph of portrait in the home of Marian Floredia Wilson Turner, with permission of the owner.
7-7 & 7-8.	James Hembray Wilson's personal collection.
7-9.	James Hembray Wilson's personal collection. *The Normalite 1919*, v. 3 (Normal, AL: Alabama Agricultural and Mechanical College, 1919), p. 5. [public domain]
7-10.	Library of Congress, http://memory.loc.gov/diglib/ihas/loc.nat-lib.ihas.200187072/default.html [public domain]
7-11 & 7-12.	James Hembray Wilson's personal collection.

7-13.	U. S. Census, 1910, Madison County, Alabama, Meridianville Precinct 1.1 [public domain]
7-13 to 8-5.	James Hembray Wilson's personal collection.
8-6.	Morrison, Richard David, *History of Alabama Agricultural and Mechanical University: 1875-1992* (Huntsville, AL: Liberal Arts Press, 1994), p. 141.
8-7.	James Hembray Wilson's personal collection. *The Normalite 1919*, v. 3 (Normal, AL: Alabama Agricultural and Mechanical College, 1919), p. 81. [public domain]
8-8.	James Hembray Wilson's personal collection. *The Normalite 1919*, v. 3 (Normal, AL: Alabama Agricultural and Mechanical College, 1919), p. 79. [public domain]
8-9.	James Hembray Wilson's personal collection. *The Normalite 1919*, v. 3 (Normal, AL: Alabama Agricultural and Mechanical College, 1919), p. 72. [public domain]
8-10.	James Hembray Wilson's personal collection. *The Normalite 1919*, v. 3 (Normal, AL: Alabama Agricultural and Mechanical College, 1919), p. 102. [public domain]
8-11.	James Hembray Wilson's personal collection.
8-12.	James Hembray Wilson's personal collection. *The Normalite 1919*, v. 3 (Normal, AL: Alabama Agricultural and Mechanical College, 1919), p. 94. [public domain]
8-13.	James Hembray Wilson's personal collection. *The Normalite 1919*, v. 3 (Normal, AL: Alabama Agricultural and Mechanical College, 1919), p. 98. [public domain]
8-14.	James Hembray Wilson's personal collection. *The Normalite 1919*, v. 3 (Normal, AL: Alabama Agricultural and Mechanical College, 1919), p. 54. [public domain]
8-15 to 9-3.	James Hembray Wilson's personal collection.
9-4.	Courtesy of Alabama A&M University Archives, Alabama A&M University.
9-5 and 9-6.	James Hembray Wilson's personal collection.
9-7.	Morrison, Richard David, *History of Alabama Agricultural and Mechanical University: 1875-1992* (Huntsville, AL: Liberal Arts Press, 1994), p. 159.
9-8.	James Hembray Wilson's personal collection. *The Normalite 1919*, v. 3 (Normal, AL: Alabama Agricultural and Mechanical College, 1919), p. 7. [public domain]
9-9.	Frank Tirro photograph. Courtesy of Alabama A&M University Archives, Alabama A&M University.

LOCATIONS AND ACKNOWLEDGEMENTS FOR ILLUSTRATIONS

10-1.	Morrison, Richard David, *History of Alabama Agricultural and Mechanical University: 1875-1992* (Huntsville, AL: Liberal Arts Press, 1994), p. 259.
10-2 to 10-4.	James Hembray Wilson's personal collection.
10-5.	Courtesy of Alabama A&M University Archives, Alabama A&M University.
10-6.	James Hembray Wilson's personal collection
10-7 & 10-8.	Courtesy of Alabama A&M University Archives, Alabama A&M University.
10-9 to 11-14.	James Hembray Wilson's personal collection.
11-15.	Courtesy of Alabama A&M University Archives, Alabama A&M University.
11-16 to 12-7.	James Hembray Wilson's personal collection.
12-8.	Courtesy of Alabama A&M University Archives, Alabama A&M University.
12-9 to 12-14.	James Hembray Wilson's personal collection.
12-15 & 12-16.	Frank Tirro photograph.
12-17 to A7.	James Hembray Wilson's personal collection.

INDEX

A&M: Alabama Agricultural & Mechanical College/Institute;
JHW: James Hembray Wilson
a, b: left, right column; **bold numerals**: illustrations

Abercrombie, John William, 187
Aberdeen (Miss.), 290a, 328a
Ackerman (Miss.), 289b-290a, 328a
"Acushla Machree" (Irish song), 137
Adair, Dora W., 179
Adair, Frank, **154**
Adams, Rev. ——— (Canton, Miss.), 289b
Adams, Julius J., 235
Adams, Oscar W., 175
"Adrift" (song), 139
African-American
    composers, 138. *See also* Handy, William C; *and under* JHW.
    culture & education, vii, 51, 115, 132, 153, 197, 221, 223, 225, 299b
    employment opportunities, ix, 18, 25, 40, 162
    military service, 1, 30-31, 48, 157, 224-225
African Methodist Episcopal Publishing Co. (Nashville, Tenn.), 175
Afro-American Fair (Lexington, Ky.), 64, 65
Alabama, vii, 52, 74, 123, 132, 164, 175, 179, 185, 187, 188, 218, 276
Alabama Academy. *See* Central Alabama Academy.
Alabama Agricultural & Mechanical College / Institute, vi, 49, 51, 52, 53, 57, 59, 60, 63, 114-115, **122**, 123-128, **124**, 134, 143, 146, 150, 153, 163, 165, 167, 175, 179-180, 184, 185, 224, 229, 291b, 294a, 296b, 298-314 *passim*
Adelphic Literary Society, 113, 298b, 300a, 306b
administration, 179, 190, 203
bandmasters, 51, 55, 56-57n, 101, 238, 264, 267, 270. *See also* Cooper, Phillip; Dawson, Thomas V.; Ford, Jonathan; Handy, William C.; Robertson, Wilton V.; *and under* JHW.
bands, vi, **viii**, **ix**, 51, 102-103, 107, 108, 112, 113, 133, 144, 157, **158,** 159, 179, **194**, 205, 206, 216, 223, **224**, 227, 233, 234, 235, 238-240, 255, 257-259, **258**, 267, 277, 298-299a, 300b, 302-306 *passim*, 308b, 314a
baseball team, 161, **161**
Ben Macato Club, x, 207-208, 215
Bibb Graves Auditorium, 212, 221, 227n, 274, 277
Bible Training classes, 155, **156**. *See also under* JHW.
buildings, 52, 60, 163, 164, 175, 189
Carnegie Library, 133, 189, 304a
chapel, 57, 104, 113, 114, 134, 137, 159, 187, 213, 257, 298b-313 *passim*

351

Chase Hall, 300a
choir, vii, 114, 251, 269, 270, 277, 281, 299a, 300b, 301a, 306b, 310b, 311a, 312
commercial orchestra, **158**, 159, 180
Councill Domestic Science Building, 163, 175, 189
curriculum & courses, 52, 54, 59, 60, 105, 146, 185, 224
disciplinary actions, 306a
Drake Library, 185, 192
faculty, 125, 146, 148-149, 150-151, 163, 164, 167, 184, 196, 200, 203, 229, 239
faculty housing, 52, 60, 273
fees, 59, 191, 202, 204
Female Industries, 60, 162, 179
finances, 163-165, 175, 183-184, 191, 200, 202, 246
Frederick Douglass Debating Society, 113, 303a
glee club & chorus, 103, 113, 115, 269, 298b, 299, 300b, 302a, 303a, 304a, 307-313 *passim*
goals & aims, 60, 146, 193
Industrial School, 115, 146-148
JHW Appreciation Day, 245, 249-255
JHW State Black Archives Research Center and Museum, **278**, 280-282, **281**
laboratory school, 54, 153-154
Langston Hall, 300a
laundry, 60, 161-162, **162**
McCormick Hospital Building, 163, 175, 184, 189
Minstrelnola Club, 114, 115, 133, 138, 139, 157, 159, 302a, 310b, 311, 312b, 313a
music, vi-vii, 28, 30, 51, 60, 101, 102-103, 125, 128, 134, 143, 149, 151, 206, 251

Normal School, 52, 54-55, 105, 107, 114, 115, 123, 127, 128, 139, 148, 299b, 307, 311a
Nurse Training, 184
Palmer Hall, 133, 166, 311a
Peabody Literary Society, 127, 301b, 302a
Phyllis Wheatley Literary Society, 307b
Preparatory Department, 60, 100, 105, 107, 108, 123
religion, 63, 102, 104-105, 168, 198-199, 225-227, 298-313 *passim*
R.O.T.C., ix, 102n, 155, 157, **158**
salaries, 56, 163, 164, 184, 191-193
sanitation, 52, 163
schedule, 104
Secretary of the Faculty, 125-127. *See also under* JHW.
Sunday School, x, 155, 168, 196, 217, 267, 299-311 *passim*.
Sunday School Teacher Training, x, 155, **156**, 157, 168, 196, 198, **200**, 215, 227, 268, 269
swing orchestra, 227, 229
Treasurer, 189, 245-246. *See also under* JHW.
Treble Clef Club, 108
vocal & choral music, vii, 52, 55, 107, 113, 125, 128, 227, 303a, 304b
water supply, 52, **54**, 153
Y.M.C.A., 105, 157, **157**, 168, 198-199, 215, 227, 299a, 300-311 *passim*
Y.W.C.A., 198, 215, 227, 300a, 311a
Alabama Black History Museum, 282

INDEX

Alabama Board of Commissioners, 134, 146, 163, 164, 167, 187, 231, 282
Alabama Quartette, 40, 41, 70
Alabama State Teachers Association, 175, 267
Alabama State (Teachers) College (Montgomery), 49, 175, 185, 267
Alex, Jack, 326a
All in the Family (TV series), 21
"All Through the Night" (chorus; Owen), 159
Allen's Minstrels, 326a
"American Indian Operetta," 208
"American Patrol" (march; Meacham), 239, 240
"Americans We" (march; Fillmore), 239
Amory (Miss.), 290a, 328a
Anaconda Standard, The (Montana newspaper), 39-40, 41
Annabel (correspondent), 291b
Anniston (Ala.), 175
Archer, Henrietta M. F., 125-127, 291a, 305a
Archer, Hiram E., 100, 101n, 125, 302b, 304b, 310a, 313b
Ardis, Harriet, 139
Ardis, Mollie, 139, 312a
Ardmore (Okla.), 326b
"Arrah Wanna" (song; Dislane & Morse), **109, 110**, 111-112, 303b
Arvey, Verna, viin
Asher, Miss ——— (Decatur, Ala.), 300a
Asher, Delanare, 313a
Asher, Hanna, 300a
Atlanta (Ga.), 1, 170, 292b-293a, 328b
Atlanta University, 149, 245

Auburn (Ala.), 164
Audran, Edmond. The Torpedo and the Whale (song), 159
Austin (Tex.), 327a

Bach, Johann Sebastian, 221
Bach-Gounod. Ave Maria, 243
Bailey, Dr. ——— (Jefferson, Ind.), 316b, 317b, 319a
Bailey, James, 313a
Baily, W. S., 290b
Ballard, E. C., 325a
Ballard, Thomas, 325a
Baltimore (Md.), 242
Band of America (Lavalle), 264
bands & band music, 22, 24, 64, 72, 74, 261, 264
    military, 31, **32**, 35, **46**, 48-49, 66, 112, 117, 179. *See also* Hamilton's Military Band.
banjo, x, 10, 66
Baptist Church, 5, 114, 217n, 226
Barili, Armand De C. Tender Little Flower (song), 144, 145
baritone (instrument), 64, 71, 119, 257, 320, 323, 325
Barnby, Sir Joseph. Paradise (hymn tune), 108
Barnett, Miss ——— (Chattanooga, Tenn.), 314b
Barnett, Richard H., 36
Barney, Carolyn, 139
Barry, Jeff (Joel Adelberg), 21
baseball, 42-43, 107, 113, 121, 170, 300a, 304b, 309a. *See also under* A&M *and* JHW.
bass, string, 40, 70, 71, 88, 119, 323, 325a
bathing, 89-90, 153
Baton Rouge (La.), 83, 327b
baton(s), 35, 66, **67**, 118, **118**, 119, **119**

353

Bayliss, Edwin H., 203
"Believe Me If All Those Enduring Charms" (song), 159
Belle, Richmond, 223
Benton, J. M., 140, 141
Berea College (Ky.), 149
Berlin, Irving. God Bless America (song), 243; Remember"(song), 180
Berry, Elder ——— (Oakwood College), 305b
Bessemer (Ala.), 262-263
  Canaan Baptist Church, 180
Bible, 17, 95, 103, 155, 169-171, 172-173, 196, 208, 253, 268, 271-273. *See also under* JHW.
"Big Stick Blues March, The" (Handy), 259
"Billowey Sea, The" (song; Nowlin), 180
Binford, Ruth P., 203
Birmingham (Ala.), 175, 238, 263
  bombings, 271
Birmingham Reporter, 175
Bizet, Georges. Agnus Dei, 243
Black, H. W., 159, 175
Black Watch Drill (minstrel act), 40
Blake, James Hubert (Eubie). *Shuffle Along* (musical), 259, 260
blues (music), 50, 275
Bolton, Ina A., 203
bones (rhythm instrument), x
Bonham, Jack, 250
Bonham (Tex.), 326b
Bonimor, Simon, 36
Booneville (Miss.), 291a, 328a
Boothe, Emmer, 139
Bose, Lucenda, 108
Boston (Mass.), 55

Boulder, Henry, 320b
Bowling Green Academy (Ky.), 175
"Boy Detective, The" (1908 movie), 293b
Bradford, Henry, Jr., 56n, 225-227, **226**, 242, 243, 250, 255, 267, 270, 272, 277, 283
Bradford, Nell Lane, 243, 250, 270, 272
Brahms, Johannes, 270
Bramlet, Miss ——— (A&M), 312a
Bray, James L., 203, 250, 253, 255
Breda, Malcolm Joseph, 274
Breil, Joseph Carl. Song of the Soul, 214
Brenham (Tex.), 327a
Bridal Rose overture (Lavallée), 33
Bright, Roy, 325b
Bright, Sara, 312a
Britton, Elder ——— (Nicholasville, Ky.), 318b
Broad Axe (Chicago, Ill. newspaper), 150
Broad Axe (St. Paul, Minn. newspaper), 25-26
Brooks, ——— (Nicholasville, Ky.), 316a
Brooks, R. E., 312b
Brooks, Reuben, 11
Broughton, Virginia Walker, 309a
Browder, Mr. ——— (A&M), 250
Brown, Ed, 323a
Browne (Brown), ——— (A&M), 12, 196-197n
Bryan (Tex.), 327a
Bryant, George, 325a
Bryant, Ira R., 175
Bryant-Stratton College (Chicago, Ill.), 197n
Bryson, Mr. ——— (Chattanooga, Tenn.), 293b

Buchanan, Ida Councill, 123, 125, 128, 134, 137-139, 148, 149-150, 151, **158**, 159, 165, 175, 299a

Buchanan, William Solomon, 92, 134, **135**, 138-139, 143, 146, 148-149, 150, 151, 155, 163-165, 167, 175, 183, 193

Buck, Dudley. Kentucky Babe (lullaby), 159

Buckeye Band (Cincinnati, Ohio), 65

Buckner, Mrs. ——— (Lexington, Ky.), 315b, 318a

Buffalo Bill's Wild West Show, 36

Buffalo Soldiers. *See* U.S. Army. Ninth Cavalry.

Bulldog (A&M yearbook), 229, 230

Bulls, Mrs. ——— (A&M), 250

Bunche, Ralph, 263

Burleigh, Harry Thacker. If Life Be a Dream (song), **136**, 137, 138

Bush, Mr. ——— (A&M student), 250

Bush, W. T., 250

Butler, Addie M., 203

Butte (Mont.), 39

B.Y.P.U., 50, 93, 94, 289b, 295b, 296a, 315b, 316b, 317b, 319a

Cairo (Ill.), 327b

"Calvary" (song; Vaughan & Rodney), 180-181

Calvert (Tex.), 327a

Camp Ellis (Ill.), 244

Camp Nelson (Ky.), 1, 51, 120, 317, 325b

Campbell, Bunk, 96n

Campbell, Fred., 326a

Campbell, Manzy (Manzie), 87, 88, 95, **96**, 96n, 97, 287a, 294b, 326a

Campbell Brothers, 88, 96n

Canada, 28, 39, 41-43, 61, 132

Canton (Miss.), 97, 289b, 328a
  Mt. Zion Baptist Church, 289b

Carnegie, Andrew, 189

Carpenter, E. J., 35

Carter, Henrietta J., 203

Carter, Nick (character), 47

Carter, Robert A., 190, 191, 203, 204, 250

Casey, John Oscar. Naukeag Polka, 214

cello, 40, 80

Central Alabama Academy (Huntsville), 302a, 303b

Chambers, Isaiah Mench. *The Devil of Today*, 295b

Chambers, Mary, 250

Chambers, William Paris, 180

Chandler (Okla.), 326b

Chattanooga (Tenn.), 101, 115, 150, 292a, 293-294a, 296b, 308a, 314, 328b
  Bijou Theatre, 293b
  Central Shed, 293
  East Side Pharmacy, 293b, 294a
  hippodrome, 294a
  Howard High School, 293b
  James Building, 293b
  Scott & Westbrook blacksmiths, 314b
  Y.M.C.A., 293b

Chatwell, Jallie, 296b

Cheyney (Pa.), 49

Chicago (Ill.), 1, 33, 44, 48, 78, 79, 92, 175, 289a

Chicago, University of, 149, 188

Chicago Heights (Ill.), 79, 326a

Chicago World Fair (1893) (World's Columbian Exposition), 263

355

Chopin, Frederic, 137
Christian, ——— (minstrel), 40
Christian Recorder (Philadelphia, Pa.), 311a
Cimbala, Paul Alan, 10
Cincinnati (Ohio), 12, 18, **20**, 21-23, **23**, 49, 61, 65, 83, 84, 287a
   Games High School, 24, 178
   Gray's Armory, 64, 65
Cincinnati Southern Railroad, 4, 18
Cissell, Celia, 315b, 316a
Civil War (U.S.), 1, 11
Clanton, Dwight Lormar, 108
clarinet, 71, 118, **158**, 209, 257, 261, 264, 320, 323, 325a
Clark, Augusta (Gus), 311b, 312a, 313
Clark, Harvey, 108
Clark, Lucy, 317b
Clark University, 150
Clarksdale (Miss.), 262, 288, 328a
Clay, Charles, Jr., 325b
Clay, Cora, 317b
Clayborn aggregation (Nicholasville, Ky.), 51
Clayborne, Mrs. Herman G., 263
Clays, Miss ——— (Camp Nelson, Ky.), 317a
Cleburne (Tex.), 327a
Cleveland, Grover, 262
Cleveland (Ohio), 65, 269
Cleveland Gazette, 65
Cochran, J. P., 250
Coffeyville (Kans.), 80, 326a
Collins, Arthur Francis, 111, 112n
Columbia University (New York City), 150, 188, 203, 242
Columbus (Kans.), 326b
Columbus (Ohio), 64, 65
Competitor, The (Pittsburgh newspaper), 165, 167, 175

Conley, S. H., 320a
Conway, Harry, 290a
Cook, Mrs. ——— (Lexington, Ky.), 318a
Cook, Denis J., 320
Cooke, Charles L., 259, 260
Cooke (Cook's) Peerless Band, 49, 320b-321a
Cooley, MahLon, 139
Coons, William, **119**, 323a
Cooper, Lloyd, 70, 71, 87, 88, 287a, 288a, 289a, 292b, 323b, 325b
Cooper, Phillip (A&M bandmaster), 57n, 257, 258
Cooper, Phillip (A&M student), 223
Corinth (Miss.), 79, 290b-291a, 328a
   St. Mark Baptist Church, 290b
Cornell University (Ithaca, N.Y.), 150, 203
cornet, vii-viii, ix, 24, **42,** 47n, 49, 61, 64, 71, 73, 80, 112, 118, **158,** 159, 220, 261, 265, 293b, 320, 323, 325. *See also under JHW.*
Corona Industrial Institute (Ala.), 134
Corsicana (Tex.), 327a
Coryell, John Russell, 47n
Councill, Dement H., 101n, 139
Councill, Ida. *See* Buchanan, Ida.
Councill, Maria Howard, 133-134, 139
Councill, William Hooper, vin, vii, 51, 55-56, **58**, 59, 60, 63, 101-103, 104, 113, 127, 132-133, 134, 143, 146, 150, 167, 175, 189, 225, 290b, 291a, 293a, 294b, 296b, 298a, 301a, 307a, 313a
Councill School (Ensley, Ala.), 175
Count Basie Orchestra, 96n

Courtland (Ala.), 291b, 328a
Covington, B., 326a
Covington, H. Douglas, 282
Cowin(s), Abe, 7, 8, 10
Crockett, Miss ——— (A&M), 308b
Crossen, Charles S., 71, 323b
"Crossing the Bar" (song; Tennyson), 133
Crowley (La.), 327b
Cuba, 46, 48-49
Curd, Richard, 118
"Curly Head" (waltz), 148
Cyclone Band. *See* Elmore's Cyclone Band.
cymbals, 71, 257, 323b

Daily Advertiser (Montgomery newspaper), 69
Daily News (New York newspaper), 11
Daisy (correspondent), 287b, 290a, 294b, 314a
Dalbey, Clarence W., 239
Dallas (Tex.), 1, 80, 327a
Dalton (Ga.), 292a
dancing, 90-91, 169-173, 208, 229
Daniels, Lucius, 223
Danks, Hart Pease. Silver Threads Among the Gold (song), 72
Danville (Ill.), 80, 326a
Dartmouth College (Hanover, N.H.), 150
David, King of Israel, 170
Davis, A. U., 315b
Dawson, Thomas V., 270, 277
Dazey, Charles Turner, 27n
Decatur (Ala.), 291b, 300a, 312b, 328b
   Presbyterian Church, 217
   Steers Infirmary, 291b

Decatur (Ga.), 328b
Decatur (Ill.), 80, 326a
DeLamater, Eugene. Universal March, 209
Delcarte entertainment, 304a
Denison (Tex.), 326b
Dennis, Mrs. ——— (Lexington, Ky.), 295b
Denton (Tex.), 327a
Depression, The, 192, 195, 200
Desdunes, Daniel, 35, 36, 325a
DeVaughn, Annie Ruth, 223
Devil of Today The (Chambers), 295b
Dickerson, Elder ——— (Nicholasville, Ky.), 116, 290b, 296b, 316a
Dickerson, Sister ——— (Nicholasville, Ky.), 116, 315b
Dismuke, Willie Mae, 159
divorce, 170, 171, 172. *See also under* JHW.
dogs, 28, 231
"Dollar Princess" (waltz; Fall), 148
Donaldsonville (La.), 327b
Donigan, Delia, 301a
Dora (Nicholasville, Ky.), 296b
Dortch, David Elijah, 134
Doss, Rubye, 243
Douglas (Ariz.), 30, 31, 49
Douglass, Frederick, 113
Drake, Anne Q., 186, 187
Drake, Harold, 209
Drake, Joseph Fanning, 185-190, **186**, 191-193, **192**, 198, 199, 200, 202, 203, 205, 224, 234, 238, 239, 240, 249, 253, 255, 257, 262, 264, 277, 282
Drislane, Jack. Arrah Wanna (song), **109**, **110**, 111-112, 303b

drum major(s), 35, 117, 118, **118,** 119, **119,** 240
drums, 47n, 71, 88, 96n, 119, 182, 209, 211, 257, 320b, 323, 325
Dubois, Ja'net, 21
Dunbar, Paul Laurence. In the Morning (poem), 159
Dunlop, Olivia E., 203
Durand, Auguste. Valse No. 1, op. 83 (piano), 180
Durant (Miss.), 289a, 328a

Earthquake, Billy, 69
East St. Louis (Ill.), 80, 326a
Edgefield (Tenn.) Odd Fellows Band, 101n
Edwards, O. B., 272
Elgar, Sir Edward. Where Corals Lie (song), 137
Elliott, S. J., 175
Elman, Dave (David Kopelman), 232, 233
Elmore, Mrs. ——— (Nicholasville, Ky.), 116, 315a
Elmore, Ollie, 165, 253, 325a
Elmore, T. M. (A&M student), 253, 254
Elmore, Thomas M., 165, 167, 175, **182,** 209, **228,** 229, 250, 253, 277
Elmore's Cyclone Band, 11, 24, 37, 38, 39, 49, 74, 165, 253, 323b-325a
Emancipation Proclamation, 5
Emporia (Kans.), 80, 326a
Enid (Okla.), 326b
Episcopal Church, 5
euphonium, 47n
Evansville (Ind.), 294b-295a, 328b
"ex 'thre' act," 79

Fagala, J. D., 293b
Fall, Leo. Dollar Princess (waltz), 148
Falla, Manuel de. Ritual Fire Dance, 243
Famous Georgia Minstrels (Richards & Pringle's), 33, 39-45, 47, 49
"Fantasia on Tramp, Tramp, Tramp" (Goldman), 267
"Fare You Well" (spiritual), 221n
Farrel, Skip, 71, 323b
Faust Overture (Wagner?), 33
Fayette County (Ky.), 1
Fayetteville (N.C.), 132
Fearns (Ala.), 296b, 310a, 313b
Federation of the Churches of Christ, 175
Fennoy, William, 108, 175
Fentress, ——— (A&M musician), 138, 139
fiddle, x, 10. *See also* violin.
Fidler, J. H. (Harry), 40, 41
Fields, W. L., **119,** 320a, 323a
Fields, William, 295b
Fillmore, Henry. Americans We (march), 239
Fillmore, Millard, 3
Fisher, John, 94, 296
Fisk Jubilee Singers, vii, 52
Fisk University (Nashville, Tenn.), 51-52, 117, 308a, 316b
Florence (Ala.), 180, 233, 242, 263, 291b
   St Martin de Porres Church, 242, 243
"Flower Song, The" (piano; Lange), 139
flute, 325a
Foilet, 311b
Ford, J. E., 310a
Ford, Jonathan, 57n, 240, 250, 251-252, 257, 259

Ford, Patricia, **279**
Ft. Pierce (Fla.), 218
Fort Smith (Ark.), 326b
Fort Worth (Tex.), 80, 327a
Foster, Stephen Collins. My Old Kentucky Home, 12, 17, 107, 108, 159, 214, 239, 270; Nelly Bly, 180
Foxx, Martha Louise Morrow, 262
Frankfort (Ky.), 120
Franklin, Mrs. ——— (Chattanooga, Tenn.), 293b
Franklin, George Washington, 293
Franklin, Mable, 293b
Franklin (La.), 327b
Franz, Robert. Im Herbst (song), 137
Frazier, ———, 205, 206
Freeman, Miss ———, 304a, 318a
Freeman, Harriet F., 148
Freeman, Maggie L., 294b
Freeman, The (Indianapolis newspaper), 17, 34, 35, 36, 37, 38, 41-42, 44-45, 47, 48, 50, 61, 65, 72-74, 78-79, 80-82, 90-91, 101, 132, 168
Fry, Thomas, 317a, 320a, 325b
Fussnecker, Isidore Louis, O.S.B., 243

Gainesville (Tex.), 326b
Galveston (Tex.), 327a
Garrett, Isora Rogers, 133
Garrett, Mary, 305a
Garrett, W. L., **119**
Gaten, Blaine S., 71, 323b
Gay, Miss ———, 316a
Geiger (C.F.) & Co., 104, 299a
Genyelar band, 318b
Georgia, 74

Georgia Minstrels (Callender's), 67. *See also* Famous Georgia Minstrels.
Germany, 123, 128
Gettysburg (Pa.), 293b
Gibson, Mary J., 105, 126, 139, 299b, 300b
Gideon's Minstrel Carnival, 33, 34, 35, 36
Gill(s), Glendora, 315b, 317a
Gill, Theodore R., 148
Gilmore, Patrick, band, 24, 73, 74
Glad Tidings, The (A&M newsletter), 267-268, 270, 272
Glover, Henry Barnard ("Lil Henry"), 216, 227, 229, 281
"Go Down Moses" (Handy), 233
"God Be with You Till We Meet Again" (hymn), 133
"God Bless America" (song; Berlin), 243
Goines, C. C., 48, 91, 93
Goines, R. M. 89, 90, 91, 93, 287b, 289b, 300b
Goldman, Edwin Franko. Fantasia on Tramp, Tramp, Tramp, 267
"Good-Bye" (song; Tosti), 180, 242, 243
Grainger, Percy. Country Gardens, 243
Grant, Ulysses S., 1
Grant, William, 326a
Graves, Mrs. C. B., 290b
Graves, Henry, 325b
Gray, Jerry, 240
Gray, Mollie, 295b
Grayson, David Allison, 148, 185, 187-189, **188**, 304b
Green, Lucy Nell, 272
Green (Silas) Show, 96n

Greene, A. B., 180
Greenville (Miss.), 288b, 328a
  Star of Bethlehem Baptist Church, 288b
Greenville (Tex.), 327a
Grenada (Miss.), 288b, 328a
Griffin, Marquis H., 102, 175, 296b, 298a, 309a
Guin, George, **119**, 320a, 323a
Guthrie, A. L., 68
Guthrie (Okla.), 326b

"Hail to the Spirit of Freedom" (Handy), 233
Haines. *See* Haynes.
Haley, Simon A., 203
Half-Century Magazine, The, 168, 170
Hall, Rev. ——— (Tupelo, Miss.), 290b
Hall, James, 64
Hall, John T. Wedding of the Winds (waltz), 239
Hamilton, Mrs. ——— (A&M), 307a, 308a
Hamilton, Ernest F., 203
Hamilton, Henry S., 64, 66, **67**, 117, 118, **118**, 119, **119**, 120, 317a, 320, 323a
Hamilton, Sid., 323a
Hamilton's Military Band (Lexington), 49, 64, 66, **67**, 74, 117-120, **118, 119**, 316b, 317a, 318, 320, 323a
Hammond, Wade H., 57n, 101
Hampton Institute (Va.), 242
Handel, Georg Friedrich. *Rinaldo*. Lascia ch'io pianga, 137; *Xerxes*. Largo, 316a
Handy, William Christopher, vii-viii, **viii**, ix, x, 11, 27, 28, 30, 51, 54, 55-56, 57n, 230-238, **232**, 241-243, 259-263, 277.
  See also titles of individual works.
Handy Brothers Music Co., 236, 259, 261
Hantham, E. U., 116, 315b
Harlan, Byron G. 111, 112n
Harlem Renaissance, 177, 213, 221
Harris, E. A., 175
Harris, Minnie D. Somebody Misses You Every Day (song), 139
Harrison, Annie Fortescue, 221n
Hartman, John. Lizzie Polka, 180
Hartmann, Thomas Alexandrovich de. Russia, 206
Harvard University, 27n, 150
Hassler, Hans Leo. Cantate Domino, 281
Hawkins, R. C., 293b
Hawthorne, Mrs. ——— (Lexington, Ky.), 97, 99, 295b, 317a
Hayden, Miss ——— (Rockport, Ind.), 295a
Hayes, Al (Henry Fillmore), 239
Haynes, Bennie, 144
Haynes (Haines), George Edmond, 175, 309
"He Didn't Know But One Tune," 267
Hedgepath, William, 64
Helm, William, 320, 323a
Henderson, Miss ——— (A&M), 309a
Henderson, Charles, 144, 145
Henderson, L. D. ("Slim"), 69, 81, 92, 289a
Henderson, L. W., 293b
Henry (A&M student), 191
Henry, Prof. ——— (Oakwood College), 305b
Herbert, Victor. Italian Street Song, 243

INDEX

Hérold, Ferdinand. *Zampa* overture, 70
Hervey, James O., 8, 9n, 10
Hicks, A., 325a
Hill, George F. [E. Hill], 57n, 101
Hill, Samuel W., 227
Hillsboro (Tex.), 327a
"His Eye Is on the Sparrow" (hymn; Martin), 281
Hobby Lobby (radio program), 232, 233
Hobson, Mrs. A. K., 250
Hobson, Pearl, 81
Hofmann, Josef, 90n
Hollins, W. H., 250
Holloway, Spencer E., 140, 141
Hollywood (Calif.), 262
Hopkins, Miss ——— (A&M), 111, 154-155, 298b, 303a
Hopkins, Henry C., 101n, 111, 114, 126, 127, 133, 144, 148, 175, 299, 300b, 302b, 306b, 312a, 314a
Hopkins, William, 325b
Hopkins-Randall, Lula, 213, 214
Hopkinsville (Ky.), 68
   Holland's Opera House, 69
horn, 11, 12, 24, 70, 71, 112, 118, 223, 257, 320, 323, 325
horn, alto, 47n, 64, 119
Horne, Lena Mary Calhoun, 262
horse shoes (game), 107-108, 113, 121, 302, 307b, 310a
Hot Springs (Ark.), 83, 327b
Houma (La.), 327b
Housley, Angelo, 47n
Housley, Beverly A., 47, 325b
Housley, Goldie (George W.?), 47n, 49, 325
Housley, Matt, 47n
Housley brothers, 40, 64
Houston (Tex.), 327a

Howard, Thomas, 64, 65
Howard University (Washington, D.C.), 150, 203
Huff, Wallace, 223
Hughes, Langston, viin, 222; I, too, sing America (poem), 221-222
Hunt, Benjamin P., 304b, 305a
Hunter, Charles (flutist), 325a
Hunter, Charles (St. Louis, Mo.), 291a
Hunter, Minnie, 139
Huntsville (Ala.), vi, 12, 114, 115, 133, 161, 175, 177, 184, 206, 260, 296b, 298b, 301a, 302a, 304b, 305a, 311a, 312a, 313
   Brandontown Cemetery, **276, 277**
   First Baptist Church, 12, 15, 274-275, **274**
   St John A.M.E. Church, 133, 310b, 312b
Hutchison, Katherine, 296b
Hyde, Robert L., 175
hyphen, 268-269

"I Shall See Him Face to Face" (hymn), 133
"I, too, sing America" (poem; Hughes), 221-222
"I Want to Be Ready" (spiritual), 148
"If Life Be a Dream" (song; Burleigh & Stanton), **136,** 137, 138
Illinois, 69, 74, 80, 83
Illinois, University of, 149, 150
Illinois Central Railroad, 79
Illinois Colored Regiment Band, Eighth, 48, 49
"In May Time" (chorus; Speaks), 108

"In Old Kentucky" (minstrel show; Litt), 25-26, **26**, 39
"In Silent Thought" (piano reverie; Morrison), 159
"In the City of Sighs and Tears" (song; Sterling & Mills), 144, 145
"In the Gloaming" (song), 221n
"In the Morning" (poem; Dunbar), 159
Independence (Kans.), 326b
Independent Order of Odd Fellows, 68, 120, 310a, 318b
Indian Territory, 35, 74, 80, 326b
Indiana State Teachers College, 203
International Sunday School Association, 197
"Iola" (intermezzo; Johnson), 108
Iowa, 35
Iowa State Bystander (Des Moines newspaper), ix
Isler, Arthur, 326a
"Italian Street Song" (Herbert & Young), 243

Jackson, Mrs. ——— (Queensboro, Ky.), 295a
Jackson, Mrs. ——— (Rockport, Ind.), 295a
Jackson, C. H., 242, 243
Jackson, Elliott, 296b
Jackson, Emma, 108
Jackson, William, **119**, 323a
Jackson (Miss.), 289a, 310b, 328a
Jackson (Tenn.), 328a
Jackson Citizen Patriot (Michigan newspaper), 27-28
Jamaica, 311b
James, Henrietta, 108
jazz, 50, 90n, 96n
Jefferson, H., **119**
Jefferson (Ind.), 316b

Jeffersons, The (TV series), 21
Jelks, William Dorsey, 123
Jenerette (La.), 327b
Jennings (La.), 327b
Jessamine County (Ky.), 1, 2-3, 5, 6, 7
Jesus Christ, 170, 173, 222-223
"Jesus Lover of My Soul" (hymn), 159
Jevis family, 317a
John the Baptist, Saint, 170, 172
Johnson, Sec. ——— (Chattanooga, Tenn.), 293b
Johnson, Albert, **119**, 320b, 323a, 325b
Johnson, Charles, 71, 323a
Johnson, Charles Leslie. Iola (intermezzo), 108
Johnson, Edward, 213, 214
Johnson, Florence T., 100, 105, 294a, 298b, 299b, 300, 306a, 308b, 309a, 312a
Johnson, George, **119**, 323a
Johnson, James, **119**, 323a
Johnson, James Weldon, 213n
Johnson, John Rosamund. Since You Went Away, 213, 214; Song of My Heart, 213, 214
Johnson, "Juggling," 69
Johnson, Minnie, 290b, 291a
Johnson, Roy, 294b
Johnson, Samuel Abraham, 300a
Johnson's Superb Band, 325b
Jones, Rev. ——— (Nicholasville, Ky.), 317b
Jones, Clarence P., 64
Jones, D. P., 302a
Jones, Gertrude, 304a
Jones, Papa Jo, 96n
Jones, W. M., 133
Jones, Willie, 180
Joplin (Mo.), 326b

Jordan, O. J., 126
jubilee hymns, 114, 138, 303b, 313a
jubilee singers, 28, 293b. *See also* Fisk Jubilee Singers.

Kansas, 74, 80
Kansas, University of, 203
Keene (Ky.), 51
Kendrick, Mr. ——— (A&M), 216, 250
Kendricks, Carrie, 299a
Kentucky, 1, 3-4, 5, 7, 47, 74, 114, 117
"Kentucky Babe" (lullaby; Buck), 159
Kersands, Billy, 66, **67**, 69, 78-79, 82, 91, 92, 97, 106
Kersands, Louisa Strong, 69, 80, 91-92, 106, 287b, 289, 290b, 291a, 292b, 293a
Kersands Minstrels, 63, 66, 68-71, 72-74, 75, 77, 78-83, 88, 95, 97, 112, 287-295a *passim*, 320a, 323b
King, Celestine, 296b
King, Karl. Princess of India, 239
King, L. R., 310b
King, Lula M. 299, 301, 302, 305a, 306a, 307a, 308b, 309, 311b, 314a
Kingfisher (Okla.), 326b
Kiser, M. L., 179
Knights of Pythias, 315b
  Uniform Rank, 119
Kryl, Bohumir, 73
Ku Klux Klan, 132, 218

Lacy, James S., 70, 71, 73, 74, 103, 295a, 298b, 317b, 323
  band & orchestra, 49, 72, 79, 323
Lacy, Vida, 108
La Grange (Tex.), 327b

Lake Charles (La.), 81, 327b
Lancaster (Ky.), 315a
land grant colleges, 102, 155, 164, 190
Lange, Gustav. Flower Song (piano), 139
Langford, Kid, 40, 41, 82
Langford, Nathan A., 203, 204, 205, 206
Lavalle, Paul, 264
Lavallée, Calixa. *Bridal Rose* overture, 33
Law, W. A., 71, 323b
Lawlah, Evelyn, 180
Lawler, William Thomas, 125
Lawrence (Kans.), 80, 326a
"Lead Me" (song), 148
Leak, Elder ——— (Oakwood College), 105, 305b, 306a
"Leaning on the Everlasting Arms" (hymn), 254
Leavel, Walter, 325b
Leavenworth (Kans.), 80, 326a
Lee, Miss ——— (Chattanooga, Tenn.), 293b
Lee, Benjamin W., 71, 323b
Lee, Harrison, 272
Lee, Ralph H., 250
"Let Us Break Bread Together" (hymn), 243
Levy, Jules, 73, 74
Lexington (Ky.), 1, 4, 37, 38, 49, 51, 64, 65, 66, 93, 97, 99, 116-117, 120, 295b, 315b-316a, 316b-317, 318, 319b, 320b, 323a, 328b
  Campbell's Restaurant, 97, 295b, 315b, 316a
  Cincinnati Southern depot, 295b
  Phoenix Hotel, 38
  Pleasant Green Church, 318a
  Union Station, 117, 120, 316a, 318b

Lexington Colored Fair. *See* Afro-American Fair.
Liberati, Alessandro. Salute Polka, 214, 215
Liberia, 168
Lincoln, Abraham, 5
Lincoln University (Jefferson City, Mo.), 149
Lindsay, Rev. ——— (Greenville, Miss.), 288b
Liszt, Franz. Rhapsodie Hongroise, 213, 214; Wanderer's Night Song, 137
literacy, 4, 10, 21-22, 37, 63, 78, 92, 272
Litt, Jacob, 25-26, 27n
Little Rock (Ark.), 83, 327b
"Little While, A" (song; Salter), 137
"Lizzie Polka" (Hartman), 180
Locket, Jessie, 139
Lockhart, Eugene (Gene). The World is Waiting for the Sunrise (song), 211
Logan, P. M., 71, 323a
Longfellow, Henry Wadsworth, 221
"Lost Chord, The" (song; Sullivan), 239, 240
Louisiana, 35, 74, 80, 81, 83
Louisville (Ky.), 97, 295, 328b
  Tenth St. Depot, 295b
"Love Untold, The" (poem), 128-130
Lowery, George L., 299b
Lutheran Church, 5
Lyman, Homer C., 197-198
lynching, 43-44, 47
Lyons, Lulu, 316b, 317b

McCain, Ella Byrd, 204, 206
McCalep, George O., 203
McCarter, Mrs. ——— (Queensboro, Ky.), 295a
McCarthy, Joseph Raymond, 268
McConico, John Hamilton, 175
McCormick, Virginia, 163, 184, 189, 304b, 305b
MacDowell, Edward Alexander, 267; To a Wild Rose, 302a
McGregor (Tex.), 327a
Mack (Versailles, Ky.), 316a
McKinney, A. W., 302a, 303b
McKinney (Tex.), 327a
McMahon, Mrs. ——— (Chicago, Ill.), 92, 289a
Maddux, Thomas W., 148
Madison County (Ala.) Democratic Party, 189
Mae (correspondent), 298b
Maggie (aunt), 99, 296b, 328b
"Maggie" (brass quartet), 208
Mahara, Frank L., 51, 55
Mahara's Colored Minstrels, viii, ix, x, 28, 30, 36, 39, 51
malaria, 219, 220
Malotte, Albert Hay. The Lord's Prayer, 243
Manning, M. C., 292b
Marbury, Carl Harris, 281, 282, 283
Marlin (Tex.), 327a
Marshfield (Wis.), 43
Martin, Mr. ——— (Nicholasville, Ky.), 319b
Martin, Al W., 27, 28, 29, **29**, 36, 37
Martin, Mrs. C. D. His Eye is on the Sparrow (hymn), 281
Martin, Willie M., 148
Mason, Emmit, 325b
Mason, Lowell, 55
Mason, Winona Agatha, 134, 137, 138

INDEX

Massenet, Jules Émile Frédéric. Elegy, 213, 214
Mastin, Harry (?). My Old Kentucky Home (Air Varie), 214
Mathews, E. Z., 175
Mayfield, Mrs. ——— (Corinth, Miss.), 291a
Mayhew, Sydney J., 146, 304b, 305a
Meacham, Frank White. American Patrol (march), 239, 240
Meharry Medical College (Nashville, Tenn.), 304b
mellophone, 118
Melroy, Leland, 36
Melroy (Leland) Minstrels, 36
Melroy, Chandler & Co., 35
Memphis (Tenn.), 79, 83, 84, 87, 89, 97, 260, 287-288a, 328a
  Avery Chapel A.M.E., 287b
  Church's Auditorium, 288a
  Fraternity Bank, 175
  Metropolitan Baptist Church, 287b
  Nikelodeon, 88, 89, 287a
  Orpheum Theater, 87, 88, 287a, 288a
Mendelssohn, Felix. *Athalie.* War March of the Priests, 221n
Methodist Church, 5, 226
Meyers, Miss ——— (Chattanooga, Tenn.), 293b
Michigan, 27
Michigan, University of, 203, 262
"Mighty Lak a Rose" (song; Nevin), 108
Miller, Bessie, 315a
Miller, Calvin (W. Cal), 70, 71, 323, 325a
Miller, Earl(e) L. ("Old Kentucky"), 38n, **42**, 81, 82, **119**, 320a, 323a, 325b

Miller, Georgia. *See* Wilson, Georgia Miller.
Miller (Glenn) Orchestra, 240
Milliner, Lucius Venable ("Lucky"), 229n
Mills, Mrs. ——— (Lexington, Ky.), 295b
Mills, Kerry. In the City of Sighs and Tears (song), 144, 145
Minnesota, 35
minstrelsy, viii, ix, x-xi, 17, 22, 25, 27, 33-35, 39, 40, **42**, 43, 45, 47, 50-51, 55-56, 66, 69-70, 72, 73, 74, 78-79, 90, 106, 112, 151, 171, 179
  whites in, viii, 27, 40
Mississippi, 74, 83, 262
Mississippi Agricultural and Mechanical College (Starkville), 290a
Mississippi School for the Blind (Piney Woods), 262
Missouri, 35, 74, 80, 83
Mitchell, Doris Mae, 225
"Mon desir" (song; Nevin), 137
Monroe, Hester. *See* Wilson, Hester Monroe.
Monroe (La.), 83, 327b
Montgomery (Ala.), 68, 69
  McDonald's Theatre, 69
  St. John's A.M.E. Church, 175
Montgomery Journal (Alabama newspaper), 185, 187
Montreal (Quebec, Canada), 68
Moody Bible School / Institute (Chicago, Ill.), 196, 248
Moore, Clara Frieson, 175
Moore, James, 40
Morehouse College (Atlanta, Ga.), 245
Morgan City (La.), 327b
Morganfield (Ky.), 97, 294b, 328b

365

Morning, Noon and Night in Vienna overture (Suppé), 70
Morris, Mr. ——— (Chattanooga, Tenn.), 293b
Morris, Thomas, 250
Morrison, Elder ——— (Nicholasville, Ky.), 94, 99, 296, 316b
Morrison, C. S. In Silent Thought (piano reverie), 159
Morrison, Richard David, 146, 184-185, 282
Morrison, Toula J., 38n, 81, **82**, 87, 88, 89, 92, 93, 94, 99, 102, 103, 107, 108, 113, 121, 128, 287-310 *passim*, 314-319 *passim*
Morse, Theodore F. Arrah Wanna (song), **109, 110**, 111-112, 303b
Mosaic Templars of America, 175
"Mother O' Mine" (song; Tours), 137
Mt. Carroll (Ill.), 35
movies, 24, 74, 88-89
Murdoch, Elias J., 148
music, vii, 90, 179, 180. *See also under* A&M.
  "classical," ixn, 90, 137, 138, 221, 238, 240
  popular, viii, 22, 64, 70, 72, 90, 111, 114, 145, 215, 238
music education, 10-11, 51, 55, 112
Muskogee (Okla.), 326b
"My Old Kentucky Home" (song; Foster), 12, 17, 107, 108, 159, 214, 239, 270
"My Spanish Rose" (song?), 159
Myers, J.W., 145n

NAACP, 263
Nalls, C. F., 175
"Narcissus" (Nevin), 308b
Nashville (Tenn.), 17, 107, 128, 133, 140, 150, 181, 182, 258, 294
  Fair View Baptist Church, 294
Nashville Students (minstrels), 33, 34, 35, 36, 37, 39, 325a
National Education Association, 55
"Naukeag Polka" (Casey), 214
"Nazareth" (song), 108
Neighbors, Jesse Robert, 97, 295b
"Nelly Bly" (song; Foster), 180
Nelson, P., 325a
Nevin, Ethelbert. Mighty Lak a Rose, 108; Mon desir, 137; Narcissus, 308b
New Iberia (La.), 327b
New Jersey, 28
New Madrid (Mo.), 43-45
New Orleans (La.), 79, 80, 81-82, 103, 327b
  Elysium Theater, 81
New Orleans Minstrels, 36-37, 39
New York (N.Y.), 55, 232, 235, 262
  Carnegie Hall, 262
  Diamond Horseshoe, 234, 235
  Madison Square Garden, 263
  Waldorf Astoria, 263
New York Academy of Music, 25
New York Amsterdam-News (newspaper), 235
Newport (Ark.), 83, 327b
Nicholasville (Ky.), 1-3, **2, 3,** 4, **9**, 10, 11, 12, 17, 22, 48, 49, 50, 51, 61, 64, 66, 68, 74, 83, 84, 85, 90-91, 93, 99, 116, 117, 120, 140, 165, 181, 209, 229, 253, 287a, 295b-296, 315-319 *passim*, 325a, 328b
  Bethel A.M.E. Church, 13, **15**, 68, 94, 99, 296, 316b, 318b-319a

Colored Christian Church, 13, **14**, 50, 68, 91, 93, 94, 99, 116, 295b, 296a

Dunbar School, 12, 296b

First (Colored) Baptist Church, 15, **16**, 48, 68, 90, 91, 93, 94, 99, 116, 296a, 315b, 316b

Hervey Town, 8, **8**, 9, **9,** 10, 12, 13, 16, 84

nickelodeon, 88

"No Love Like Thine" (brass prelude), 243

"None But a Weary Heart" (song; Tchaikovsky), 213, 214

Normal (Ala.), x, 59, 101, 150, 183, 224, 298, 299a, 304a, 305b, 310a, 312b, 313, 314a

Normal Index, The (A&M newsletter), 174-177, 196, 213, 215, 225, 238, 257, 261, 268

North Carolina, University of, 245

Norton (Va.), 209

Nowlin, Dave. The Billowey Sea (song), 180

"O Dry Those Tears" (song; Riego), 242, 243

Oakwood School / College (Huntsville, Ala.), 105, 205, 206, 239, 249, 250, 258, 269, 272, 305b, 306a

Oberlin College / Conservatory (Ohio), 123, 128, 150, 151

Odd Fellows. *See* Independent Order of Odd Fellows.

Ohio, 4

Ohio National Guard. Ninth Infantry Band, 49, 66

Ohio State Agricultural College (Ames), 151

Ohio State Fair, 64, 65

Ohio State University (Columbus), 65n, 150, 203

Ohio Wesleyan University (Delaware), 150

Oklahoma, 35, 74, 80

Oklahoma City (Okla.), 326b

"Old Kentucky" (alias). *See* Miller, Earl.

Olden, Mamie, 293b

Olden, Nettie, 293b

Oliver, Edward, 250

Olympia (Wash.), 39

O'Neal, Emmet, 164

Opelousas (La.), 327b

orchestra(s), 35, 40, 70, 71, 112, 323b, 325

organ, 88, 93, 227. *See also under* JHW.

Original Nashville Students (minstrels), 33. *See also* Nashville Students.

Orpheus Jubilee Singers, 293b

Orr, Charles Walter (son-in-law), 198, 242

Orr, Hester Elizabeth Wilson (daughter), 77n, 151, **152, 154**, 182, 195, 206, 208, 209, 242, **256**, 281, 283

Oswego (Kans.), 326b

Ottawa (Kans.), 44, 80, 326a

"Our God, Our Help" (hymn; Watts), 281

Overstreet, Ed., 323b

Owen, David. All Through the Night (chorus), 159

Owens, Mattie, 312a

Owens Cross Roads (Ala.), 202

"Palms" (music; Fauré?), 308b, 309a

Paris (Ky.), 120, 318

Paris (Tex.), 327a

Parker, Mary, 202

Parker, Theophilus R., 167-168, 175, 179, 183-185, 191, 193

Parrish, Charles H., Sr., 114-115, 312b
Parsons Weekly Blade (Kansas newspaper), 25
Patrick, Henrietta K., 296b
Patterson, Katherine J., 274
Patton, Leander R., 245, **246**, 247, 250
Pauls Valley (Okla.), 326b
Payne, Dorsey E., 148
Pearson, Urtha, 223, 224, **224**
Pendleton, James Madison, 315a
penmanship, 105, 106, 139, 299b, 304-311 *passim*
People's Band (Columbus, Ohio), 64, 65-66
Perkins, Theron D. Scintilita (trumpet solo), 159, 214
Perry, Oliver, 37
Philadelphia (Pa.), 49
"Phillipina Dance, The" (minstrel sketch), 69
piano, 60, 125, 128, 138, 153, **158**, 182, 208, 209, 293b, 305b, 325a. *See also under* JHW.
"Pickaninny Band" (ensemble), 25
Pickett, J. B., 300a
Pine Bluff (Miss.), 83, 327b
Pittman, W. S., 304b
Pitts, Mrs. ⸺ (Chattanooga, Tenn.), 294a, 314b, 317b
Pitts, E. M., 304a
Pitts, Jerry, 79n
Pitts, John, 292a, 293a, 294a, 295a, 314b, 317b
Pittsburg (Kans.), 72, 326b
Pittsburgh (Pa.), 165, 175
Plaquemine (La.), 327b
Pocahontas (Indian princess), 111
Poet and Peasant overture (Suppé), 239, 240
Polk, Austin, 140

Polk, Elizabeth Litton, 140, 151, 181-182
Polk, Exeline. *See* Wilson, Exeline Polk.
Poplar Bluff (Mo.), 327b
Port Arthur (Tex.), 80, 81, 327b
Port Gibson (Miss.), 83, 327b
Porter, Dr. ⸺ (Memphis, Tenn.), 287b
Porter, Maune, 316a
Porter, W. Ellis, 292b
Prairie View State College (Tex.), 203
Prampin, Harry, 33, 35, 36, 292a, 325a
Prampin, Laura, 302b, 325a
Prampin Peerless Band, 49
Pratt City (Ala.), 175
Prentice, R. B., 175
Presbyterian Church, 4, 5
Price, Elder ⸺ (Memphis), 287b
Price, Beulah, 117, 308a, 316b, 317a
Price, S., 295a
"Princess of India" (King), 239
Princeton (Ky.), 17, 294b, 328b
"Professor" (honorific), 37, 146, 195
Puccini, Giacomo. *La Bohème*, 148
Pulley, Joyce, 272
Pulliman, Lillian, 293b

Queensboro (Ky.), 295a, 328b

race & racism, x, 3, 7, 10, 21, 25, 27, 31, 43-44, 48, 57, 60, 66, 69, 103, 115, 146, 150, 164, 176-177, 181, 184, 187, 217, 218, 221-222, 271, 276, 291a
Rachmaninoff, Sergei. Prelude (piano), 137

radio, 24, 74, 240, 263, 264, 268
ragtime, x, 22, 50, 70, 72
railroad, 4, 27-28, 33, 79, 89, 91-92, 289a
  palace cars, 28, 40
Rairy family, 316a
Ramsey, J. Walter, 126, 148, 299, 300a, 301a, 307, 308a, 311a, 314a
Real Negro Minstrels, 35-36
recording(s), 24, 73, 74, 111, 112-113, 240
religion & churches, 4-5, 50, 55, 90-91, 169-171, 175, 197-199, 242, 268-269, 270-273. *See also under* A&M *and* JHW.
Rexford, Eben Eugene. Silver Threads Among the Gold (song), 72
Reynolds, William, 291b
Rheinberger, Josef Gabriel. Ballade (piano), 137
rhetoric, 105, 106-107, 113, 139, 299b, 306, 307a
Richard, Mrs. ——— (Nicholasville, Ky.), 316a
Richards, D. J., 180
Richards, W. M., 91
Richards & Pringle (minstrel managers), 33, 34, 39, 43, 44, 47
"Ride the Chariot" (spiritual; arr. Smith), 281
Riego, Teresa del. O Dry Those Tears (song), 242, 243
Rink, Johann Christian Heinrich, 159
Rison (W.R.) Banking Co. (Huntsville, Ala.), 163
Roberts, Gertrude, 144
Robertson, Wilton V., 57n, 238, 240

Robinson, Alma, 243
Robinson, Mary, 144
Robinson, Odell, 133
Robinson, Sam, 35
Rochelle (Ill.), 47
Rockport (Ind.), 295a
Rodney, Paul. Calvary (song), 180
Rogers, E. E., 272
Roman Catholic Church, 5, 242, 243
Rome (Ga.), 292, 328b
Rose, William ("Billy"), 234, 235
Rosie (cousin), 99, 296b
Ross, Miss ——— (A&M), 291b
Rossini, Gioachino Antonio, 221; *Stabat Mater*. Inflammatus, 221n; *William Tell* overture, 22, 33, 70
R.O.T.C., 102n. *See also under* A&M.
Roten, Miss ——— (A&M), 314a
Rubinstein, Anton Grigorevich. Melody in F, 89, 90, 287b
Rusco & Holland (Chicago agency), 33, 34
Russell, Hannah (cousin), 316a
Russell, Sylvester, 78, 175
"Russia" (trumpet solo; Hartmann), 206

Saffold, Elizabeth, 108
St. Joseph (Mo.), 80, 326a
St. Louis (Mo.), 175, 291a
"St. Louis Blues" (Handy), 233, 234, **236, 237**, 263
St. Paul (Minn.), 26
Saint Saens, Camille. Were I Sunbeam (song), 137
salaries, 56, 64, 65, 125. *See also under* A&M.
Salter, Mary Turner. A Little While (song), 137

Salter & Martin (theatrical company), 27
Saltzman, Alfred A., 119n
"Salute Polka" (Liberati), 214, 215
Samuels, N., 295a
San Antonio (Tex.), 80, 327a
San Marcos (Tex.), 327b
Sanders, Charles W., 250
Sanford, Smith, 320b
Sapulpa (Okla.), 326b
Satie, Eric, 270
saxophone, 64, 71, 118, 209, 257, 323b
Schott, ———. Valse (piano), 137
Schubert, Franz Peter, 221; Ave Maria, 214, 243, 269, 300a
"Scintilita" (trumpet solo; Perkins), 159, 214
Scott(e), C. J., 37
Scott, G. W., 175
Scottsboro (Ala.), 291b-292a, 328b Baptist Church, 291b-292a
Searcy, Thomas Jefferson, 287b
Secchi, Antonio. Lungi dal caro bene (song), 137
Sedalia (Mo.), 80, 326a
Segura, Marion, 144
Seitz, Ernest Joseph. The World is Waiting for the Sunrise (song), 211
Selective Military Service Act, 224-225
sermons, 87, 91, 93, 94, 105, 114-115, 116, 170, 173, 287b, 289b, 290b, 292a, 294a, 296a, 299-307 *passim*, 310-319 *passim*
Seventh-Day Adventists, 206
sexism, 22, 172, 183, 225, 227
Shakespeare, William, 221
Shawnee (Okla.), 326b
Sheffield (Ala.), vii, 175, 180, 291, 308b, 328a

Sheids, "the only," 40
Sheridan, Philip Henry, 30
Sherman (Tex.), 326b
Showalter, Anthony J. Leaning on the Everlasting Arms (hymn), 254
Shuffle Along (musical; Sissle & Blake), 259, 260
Sibelius, Jean, 267
"Silver Threads Among the Gold" (song; Rexford & Danks), 72
Simmons, Isora, 108
Simmons College (Kentucky), 114
Simms, R., 289b
Simpson, Fred W., 233
Simpson, Samuel, 323a
"Since You Went Away" (song; Johnson), 213, 214
Singleton, George G., 218
Singleton, J., 326a
Singleton, Mary, 312a
Sissle, Noble Lee. *Shuffle Along* (musical), 259
Six Campbell Brothers (group), 88. *See also* Campbell.
Six Whirlwinds (act), 36
slaves & slavery, vin, vii, 3, 4, 5-7, 10-11, 27, 114, 132, 189, 269
Sledge, D. B., 274
smallpox, 68
Smally, Ed., 325a
Smally (Smalley), M. E., 94, 289b, 290b, 294b, 296, 300b, 315b, 316b
Smith, Mrs. ——— (Chattanooga, Tenn.), 308a, 314b, 315a, 317a
Smith, David, 115, 290b, 294a, 314b
Smith, David D., 290b
Smith, David P., 296b
Smith, J. J., 80
Smith, Jakie, 71, 323b

Smith, Jean Voltaire, 169n
Smith, John (Nicholasville, Ky.), 296b
Smith, John (Virginia colonist), 111
Smith, Miss M. A., 250
Smith, Morton, 313b
Smith, William Henry. Ride the Chariot, 281
Smith-Lever Act, 164
Sneed, Mr. ———, 10
Snodgrass, Horace P., 274
"Somebody Misses You Every Day" (song; Harris), 139
Somerset (Ky.), 116, 314b-315a
　First Baptist Church, 315a
　Kyle Barber Shop, 315a
"Song of My Heart" (song; Johnson), 213, 214
"Song of Nature, A" (chorus), 144, 145
Sousa, John Philip, 24, 74, 267
Spanish-American War, 48
Speaks, Oley. "In May Time" (chorus), 108
spirituals, 138, 270
Springfield (Mo.), 326b
Stamfis, Miss ——— (Chattanooga, Tenn.), 293b
Stanton, Frank Lebby. If Life Be a Dream (song), **136,** 137, 138
"Star Spangled Banner, The" (song), 159, 239, 243
Starkville (Miss.), 290a, 328a
Staunton, Bertha, 293b
"Steal Away to Jesus" (Handy), 233
Steel, Robert, 325b
Steele, Paul, 81
Steers, Willis Wood, 291b
Sterling, Prof. ——— (Sheffield, Ala.), 308b

Sterling, Andrew B. In the City of Sighs and Tears (song), 144, 145
Stevens, Thomas, 320b
Stevenson, Arnie, 40, 41
Steward, L., 295a
Stewart, Charles, 306b
Stewart, John, 325a
Still, William Grant, Sr., vii, 57n
Still, William Grant, Jr., vii, 11
Stitt, Edward Boatner, Jr. ("Sonny"), 229n
Stone's Cornet Band, 87, 287a
Storksville (Miss.) *See* Starkville.
Story of Ruth, The (drama), 227
Stowe, Harriet Beecher, 27
Stratton, Linnie, 144
Strong, Mr. ——— (A&M), 215
Student Army Training Corps, 155
Stump, Charles E., 150
Sues, Leonard, 234, **236**
Sullivan, Sir Arthur. The Lost Chord (song), 239, 240
Sunday school, 199, 267-268. *See also under* A&M *and* JHW.
Suppé, Franz von. *Morning, Noon and Night in Vienna* overture, 70; *Poet and Peasant* overture, 239, 240
Sutton, Dick P., 41
Swan, George A., 45
Swift, Hugh, 323a

Talladega College (Ala.), 150, 203
Tandy, Vertner, 320b
Tappey, Francis, 148
taps (melody), 159, 239
Tate, William, 311a
Tatman, Mr. ——— (Lexington, Ky.), 317a
Tatman, Frank, 320b, 323a
Tatman, Mattie, 315b, 316a

Tatnall, Hazel, 313a
Taylor, Richard, 325b
Taylor, Zachary, 3
Taylor (Tex.), 327a
Tchaikovsky, Petr Ilich. None But a Weary Heart (song), 213, 214
television, 21, 263
"Tender Little Flower" (song; Barili), 144, 145
Tennessee, vii, 74, 83
Tennyson, Alfred Lord. Crossing the Bar, 133
Teo, L., 325a
Terrel, Hazel, 175
Terrell (Tex.), 327a
Terry, Harriet J., 203, 255
Tevis, James, 325b
Texas, 31, 35-36, 72, 74, 80
Thadius (cornetist), 49, 320b
"They That Sow in Tears" (Handy), 277
Thibodaux (La.), 327b
Thigpen, Placidia E., 227, 250
Thomas, Dick, 40, 41
Thomas, J. Pompey, 175
Thompson, Marguerite, 113, 306b
Timblake, Dr. ——— (Lexington, Ky.), 315b
"To a Wild Rose" (MacDowell), 302a
Toney, Harry, 290a
Toney (*or* Tony) Trio, 80, 82
Topeka (Kans.), 80, 326a
"Torpedo and the Whale, The" (song; Audran), 159
Tosti, Sir Francesco. Good-Bye (song), 180, 242, 243
Toula. *See* Morrison, Toula J.
Tours, Frank E. Mother O' Mine (song), 137
Trammell, E., 139
"Tramp, tramp, tramp" (song), 267
Tramps (New Orleans social club), 81
"Traumerei" (unidentified solo), 300b
travel, 4, 45. *See also under* JHW.
Trenholm, George Washington, 175
Tribble, Burritt, 325b
Trimble, J. F., 293b
trombone, **42,** 70, 71, 119, **158,** 223, 257, 270, 320a, 323, 325
Troupe of Arabs (minstrel act), 36
trumpet, 24, **158,** 182, 209, 220, 229n, 230, 257. *See also under* JHW.
Trusty, Ray, 36
Tryser, George A., 45
tuba, 70, 71, 112, 119, 320, 323, 325
tuberculosis, 144, 313b
Tuckahoe (N.Y.), 263
Tucker, James, 325a
Tucker, Richard, 281
Tull, Rev. ——— (Nicholasville, Ky.), 315b
Tulsa (Okla.), 326b
Tupelo (Miss.), 290b, 291a, 328a
  Rising Star Baptist Church, 290b
Turner, ——— (Lexington, Ky.), 315b
Turner, Allie, 144
Turner, John Brister (son-in-law), 245, **245,** 258
Turner, Marian Elizabeth (granddaughter), **256,** 258
Turner, Marian Floredia Wilson (daughter), 11, 77n, 151, 153-155, **154,** 181, 183, 195, 209, 210, 215-220, 229, 230-231, 245, **245,** 249, **256,** 258, 261, 264, 269, 273, 277

Tuscumbia (Ala.), 180, 291b
Tuskegee Airmen, 245
Tuskegee Institute (Ala.), 49, 52, 164, 204
typewriter, 115, 216, 314a, 316a, 318a

Uncle Tom's Cabin (play), 27-28, **29**, 36, 37, 39
United States Army, 30, 31, 119n, 188, 225, 242
    Ninth Cavalry Band, 30-31, **32**, 45, 49
United States Postal Service, 183
"Universal March" (DeLamater), 209

Vaughan, Henry. Calvary (song), 180-181
Vaughan, Sarah Lois, 229n
Verdi, Giuseppe. *Rigoletto*. Caro nome, 72; *Il Trovatore*, 239
Versailles (Ky.), 316a
Vicksburg (Miss.), 11, 83, 327b
Victoria (Tex.), 327a
viola, 70, 71, **158,** 323b
violin, 40, 64, 70, 71, **158,** 209, 323b, 325a
Virginia, 218
Virginia State College, 215, 218, 219

W ———, L ———, 314b
Waco (Tex.), 327a
Wagner, Richard. *Faust Overture*, 33
Waide, D. S., 296b
Waide, Lulu, 318b
Walker, Belle, 10
Walker, Phillip, 7, 9, 10
Wallace, Elsie Hall, 250, 254
Wallace, Wendolyn, 243

Ware, Benjamin E., 108
Washburn College (Topeka, Kans.), 203
Washington, Booker Taliaferro, 52, 132
Washington, Dinah (Ruth Lee Jones), 229n
Washington, George (drummer), 320b, 325a
Washington, Mrs. J. M., 180
Washington (state), 41
Washington (La.), 327b
Watkins, Doris M., 243
Watkins, Emmer, 139
Watkins, Walter, 71, 323b
Watson, James, 175
Watts, Charles T., 70, 71, 323b, 325b
Watts, Isaac. Our God, Our Help (hymn), 281
Watts, J. A., 71, 323b
Waxaha(t)chie (Tex.), 327a
"Way of the Wise, The" (reading), 269
"Wedding of the Winds" (waltz; Hall), 239
Weir, Charles, 320a, 323a
Weltraus, Amanda (cousin), 315b
"Were I Sunbeam" (song; Saint Saens), 137
West (Tex.), 327a
West Point (Miss.), 290a, 328a
Western Electric Company (Baltimore, Md.), 242
"Where Corals Lie" (song; Elgar), 137
White, Berthonia S., 272
"Whiter than Snow" (hymn), 176-177
whites, viii, 4, 80, 189, 258, 291a
Whitesboro (Tex.), 35

Whiteside, Ernestyne, 243
Whitfield, Nannie B., 144
Whitfield, Susan T., 159
Whitman, Walt, 222n
Wichita (Kans.), 80, 326a
Wilberforce College (Ohio), 262, 263
Wilkins, Nathan, 37, 325b
William Tell overture (Rossini), 22, 33, 70
Williams, Mrs. ——— (Chattanooga, Tenn.), 294a
Williams, Charles, 325b
Williams, Charlie (A&M), 144
Williams, L. D., 298b, 302a, 310b, 313a
Williams, Robert, 325b
Williams, W. H., 315a
Wilson, Mr. ——— (Jamaica), 311b
Wilson, Charles, 326a
Wilson, Cornelius W., **119**, 320a, 323a
Wilson, Exeline Polk (second wife), 94, 107, 108, 121, 128-132, **129**, 130, 131, 140, 143, 151, 153, 154, 161-162, 181, 183, 215-216, 218, 219, 238, 253, **256**, 268, 269, 273, 276, 277
Wilson, Georgia Miller (first wife), 17, 37-38, 47, 49, 50, 51, 59, 63, 68, **82**, 84, 92, 93, 94, 99, 107, 116, 117, 121, 140, 141, 172, 289, 290b, 292, 296b, 299, 302b, 305b
Wilson, Hester Monroe (mother), 5, 7, 18, 21-22, 23-24, 83, 84, 99, 151, 287a
Wilson, J. A. (A&M), 313a
Wilson, Jacob (father), 2-3, 5, 8, 10, 11-13, 15, 17, 18, 22, 24, 47, 84, 93, 94, 99, 116, 181, **182**, 183, 295b, 296a, 307b, 325a

Wilson, James Hembray, ix-x, **61, 98, 154, 157, 178, 192, 201, 230, 232,** 248, 248, 252, 253, **256, 279**
  arranger, 61, 71, 74, 80, 89, 90, 103, 108, 111, 112, 157, 209, 240, 257, 261, 267, 287b, 295a, 298b, 301a, 302, 303, 304, 307a, 308b, 311b, 316a, 319a
  Band and Tour Booklet, 49, 70, 77n, 320-328, **321, 322, 324**
  bandmaster, 11, 17, 25, 27, 36, 37, 38, 39, 48, 49, 63, 64, 66, **67,** 79, 118, **118,**119, **119,** 121, 165, 320, 323, 325b
  bandmaster at A&M, 30, 54, 56-57, 59, 61, 101, 102-103, 113, 128, 133, 138, 144, 149, 157, **158,** 159, 179, 196, 206-209, 215, 216, 223, **224,** 227, 238-240, 257-259, **258,** 262, 298, 300-305 *passim*, 308a, 314a
  baseball coach, 161, **161**
  Bible teacher / scholar, 151, 155, **156,** 171, 172-173, 177, 196-197, 248, 289a, 303b
  birth, 7, 12
  bookkeeper & Financial Secretary (A&M), 151, **160,** 160-161, 179, 190-191, 195-196, 197n, 200, 202, 203, 204, 205, 206, **207,** 215, 229. *See also* Treasurer.
  character & abilities, 39, 70, 91, 92-93, 95, 108, 145, 154, 177, 198, 204, 215, 269, 283
  church musician, 48, 50, 51, 93. *See also* organist.
  composer, 25, 61, 71, 72, 73, 74, 79, 103, 157, 240, 258, 259, 261, 305a
  cornetist, ix, x, 12, 24-25, 27, 28, 30, 35, 36, 38, 39, **42,** 43, 48, 61, 63, 65, 66, 71-73, 74,

INDEX

79, 80, 82, 90, 115, 116, 117, 118, 121, 138, 139, 305a, 312a, 313a, 314b, 315, 316, 317a, 323a
cousins, 99, 296b, 315b, 316a
death & burial, **276**, 277, 282
disciplinarian, 113-114, 205, 310a
divorce, 38, 49, 84, 94, 102, 117, 121, 128, 138, 140-141, 172
dress & toilet, 61, 95, 97, 288a, 289, 294b, 295a, 311a, 313b, 315a, 316a
education, 12, 24, 106, 128, 145-146, 151, 196, 229
eyeglasses, 119
family concerts, 182, 209, 211-213
family life, 83, 123, 151, 153, 181, 206, 209, 215-217
finances, 49, 50, 51, 63, 68, 97, 182-183, 192-193, 195, 196, 273
Freeman agent, 17, 48, 50, 51, 91
health, 108, 219, 220, 223, 229, 238, 249, 258, 259, 269, 273
homes & houses, 22-24, 84, 116, 138-139, 143, **152**, 153, **154, 182,** 253, **256,** 273
Homilies Booklet, 77n
Journal, **76**, 77, 83, **84, 85, 86,** 87-95, 97, 284-319, **285, 286, 297**
musical education, 11-12, 24
organist, 13, 93, 94, 114, 116, 296a, 311a, 312b, 315b, 316b
penmanship, 91, 106
pianist, 115, 294a, 314b, 317a
postmaster, x, 183, 215, 238
preacher, 77n, 173, 217

publication (music), 258, 259-261
religion & religious life, 12-13, 15, 17, 87, 93, 94, 95, 99, 104, 116, 121, 168-173, 175-178, 180, 196, 206, 222-223, 267-269, 271, 273, 287-319 *passim*
resignation from A&M (1904), 61, 63
retirement, 185, 249, 257
Secretary of Faculty (A&M), 160, 178, 179, 190
shot & jailed, 43-45, 47
speaker, 106, 177-178
Sunday School & Sunday School Teachers Training teacher, x, 15, 93, 105, 116, 155, **156**, 196, 197, 198, **200**, 215, 227, 267-268, 272, 290b, 296a, 299a, 300a, 301a, 302, 304b, 307b, 309b, 315a, 316b
traveller, 28, 61, 68, 74, 83
Treasurer (A&M), x, 160, 189, 245-247, **246**
trombonist, 35, 36, 39, 325a
trumpeter, **ix,** 30, 31, **32, 33,** 49, 66, **67**, 133, 138, 139, **158**, 159, 179, 180, **194,** 197n, 206, 211, 213-214, 219, 220, 229, 232, 233, 242, 243, 262, 264, 267, 269, **270**, 274, 299b-300, 301a, 302a, 304b, 307b, 308b
vocal teacher & conductor, 59, 101, 103, 113, 114, 115, 128, 138, 139, 144, 149, 157, 207, 298b, 299, 300b, 302a, 303a, 304, 305a, 307-313 *passim*
writer, 50, 91, 92, 168-177, 198-199, 215, 267-269, 293a

Wilson, James Hembray.
LITERARY WORKS:
The Church and Dancing, 169-173
The Day the Lord Made, 176
Getting Back on the Job, 176
The Harvest and Laborers, 176
If I Was a Crying Man (poem), 275-276
"The Little Foxes" Song of Solomon 2:15, 268-269
Putting Old Wine in New Bottles, 267-268
Three Men—Three Philosophies, 270-272
The Two Fruit Cakes, 175, 176
Watch Your Step, 176
Whiter Than Snow, 176-177

MUSICAL WORKS. *See also* Appendix 3.
Alabama A and M College March, 261, **266,** 267
The Bugle Call (march), 73, 253, 255
Carmena, 180
Drag Lotz, 72
Gloomorian, 74
Kentucky Blue Grass, 261, 263
The Normal Students (march), 159
Reveille, 79
Roberteen Polka, 239, 240
Shame Lotz, 72
Silas Green March, 206, 261, **264**
United (march), 72, 239, 259, 260, 261, **265**
Wilson, James Hembray, Jr. (son), 151, **152, 154, 161,** 182, 195, 209, 211, 218, 219, 233, 242, **256**
Wilson, James Hembray III (grandson), **256**
Wilson, Karl Talmadge (son), 151, **154, 161,** 182, 209-211, 217, 218, 219, 242, **244, 256**
Wilson, Maggie (sister), 13, 18, 22, 24, 99
Wilson, Marian Floredia (daughter). *See* Turner, Marian.
Wilson, Sophia, 5
Wilson, Theodore Shaw ("Teddy"), 90n
Wilson, W. J., 310a
Wilson, Woodrow, 268
Winchester, Harrey, 320b
Winfield (Kans.), 80, 326a
Winnipeg (Manitoba, Canada), 41
Winona (Miss.), 289a, 328a
Wisconsin, 35
women, 183, 223, 225, 272. *See also* sexism
Wood, Walker R., 312b
Woods, W. T., 175
Wordsworth, William, 221
"World is Waiting for the Sunrise, The" (song; Lockhart & Seitz), 211-212
World War I, 155, 169, 267
World War II, viii, 200, 220, 221, 225, 234, 240
World's Columbian Exposition (1893), 263
Worthy, Nicholas, 22, 24
Wright, Miss ——— (A&M), 299a
Wright, Charles, 87, 88, 287a, 326a
Wright, Louis F., 43-44, 47

Yazoo City (Miss.), 94, 289, 328a
Yeilding, Ency F., 242, 243
yellow fever, 35
Y.M.C.A., 309a. *See also under* A&M.
York, Henry J., 144

Young, Rida Johnson. Italian Street Song, 243
Young, Robert, 325a

Zampa overture (Hérold), 70
Zurich (Switzerland), 197

With Trumpet and Bible